The Daily Telegraph
Century of County Cricket
The 100 Best Matches

The Daily Telegraph

Century of County Cricket
The 100 Best Matches

Edited by Simon Heffer
Introduction by E. W. Swanton

SIDGWICK & JACKSON
LONDON

ACKNOWLEDGEMENTS:

We would like to thank the following for their invaluable help in producing this book: Brian Coulon, Robert Gray, Andrew Hutchinson, Teresa Moore, Hugh Montgomery-Massingberd, George Plumptre, Harry Smith, E. W. Swanton, Marilyn Warnick, Mr. and Mrs Frank Wheeldon and Graham Windram.

PICTURE CREDITS

We are grateful to Roger Mann for the photographs for matches 1–7, 10–14, 16–35, 37–44, 46–49, 51–59, 63, which came from his private collection. The remaining photographs came from *The Daily Telegraph's* own library.

Picture Research by Diana Heffer

First published in Great Britain in 1990
by Sidgwick & Jackson Ltd.
1 Tavistock Chambers
Bloomsbury Way
London WC1A 2SG

ISBN 0283 06048 4

Designed by Bob Hook

Typeset by Florencetype Ltd, Kewstoke, Avon
Printed by Butler and Tanner Ltd. Frome and London.

CONTENTS

Foreword

The inspiration to compile this book came from two sources. First, my wife had recently compiled *The Daily Telegraph Record of the Second World War*, publishing for a new generation of readers some excellent reports from the newspaper from the years 1939–45. Both she and I were provoked to think that other less bellicose themes could be pursued in this way. Second, the link with cricket was made during frequent browses through the records section of *Wisden*. I had so often, for example, read of the achievements of Holmes and Sutcliffe in scoring 555 for the first wicket for Yorkshire against Essex at Leyton in 1932: but what about the rest of the match? I therefore sat down with a pile of old *Wisdens* and, after weeks of most enjoyable research, chose 100 of the most notable games ever played in the County Championship, and then selected the reports that appeared in *The Daily Telegraph* at the time with a view to compiling them in this book.

Some words of explanation are necessary. I chose to base the book on the County Championship alone for several reasons. There is a surfeit of books about Test cricket and, however much enjoyable reading the *Telegraph* reports of great Tests might provide, I thought it was more than the market could bear. In any case, many of the best are already anthologised by E.W. Swanton, the *Telegraph's* most renowned cricket correspondent, in the indispensable collections of his work. By contrast, there are few books purely about county cricket, fewer still in print, and none I could find that took such an approach as this. As Mr Swanton says in his introduction, 1890 is an appropriate year in which to start the 100 games. I took it as my starting point principally because it was the year in which the Championship was properly established, and all doubts about the scoring of points – and therefore about who, in some years, had

actually been champions – were cleared up.

I bore several points in mind when choosing the matches. The well-known 'great games' should mostly be found within – matches in which remarkable feats had been accomplished, or in which sensational victories had been won, or reverses achieved. I added to these a good measure of games that, from a few weeks spent in the company of *Wisden*, struck me as being simply good cricket. Finally, I am indebted to Mr Swanton for drawing to my attention several games whose absence from this book would have seriously diminished it.

For each game I have given the full scorecard of the match as published in the newspaper. Over the century they have varied in the extent of their detail – it was not until comparatively recently, for example, that the total at the fall of each wicket was given – and this will explain the stylistic variations the discerning reader will find in the statistical parts of the book. Then I have published as much of the original reports as space will allow. In many cases this is everything for the whole three days; in some drastic cuts have had to be made. I could not include every game I wanted to. In the five or six seasons after the second world war newsprint rationing led to some of the best matches hardly being reported at all.

For each match I have written a brief but, I hope, thorough introduction. Much of my own love of cricket was fed, as a small boy, by reading copiously about it (and often to the exclusion of anything else). While this book is aimed at (as the phrase goes) small boys of all ages, I have tried to make it a perfect introduction to the history of the Championship for anyone already familiar with cricket today. In the 100 introductions the reader will find potted biographies of the principal players, with their career records. Reading from beginning to end the book should provide the reader with a comprehensive picture of first-class cricket and first-class cricketers in England over the last 100 years. Much of the detail in the book has come from reading our own reports, from a succession of distinguished correspondents. All statistics have been verified in *Wisden* and double-verified in the excellent and indispensable *Who's Who of Cricketers*, published by the Association of Cricket Statisticians. In the rare instances where these two magisterial works of reference did not agree I deferred to age and chose *Wisden*. All statistics are correct to the end of June 1990, when the proofs were being checked. Career figures of cricketers have been included only where that career is complete. At proof stage I was tempted to make one change, and include the Surrey vs Lancashire match of May 1990, where the visitors made 863 in reply to the home side's 707 for 9. Noting Mr Swanton's strictures on statistical freaks, I thought better of it, and in any case, the feat may well be upstaged in the end-of-season 1990 round of 4-day matches.

It is not the purpose of this foreword to dwell on the nature of county cricket; that is done more splendidly than I could hope to do by Mr Swanton in his introduction. I would, though, confine myself to three points. First, my researches for this book have convinced me that cricket reached a nadir in the late 1960s from which it is still recovering. One hopes that the novelty of one-day cricket is wearing off, and that we are experiencing a return by spectators to the traditional three-day game. In most respects the attitudes of players have improved. Less negative cricket is being played, and more concern is shown to reward the devotion of supporters by providing them with good cricket. There is room for further

improvement – over rates must be higher, there must be a return of spin bowling (these two points are, of course, inter-related), and wickets should be uncovered in order to make the balance of the game fairer. In other respects, the lesson to be learned from the past is that undue tinkering with the game inevitably ends in tears.

There have always been complaints that cricket is in decline. While researching this book I came across articles in the *Telegraph* every few years of the 'things were much better when I was a boy' variety. No-one who was a boy in the 1960s or 1970s can possibly say that now, though I can imagine that a browse through this book may make many of us wish we had been boys somewhat earlier than we were.

My main acknowledgment must be to my wife, Diana, who did much of the textual research for me, and virtually all of the picture research. Her experience in such matters was invaluable, and ensured that the book progressed far more smoothly than it would otherwise have done, and she helped in most other respects of producing the book too. As well as writing his introduction, Mr Swanton gave me more good advice than I can remember, though he will be glad to know that I took almost all of it. I am particularly happy that so much of his work appears in the later pages of this book, for he is a towering figure in modern sporting journalism. There is, also, the debt owed to all the other writers whose reports – many of them anonymous – appear in the book, and to the Librarian of *The Daily Telegraph* and her staff, whose help and facilities were given freely.

Simon Heffer

Introduction

by E.W. Swanton
Cricket Correspondent of *The Daily Telegraph* 1946–75

There are aspects of English cricket today to which many followers of the game react with indifference or even hostility. Attitudes and behaviour at the level of Tests and overseas tours in recent years have distressed those brought up to believe that cricket and the old decencies are synonymous. The international game, they are inclined to say, is over-exposed, the top players over-glamorised. To all such, as indeed to supporters of every generation and persuasion, this celebration of a century of county cricket should make a broad appeal.

For we followers, aficionados – 'fans' if you can bear the term – all started surely by identifying with a county. If we were not lucky enough to be born within the borders of any of the favoured seventeen we adopted one of them, attracted probably by one or other of the household names of our youth.

The greats were the heroes of our boyhood, and, as one looks back, one's spectacles perhaps tinted slightly pink, there seems small reason to amend those early judgements. To me the average county cricketer, whether amateur or professional, has been with very few exceptions a good sportsman and an amusing companion. If the fellowship of cricket seems to some a blimpish phrase, so be it. Of the present generation I should express reservations only in that my contact has naturally grown less with the years. If the moderns are more mercenary then their predecessors, and if their sense of loyalty is scarcely what it used to be, their attitude is no more than a reflection of the times and manners of today.

The abolition of amateur status in 1962 – an economic necessity in the long term – altered the character of county sides in an important way because it caused the disappearance of the *independent* cricketer: independent of committees and therefore natural captaincy material. Leaders are accordingly hard to come by. Yet the moderation and common sense of the players' trade union, the Cricketers' Association, ever since its foundation in 1968, are qualities to be deeply thankful for. If a few at the top have grown too big for their boots the generality of county cricketers still have their feet on the ground.

The editor begins his story with the season of 1890, not merely a convenient round number but a significant date for several reasons. Although the Golden Age had no precise starting point the quarter century that ended with the onset of the First World War is generally regarded as marking its limits.

If there is one building in the whole wide world of sport that is instantly recognizable as symbolizing a national game it is Lord's pavilion. That splendid edifice which is at once a monument to cricket's place in Victorian England and a pledge today of its future opened its doors in May 1890.

Most significantly, however, it was in 1890 that the counties, who of course had been playing one another since the early 1870s, and in an irregular way for many years before that, contested an officially-designated County Championship. Hitherto a table had been compiled by the press, the fewest matches lost being the yardstick for the title – a palpably unsatisfactory method when one side might play twice as many matches as another. In December 1889 the county secretaries, meeting at Lord's, decided on the identity of counties to be designated as first-class, and that the Championship should be determined simply by subtracting defeats from victories and awarding points accordingly. Draws were ignored. So we have Surrey as champions in 1890, having played 14 matches, won 9, drawn 2, lost 3. Points 6. Poor Sussex landed bottom with minus 10 points, having won once and been beaten 11 times! There were nevertheless suffered to continue in the Championship, which in 1890 consisted of eight counties: those always regarded as 'the big six', Yorkshire, Lancashire and Nottinghamshire in the north, Surrey, Middlesex and Kent in the south, plus Gloucestershire and Sussex.

A strange anomaly may be noticed here. At this time of emerging county activity a body was formed in 1887, independent of MCC though meeting at Lord's, called the County Cricket Council. Some twenty-odd counties attended its meetings under the Presidency of the captain of Kent and benevolent autocrat of its affairs, Lord Harris. It busied itself with fixture-making and the always vexed matters of county qualifications and Australian visits. It seems theoretically and in retrospect a useful administrative instrument. Yet at a meeting in 1890 it dissolved itself on the casting vote of its Yorkshire chairman, following a debate on a motion which ended in a tie to suspend its activities *sine die*. The key to this curious business, I think, can only be that Harris, the Council's founder and guiding spirit, had gone off to be Governor of Bombay. He left a void which no other county figure had the stature to fill.

So the regulation of county cricket fell *faute de mieux* into the hands of MCC who throughout history have never initiated new areas of responsibility but always respond when invited. It was they who approved the agreement of the county captains that as from 1895 five counties be added to the list: Derbyshire, Essex, Leicestershire, Warwickshire and Hampshire. Somerset had already joined the hallowed circle in 1891. Thus the Championship assumed something near its present form, Worcestershire being subsequently admitted in 1899, Northamptonshire in 1905 and Glamorgan in 1921. In 1904 MCC set up the Advisory County Cricket Committee, having in 1898 regularized a haphazard situation by forming the Board of Control for Test Matches at Home. Both these bodies performed under MCC's benevolent umbrella until 1968 when the Club opted to devolve its authority: hence the Test and County Cricket Board came into being.

So much, in brief, for the evolution of county cricket which is today and has been throughout cricketing history the backbone of the game. There is school, then village and town club and University cricket. All feed their best into the county sides which in turn provide the players for the England XI. Test Matches are the game's highest expression, and the county clubs their essential nurseries, and thus the focus of patriotic interest and support.

Our century, 1890–1990, divides itself naturally and conveniently into four more or less equal phases. The second break occurred in 1939. The third phase takes us to 1968 at which date not only did the governance of the game change hands but the limited-over one-day explosion gathered pace. The Sunday League idea was accepted and its operations began in the following year.

Born in 1907, I can write at first hand of the last three periods but, obviously, not of the first. Yet those Edwardian summers have inspired so much nostalgic writing, and older generations have talked so evocatively about the game in those halcyon days, that one can at least conjure a picture of the era on which the curtain came down with such utter finality in August 1914. To two colleagues of that time especially I listened and learned. One was the great C.B. Fry, with whom I was associated when we were covering the game together for the *Evening Standard*, the other Colonel Philip Trevor, CBE, whose name as cricket correspondent of *The Daily Telegraph* went back to around 1910. He went on writing until close on his death in 1932, latterly guided by a daughter. I only too happily aided his failing sight while absorbing the memories of a kindly old fellow who, after fighting in the Boer War, managed the MCC tour of 1907/8 to Australia (Hobbs's first of five) and then took to journalism.

Cricket came to its full flowering in the Golden Age. The multiplicity of clubs of all sorts founded in the last quarter of the 19th century took root and throve. It was the heyday of public school cricket, with the straitjacket of 'A'-levels unimaginable and little competition from lesser forms of exercise other than on the river. Village and country-house cricket abounded, the butcher, the baker and the candlestick maker rubbing shoulders with the gentry, joined by the bond of comradeship in cricket. At Oxford and Cambridge the standards were such in the 1890s that within the decade 15 blues won Test caps, including such legendary names as Jackson, Jessop, Fry, 'Ranji', Wood and Warner. In county cricket, with a few northern exceptions, the fusion of amateur and professional tended to bring the best out of both. Test matches were occasional treats, Gentlemen v. Players the high point of the domestic summer. An idealized picture? Slightly so maybe, but I make no apology for presenting it.

Many of the attractions of pre-1914 county cricket persisted between the wars. The amateur strain weakened somewhat, but in most counties was still much in evidence. Moreover the great professional batsmen had mostly developed alongside high-class amateurs, and each had benefited from the other. When Jack Hobbs and Frank Woolley had been teenagers, J.T. Tyldesley and Tom Hayward were the only pros to get near the England XI as batsmen. Hobbs and Woolley, the most prolific run-getters in history, inherited the philosophy that the batsman must aim to dominate the bowler or the converse would occur. The best of the inter-war generations tended to follow their lead, most notably in the shape of Walter Hammond and Denis Compton. English cricket was in good shape when the second war intervened, the Test bowling well varied and the batting led in the classic mould by Len Hutton.

The third phase of our century (from 1946 to 1968) declined from a euphoric start wherein bumper crowds celebrated the peace. England in the 1950s enjoyed the winning of three successive rubbers against Australia, a phenomenon that last happened in the reign of W.G. Grace. County cricket has never known such support as in the decade after the war. The 1960s were a poor time for cricket, as for much else in our society: hence the revolutionary effort to revivify the county game by the infusion of fresh blood from overseas and the regular diet of 40-over cricket every Sunday.

Experience has shown that the medicine was too drastic. Yet as we survey the current scene it should not be forgotten what pleasure was given by some of the bright stars from overseas: Barry Richards, Clive Lloyd, Mike Procter, Majid Khan, Eddie Barlow, and the greatest of the constellation, Gary Sobers. It was the presence of such as these which got the age of sponsorship underway.

The summer's fixture structure, complicated by the fitting-in on economic grounds of four competitions instead of the one hitherto, is a subject of running debate. For the moment let us be thankful that at their 1990 spring meeting the TCCB decisively turned down the dreary and maybe fatal proposal to limit the Championship to sixteen 4-day matches. By 14 votes to 4 the counties and MCC opted to retain until at least 1993 the present format of sixteen 3-day and six 4-day fixtures per county.

The hundred matches the editor has chosen illustrate beyond all else that quality in cricket expressed in the age-old cliché, its 'glorious uncertainty'. Here we find recorded from the pages of *The Daily Telegraph* many unforgettable feats with bat and ball and a due proportion of tight finishes. Some perhaps might have preferred a choice less influenced by statistics. Great deeds are not specially conducive to great matches. Over the span of a century the hundred might clearly have been multiplied many times. I prefer to congratulate Simon

Heffer on the result of much diligent research, and to commend particularly the way in which he has woven into his text biographical notes on most of the outstanding cricketers of the century.

I am tempted to add a marginal note to a few of the games chosen. As a boy I recall first perhaps the most extreme of all reversals of fortune, Hampshire's victory at Edgbaston in 1922 after being bowled out for 15 (game 36). As I learned much later, Lionel Tennyson's determination to fight back from utter disaster was multiplied by his opposing captain's proposal to use the third day by playing golf. Nettled by this, the poet's grandson answered pithily in the vernacular.

The circumstances of Gubby Allen's ten for 40 against Lancashire at Lord's in 1929 are familiar ground to me as his biographer (game 46). He was employed at Debenham's stores at the time, and his captain was aware he was required to work on Saturday morning and would therefore be late. Lancashire, champions for the three preceding years, were batting on a plumb pitch when Gubby took the field shortly before noon. In 25.4 overs he clean bowled eight, had one caught by Fred Price, the keeper, while Ted McDonald, the great fast bowler, coming in last, was, astonishingly, stumped. McDonald (not his favourite cricketer) advanced down the pitch, the bowler saw him coming and delivered a slower, wider one which enabled Price to rush up to the stumps and do the necessary.

There was a keen background to Duleep's devastating batting at Hastings in 1929 (game 45). Three weeks earlier during a spell of fine weather, Sussex arrived at Mote Park, Maidstone, and found a pitch which at one end had apparently been hit by a very local storm. Result, Freeman seven for 16, Sussex all out 69 and defeated by 12.30 on the second day. Duleep, most sweet-tempered of men, declared, 'They are cheats. Wait until they come to Hastings.' I relate the story while as a Man of Kent, naturally deploring the implication . . . But what a match at Hastings! What would I not have given to see it on that ground, under the

castle ruins, which is, sadly, no more – and on which, to strike a note of pure bathos, I once made a hundred myself.

Essex v. Yorkshire at Leyton in 1932 (game 48) I saw and can never forget because as a result of my getting last to the only telephone to relate the story of the record, and so missing an edition, the *Evening Standard* reversed their decision to send me to Australia to cover what was to become the Bodyline tour. 'If the young fool can't get us a story from Leyton how can we rely on him from Sydney and Melbourne?' So ran the thinking. Incidentally, in cold fact the record was only equalled. The scoreboard had been a run ahead of the scorers, who after some palaver were eventually persuaded that they had not noticed the signalling of a no-ball.

The Essex match at Brentwood two years later (game 52) remains clear for a different reason. A few days before this first-ever Brentwood Week I was playing there for MCC in a one-day match against the Club Cricket Conference and the pitch had started to powder by teatime. When I asked B.K. Castor, the Essex secretary, how he thought the pitch would stand up to a three-day match he laughed and said, 'Oh, we can take care of that.' In a way they did – Kent declared after an hour on the second morning at 803 for four. The answer had been a liberal application of liquid cow-dung – the same sort of dressing of which Bill O'Reilly said, with some feeling, when England made 903 for seven at the Oval a few years later: 'You could smell it from the pavilion gate'. I quote the expurgated version.

'Bosser' Martin's perverted ambition had been that either England or Australia should make 1,000. A more creditable example of his art was that on which Surrey played Kent for Andrew Sandham's benefit in 1935 (game 53). Here was another game I might have seen but did not – an illustration of county cricket and Woolley at their respective best. The incomparable one batted only 190 minutes for his 229, and Alf Gover recalls how Frank enjoyed pinging him straight over his head on to the canvas awning which then stretched above the pavilion seats.

Pat Hendren's last match which brought the Lord's season of 1937 to a close I did see (game 57). On the second day a crowd of 17,000 had savoured the emotional moment when Pat – a prime favourite throughout his career – obliged with a hundred. On the last evening Errol Holmes provoked a noisy protest by bowling an over of wides and byes in order to get the new ball at 200. Thereupon, though the sun was shining, Walter Robins and 'Gubby' Allen both appealed against the light to Bill Reeves, the umpire, who promptly took off the bails and so ended the match with Surrey three wickets short of victory. I wrote in strong disapproval, on the grounds that the Surrey captain had spoiled a memorable occasion and brought the game into disrepute. This severed a friendship I much valued – until in the middle of the following summer we met over a drink and all was forgiven. Something must have provoked Errol, who was the very essence of an amateur cricketer and a model county captain.

Ten years on Middlesex, though they went on to win the Championship, were thwarted at Lord's by Kent in a match of vintage quality dominated by Denis Compton on one side and Doug Wright on the other (game 62). I am reminded how the shortage of newsprint meant short reports in 1947 and even shorter ones in 1948. By 1959, in contrast, I was given a free rein, as may be seen from my next report from Lord's in this book (game 75) – 23 inches to describe a one-run win by Middlesex over Sussex in the Whitsuntide match. The occasional telephonic error is inevitable, but 'chicken-hearted' as applied to Sussex, instead of 'chicken-headed' was a real embarrassment, demanding the apology that the paper duly printed next day.

Meanwhile in 1950 came the classic Roses' Match at Bramall Lane (game 65). The grinders always rolled up in force to that unlovely yet somehow well-loved arena long since surrendered to Sheffield United. Note the crowd of 16,000, the biggest I recall for

E. W. Swanton

the third day of a county match. I was broadcasting as well as writing, which one did there at a table in the pavilion surrounded by and in the hearing of Yorkshire members. It was 'Nah then, Jim: careful what tha' says, lad'. I enjoyed the proximity – it kept you on your toes. On and on one went on the old Home Service, half an hour at a stretch with a mug of tea or a drink handy but no scorer. On this Tuesday morning I urged all who could do so to come along in the afternoon because it was a great fight and there would probably be a tight finish. John Nash, the Yorkshire secretary, most delightful of men, was astonished when over the lunch interval the crowd just about doubled.

The 1950s belonged to Surrey, but the Oval pitches were often far less good than they should have been, let alone than they used to be, as games 67 and 68 make clear. It is good to be reminded of fine cricketers who were near the top rungs of the ladder but never quite got there: Maurice Hallam, of Leicestershire (game 74) for instance and Ian Thomson, of Sussex (game 78). Apart from being the most recent bowler to take all ten wickets in England, Thomson is remembered as the man who bent the ball around like a boomerang at Lord's one morning and virtually decided a Gillette final in an hour or so. County cricketers are seldom short on humour and the story went the rounds how Hallam, a splendid slip-fielder, explained his missing a comfortable catch. His captain being the super-enthusiastic but over-effusive Tony Lock, he said he couldn't bear the thought of being kissed by him so early in the morning.

So one might reminisce further. But it must be on with the play, with a final word of gratitude of having had the opportunity to see so much and to have enjoyed so many happy days in the sun.

E.W. Swanton

1. *Nottinghamshire v Sussex*
NOTTINGHAM, 16–18 MAY 1890

Eight counties contested the Championship in 1890. Although they did not win the title until 1907, Nottinghamshire were, in the Nineties, one of the most formidable sides, particularly on account of their batting. As the report says, the partnership between Shrewsbury and Gunn of 398 for the second wicket was 'a larger number than a partnership in a first-class match has ever produced'. It stood as a world record until 1934, when Bradman and Ponsford overtook it for Australia in their stand of 451 against England at the Oval, and was not surpassed in the Championship until Jameson and Kanhai's 465 for Warwickshire in 1974, more than a lifetime later (see game 85).

Arthur Shrewsbury (1856–1903) was one of Wisden's cricketers of the year in 1890, and as (in W.G. Grace's opinion) the finest professional bat in England then was a regular test player. He appeared in 23 tests, and toured Australia four times, twice as captain. He played from 1875 until his death, scoring 26,505 runs at an average of 36, at a time when conditions so often favoured the bowler (W.G. Grace, a contemporary, averaged 39). Despite heading the averages in 1902, his last season, he killed himself partly out of despair that ill-health would end his career. His 267 in this match equalled the highest score of his career. William Gunn (1858–1921) was also one of Wisden's cricketers of the year, another regular test batsman, and part of a dynasty that dominated Nottinghamshire cricket for half a century. He made 25,691 runs at an average of 33 in a career that lasted from 1880 until 1904. In an age where the all-rounder was supreme, he also played football for England, and founded the bat-making firm that still bears his name.

Nottingham, Thursday

The opening match of the Notts season at Trent Bridge yesterday was characterised by some remarkable cricket. Out of some five hours and fifteen minutes' play the home team only lost one batsman, who was dismissed when the score had reached 26. At this point Gunn joined Shrewsbury, and so well did the pair bat that they occupied the wicket during the remainder of the day, carrying the total to 341, or 315 since the fall of the first wicket, with Shrewsbury (not out) 164, and Gunn (not out) 152. The partnership of 340 runs made by Messrs K. J. Key and H. Philipson for Oxford University against Middlesex at Chiswick Park in June 1887, therefore, looks like being beaten.

From the time that Gunn joined Shrewsbury runs came at a good pace, although occasionally the pair took matters quietly. It was, however, a race between them for scoring honours as Gunn gradually ran his figures up to those of his partner. An hour and forty minutes' play realised 100 runs and 34 runs later Shrewsbury should have been caught by McCormick, when he had made 74, and the let-off was clearly paid for. After this, numerous changes in the attack were made, but without effect, and when stumps were drawn for the day the batsmen were still together. With the exception of the chance mentioned, the batting display of both men was of the most brilliant description.

Friday

A performance that may not be equalled for a long time was yesterday accomplished in this match at Nottingham by Gunn and Shrewsbury. Getting together on the first day of a contest, when one wicket had fallen for 26 runs, they defied all the bowling

Gunn and Shrewsbury

brought against them, and at the end of the day had carried the total to 341, Shrewsbury's score being 164 and Gunn's 152. In beautiful weather the game was continued, but the attendance of spectators was again small. A start was made at twenty minutes past eleven, and although four bowlers were tried, Gunn and Shrewsbury continued to hit hard and well. Just before noon 400 was telegraphed and a quarter of an hour later Shrewsbury completed his second century. At length, however, Gunn was smartly caught at mid-on by Gibb, and retired for a faultlessly played 196.

In all he had been associated with Shrewsbury for six hours, and during that period 398 runs were scored. This is a larger number than a partnership in a first class match has ever produced, the next best being 340, made by Key and Philipson, in an Oxford and Middlesex match in 1887. Gunn's chief hits were eleven 4's, eleven 3's, and twenty-one 2's. Shrewsbury continued until he had made 267, which ties the one he made against Middlesex in 1887. He went in first and was out with the total at 569, being cleverly caught at the wicket. Altogether he was batting eight hours and fifty minutes, and during that time played grand cricket. Shrewsbury's innings included nineteen 4's, sixteen 3's and thirty-nine 2's.

As might have been expected, after their tiring time in the field, Sussex made a bad start, Tebay being bowled with the total at 3, whilst Quaife left at 30. Newham and Bean hit with rare vigour, and, although Shacklock, Attewell, Richardson and Flowers were tried, 100 were scored in less than two hours. At the close, however, half the side were out for 126.

Saturday

As anticipated, Notts on Saturday gained a very easy victory over Sussex, defeating them by an innings and 266 runs. The cricket witnessed on the first two days was of the most remarkable character. On Saturday the first innings of Sussex, which overnight had stood at 126 for five wickets, was resumed and terminated for an addition of 50 runs, Newham, Bean and Jesse Hide being the top scorers. With the heavy task of wiping off 404 runs to avoid a single innings' defeat, Sussex entered upon their follow on at a quarter to one, but although several members of the team made a plucky stand, they could not get anywhere near that total and at five o'clock the whole side were out for 138 runs, leaving the home team victorious as stated. Score:

Notts

J. A. Dixon, c Butt, b Bean 13	Shacklock, c Butt, b Humphreys 3
Shrewsbury, c Butt, b Humphreys 267	Richardson, b Gibb 4
	Sherwin, b Quaife 14
Gunn, c Gibb, b Humphreys 196	Scotton, not out 5
Barnes, lbw, b Humphreys 4	B 12, 1 b 3 15
Flowers, b Smith 44	
F. Butler, c Butt, b Bean 15	Total 590
Attewell, b Bean 10	

Sussex

Quaife, b Shacklock 10	run out 0
Tebay. b Shacklock 3	b Barnes 9
W. Newham, c Shrewsbury, b Shacklock 36	lbw, b Barnes 19
Bean, c Hart, b Flowers 50	c sub, b Barnes 10
Jesse Hide, c Dixon, b Shacklock ... 37	c Scotton, b Barnes 44
Butt, lbw, b Attewell 6	lbw, b Attewell 1
E. J. McCormick, b Flowers 17	c Attewell, b Barnes 9
C. A. Smith, c Shrewsbury, b Shacklock 14	c and b Attewell 32
Charlwood, c Shrewsbury, b Barnes 3	b Barnes 6
Humphreys, not out 3	b Attewell 2
Gibb, c Gunn, b Shacklock 0	not out 4
B 2, 1 b 5 7	B 2
Total 186	Total 138

Notts – First Innings

	O	M	R	W		O	M	R	W
Hide	65	22	135	0	Humphreys	31	1	72	4
C. A. Smith	61	17	130	1	E. J. McCormick ...	9	4	10	0
Bean	45	14	77	3	W. Newham	8	2	16	0
Gibb	51	16	101	1	Quaife	14.4	1	34	1

Sussex – First Innings

	O	M	R	W		O	M	R	W
Attewell	45	23	45	1	Flowers	12	2	25	2
Shacklock	33.4	8	87	6	Barnes	6	3	4	1
Richardson	8	2	18	0					

Second Innings

	O	M	R	W		O	M	R	W
Shacklock	15	5	42	0	Richardson	7	3	4	0
Barnes	22.4	8	60	6	Flowers	10	6	11	0
Attewell	33	20	18	3	J. A. Dixon	2	1	1	0

Umpires – R. Humphrey and F. Silcock

2. Sussex v Lancashire
HOVE, 15–16 AUGUST 1890

'The weather was cold and boisterous' wrote *The Daily Telegraph's* correspondent. From his other remarks one senses that he might well have been aware of the potential of A.C. MacLaren, who had only just left Harrow (where he had captained the XI) and was making his debut for Lancashire. Not since 1875 had a cricketer in the Championship made a century on his debut, and MacLaren was the first batsman to do so since the Championship had been constituted officially in 1890. MacLaren (1871–1944) was to become one of the finest amateur batsmen of the Nineties. He is best remembered for his 424, still the highest score ever made in England in a first-class match (see game 7). In a career lasting from 1890 until 1922 he made 22,237 runs at an average of 34, and played 35 tests, 20 of them as a highly-regarded

A.C. MacLaren

captain. Perhaps the second most remarkable feat of his long career came at its end. He decided, in 1921, that he could pick an amateur XI that would beat Warwick Armstrong's all-conquering Australian tourists. He did, and they did.

It might be thought that Lancashire's easy victory over Sussex was only to be expected of a side that would be runners-up in the Championship, whereas Sussex were bottom. However, Sussex had no fewer than four players who had represented or would represent England (Newham, Bean, Smith and Butt), so were far from bereft of talent. There is a literary interest in the Lancashire side: both players named in Francis Thompson's famous poem *At Lord's* are to be found on the scorecard: 'As the run-stealers flicker to and fro/To and fro:/ Oh my Hornby and my Barlow long ago!'

Brighton, Thursday

Representative teams opposed each other in this return match which was commenced at Brighton yesterday in delightful weather. The visitors are leaving out Yates and F. Ward, a place being found in the team for A. MacLaren, this season's Harrow captain, who more than justified his selection. Sussex were without the services of W. H. Andrews, who was selected to play, but was unable to at the last minute, and the vacancy was filled by W. C. Holloway, a Brighton amateur. The home side, who batted first, made but a poor show as they were all got rid of in two hours for the meagre total of 85, Jesse Hide, with 25 to his credit, being the only one to offer any resistance to the visitors' bowling.

Lancashire on the other hand were seen to great advantage, although the start was not at all a good one, the first two wickets falling for nine runs. Then, however, MacLaren and Briggs, on being partnered, completely altered the aspect of the game. Hitting in brilliant style the pair scored at a very rapid rate, and despite numerous changes in the bowling, 91 runs were added before Briggs was got rid of for a useful 54, whilst soon afterwards MacLaren's admirable innings was brought to a close. He had been batting two hours and ten minutes for a grand 108, made without the slightest chance, his hitting hard and clean. The total was taken to 248 ere the innings terminated, stumps being then drawn for the day. The home team today have the hard task set before them of hitting up 162 runs, to save a single innings defeat.

Friday

As was anticipated at the end of Thursday's play at Brighton, this match terminated yesterday afternoon. The result was favourable to the visitors, who won by an innings with 62 runs to spare. Yesterday Sussex when they had to commence their second innings, required 162 to save the single innings defeat, but never looked likely to obtain the number. On a wicket that suited them well Mold and Watson were almost unplayable. Smith was the only one who batted with any confidence and his 39 were not obtained until several chances had been given. In less than two hours the whole of the side were sent back for 100 runs. The weather was cold and boisterous, and very few people witnessed the finish. Score:

SUSSEX

Quaife, run out	13	c Kemble, b Watson	7
Humphreys, b Mold	3	retired hurt	0
W. Newham, c MacLaren, b Mold	4	b Mold	15
Bean, b Mold	7	b Watson	10
Hide (J.), b Mold	25	b Mold	13
C. A. Smith, b Mold	5	b Mold	39
G. L. Wilson, b Watson	11	b Watson	0
C. J. M. Godfrey, b Mold	11	c Briggs, b Mold	0
Hide (A.), b Watson	0	b Watson	4
Butt, not out	2	not out	1
W. D. Holloway, b Watson	1	b Watson	10
B	4	B	1
Total	**86**	**Total**	**100**

LANCASHIRE

Barlow, b Godfrey	3	A. N. Hornby, c Butt,	
Sugg, b Godfrey	1	b Humphreys	14
A. Ward, c Godfrey, b A. Hide	19	A. T. Kemble, b Humphreys	17
A. C. MacLaren, c Holloway,		Watson, c Godfrey, b Wilson	7
b Humphreys	108	Mold, not out	0
Briggs, b Wilson	54	B 6, 1 b 1, n b 1	8
Paul, l b w, b Wilson	0		
Baker, c Butt, b Wilson	17	**Total**	**248**

SUSSEX – First Innings

	O	M	R	W		O	M	R	W
Watson	27.4	15	23	3	Mold	27	6	59	6

Second Innings

	O	M	R	W		O	M	R	W
Watson	26.2	11	41	5	Briggs	4	1	6	0
Mold	22	9	52	4					

LANCASHIRE – First Innings

	O	M	R	W		O	M	R	W
A Hide	16	6	23	1	Bean	7	0	28	0
Godfrey	12	3	54	2	Holloway	4	1	12	0
Smith	7	1	24	0	Wilson	11	2	47	4
J. Hide	4	0	10	0	Humphreys	10	1	42	3

Godfrey bowled one no ball.

3. *Lancashire v Somerset*
OLD TRAFFORD, 9 AUGUST 1892

In the list of 25 first-class matches in the world since 1890 finished on the first day, Somerset featured in no fewer than seven, losing each time, and in four of them to Lancashire, of which this was the first. The humiliation was repeated, for the first time, on the same ground two years later (and see game 39). A combination of higher over rates and more flexibility about finishing times – this match was extended 40 minutes beyond the usual close to stop the players having to come back – made one-day finishes more commonplace before the Great War. Somerset were the newest side in the Championship – they had joined only in 1891 – and enjoyed far more success than this thrashing would suggest, finishing third in the season, one place ahead of Lancashire.

Two bowlers, Briggs and Mold, accounted for Somerset. Arthur Mold (1863–1921) would play his only three tests for England the following summer, but was a prolific wicket-taker, with 1,673 wickets at 15 each in his career. However, there was constant controversy about

his action, and he was called for throwing in 1900. When called again in 1901 he retired. 'Boy' Briggs (1862–1902), so called because of his short stature, was a slow left-arm bowler who was originally a batsman. As with several other Victorian professionals, his life was short and tragic. Despite being plagued from his late twenties with epilepsy he enjoyed a successful test career (playing 33 times for England and taking 118 test wickets), ended – as it seemed his whole career would be – by a bad fit in the 1899 Leeds test. He played one more season before recurring severe fits led to him being taken to an asylum, where he died in his 40th year. He had taken 2,221 wickets at an average of 16.

Manchester, Monday

The Old Trafford Ground, Manchester, yesterday was the scene of some remarkable cricket, the return fixture between these two counties being begun and finished in a single day, an event that occurs but seldom in the annals of first-class cricket. Only about a dozen instances are on record during the last half century, the

'Boy' Briggs

first as far as can be traced, being the North and South match at Lord's on July 16, 1850, whilst the more recent matches were Lancashire v Surrey, at Manchester, in August 1888, Surrey v Leicestershire, at the Oval, in May 1890; and MCC and Ground v Notts in June 1891.

The result in the present instance was brought about through a hot sun which so affected a soddened wicket that the batsmen could practically do nothing. The ball at times got up in an alarming manner, and the wonder is that the whole of the players got off scot free. During the day no fewer than thirty two wickets fell for 294 runs – an average of less than 10 each.

The cricket calls for little comment. Somerset who went in first, started well by contributing 50 for two wickets; but a rot setting in, the whole side were out for an addition of 28 runs. The home county, on the other hand, fared badly at the commencement, losing four wickets for 21; but double-figure contributions by MacLaren, Yates and Kemble enabled them to exceed their opponents' total by 28. Somerset did even worse in their second venture, and the innings can only be termed a procession to and from the wickets, as in less than an hour and a half the lot were got rid of for the meagre total of 58. Lancashire with 31 to get to win, lost two wickets, play having been extended forty minutes in order to finish the game. As will be seen from the analysis given below, the bowlers on each side had remarkable averages. Score:

SOMERSETSHIRE

Batsman	1st	2nd
H. T. Hewett, c Sugg, b Briggs	35	c. Mold, b Briggs — 6
L. C. H. Palairet, c Sugg, b Briggs	22	not out — 22
J. B. Challen, c Mold, b Briggs	13	b Briggs — 8
W. C. Hedley, b Mold	1	b Briggs — 1
S. M. J. Woods, c MacLaren, b Briggs	3	b Mold — 4
C. E. Dunlop, b Briggs	2	b Mold — 0
G. B. Nichols, l b w, b Briggs	2	b Mold — 4
W. N. Roe, l b w, b Briggs	3	c Yates, b Briggs — 3
A. E. Newton, c Smith, b Mold	3	c Watson, b Mold — 0
E. J. Tyler, b Mold	0	b Mold — 0
C. J. Robinson, not out	4	c and b Briggs — 0
Extras	0	Extras — 10
Total	**88**	**Total — 58**

LANCASHIRE

Batsman	1st	2nd
Ward, A., b Tyler	8	not out — 12
Sugg, F., c Nichols, b Tyler	2	b Hedley — 5
Smith, A., b Woods	6	b Hedley — 4
A. C. MacLaren, b Hedley	27	not out — 10
Baker, c and b Hedley	13	
Yates, by Woods	27	
S. M. Crosfield, c Newton, b Hedley	1	
A. T. Kemble, b Hedley	23	
Watson, b Woods	3	
Mold, not out	1	
Extras	5	Extra — 1
Total	**116**	**Total (2 wickets) — 32**

SOMERSET – First Innings

	O	M	R	W		O	M	R	W
Briggs	24	6	62	7	Mold	15	8	13	3
Watson	8	3	13	0					

Second Innings

	O	M	R	W		O	M	R	W
Briggs	18	11	21	5	Mold	17.2	7	27	5

LANCASHIRE – First Innings

	O	M	R	W		O	M	R	W
Woods	23	9	50	4	Nichols	8	3	17	0
Tyler	19	8	26	2	Hedley	11.4	5	18	4

Second Innings

	O	M	R	W		O	M	R	W
Woods	9	2	15	0	Hedley	8.1	4	16	2

4 Somerset v Yorkshire
TAUNTON, 25–27 AUGUST 1892

Somerset's good opening run in the Championship – they were not to equal their third place this year until 1958 – coincided with comparative barrenness for Yorkshire. The visitors were still building the team that would win the Championship the following summer, and would finish out of the top three only once in the next 17 seasons. Somerset were better as a batting than a bowling side, as this performance proved, and depended more heavily than any other county on the services of amateurs, nine of whom are on the card for this match. While the opening partnership world record by Hewett and Palairet of 346 stood for just five years it remains the Somerset record for any wicket. Somerset have only twice made more than they did in this game, and never before had three centuries been scored in the same first-class innings. Had the rain not

defeated them on the final day, Somerset must have had a good chance of beating Yorkshire, and improving still further on their Championship placing.

Herbert Hewett (1864–1921) was a former Oxford blue and the Somerset captain, though he resigned the following year after an argument over his tactics in the tourist match. He scored 1,407 runs in 1892, his best season, with his 201 in this game his highest score. However, so unamicable was his departure from the captaincy that he played only a handful of games for Somerset after that. Lionel Palairet (1870–1933) was still an Oxford undergraduate, and a blue in each of his four seasons there. He played for Somerset until 1909, scoring 15,777 runs at an average of 34 in his career, and played twice for England. He occasionally went in first for Somerset with his brother Richard.

Taunton, Thursday

The above fixture, which is the fourth of a series of five matches on the Taunton ground, was commenced yesterday in fine weather and as it was the weekly half-holiday of the townspeople, there was a large attendance of spectators.

Somerset played the team that defeated both Notts and Middlesex whilst on the visiting side F. S. Jackson, the old Blue, still played *vice* Lord Hawke.

The first match of the season between the two counties, played at Sheffield a few weeks ago, resulted in a victory for Somerset by 87 runs, so that additional interest attached to the present fixture.

Yorkshire yesterday were fortunate enough in winning the toss, and going in on a splendid wicket, kept their rivals in the field for four hours and a quarter, during which period they compiled a total of 299 runs. The batting was of a very even character, no fewer than nine of the players getting into double figures. Smith and Jackson, the first pair, put on 83 before being separated, whilst Peel and Wainwright also distinguished themselves by adding 80 runs for the sixth wicket.

Nothing daunted, the home batsmen were seen to equal advantage, as in the hour and ten minutes left for play, Hewett and Palairet, playing in brilliant style, knocked up 78 without being separated. The game, therefore, at present stands in a very interesting position.

Friday

Since their inclusion in the ranks of first-class counties the Somersetshire eleven have accomplished some remarkable performances, but all these pale before their marvellous achievement yesterday in the second day's play of the above match at Taunton. Not only did the team compile the huge total of 592, which is the highest this season, but the first pair of batsmen, Hewett and Palairet, put on the remarkable number of 346 runs before being separated, which beats the first wicket record of 283 established as far back as 1869 by W. G. Grace and B. B. Cooper in the match played by the Gentlemen of the South against the Players of the South at Kennington Oval. The total of 593 is also the biggest the Westerners have ever made in a first-class match, and the present fixture is unique at Taunton from the fact of its containing three individual efforts of over a century in one innings. Enough praise cannot be given to Hewett and Palairet for their wonderful performance, and the pair throughout played in exhilarating style. Overnight, against a completed innings of 299 by the visitors, Somerset had scored 78 without the loss of a wicket – Hewett (not out) 42, and Palairet (not out) 32. Resuming yesterday the two batsmen soon collared the bowling, and, hitting with the greatest confidence and freedom, runs were added at a great rate. The hundred and 200 were

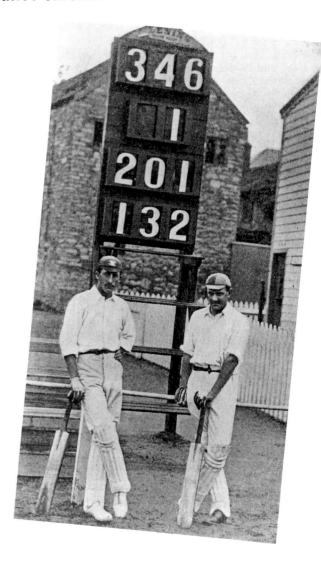

Hewett and Palairet after their stand

soon hoisted, while about one o'clock the record of 283 for the first wicket disappeared, and before lunch the Yorkshire total (299) was passed, with the balance still together. After the interval the pair continued to score very fast, and with the total at 334 Hewett gave his first and only chance to deep square leg, the fieldsman, who had previously injured his hand, dropping the ball, the left-hander having at this period compiled 189. With 12 runs added to his credit, and with the total at 348, Hewett was clean bowled by Peel. His 201 had taken him three hours and a half to put together, and throughout his cricket had been of a most brilliant character, and the vigour of his batting may be judged from the fact that he hit thirty 4's, three 3's, and fifteen 2's. Palairet ultimately succumbed to a grand catch in the slips by Sellers, the outgoing batsman having compiled 146, which, with the exception of a chance on the previous evening, was faultless. He was in three hours and fifty-five minutes, while 372 runs were put on, and his hits included one 6, nineteen 4's, five 3's and six 2's. Several of the remaining batsmen followed the example of their predecessors by contributing double figures, Hedley in particular being the most prominent. He added 102 in dashing style, and hit ten 4's four 3's, and seven 2's. Just before the time fixed for the drawing of stumps the innings, after an existence of six hours and thirty-five minutes, came to a close for the immense total of 592, which leaves the home county with a substantial advantage.

Saturday

After compiling the huge total of 592 in their first venture, it was most unfortunate for Somerset that rain at Taunton on Saturday prevented cricket being proceeded with. Score:

YORKSHIRE

E. Smith, b Tyler	45	Wardall, c Hill, b Tyler	14
F. S. Jackson, run out	56	Brown, not out	11
Tunnicliffe, l b w, b Tyler	30	Moorhouse, c Woods, b Tyler	11
A. Sellers, c Hewett, b Tyler	29	Ellis, b Nichols	0
Ulyett, b Hedley	6	B	7
Peel, c Nichols, b Tyler	47		
Wainwright, c Palairet, b Tyler	43	Total	299

SOMERSETSHIRE

H. T. Hewett, b Peel	201	S. M. J. Woods, c Wardall, b Wainwright	31
L. C. H. Palairet, c Sellers, b Jackson	146	G. Fowler, not out	33
J. B. Challen, b Peel	5	Nichols, c Sellars, b Peel	7
W. C. Hedley, c Wardall, b Peel	102	C. J. Robinson, st Ellis, b Peel	2
A. K. Newton, c Sellers, b Jackson	4	Tyler, b Peel	1
V. T. Hill, c Brown, b Peel	39	B 19, l b 2	21
		Total	592

YORKSHIRE – First Innings

	O	M	R	W		O	M	R	W
Tyler	50	13	111	7	Hedley	28	6	87	1
Nichols	22.4	7	62	1	Woods	18	7	32	0

SOMERSETSHIRE – First Innings

	O	M	R	W		O	M	R	W
Jackson	30	8	148	2	Wardall	9	1	26	0
Peel	19.3	15	133	7	Brown	2	0	8	0
Wainwright	33	6	117	1	Clyett	3	0	12	0
Smith	23	1	97	0	Moorhouse	6	0	21	0

Umpires – Pullin and Lilywhite.

5. Gloucestershire v Somerset
CHELTENHAM, 14–16 AUGUST 1893

Only three times in the history of first-class cricket has a wicket-keeper 'taken' a hat-trick of dismissals. This match includes the first of these, a feat that remains unique because it was a hat-trick of stumpings. William Brain (1870–1934) had just come down from Oxford, where he had won a blue in each of his three years, and had also won a blue for soccer as the University's goalkeeper. This was the only season that he played county cricket. The unusual quality of his feat seems to have escaped *The Daily Telegraph's* correspondent, who regarded it merely as 'curious': almost a century later, it has never been emulated, and the change in wicket-keeping styles and the infrequency of stumpings make it most unlikely that it ever will be. The bowler who took the hat-trick, Charles Townsend (1876–1958), was still a schoolboy at Clifton. A leg-spinner, this was only his second match for Gloucestershire, for whom he played regularly until the turn of the century, and sporadically until 1909. He topped the bowling averages in 1895, having just left Clifton, and was also a very capable batsman, doing the 'double' of 100 wickets and 1,000 tuns in a season in both 1895 and 1899. After 1900 his cricket had to take second place to his work as a solicitor, and he became the Official Receiver for Stockton-on-Tees. In his career he made 9,512 runs at an average of 30 and took 725 wickets at 23 each, and played twice for England.

W.G. Grace was absent, playing against Australia at the Oval. His elder brother E.M. was nearing the end of his career, but his son, W.G. junior, was in his first season for the county, and would win a blue at Cambridge for the following three seasons. Nowhere near as talented as his father, he died aged 30 after a failed appendectomy.

Cheltenham, Monday

Brilliant weather favoured the opening of the annual cricket festival at Cheltenham. This year Gloucestershire meet the adjoining shire and also the Australians, but in the first match started yesterday, they were not fully represented, as they suffered from the absence of W. G. Grace, who was doing duty at the Oval, Captain Luard, and Mr O. G. Radcliffe: whilst, on the other hand, Somerset have their best eleven. The latter were fortunate in winning the toss, but on batting first they did not make a very promising start, as the first half a dozen batsmen were all got rid of for 74 runs. When Woods joined Roe, however, the game underwent a change: for, hitting Murch's deliveries pretty freely, the former was not dismissed until the total had reached 118, and of the 44 added during the partnership Woods claimed 26.

In the meantime Roe had been playing very finely, and on the advent of Newton he continued to hit in very good style, 37 more runs being added to the total before Newton was caught, but Roe stayed on until the score was 191, being the ninth man out, after compiling a brilliant 75. He was at the wickets only an hour and thirty-five minutes, and among his chief hits were nine 4's, one 3 and eight 2's. The innings eventually closed for 197.

Gloucestershire, like their rivals, did badly at the commencement, losing Rice before a run had been made, whilst young W. G. Grace, after staying at the wickets forty minutes, was dismissed for 7. Ferris and De Winton improved matters by contributing double figures, but the last-named could get no one to stay with him and when stumps were drawn for the day five wickets were down for 83 runs.

Tuesday

Set with 302 to get to win, Gloucestershire to-day in the above match at Cheltenham have a very uphill task before them, and with a dearth of good batsmen, which they are suffering from at the present time, it is very unlikely that they will accomplish the perfor-

mance. On continuing their yesterday's innings the home county were 109 runs behind their rivals with only half their wickets in hand, but thanks to the very plucky stand by De Winton and Page the majority of these runs were knocked off in spite of repeated changes in the visitors' attack. The partnership, which had commenced overnight, lasted about an hour and a half, during which period 72 runs were added to the total, and, though Page was only credited with 22, he was loudly cheered for his invaluable defence. De Winton was not displaced until he had compiled a brilliant 80 which had occupied two hours and fifty minutes to put together, with best hits of five 4's, five 3's, and twelve 2's. After his dismissal the innings soon closed for a total of 165. Aided by some luck, Hewett and L. Palairet, who opened the visitors' second venture, scored 58 for the first wicket, whilst the latter and Challen, hitting very vigorously, put on 64 for the second. Hedley and R. Palairet contributed double figures, but it was left for L. Palairet to carry off the honours of the day, as he scored a fine item of 72 before being got rid of. He gave a chance when he had made only two, but afterwards played sterling cricket, his hits being eight 4's, two 3's, and seven 2's. All the Somersetshire players continued to bat very finely, and

William Brain, holding the glove

it seemed as if they would contribute a big innings, as the total had reached 270 for seven wickets. Then followed, however, a remarkable and sensational performance on the part of young Townsend, who, it will be remembered, was only tried for Gloucestershire for the first time last Thursday. With three successive deliveries he got rid of Newton, Nichols, and Tyler, and thus accomplished the 'hat trick', a very rare feat in first-class cricket. Curious to relate, each batsman was very smartly stumped by Brain, so that great credit belongs to him. With the abrupt termination of the Somersetshire innings play ceased for the day.

Wednesday

As anticipated, the task set Gloucestershire yesterday of obtaining 302 runs to give them victory proved too much for their powers. Although brilliant weather again favoured proceedings few spectators attended on the College Ground to witness the close, as very little interest was taken in the finish, so hopeless did the home county's task appear.

They started very badly, and with half their wickets down for 47 runs it seemed as if the innings would not realise 100. Page and E. M. Grace, however, made matters a little more lively, and took the total to 82 before the sixth wicket fell, whilst in spite of repeated changes in the bowling Page and Brain kept together until the first-named had contributed a sterling 40, for which he had been batting just over an hour, his best hits being four 4's, two 3's and five 2's. Murch and Roberts gave some trouble, but the end soon came, the innings closing for 174, leaving Somersetshire victorious by 127 runs. Score:

SOMERSET

W. C. Hedley, b Murch 8	c Brain, b Ferris 14
L. C. H. Palairet, b Roberts 27	c Painter, b Ferris 72
J. B. Challen, b Murch 14	st Brain, b W. G. Grace, jun. 30
R. C. N. Palairet, c Brain, b Roberts 16	c W. G. Grace, jun., b Roberts 39
V. T. Hill, b Roberts 0	c Page, b Murch 29
W. N. Roe, b Roberts 75	not out 9
H. T. Hewett, c Page, b Murch 0	c Painter, b Murch 33
S. M. J. Woods, st Brain, b Townsend 26	c De Winton, b Townsend 22
A. F. Newton, c De Winton, b Murch 13	st Brain, b Townsend 4
Nichols, not out 9	st Brain, b Townsend 0
Tyler, b Ferris 1	st Brain, b Townsend 0
Byes 8	B 15, l b 3 18
Total 197	Total 270

GLOUCESTERSHIRE

J. J. Ferris, b Nichols 32	b Tyler 1
R. W. Rice, c and b Tyler 0	c Roe, b Tyler 2
W. G. Grace, jun., c Newton b Nichols 7	c and b Woods 14
G. S. De Winton, l b w, b Tyler 80	run out 10
J. Painter, c R. Palairet, b Hedley ... 6	c Newton, b Woods 11
E. M. Grace, b Hedley 0	c L. Palaired, b Tyler 28
H. V. Page, c L. Palairet, b Nichols 22	b Nichols 40
W. H. Brain, c Woods, b Tyler 5	c Hewett, b Tyler 17
C. L. Townsend, not out 1	c R. Palairet, b Tyler 4
Murch, b Tyler 2	c R. Palairet, b Hedley 26
Roberts, c Hill, b Tyler 1	not out 11
B 9, l b 1 10	B 10
Total 166	Total 174

SOMERSET – First Innings

	O	M	R	W		O	M	R	W
Townsend	20	3	71	1	Roberts	17	2	43	4
Murch	24	5	67	4	Ferris	10.3	1	8	1

Second Innings

	O	M	R	W		O	M	R	W
Murch	20	2	88	2	W. G. Grace Jr. ...	12	3	30	1
Roberts	15	3	44	1	Townsend	8	1	16	4
Ferris	19	2	74	2					

GLOUCESTERSHIRE – First Innings

	O	M	R	W		O	M	R	W
Tyler	33.2	12	39	5	Nichols	33	15	48	3
Woods	13	2	32	0	Hedley	23	6	37	2

Second Innings

	O	M	R	W		O	M	R	W
Tyler	35	10	71	5	Hedley	7.2	2	23	1
Woods	21	4	46	2	Nichols	10	4	24	1

Umpires – J. Street and S. Talbeys.

6: *Surrey v Essex*
THE OVAL, 18–20 JUNE 1894

Surrey were the pre-eminent side of the Nineties, winning six Championships between 1890 and 1899, including in this year. However, although this was a first-class match, Essex were not to enter the Championship until the following season. Surrey's dominance is all too clear from the fashion in which they – or rather Richardson – disposed of their opponents, and then scored with such ease on a bowler's wicket, leaving Essex in a position aptly described by *The Daily Telegraph's* correspondent as 'hopeless'.

From 1893 to 1898 Tom Richardson (1870–1912) took more than 160 wickets each year, including 196 in this season and a record 290 in 1895, which only 'Tich' Freeman subsequently overtook. He played 14 tests for England and toured Australia twice, and was without question England's leading fast bowler. Herbert Strudwick, who kept wicket for Surrey for the first quarter of the 20th century, said Richardson remained the finest bowler he had ever seen. His return in the first innings of this match – 10 for 45 – was the best bowling of his career, and has only once been bettered for Surrey. No bowler ever took more wickets in a season or in a career for the county, despite Surrey being the team of Bedser, Laker and Lock.

Although the Surrey batting in the 1890s is what the side is remembered for (see games 12, 13 and 14), Richardson's role as spearhead was if anything more crucial. Troubled in his thirties by severe obesity, he disappeared from the Surrey side in 1904. He played once for Somerset, in 1905, but his glorious, short career – in which he took 2,104 wickets at 18 each – was at an end. He died, tragically young, of a brain haemorrhage before his 42nd birthday.

The Oval, Monday

Showery weather greatly curtailed the play in this match yesterday at the Oval, where these counties met for the first time this season. Rain not only caused a temporary cessation early in the match, but later put a stop to the game. Only seventy minutes' cricket was possible, during which time Essex completed their first innings for the moderate total of 72. The wicket was slow after the overnight rain, and Richardson proved a terror to the visitors. He and Smith went on to bowl, and Essex had a very bad time of it. One after another fell before Richardson's fast deliveries, and after an hour's play, when rain caused a cessation, eight wickets had fallen for 55 runs, all being credited to Richardson, while only one batsman, Burrell, obtained double figures. Another fifteen minutes' play subsequently finished off the venture for 72, Richardson having taken all ten wickets, eight being bowled, for 45 runs. Just as they concluded the innings rain came on again, and the downpour continued the remainder of the afternoon. At half-past five stumps were drawn for the day.

Tuesday

On a wicket which had dried considerably after the previous night's heavy downpour, the Surrey eleven yesterday kept their opponents fielding for close upon six hours. The Surrey batsmen hit out with great freedom and compiled a total of 438 runs. All the side scored, and only two failed to obtain double figures. Brockwell, batting for a little over two hours, ran up 108 by vigorous play, and D. L. A. Jephson, the only amateur on the side, came very near his century, carrying out his bat for a finely-hit 94. Abel and Read opened the venture, and they scored 92 runs in an hour and ten minutes before being separated. Another 44 were put on by Abel and Hayward, and then, with Brockwell and Abel together, runs were piled up at a fast pace, and it was not until the total had been carried to 202 that the third wicket was obtained, Abel being easily caught for a finely played 65, which had occupied him two hours and three-quarters. Among his hits were one 5, six 4's, four 3's and three 2's. Jephson was an able partner to Brockwell, the latter realising his hundred as the result of an hour and fifty minutes at the wickets. A third century was hooked by

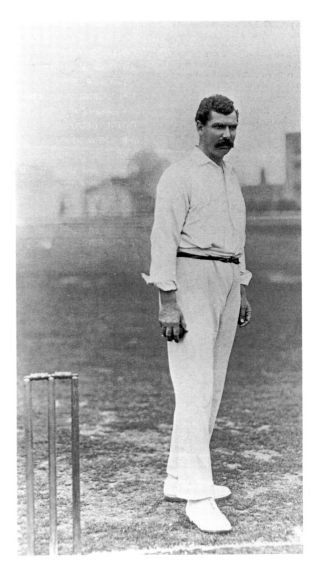

Tom Richardson

this pair without further loss, and it was not until 322 had been scored that Brockwell was dismissed, his 108 including twelve 4's, four 3's, and fourteen 2's. The next two wickets gave the least trouble, but subsequently Jephson had Street and Ayres to assist him. After eight wickets had fallen for 376, Marshall became associated with the amateur, and further vigorous hitting carried the score past a fourth hundred, the ninth wicket adding 49. The innings closed, just as Jephson looked like realising his hundred, for a total of 438. Jephson had been in over three hours for his not-out contribution of 94, which contained two 5's, seven 4's, five 3's, and six 2's. Surrey were 366 on when Essex went in a second time. They had a very bad time of it, losing three wickets for 25 runs, and now require 341 to save a single-innings defeat.

Wednesday

The weather yesterday morning was dull and threatening, and with absolutely no interest left in the game, only a few spectators witnessed the final stage, which extended over sixty-five minutes, during which period the remaining seven wickets fell for an addition to the total of 80, which left Surrey victorious by an innings and 261 runs. Carpenter (13) was joined at the wicket by Burrell, and Richardson and Smith took up the bowling. With the score of 27 (2 added) Burrell was bowled by Richardson, and that player also got rid of Lucas and Carpenter, who played steadily for his 25, and six men were out for 46. With 7 added Russell was run out, but on Kortright joining M'Gahey the rot was stayed for a time. The Essex fast bowler hit in splendid style, whilst M'Gahey played a defensive game. Jephson and Brockwell had a turn with the ball, but the hundred was hoisted at half-past twelve, and not until the partnership had yielded 52 runs was it dissolved by Jephson, who bowled M'Gahey. Pickett came in, and Richardson resumed bowling vice Brockwell. The change at once worked, as without addition Kortright, who had played excellent cricket, was caught in the long field, and Hailey being absent, the innings closed for 105. Score:

ESSEX

Burns, c Marshall, b Richardson	9	b Smith	6
Carpenter, b Richardson	0	b Richardson	25
H. G. Owen, b Richardson	5	st Marshall, b Smith	4
H. Hailey, b Richardson	3	absent ill	0
R. J. Burrell, b Richardson	31	b Richardson	1
Russell, b Richardson	0	run out	12
C. M'Gahey, b Richardson	1	b Jephson	16
A. P. Lucas, b Richardson	5	b Richardson	3
C. J. Kortright, c Hayward, b Richardson	5	c Read, b Richardson	34
Mead, b Richardson	11	b Richardson	1
Pickett, not out	1	not out	0
L b	1	B	3
Total	72	Total	105

SURREY

Abel, c Pickett, b Mead	65
Read, b Burns	59
Hayward, b Owen	35
Brockwell, h w, b Burns	108
D. L. A. Jephson, not out	94
Henderson, c Burns, b Mead	1
Street, b Mead	10
Ayres, b Kortright	16
Smith (F.), c Lucas, b Kortright	4
Marshall, b Owen	22
Richardson, c and b Mead	6
B 13, l b 4, n b 1	18
Total	438

ESSEX – First Innings

	O	M	R	W		O	M	R	W
Richardson	15.3	3	45	10	Street	2	0	4	0
Smith	13	4	22	0					

Second Innings

	O	M	R	W		O	M	R	W
Richardson	16.3	5	50	5	Jephson	5	1	17	1
Smith	14	4	27	2	Brockwell	3	1	8	0

SURREY – First Innings

	O	M	R	W		O	M	R	W
Kortricht	38	10	96	2	Pickett	14	2	28	0
Mead	48.3	11	139	6	Owen	13	2	37	2
Burns	47	12	104	2	Carpenter	4	0	16	0

Owen delivered one no ball.
Umpires – Thomas and Lillywite.

7: Somerset v Lancashire

TAUNTON, 15–17 JULY 1895

No batsman has yet scored more in a single innings in an English first-class match than Archie MacLaren in Lancashire's defeat of Somerset in 1895, though Graeme Hick would come close over 93 years later on the same ground, the next time 400 was passed in England (see game 99). It would be 27 years before Ponsford – who accomplished the feat twice – would match MacLaren anywhere else on earth. At this time declarations in the first innings were still not allowed, so unless batsmen were prepared to throw their wickets away gargantuan totals would be built up on wickets as friendly as Taunton's appears to have been. Three of the four scores of 800 or more in the Championship up to 1990 were made between 1895 and 1899 (see games 8 and 13); the fourth was in 1934 (see game 52). Lancashire's total was the highest ever made in county cricket (though it would be surpassed the following year by Yorkshire), and was the county record until the 863 at the Oval in 1990.

MacLaren, by now the captain of his county, also made what was at that point the second highest second-wicket stand in the world with Arthur Paul. Paul (1864–1947) had toured Australia with England's Rugby team, and had been goalkeeper for Blackburn Rovers; after his retirement he became the Lancashire coach. His 177 was to be the highest score of his career, and 1895 was his most successful season with the bat. Lancashire had a fine season too, coming second in the Championship, which was that year expanded to 14 counties with the inclusion of Derbyshire, Essex, Hampshire, Leicestershire and Warwickshire. Somerset, who finished ninth, continued to suffer from weak bowling. As the reports tell, Essex had taken 692 off them in the previous match, and W.G. Grace had that year scored 288 against them.

Taunton, Monday

A good many remarkable batting performances have so far been accomplished during the present cricket season, but none to compare with that done by

Lancashire on the opening day of the above match at Taunton yesterday. Going in first on a splendid wicket, the visitors kept their rivals in the field during the whole of the time available for play, and ran up the wonderful total of 555 for the loss of only three batsmen. After MacLaren and Albert Ward had put on 141 runs for the first wicket, of which number the professional claimed 64, a sensational partnership took place between MacLaren and Paul. The pair flogged the weak Somerset bowling with such effect that they augmented the score to the extent of no fewer than 363 runs in just three hours. This constitutes the second highest stand on record for the second wicket, the best being that of Shrewsbury and Gunn, who together made 398 for Notts against Sussex, in 1890. Paul, whose hits included one 6, thirty 4's, two 3's, and nine 2's, contributed a brilliant effort of 177, made in three hours, and as MacLaren is at present not out with 289 to his credit, a further opportunity will be offered to-day to refer to his display.

Tuesday

After the huge score of 555 for three wickets made by Lancashire on the opening day of the above fixture at Taunton no one was yesterday surprised to find two new records had been established as far as first-class cricket is concerned. The first was when A. C. MacLaren, who overnight had 289 not out to his credit, ran his figures into 424. This wonderful compilation is the highest ever made in first-class county cricket, the previous best having been 318, made by W. G. Grace as long ago as August, 1876, for Gloucestershire against Yorkshire, at Cheltenham, whilst it stands second to the highest individual score made in any match, A. E. Stoddart being credited with 485 for Hampstead v. Stoics, in August, 1885. Though the young Lancashire amateur gave two chances during his lengthy stay of seven hours and fifty minutes at the wickets, the first before he reached his century, and the second at 262, his contribution is all the more remarkable when it is taken into consideration that he is not yet twenty-four years of age, having been born

on Dec. 1, 1871. All through his innings he displayed wonderful command over the bowling, and his cutting in particular was remarkably fine. His hits included one 6 (out of the ground), sixty-two 4's, eleven 3's, thirty-seven 2's, and 63 singles. At the close he was the recipient of an immense number of congratulations from friends and opponents alike. When the Northerners' venture closed for the immense total of 801 another record had been passed, as this is the highest aggregate ever obtained in first-class county cricket, the best previously being 726 made by Notts, at the beginning of the present season, against Sussex, at Nottingham, while not far behind was Essex's 692, compiled on the Taunton ground last week. As may be imagined, Somerset had a very thankless task when they went in to bat after such a long time in the field. Their first innings only realised 143, and going in a second time they lost one wicket for 68 runs ere stumps were drawn for the day.

Wednesday

When stumps were drawn at Taunton, on Tuesday, Somerset were in a hopeless position, as, with nine wickets to fall, they required 600 runs to avoid a single-innings defeat; the Somerset second innings total then standing at 58. Two more wickets fell when it amounted to 73, but, thanks to Fowler, Woods, and Tyler, a very fair struggle was made, and the venture lasted over three hours and realised 206. Score:

LANCASHIRE

A. C. MacLaren, c Fowler, b Gamlin 424	Baker, st Wickham, b L. Palairet ... 23
Ward (A.), c R. Palairet, b Tyler 64	Briggs, not out 9
Paul, c Gamlin, b. L. Palairet 177	Smith (C.), c Trask, b L. Palairet ... 0
Hallam, c Fowler, b L. Palairet ... 6	Mold, c R. Palairet, b Gamlin 0
C. H. Benton, c and b Fowler 43	B 9, l b 4, w 1 14
Sugg (F. H.), c Wickham, b Woods 41	
Tinsley, c Gamlin, b Woods 0	Total 801

SOMERSET

L. C. H. Palairet, b Briggs 30	b Mold 4
G. Fowler, c sub, b Hallam 39	c MacLaren 46
H. C. N. Palairet, c Hallam, b Mold 2	st Smith, b Briggs 7
H. T. Stanley, c Smith, b Briggs 8	c Smith, b Mold 12
H. R. Porch, run out 18	c MacLaren, b Mold 1
S. M. J. Woods, c Smith, b Mold ... 11	b Briggs 55
Dr. J. F. Trask, c Ward, b Mold ... 11	c and b Mold 26
Rev. A. P. Wickham, b Mold 3	not out 0
Tyler, not out 15	b Briggs 41
E. W. Bartlett, b Briggs 4	c Mold, b Briggs 6
Gamlin, st Smith, b Briggs 0	hit wicket, b Briggs 0
L b 2	B 4, l b 4 8
Total 143	Total 206

LANCASHIRE – First Innings

	O	M	R	W		O	M	R	W
Tyler	59	5	212	1	H. Palairet	11	3	41	0
Woods	46	5	163	2	Trask	2	0	9	0
L. Palairet	44	10	133	4	Porch	5	3	16	0
Gamlin	26	8	100	2	Bartlett	6	0	16	0
Fowler	23	5	97	1					

L. Palairet delivered a wide.

SOMERSET – First Innings

	O	M	R	W		O	M	R	W
Briggs	37.3	15	59	4	Hallam	2	1	7	1
Mold	35	15	75	4					

Second Innings

	O	M	R	W		O	M	R	W
Briggs	37	17	78	5	Mold	33	11	76	5
Hallam	8	2	19	0	Baker	5	8	25	0

Umpires – J. Wickers and Howe.

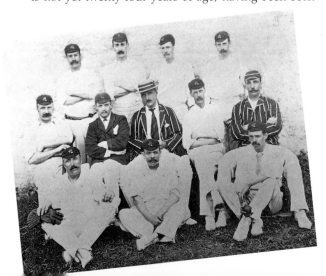

The Lancashire side of 1895

8: *Warwickshire v Yorkshire*
EDGBASTON, 7–9 MAY 1896

Lancashire's record for the highest county score was to survive less than 10 months, until Yorkshire, who would finish the season as champions, batted for the first two days of this match to amass 887. It was, at the time, the highest score to be made in a first-class match, though held for only four years until New South Wales took 918 off South Australia at Sydney. It remains the highest score ever made in a county match, and only England's 903 for 7 in Hutton's Test in 1938 has surpassed it in England. Never before had four batsmen made hundreds in the same innings. The rule about not declaring in first innings still applied, and it was somewhat typical of the determination with which mighty Yorkshire sides ground down their opponents over the next half-century that there was no throwing away of wickets in order to get the opposition in.

Peel and Lord Hawke put on 292 for the eighth wicket, still an English record, and bettered only once in all cricket. Hawke (1860–1938), who succeeded to his father's barony in 1887, captained Yorkshire from 1883 to 1910 and was the county's president from 1898 until his death. He was the dominating voice in Yorkshire cricket for over half a century, and through his involvement with MCC a major influence on the game nationally and internationally. A particular concern of his was to drive heavy-drinking players out of the game. One of those to be affected by this policy was Peel (1857–1941), whom Hawke abruptly sacked for drunkenness in 1897, after 15 years on the staff. Peel was principally a bowler and Hawke never more than an ordinary lower-order bat, and the scores they made in this match were the highest of their careers.

Lord Hawke

work; 50 runs were the result of half an hour's play. Thirteen runs later the professional was caught at mid-off. Brown joined Jackson, the latter registering his 50 in fifty-five minutes. Brown was soon sent back, and Denton only assisted to the extent of 5. Moorhouse now came in, and a lengthy stand was made. Despite frequent changes in the attack, the batsmen hit with great freedom. It was not until Jackson had made 117 that he was secured by Law. He had been at the wickets two hours and a half, and hit thirteen 4's. His only mistake was when he had made 71. Wainwright next partnered Moorhouse, and made things very lively, scoring 26 in three overs. With the score at 339 Moorhouse was clean bowled for 72. A few minutes before six the 400 went up, but 5 runs later Wainwright was run out, through a quick piece of fielding, by the younger Quaife. He had batted in excellent fashion for 126, and never gave a chance. His chief hits were sixteen 4's. Peel and F. W. Milligan became partners. The former was easily missed when he had made 17, and the pair kept at the wickets until a few minutes before time, when the amateur played on. Lord Hawke and Peel were together until the close, the score standing at 452 for seven wickets.

Birmingham, Thursday

The Midlanders opened their home encounters yesterday at the County Ground, Edgbaston, against Yorkshire, who, after a sensational finish, defeated Lancashire at the beginning of the week.

The Northerners won the toss, and, taking advantage of an excellent wicket, kept their opponents in the field all day, two 'centuries' being recorded. F. S. Jackson and Tunnicliffe started the game, and quickly got to

Friday

For the second time this week Warwickshire have had their full share of fielding, and yesterday, at Birmingham, had to spend a second full day in succession leather hunting, while Yorkshire established a new record in first-class cricket by putting together 887. This is the highest total ever made in first-class cricket, the previous best being 843, Australians v. Cambridge University Past and Present, in 1893. Four separate three-figure innings were recorded, Peel being credited with 210 not out, a grand performance. When play finished on Thursday, the score stood at 452 for seven wickets, so that yesterday the remaining three wickets put on 435. Peel (37) and Hawke (3) were the not-outs, and at 11.35 those batsmen resumed their innings to the bowling of Ward and Santall. Runs came rapidly, and despite frequent changes they were still together at the luncheon interval, when both had completed their centuries. Each played sterling cricket, and with the exception of Law all the Warwickshire team were tried to bring about their downfall, but without avail until 292 had been added to the score, when Lord Hawke, who had given his first chance when he had made 151, played on to his wicket. He had been batting three hours fifty minutes for his 166, which is the best that he has made in first-class cricket, his previous having been 157 for Mr. Thornton's Eleven against Cambridge some years ago. He hit twenty-one 4's, seven 3's, and thirteen 2's. Hirst filled the vacancy, and soon got to work. He hit vigorously for 85, when, with the total at 876, he was caught in the slips. He hit fifteen 4's. Hunter was last man in, and after making 5 was bowled, and the innings closed for 887, Peel being not out, 210, which exceeds his previous best by 2 in first-class cricket. He gave a chance early in his innings, but otherwise it was faultless. Included in it were one 5, sixteen 4's, fourteen 3's, and seventeen 2's. He was at the wicket in all seven hours and a quarter, and his effort must be considered a brilliant one. The Tykes will have all their work cut out to-day to get rid of their rivals twice in succession in a little over six hours.

Saturday

The North Countrymen set about the task of getting the home team out twice in one day, but failed, the match eventually ending in a draw. But for W. G.

Quaife, the game might have finished disastrously for Warwickshire, as, with the exception of his 92, only three others got into double figures. The young professional gave a splendid display, and his not-out innings is deserving of great praise. Santall's 29 was the next best score. The innings closed, at five o'clock, for 203. An arrangement having been made to draw at six, there was but half an hour left for play when Warwickshire followed on, 684 runs in arrear, and they lost one wicket for 48. Score:

YORKSHIRE

F. S. Jackson, c Law, b Ward 117	F. W. Milligan, b Pallett 34
Tunnicliffe, c Pallett, b Glover 28	Lord Hawke, b Pallett 166
Brown, c Hill, b Pallett 23	Hirst, c Glover, b Santall 85
Denton, c W. G. Quaife, b Santall .. 6	Hunter, b Pallett 5
Moorhouse, b Ward 72	B 5, l b 6, w 4 15
Wainwright, run out 126	
Peel, not out 210	Total 887

WARWICKSHIRE

H. W. Bainbridge, c Hunter, b Hirst . 5	b Wainwright 29
Quaife (W.), b Hirst 0	not out 18
Quaife (W. G.), not out 92	
Law, c Jackson, b Hirst 7	
Lilley, b Hirst 0	
J. E. Hill, b Hirst 4	
Diver, b Peel 27	
Pallett, c Wainwright, b Jackson ... 25	
Santall, b Hirst 29	
A. C. S. Glover, b Hirst 1	
Ward, b Hirst 3	
B 4, l b 3, w 1, n b 2 10	n b 1
Total 203	Total (1 wicket) 48

YORKSHIRE – First Innings

	O	M	R	W		O	M	R	W
Santall	65	9	223	2	Bainbridge	6	1	17	0
Ward	62	11	175	2	Hill	3	0	14	0
Glover	30	1	154	1	Lilley	6	1	13	0
Pallett	75.3	14	184	4	Quaife (W.)	9	1	18	0
Quaife (W.G.)	8	1	33	0	Diver	10	1	41	0

Pallett bowled two wides and Hill and Diver one wide each.

WARWICKSHIRE – First Innings

	O	M	R	W		O	M	R	W
Hirst	40.1	16	59	8	Milligan	13	5	14	0
Peel	31	21	27	1	Brown	4	0	24	0
Jackson	18	9	23	1	Moorhouse	4	1	11	0
Wainwright	16	7	35	0					

Hirst and Moorhouse each bowled a no ball, and Peel one wide.

Second Innings

	O	M	R	W		O	M	R	W
Milligan	5	1	15	0	Peel	2	2	4	0
Moorhouse	4	0	24	0	Wainwright	2.1	1	4	1

Moorhouse bowled one no ball

9: *Gloucestershire v Sussex*
BRISTOL, 3–5 AUGUST 1896

Dr W. G. Grace (1848–1915) was the towering figure of English cricket in the last 30 years of the 19th century. His legend dominated the game until long after his death, his face – or rather beard – still the most famous physical image of a cricketer in the world. He played his first first-class match in 1865, aged 16, going in first and opening the bowling for the Gentlemen at Lord's; his last match was in 1908 at the age of 60. Grounds used to put up signs like 'Admission, 3d. If Dr W.G. Grace plays, admission 6d.' He was known as 'the Champion' and established and broke records as a matter of routine. He was the first batsman to score two centuries in a first-class match; the first to score a treble century; the first to score ten centuries in a season; the first to score 100 centuries in a career; the first to score 2,000 runs in a season; and so on. He was similarly prodigious as a bowler, taking nine wickets in an innings three times and ten wickets once. In his career he made 54,896 runs at an average of 39.55, and took 2,876 wickets at 18 each. In 1895, at the age of 47, he scored 1,000 runs in May. To mark his 'rejuvenation' *The Daily Telegraph* organised a shilling testimonial for him, which raised the then phenomenal sum of £5,000; a further £5,000 was raised from other sources. So much for amateurism.

Grace's treble century was his third and last. For good measure, the three wickets he took in the Sussex second innings helped secure his side's victory. Grace, together with his brothers, transformed Gloucestershire into a first-class county and he captained them from 1871 until he left, after a difference of opinion with the club's committee, in 1899.

Bristol, Monday

Between 9,000 and 10,000 people assembled at the Bristol County Ground to witness the first day's play in this match. The weather was beautifully fine, and an excellent wicket had been prepared. Sussex were without Butt (who injured his hand badly last week) and Brann, who were replaced by R. W. Fox and A. Collins. Gloucestershire were strongly represented, and, winning the toss, made such excellent use of their good fortune that Sussex had to field all day, whilst 341

W.G. – 'The Doctor'

runs were hit off their bowling for the loss of only three wickets. This state of affairs seemed hardly likely to be achieved when W. G. Grace, jun., was bowled with the score at 4. Afterwards, however, Grace, sen., had ample revenge for his son's early dismissal, and, as he was still not out when stumps were drawn, a chance exists of his beating his previous best score this season, viz., 243. His most useful partner was Rice, who remained three hours and a quarter, and helped to subscribe 211. Rice played very correct although careful cricket, and it is worth noting that whereas he was two hours and fifty minutes in scoring 50, Grace completed 100 in five minutes less time. Rice had never previously made such a big score for his county, his highest being 67, against Middlesex, in 1892. That he was not afraid to hit when opportunity served is proved by his making fourteen 4's and seven 2's. Hemingway played very well for his 30, and then Townsend stayed with his captain to the close, although he should have been caught and bowled by Tate when 3. Grace played splendidly all day, and his only bad stroke was made after his score had exceeded the century. He played all round the wicket in quite his best form.

Tuesday

It will be long before those privileged to witness yesterday's play in this match, at Bristol, will forget the treat afforded them. The day was made memorable by another great performance on the part of Dr. W. G. Grace, who exceeded all efforts accomplished by himself since 1876, and also ran up a bigger score than any cricketer has made in a first-class match this year. The weather was again beautifully fine, and a crowd of quite 10,000 people attended. How the game will result today is a difficult matter to say; the most probable conclusion would seem to be a draw, for Sussex have seventeen wickets to fall, and, in the absence of rain, the wicket will, in all likelihood, hold good to the close. Sussex can hope for nothing better than the mere averting of defeat, however, for they will start the third stage of the encounter with a deficit of 419 confronting them. On Monday Gloucestershire occupied the crease all day, and totalled 331 for the loss of only three wickets. Grace, senior (193) and Townsend (29) being the not outs. For a while yesterday Tate and Parris carried all before them, and in the first half-hour five more wickets fell for an addition to the figures of only 14. Then came the feature of the match. This was supplied by Grace, sen., and Kitcat, who remained together three hours. Kitcat proceeded very cautiously against all the bowlers, but Grace continued to play in his own inimitable fashion. Four hundred was telegraphed in six hours and a half from the start, Grace's share being 228. After batting two hours and fifty minutes, Kitcat reached 50, and at the expiration of eight hours 500 was telegraphed. Altogether, the partnership for the ninth wicket realised 196, and then

Grace was bowled. The enthusiasm evoked by the Champion's display is difficult to describe. Grace's score of 301 is notable from many standpoints. It is the highest made in first-class cricket this year – L. C. H. Palairet's 292 for Somerset v. Hampshire being the previous best – and the greatest ever compiled in the ground. Since 1876 the Gloucestershire captain has not made such a total, but in that season he scored 344 against Kent (which remained the highest individual contribution in first-class cricket up to A. C. MacLaren's 424 for Lancashire v. Somerset in July last year) and 318 not out against Yorkshire. The only other total of 300 in big matches in England is 338 by W. W. Read, for Surrey v. Oxford, in July, 1888. Probably Grace never played better cricket in his life. He made very few risky strokes, and absolutely gave nothing that could be called a chance. His hits included twenty-nine 4's, sixteen 3's, and twenty-six 2's. Roberts was soon disposed of, and Kitcat was left to carry out his bat for 77. For that number he was at the wicket over three hours, so that it will be seen he was inclined to run no risks. The crowd were almost as delighted with his performance as with that of Grace, and carried the young amateur shoulder-high to the pavilion at the close.

There was an hour and a half left for play when Sussex commenced their forlorn task. Marlow and Killick made a pretty good start, and, despite bowling changes, put on 60 before they were parted. Marlow, who obtained 50 in three-quarters of an hour, left shortly after; but Murdoch stayed some time.

Wednesday

At Bristol, yesterday, the Sussex eleven just failed to play out time by a quarter of an hour and were defeated by an innings and 125 runs. Although it was certain Sussex would have to act strictly on the defensive all day if they were to save the game, spectators were again numerous. When stumps were drawn on Tuesday Sussex had scored 132 for three wickets, against the 551 put together by Gloucestershire. Ranjitsinhji (31) and Newham (9) were the not outs, but yesterday the former caused great disappointment by merely adding seven before he was bowled. Not so Newham, however, who carried out his bat for an excellent 63, the one chance

he offered being to Grace, jun., when 60. He hit a 5, five 4's, two 5's, and six 2's. The only player to afford Newham respectable assistance was Collins, who remained an hour, and saw 51 added for the sixth wicket. Altogether the innings lasted three hours and twenty-five minutes, and closed for 250, so that Sussex had to follow on 301 to the bad. The wicket was showing signs of wear, and the visitors' second essay proved far less productive than their first. Still, they made a gallant attempt to avert defeat. The first wicket fell at 38, and the second (Killick's) at 75. Ranjitsinhji went in for hitting, and in forty minutes knocked up 50, but four later was out to a fine catch by the younger Grace at mid-off. Collins and Tate made a fine stand, and looked like saving the match; but a bit of bad play at the finish – the last two men were out l b w – gave Gloucestershire victory. Score:

GLOUCESTERSHIRE

W. G. Grace, sen., b Collins 301	C. O. H. Sewell, b Parris 4
W. G. Grace, jun., b Hartley 1	G. L. Jessop, l b w b Parris 2
R. W. Rice, c Parris, b Ranjitsinhji . 84	Board, c and b Parris 0
W. McG. Hemingway, c Killick,	S. A. F. Kitcat, not out 77
b Hartley 30	Roberts, c Parris, b Killick 2
C. L. Townsend, c and b Tate 30	B 17, l b 3 20
Wrathall, c Parris, b Tate 0	Total 551

SUSSEX

Marlow, c Hemingway,		
b Townsend 57	c and b Townsend 21
Killick, b Jessop 13	b Jessop 20
K. S. Ranjitsinhji, b Roberts 38	c Grace, jun., b Jessop 54
W. L. Murdoch, b Townsend 12	run out 9
W. Newham, not out 63	l b w, b Grace, sen. 11
Bean, c Jessop, b Townsend 8	c Wrathall, b Grace, sen. 6
A. C. Collins, c and b Roberts 23	not out 14
J. C. Hartley, c Grace, sen.,		
b Roberts 0	b Grace, sen. 0
Parris, c Townsend, b Grace, sen., . 1	b Roberts 3
Tate, b Roberts 4	l b w, b Roberts 30
R. W. Fox, b Roberts 9	l b w, b Townsend 0
B 13, l b 6, w 1, n b 3 22	B 6, l b 1, n b 3 10
Total 250	Total 178

GLOUCESTERSHIRE – First Innings

	O	M	R	W		O	M	R	W
Tate	65	24	134	2	Killick	32.2	11	57	2
Hartley	37	5	115	2	Bean	13	4	34	0
Collings	48	7	48	1	Ranjitsinhji	12	1	40	1
Parris	63	30	103	3					

SUSSEX – First Innings

	O	M	R	W		O	M	R	W
Townsend	27	4	88	3	Grace, sen.	10	3	30	1
Roberts	27	7	50	5	Grace, jin.	4	0	8	0
Jessop	19	4	52	1					

Townsend bowled one wide and Roberts three no balls.

Second Innings

	O	M	R	W		O	M	R	W
Roberts	24	10	38	2	Jessop	14	7	40	2
Townsend	26.3	3	67	2	Grace, sen.	19	11	23	4

Jessop bowled three no balls.
Umpires – Littlewood and Chester.

10: Yorkshire v Gloucestershire
HARROGATE, 29–31 JULY 1897

Gilbert Jessop (1874–1955), universally known as 'the Croucher' because of his batting stance, is one of those cricketers synonymous with the golden age of the game

before the Great War. He was one of the mightiest, and most successful, aggressive batsmen in the history of the game, blessed with the combination of physical strength and superb hand and eye co-ordination. He was also one of the greatest fielders in history. His fast scoring feats are legendary. Often overlooked, given his excellence with the bat, were his feats as a fast bowler: in his career he took 873 wickets at 23 each, twice accomplishing the double. This season, 1897, was his best with the ball. But it is with fast scoring that we are concerned here. His 101 against Yorkshire was then the fastest in the history of the game, coming in 40 minutes. Unlike at least one and possibly two of the three faster centuries scored since, Jessop was not being served up easy balls to hasten a declaration. His Yorkshire opponents were possibly the finest side in the Championship, the reigning champions, and certainly not bent on easing Jessop's existence. Jessop also scored the two fastest double centuries in first-class cricket, in 120 and 130 minutes respectively, records not matched until 1976 and not beaten until 1984–85.

Jessop played for Gloucestershire for the 20 years before the Great War, making his debut in 1894. When he scored this fast hundred he had just completed his second year at Cambridge, for which he won a blue in each of his four summers. He played in 18 tests, and toured Australia once. He made 26,698 runs at an average of 32 in his career, though was less successful in tests, where he made just 569 at an average of 22.

Jessop – 'The Croucher'

was bowled. His hits were four 6's, fifteen 4's, a 3, and fourteen singles. The total when Jessop left was 190, so that 108 had been added in forty minutes. The second hundred appeared two hours and twenty minutes from the start, but 3 later Champain, who had batted patiently for 44, was caught in the slips. Hemingway's first ball proved disastrous, but another stand was effected by Townsend and Board. In an hour and five minutes they added 77, when Board was run out after contributing a useful 43. Townsend and Goodwin brought up the third hundred, and the former completed his hundred after two hours and a half's sound batting. He was out to a good catch in the slips shortly afterwards, having, during his stay, hit seventeen 4's, one 3, and five 2's. After his retirement the end soon came, the innings closing at a quarter past six for 370, having lasted five hours. Play then ceased for the day.

Harrogate, Thursday

The Western county gave a brilliant display of batting at Harrogate, when their return fixture with the champions was commenced. The visitors played the team that suffered such a severe reverse at the hands of Lancashire, whilst on the Yorkshire side C. E. M. Wilson displaced Haigh. Winning the toss, Dr. Grace, who made his first appearance on the Harrogate ground, opened the batting with Rice. The start was a bad one, only 13 being registered when Rice fell to an easy catch in the slips. Champain joined his captain, but runs proved difficult to get, and in half an hour only 16 had been scored. Grace was particularly slow, and after staying an hour and ten minutes for 22 he was dismissed by a fine catch at short slip. Wrathall hit vigorously whilst at the wickets, his 17 including four boundary hits off Wilson. Three wickets for 72. Jessop then came in and matters became exceedingly lively. The Cantab at once got to work, and in the twenty minutes before luncheon had registered 43, including a 6 and six 4's. After the interval he scored even faster, and in six consecutive overs he placed 48 to his credit – 18 coming from Hirst in one over. In forty minutes he had completed his hundred, but the next ball saw his downfall, as, in attempting to pull one of Jackson's, he

Friday

At Harrogate on Thursday the visitors kept their opponents in the field the whole of the day, while they compiled 370. Yesterday the game continued in their favour, as, after dismissing the home side for 278, in their second venture Gloucestershire put together 85 for the loss of two men, so that, with eight wickets in hand, they hold a lead of 180. The weather was exceedingly hot when Jackson and Tunnicliffe went to the wickets to open the Yorkshire innings. The first twenty-four minutes had produced as many runs when the old Cambridge captain was beaten by Jessop, who also disposed of Tunnicliffe 23 runs later. Brown and Denton carried the total to 62 when the latter was sent back, and only one run had been added when Wainwright and Wilson left. Half the Yorkshire wickets were thus down to 63, and the prospects of the champions were gloomy in the extreme. At this point, however, Brown and Hirst effected a great change in the game. They were still in possession when the interval was taken, having increased the score to 166 for five wickets. This was the extent of their partnership, however, as the first ball after luncheon Hirst returned to Jessop. He had made 55 out of 103 in an hour. Milligan contributed 15, and then Brown, who had batted in excellent form for two hours and twenty minutes for 80, was eighth to leave at 202. His hits included fourteen 4's and three 2's. When Lord Hawke joined Collinson 49 were still required to save the follow-on. By lively cricket, however, 68 runs were put on, and the innings closed at quarter-past four for 276. With a lead of 94, Gloucestershire opened their second venture in good style with Grace and Rice, who stayed together an hour before the latter played on. Grace fell to the last ball of the day, having during the course of his innings completed his 1,000 runs. The score at his retirement was 86 for two wickets.

Saturday

On the resumption of the game, Champain failed to add to his overnight total, Jessop, whose fine display in the first innings was the feature of the match, failed to score, and, to make matters worse, Townsend was disposed of for a single. Wrathall and Hemingway, however, came to the rescue, and added 55 in less than twenty-five minutes, after which Board and Goodwin, by free hitting, added another 62 for the eighth wicket before the amateur was sent back. Then the former and Brown put on 41 more, when Board was beaten, after batting admirably for 69. With his departure, at 271, Grace declared the innings closed, leaving Yorkshire four hours and a quarter in which to get 366 runs. The home side started in disheartening fashion, Jackson playing on in the fourth over. Tunnicliffe and Brown took the total to 31 before luncheon, but after the interval the former was soon out. Brown and Denton further improved Yorkshire's prospects, and by free cricket put on 59 in three-quarters of an hour. Wainwright, however, again failed, and four wickets were down for 113. With Wilson and Denton together, both playing careful cricket, a draw seemed certain. The pair had added 46 when, at 159, Jessop beat Wilson, having thus far accounted for all the wickets.

GLOUCESTERSHIRE

W. G. Grace, c Tunnicliffe, b Wilson 22	c Wainwright, b Milligan 33	
R. M. Rice, c Milligan, b Hirst 9	b Jackson 22	
F. H. B. Champain, c Tunnicliffe, b Jackson 44	b Wainwright 26	
Wrathall, b Jackson 17	c Wainwright, b Wilson 34	
G. L. Jessop, b Jackson 101	c Denton, b Wainwright 0	
W. McG. Hemingway, c Milligan, b Jackson 0	c Jackson, b Milligan 27	
C. L. Townsend, c Milligan, b Wilson 109	run out 1	
Board, not out 43	b Milligan 69	
H. S. Goodwin, c Wainwright, b Jackson 11	c Hirst, b Milligan 26	
W. S. A. Brown, b Milligan 10	not out 12	
Roberts, not out 1		
L b 2, w 1 3	B 21	
Total 370	*Total (nine wkts.) 271	

YORKSHIRE

F. S. Jackson, b Jessop 7	b Jessop 4	
Tunnicliffe, c and b Jessop 24	c Board, b Jessop 25	
Brown, c Townsend, b Roberts 80	b Jessop 49	
Denton, c Board, b Jessop 10	c Townsend, b Brown 55	
Wainwright, c Board, b Roberts 1	c Board, b Jessop 9	
C. E. M. Wilson, c Goodwin, b Roberts 0	b Jessop 22	
Hirst, c and b Jessop 55	c Wrathall, b Brown 35	
F. W. Milligan, c and b Roberts 15	c Townsend, b Brown 2	
R. W. Collinson, c Wrathall, b Roberts 34	c Townsend, b Brown 2	
Lord Hawke, c Hemingway, b Roberts 38	not out 9	
Hunter, not out 1	c Champain, b Roberts 5	
L b 7, n b 4 11	B 5, l b 2, w 1 8	
Total 276	Total 225	

GLOUCESTERSHIRE – First Innings

	O	M	R	W		O	M	R	W
Hirst	27	7	86	1	Jackson	35	13	73	5
Wainwright	27	14	43	0	Milligan	19.1	2	96	1
Wilson	19	3	54	2	Brown	5	1	15	0

Milligan delivered one wide.

Second Innings

	O	M	R	W		O	M	R	W
Hirst	17	8	44	0	Wilson	15	7	16	1
Wainwright	24	7	83	2	Milligan	19.4	5	67	4
Jackson	17	6	40	1					

YORKSHIRE – First Innings

	O	M	R	W		O	M	R	W
Townsend	8	1	28	0	Wrathall	3	1	4	0
Jessop	37	10	106	4	Brown	3	0	12	0
Roberts	33.3	10	84	6	Grace	9	1	31	0

Jessop delivered three no-balls and Roberts one.

Second Innings

	O	M	R	W		O	M	R	W
Roberts	33	12	91	4	Townsend	9	2	24	0
Jessop	34	10	71	5	Brown	8	2	14	4
Grace	6	0	17	0					

Brown delivered one wide.

Umpires – W. Shrewsbury and W. Potter.

11: Derbyshire v Yorkshire
CHESTERFIELD, 18–20 AUGUST 1898

'No first pair have ever done so well as Brown and Tunnicliffe yesterday,' wrote our correspondent. Indeed, it was to be 34 years before any other pair could beat them, appropriately another Yorkshire opening partnership (see game 48). Their remarkable achievement of 554 for the first wicket is still the third best ever recorded. Together

Brown and Tunnicliffe shared 19 century opening partnerships for their county. Yorkshire had managed only fourth place in 1897, but would regain the title this summer. Derbyshire were one of the weakest counties at the time, although the ninth place they recorded in 1898 was not to be exceeded until 1927.

John Brown (1869–1904) in this match made

his second treble century for Yorkshire. In 1897 he had taken 311 off Sussex at Sheffield (and put on 378 with Tunnicliffe for the first wicket). He played eight times for England, but his career – and his life – were cut tragically short by ill-health. Brown died of heart trouble shortly after his 35th birthday, his illness aggravated by chain-smoking, a habit still more foolish in the light of the chronic asthma from which he also suffered. He made 17,920 runs at an average of 30 in his career. His partner, John Tunnicliffe (1866–1948), played for Yorkshire from 1891 until 1907, when he became coach at Clifton. Well over six feet in height, he was known as 'Long John of Pudsey', after his birthplace. 1898 was his best season, when he made 1,804 runs at 41. His 20,310 runs in his career at an average of 27 do not put him in the front rank of county openers, despite his achievements. His 243 in this game was the best of his career.

Chesterfield, Thursday

The opening day's play in this match will undoubtedly stand for some time to come as one of the most memorable in the annals of the game.

During the day an extraordinary record was established by Brown and Tunnicliffe, who opened the batting for Yorkshire on a good and fast wicket. The pair kept up their wickets throughout the whole of the day, and at the close had between them compiled the huge total of 503. Even now this is a long way in front of the previous best stand for the first wicket in a first-class match, which was claimed by Abel and Brockwell, who made 379 for Surrey against Hampshire at the Oval in August, 1897. Previous to that Brown and Tunnicliffe had themselves held the record, having compiled 378 for their county against Sussex at Bramall-lane. Prior to yesterday the best stand in a first-class match, irrespective of wicket, stood to the credit of Gunn and Shrewsbury, who made 398 for the second wicket for Notts against Sussex in May, 1890, but this also has been well beaten by the present performance. No first pair have ever done so well as Brown and Tunnicliffe yesterday, the best being 472, but it has not yet reached that by Captain Oates and Private Fitzgerald, who scored 623 for the second wicket whilst playing for the Royal Munster Fusiliers against the Army Service Corps at The Curragh. At present Yorkshire hold the record for the highest aggregate in first-class cricket, viz, 887 against Warwickshire in 1896, and it is quite possible that they may beat these figures to-day.

Yesterday's display of hitting was a brilliant one, and, although Brown gave four difficult chances, they scarcely detract from his grand efforts in keeping up his wicket all day for 270, which is the highest score

this season. Tunnicliffe's 214 has so far been made with only one fault, and the score is the biggest he has ever made. The receipts for the day amounted to £175.

Friday

Brown and Tunnicliffe, having stayed together all day on Thursday, and compiled 503, it was not deemed prudent to unduly prolong the innings yesterday. Thus all the wickets fell in the morning for an addition of 159. Brown and Tunnicliffe, who were not out 270 and 214 respectively, increased the total to 554, when Tunnicliffe, who had been missed in the long-field in the first over of the morning, was smartly caught in the slips. His score was 243, a grand innings, only containing two chances. He was batting in all five hours and five minutes, and among his hits were forty-eight 4's, three 3's, and seven 2's. Brown, acting under instructions, after making 300, hit down his wicket. The total was the best this season up to that time, but, as subsequent events proved, was destined to be beaten by Hayward at the Oval. The Driffield professional was at the wickets five hours and ten minutes, and, notwithstanding the four chances he gave, his display was a grand one. His hits included forty-eight 4's, six 3's, and nineteen 2's. After this, the batsmen made no pretence to stay, but hit out at everything, and at twenty minutes to one the innings closed for 662, which is the best aggregate total this season, the previous best being 645, scored, curiously enough, by Derbyshire against Hampshire. Wainwright, after all, proved too unwell to play, and at the last moment Hirst was pressed into service. Derbyshire started batting at five minutes to one, but fared badly, and at a quarter-past four the side were all out for 118. Following on no fewer that 524 behind, Derbyshire, with nothing but defeat before them, did a little better, and at the close had scored 50 for one wicket, the bad light causing play to cease at twenty minutes to six.

Saturday

As was to be expected after the first two days' play in this match at Chesterfield, Yorkshire on Saturday afternoon secured an overwhelming victory in a single innings, with 387 to spare. Some slight resistance was offered to the visiting attack, and it took Yorkshire two hours and forty-five minutes to dispose of the remaining batsmen, although the overnight total was only taken from 50 to 157. Chatterton, who joined Storer at the resumption of the game, was sixth to leave, at 128, with a well-played 54, made in two hours, whilst Sugg was batting forty minutes for three runs. The game was prolonged beyond the usual hour for luncheon, in the hope of finishing, but at a quarter-past two the interval was taken. The first ball after resuming, however, saw Walker bowled, and at ten minutes past three Yorkshire had won a memorable match, as stated. Score:

Brown and Tunnicliffe

YORKSHIRE

Brown, h w, b Storer 300	Rhodes, c Storer, b Walker 6
Tunnicliffe, c Davidson, b Storer . 243	F. W. Milligan, c Chatterton,
Lord Hawke, c Walker, b Storer 14	b Davidson (F.) 4
Hirst, c Davidson (G.), b Walker 0	F. Smith, c Storer, b Walker 4
Denton, b Davidson (F.) 45	Haigh, c Ashcroft, b Davidson (F.) 13
F. S. Jackson, c Storer, b Walker 14	Hunter, not out 0
	B 14, l b 4, n b 1 19
	Total 662

DERBYSHIRE

L. G. Wright, c Hawke, b Hirst 0	st Hunter, b Rhodes 5
S. H. Evershed, c Hunter,	b Smith 12
b Jackson 18	b Jackson 2
Bagshaw, c Haigh, b Jackson 20	c Rhodes, b Jackson 25
Storer, c Denton, b Milligan 13	c and b Rhodes 54
Chatterton, b Milligan 6	l b w, b Jackson 2
Davidson (G.), b Jackson 36	not out 21
F. M. Ashcroft, c Hunter,	b Rhodes 3
b Jackson 1	retired 5
Sugg, c Brown, b Smith 8	absent. hurt 0
Davidson (F.), c Haigh, b Smith 3	b Haigh 7
A Charlesworth, c Haigh,	
b Rhodes 7	
G. G. walker, not out 0	
B 5, l b 1 6	B 15, l b 6 21
Total 118	Total 157

YORKSHIRE – First Innings

	O	M	R	W		O	M	R	W
Davidson (G.)	1	0	3	0	Storer	26	1	142	3
Walker	55	11	199	4	Ashcroft	6	1	21	0
Davidson (F.)	39.3	9	133	3	Evershed	3	0	13	0
Sugg	5	0	27	0	Wright	3	0	24	0
Bagshaw	11	1	50	0	Charlesworth	7	0	31	0

Walker bowled a no-ball.

DERBYSHIRE – First Innings

	O	M	R	W		O	M	R	W
Hirst	10	3	19	1	Smith	7.1	6	5	2
Jackson	28	12	52	4	Rhodes	1	1	0	1
Milligan	12	5	36	2					

Second Innings

	O	M	R	W		O	M	R	W
Smith	21	10	35	1	Brown	4	1	9	0
Rhodes	29	13	47	3	Haigh	7.1	4	13	1
Jackson	37	22	26	3	Milligan	4	2	6	0

Umpires – H. Holmes (Hampshire) and J. H. Holmes (Somerset)

12: *Surrey v Lancashire*
THE OVAL, 18–20 AUGUST 1898

On the same days that Brown and Tunnicliffe were re-writing the record books at Chesterfield, Tom Hayward was making the highest score ever recorded for Surrey, though the record was to survive a mere nine months (see game 13). This match had special importance, as Surrey had been runners-up to Lancashire the previous season. They would slip to fourth this year (and Lancashire to sixth), before regaining the title in 1899. During the 1890s they were challenged only by Yorkshire for consistent success, and Hayward was the backbone of their batting efforts. This was one of 19 occasions in first-class matches that Surrey have passed 600, more than any other county.

Hayward (1871–1939) played for Surrey from 1893 to 1914. His father and grandfather had

played for the county before him. In 20 consecutive seasons, from 1895 to 1914, he made more than 1,000 runs in a season. He twice made more than 3,000, and his 3,518 at an average of 66 in 1906 was the record aggregate for the season, standing for 41 years until Compton and Edrich both overhauled it 1947, and in that season he equalled C.B. Fry's record of 13 centuries. He was the second batsman after Grace to score 1,000 runs by the end of May, and the second after Grace to complete 100 centuries. In the early part of his career he had been a useful medium-pace bowler, and achieved the 'double' in 1897. In his career from 1893 to 1914 he made 43,551 runs at an average of 42, and his 481 wickets cost only 23 each. He played 35 times for England.

Those who believe that rowdy crowd

behaviour is a product of unhappy and less genteel modern times would do well to note the last paragraph of the correspondent's final report.

The Oval, Thursday

The Surrey Eleven gave a further proof yesterday of their batting strength on fast wickets by defying Lancashire's attack all day at the Oval. Exclusive of the intervals the afternoon's cricket lasted as nearly as possible five hours, and during this period the home county reached a total of 361 for the loss of half their batsmen, but did not start in any too promising fashion, seeing that with the score at 11, Abel spooned a ball back tamely to Cuttell, whilst Brockwell and Lockwood were both out before the hundred was hoisted. They fell victims to Baker, who had taken up the attack at the Vauxhall end. Holland and Hayward ere lunch-time advanced the figures to 121 without further loss, but at 133 Holland was taken by Hartley. Jephson was the newcomer, and for over a couple of hours the Lancashire bowlers laboured in vain. Even Albert Ward and Hartley were called upon, but it was not until the total had been increased to 308 that Cuttell reached the leg-stump of the Cantab's wicket. His 54 was free from fault, and included five 4's, a 3, and half a dozen 2's. Prior to this Hayward had, after batting two hours and a quarter, secured his third 100 of the season and also completed his 1,000 runs. Key assisted Hayward to increase the home total in the last forty minutes to the tune of 53. Hayward ere six o'clock arrived had brought his figures to 163 not out – his highest contribution this summer. When 78 he offered an easy return chance to Briggs, and at 83 might have been secured in the long field had not Eccles misjudged the catch. Towards the finish, too, he offered a hot return, and a difficult chance in the long field, while he was lucky to escape being stumped with 155 to his account. A crowd of fully 12,000 watched the afternoon's play.

Friday

At Kennington Oval yesterday, the Lancashire eleven were again outplayed at all points of the game by the Surrey team. On Thursday the home side put together the big score of 361 for the loss of five wickets, and, following up the advantage gained in this way by some remarkable cricket yesterday, they eventually compiled the huge total of 634. Towards this T. Hayward contributed a wonderful not-out innings of 315. Going in third wicket down, with the score 81, Hayward saw the rest of the team depart, and carried out his bat, after a stay of six hours and forty minutes. In this time he ran no fewer than 553 runs in weather of an almost tropical nature, and it was not surprising to find a substitute doing duty for him during the first half hour of the Lancashire innings. So far, Hayward has been the hero of what looks like being a remarkable match. Never previously has he done anything so well for the county of his adoption, his previous best effort being 229 not out, against Derbyshire, in 1895. Although his display was not without fault, it was a marvellous performance. On Thursday this nephew of the most stylish batsman of his day might have been out on five occasions, and yesterday he was let off by the bowler, and should have been run out. All the same, Hayward's feat is one of which he may well be proud. Excepting when he has passed his third hundred his cricket was full of polish and effect, his driving and cutting being beautifully clean and well timed. Yesterday Hayward received valuable assistance from Braund, a younger member of the team, who, while in only seventy minutes, helped to put on no fewer than 204 runs. The Surrey innings, which commenced at five minutes after twelve on Thursday, produced eight hours and a quarter's actual cricket.

Tom Hayward

The total is the highest made at the Oval this year, and but sixty-four short of the best ever compiled by the county, viz., 698, against Sussex in 1883. As an individual innings, Hayward's 315 ranks sixth in first-class cricket to the following: A. C. MacLaren, 424; W. G. Grace, 344; W. W. Read, 338; W. L. Murdoch, 321; and W. G. Grace, 318.

As we have said, all the interest yesterday was centred in the batting of Hayward; in fact, with the exception of Braund, none of the others gave any trouble. With Mold away, the Lancashire attack was roughly treated on the excellent wicket, and it appeared to be only a question of how many runs the Southerners would make. When the venture closed the visitors entered upon their thankless task of saving the match, for of course a victory was out of the question. The batting at the start lacked spirit, and in the course of an hour four good wickets fell for but 39 runs. At this stage, however, Baker and the Oxonian, A. Eccles, came to the rescue with a stand that extended over an hour and a quarter and realised 77 runs. Yesterday's proceedings attracted about 12,000 spectators, of which number 9,128 paid for admission. A collection made for Hayward realised £71 1s 9¼d.

Saturday

After furnishing some sensational cricket in its early stages, the return match between Surrey and Lancashire ended in the tamest manner possible at Kennington Oval on Saturday, the result being a draw. The home team spent so much time during the first two days in putting together the huge total of 634, that they failed to twice dismiss the visiting side; and the Northerners, after appearing hopelessly beaten, had the satisfaction of saving the game. It will be remembered that the Surrey innings, which extended over eight hours and a quarter, did not close until nearly half-past three on Friday, and, going in to bat at a quarter to four, Lancashire had at the drawing of stumps lost four wickets for 116 runs. Of course, they had not the slightest idea of playing for anything but a draw, and the question was, could the Surrey men, in the five and a half hours left for cricket on the last day, succeed in taking the remaining sixteen wickets? The pitch was still in excellent condition, when, with the game in this position, play was resumed on Saturday morning, the not-outs being Eccles (42) and Baker (36). The opinion prevailed that Lancashire would save the game, but Surrey had in the brief space of an hour and a quarter captured the remaining six wickets, and finished off the innings by ten minutes to one, it appeared just possible that a definite result might be attained. The home eleven had got Lancashire out in three hours and twenty-five minutes, and with over four hours left for actual cricket, there was no reason why they should not be able to dismiss them a second time. A stand, however, by Albert Ward and the young professional, Hallows, who remained

together for the fifty minutes previous to the luncheon interval, practically settled the matter, and little interest was centred in what followed. With but one object, that of playing out time, Ward and Hallows adopted defensive tactics. Hallows, a left-handed batsman, played exceptionally good cricket. Early he was hit heavily on the knee, and after the interval had Briggs as a runner. For an hour and fifty minutes he and Ward kept company, and when the first wicket fell, at ten minutes to four, all hope of a Surrey victory had gone. Hallows scored 51 out of 78, and in doing so hit nine 4's. For some time after the departure of the left-hander the Surrey captain changed his bowling with marked rapidity, but nothing could tempt Ward to hit or take risks. For fifty-five minutes he and Tyldesley made good the defence, and in this time the last-named, by free and attractive cricket, scored 44 out of 57 added for the wicket. Long before Tyldesley left a draw was certain. Ward, however, still stuck to his defensive tactics, and finally he carried out his bat after a most patient and, under the circumstances, invaluable display extending over four hours. Ward was hooted and jeered at by a section of the crowd, who invaded the field of play and took possession of the ground in front of the pavilion before the last over was commenced, but he never played a more serviceable innings in his life for the county of his adoption. Score:

SURREY

Abel, c and b Cuttell	10	K . J. Key, b Lancaster	31
Brockwell, l b w, b Baker	43	Hayes, run out	22
Holland, c Hartley, b Hallows	45	Braund, c Eccles, b Briggs	85
Lockwood, c Radcliffe, b Baker	5	Wood, c Ward, b Briggs	6
Hayward, not out	315	Richardson, b Briggs	0
D. L. A. Jephson, b Cuttell	54	B 13, l b 4, w 1	18
		Total	634

LANCASHIRE

C. R. Hartley, c Wood, b Lockwood	0	b Braund	32
Ward, b Richardson	10	not out	63
Tyldesley, b Richardson	21	c Jephson, b Brockwell	44
A. C. MacLaren, b Richardson	3	c Brockwell, b Abel	15
Baker, b Lockwood	42	c Abel, b Hayward	51
A. Eccles, b Richardson	51		
Cuttell, c Holland, b Lockwood	5		
Briggs, b Brockwell	18		
Hallows, not out	19		
Lancaster, c and b Brockwell	0		
Radcliffe, c Holland, b Lockwood	0		
Byes	4	B 4, n-b 1	5
Total	173	Total	210

SURREY – First Innings

	O	M	R	W		O	M	R	W
Lancaster	45	13	126	1	Hallows	29	8	68	1
Cuttell	54	15	121	2	Ward	13	5	38	0
Briggs	56	8	142	3	Hartley	13	1	42	0
Baker	28	7	75	2	MacLaren	1	0	4	0

Cuttell delivered a wide.

LANCASHIRE – First Innings

	O	M	R	W		O	M	R	W
Richardson	32	13	62	4	Brockwell	7	4	12	2
Lockwood	28.2	4	77	4	Jephson	4	1	5	0
Hayes	4	0	9	0	Braund	2	1	4	0

Second Innings

	O	M	R	W		O	M	R	W
Richardson	25	12	59	0	Jephson	9	4	12	0
Lockwood	21	9	40	0	Hayward	9	2	21	1
Hayes	9	5	10	0	Abel	4	2	10	1
Brockwell	19	7	41	1	Braund	1.3	0	12	1

Lockwood delivered one no-ball.
Umpires – Draper and Tuck.

13: Surrey v Somerset
THE OVAL, 29–31 MAY 1899

Surrey were to be champions this year, though decline would set in thereafter – the title would not be theirs again until cricket came to its sudden halt in August 1914. As with, apparently, so many batting feats, Somerset were the victims as Surrey made their best score in first-class cricket, then the fourth highest in the game's history. 'The Somerset bowling was very poor', says our correspondent, with understatement. Abel's innings was (and still is) the highest for Surrey, and at the time was the second highest ever made (after MacLaren's 424). It is still the third highest score ever made in county cricket.

Bobby Abel (1857–1936), known as 'The Guv'nor', played for Surrey from 1881 to 1904. His finest form came towards the end of his career, when he scored more than 2,000 runs in consecutive seasons from 1895 to 1905, and his total of 3,309 in 1901 was a record for the time. He was troubled with eye disease throughout his playing career and ended by wearing spectacles. Ultimately, though, poor sight forced his retirement, during which he ran, for many years, a bat shop at the Oval. In his career he made 33,124 runs at an average of 35. He played 13 tests, the last in 1896, before the finest days of his career had begun. This may be partly explained by the fact that he was one of those professionals who threatened, in 1896, to go on strike unless their match fee was doubled from £10 to £20, their appetites increased by the rumours of the profits the touring Australians would be taking back with them. Abel and William Brockwell, who failed in this match, were one of the most celebrated opening partnerships of the 1890s.

The Oval, Monday

It was a day of big scoring at the Oval yesterday, for Surrey, who won the toss, remained at the wickets all day. Surrey opened their innings soon after twelve, but Abel and Brockwell, who went in for them first, were soon separated, Brockwell, after hitting up 11 in rapid style, being caught behind the wicket off Gill. Then Hayes and Abel made a splendid stand, the first-named hitting with great vigour. Thirty-five minutes from the start Abel caused 50 to be recorded with a fine off-drive from Gill, and immediately after he off-drove Cran-field, who was playing in place of Tyler, for 4. Bowling changes were soon tried, but were of no avail, and with a 4 off-drive from Robson an hour after the start, Hayes sent up the 100. With his next stroke he raised his own score to 50, he having then been in forty-five minutes. Ten minutes later, however, he was smartly caught at third man by Daniell, and a couple of wickets were down for 110. Among the hits made by Hayes in his useful 56 were nine 4's, two 3's, and a couple. D. S. A. Jephson, who took his place, remained with Abel for 18, and whilst this partnership lasted Abel reached his 50. At 145 Jephson was bowled by Captain Hedley, and Hayward then went in. The 150 was passed just prior to lunch, and at the interval the score stood at 152 for three wickets. After lunch Abel and Hayward simply did as they pleased with the bowling, which by this time had been completely mastered. Off Woods, who was put on at 188, they made 9 in one over, and the 200 was signalled two and a half hours from the start. Five minutes later Abel, who had been batting from the commencement of the game, made a 4 to leg off a full toss by Woods, thereby reaching his first century this season. With his score at 38, Hayward was missed at the wicket. Boundary hit after boundary hit was made, the bowlers being treated in unmerciful fashion, and 300 went up in three and a half hours. Amidst tremendous applause Hayward obtained his century, and a little later 400 was hoisted. With his total at 131, Hayward was missed in the slips by Daniell, but it was a very difficult chance high up. After being in four hours and three-quarters Abel took his figures to 200. Hayward kept with Abel for three and a half hours, and was then caught at cover-point, his total being 158 and his best hits twenty-one 4's, eight 3's, and eight 2's. During the partnership 334 runs were put on. H. B. Richardson, who succeeded, was caught after making a single, and then V. F. S. Crawford kept with Abel until time, the total then being 495 for five wickets. Abel, who was not out, was at the wickets over five and a half hours, and up to the present his best hits have been four 5's, twenty-five 4's, eight 3's, and fifteen 2's.

Tuesday

When the play ceased on Monday Surrey had made 495 for the loss of but five wickets, and this huge score they yesterday increased to 811. But for the failure of the tail they might have passed the Yorkshire aggregate record of 887, made against Warwickshire in 1896. Abel, who went in first, and carried out his bat, accomplished the best performance of his life, making

357 not out. The only better individual score in first-class cricket was the 424 by Mr. A. C. MacLaren at Taunton in 1895.

The game was resumed yesterday morning at half-past eleven, Abel (who was 227 not out) and Crawford being then opposed by Gill and Cranfield. The score was soon taken to 500, Crawford making a 4 and a single in the first over from Gill. With his total at 237 Abel gave a chance at stumping, but the opportunity was allowed to slip by, and, after Crawford had driven Gill to the off for 4, Abel put a ball from the same bowler to leg for 6, and followed up with a 5 to leg from Cranfield. A double change of bowling was tried at 549, but it was of no avail, and Crawford soon reached his half-century. Then Nichols was put on, but he proved most expensive, Crawford in one over scoring three 4's off him. This raised Surrey's total to 600, the game having then been in progress six hours and thirty-five minutes. At 623 Woods himself took the ball, but Abel promptly put him to leg for 5, and Crawford sent the ball through the slips to the boundary. Following this up with a couple of 4's off Gill, the Surrey amateur reached his century, this being his first in first-class cricket. He was missed when at 119 by Nichols running in from mid-off, and then Abel scored another 5 off Woods. With a 4 from Gill he increased his score to 300, having then been in at the wickets seven and a quarter hours. Stanley was tried as a change at 690, and with his second delivery

he disposed of Crawford, who, after being in a little over two hours with Abel, was caught in the slips by Daniell. The partnership realised 211, and of this number Crawford was responsible for 129, the best he has ever done in first-class cricket. Among his hits were twenty-one 4's, three 3's, and nine 2's. Key, who took his place, was not in long, but he hit freely, and before being caught by Cranfield in the deep field had put on 43. Just prior to this he had been missed by Hickley in the slips, but it was a difficult chance. When Key was dismissed the players adjourned for lunch, the total then being 759 for seven wickets, Abel being 327 not out. When play was resumed Lees became Abel's partner, and the pair took the score past 800, the game having lasted eight hours and twenty minutes altogether. Then, however, the collapse came, and the innings closed for 811 eight hours and thirty-five minutes from the start, Abel, who had been in all the time, being 357 not out. This is by far the best score he has ever made. Among his hits were a 6, seven 5's, thirty-eight 4's, eleven 3's and twenty-three 2's. A collection made for him on the ground realised £33 3s.

Somerset opened their first innings at ten minutes to four, and quickly lost two of their batsmen, Captain Hedley being bowled by Lees at 13 and Stanley by Richardson before the total was altered. Trask, who then became a partner of Robson, opened with a 4 to leg off Richardson, but at 30 lost Robson, and three wickets were down for this poor score. Next came

Abel at the wicket

38

S. M. J. Woods, who for an hour upset the Surrey attack, and in that time put on 49. He was missed at 17 at mid-off, but otherwise his display was invigorating, and his finished strokes delightful to watch. Among his hits were a 6 and eight 4's. Soon after Wood's dismissal by Hayward, who had supplemented Lees at 76, Trask reached his 50, having been in an hour and a quarter. He lost Nichols at 121, and Gill 3 runs later, six wickets thus being down for 124. When he had himself been in a little over two hours for 70 he was caught in the slips by Brockwell, the total then being 152. His best hits were a 6, five 4's, eight 3's, and five 2's. After Trask went out wickets fell rapidly, and when stumps were drawn Somerset had lost nine wickets for 165 runs, and thus, with but a wicket in hand, are 646 in arrear.

Wednesday

All the interest in this match had evaporated before play was resumed yesterday morning, as Somerset's task was an impossible one. Against Surrey's magnificent total of 811 they had lost nine wickets in scoring 165. Daniell and Cranfield made an unexpected stand, and carried the total to 234 before they were separated, but that still left the visitors 577 runs behind. Going in again at one o'clock they were all out in two hours and three-quarters for 198. Woods and Gill showed some lively cricket, and Stanley, Robson and Newton were fair contributors, but all their efforts were unavailing, and their team were beaten by an innings and 379 runs.

SURREY

Abel, not out 357	K. J. Key, c Cranfield, b Hedley 43
Brockwell, c Newton, b Gill 11	Lees, c and b Gill 20
Hayes, c Daniell, b Hedley 56	Marshall, b Gill 0
D. L. A. Jephson, b Hedley 18	Richardson (T.), b Gill 2
Hayward, c Hedley, b Cranfield . 158	B 8, l b 6, n b 2 16
H. B. Richardson, c Daniell,	
b Cranfield 1	Total 811
V. F. S. Crawford, c Daniell,	
b Stanley 129	

SOMERSETSHIRE

H. T. Stanley, b t. Richardson 8	c Marshall, b T. Richardson 33
Capt. W. C. Hedley, b Lees 1	c Crawford, b Brockwell 7
Robson, b T. Richardson 5	c Marshall, b T. Richardson 23
W. Trask, c Brockwell, b Lees 70	l-b-w, b T. Richardson 0
S. M. J. Woods, b Hayward 49	b Brockwell 53
Nichols, b Hayward 0	b T. Richardson 9
Gill, b Brockwell 3	b Jephson 36
J. Daniell, c H. Richardson,	c Crawford, b Brockwell 0
b Brockwell 50	b Brockwell 8
Lieut. Hickley, b T. Richardson 4	not out 20
A. E. Newton, c Brockwell,	b Brockwell 0
b T. Richardson 0	
Cranfield, not out 27	
B 12, l b 5 17	B 5, l b 4 9
Total 234	Total 198

SURREY – First Innings

	O	M	R	W		O	M	R	W
Gill	43.2	6	170	4	Daniell	4	1	20	0
Cranfield	56	5	180	2	Nichols	14	1	76	0
Robson	23	6	87	0	Trask	6	0	24	0
Hedley	48	16	105	3	Stanley	12	0	60	1
Woods	16	1	73	0					

Gill delivered two no balls.

SOMERSET – First Innings

	O	M	R	W		O	M	R	W
Richardson (T.) ..	28	5	77	4	Brockwell	12.4	6	25	2
Lees	23	6	52	2	Abel	7	2	14	0
Hayward	13	6	47	2	Jephson	3	1	2	0

Second Innings

	O	M	R	W		O	M	R	W
Brockwell	24.3	7	76	5	Lees	9	2	33	0
Richardson (T.) ..	21	3	59	4	Jephson	7	2	21	1

Umpires – R. Thomas and A. White.

14: Surrey v Yorkshire
THE OVAL, 10–12 AUGUST 1899

This was a titanic fixture, with the two finest sides meeting in one of the most wretched matches imaginable for bowlers. Neither side was going to allow the other the slightest chance of victory, and in three full days' play not even the first innings were completed. Abel and Hayward (see games 12 and 13), combined to record the second highest partnership in first-class cricket. It remains a Surrey record for any wicket, and was a fourth-wicket record not beaten until Worrell and Walcott passed it for Barbados in 1946. It remained an English fourth wicket record until Humpage and Kallicharran put on 470 for Warwickshire against Lancashire in 1982 (see game 92).

Yorkshire's 704 was the highest score ever made against Surrey (though Sussex overtook it three years later), and remains the second highest score Yorkshire have ever made (see game 8). Though he failed on this occasion, F.S. Jackson (1870–1946), who went in first for Yorkshire, was one of the finest all-rounders in the country, and a future England captain; though thanks to the dominance of Lord Hawke he never captained his county. He was even more distinguished outside cricket. Winston Churchill was his fag at Harrow. Jackson went from the cricket field to the Boer War after the 1899 season, and raised and commanded a battalion of the West Riding regiment in the Great War. For nine years from 1915 he was a Yorkshire Unionist MP, and in 1922 became Financial Secretary to the War Office, becoming Unionist Party Chairman in 1923. He left

Parliament to become Governor of Bengal, with a knighthood, and was almost assassinated by a girl student in Calcutta. He died shortly after being run over by a taxi in London.

The Oval, Thursday

The Yorkshire eleven are just now in wonderful batting form, and when they won the toss at the Oval yesterday morning it was taken for granted they would make a lot of runs. For what they actually did, however, not even the most sanguine of their supporters could have been prepared. They were batting for, roughly speaking, five hours and a half, and in that time they scored 478 runs and only lost four wickets. When at lunch time they had Jackson, Tunnicliffe, and Denton out for 153, it was not thought – in view of Surrey's strength in batting and the perfection of the wicket – that they had done any too well, and no one would have been greatly surprised if their innings had been finished off before the end of the afternoon. After lunch, however, the bowlers were soon mastered, and as time went on runs came at a tremendous rate. The turning point of the innings was the partnership of Mitchell and Wainwright, who, in about two hours, carried the score from 142 to 302. By the time Mitchell was out the bowlers had done the best of which they were capable, and on Hirst going in they had a terribly rough time of it, 176 runs being added without further loss in about a hundred minutes.

As is usual at the Oval on the first day of a match, the wicket became faster as the afternoon went on, and of this fact the batsmen naturally made the most. Wainwright outstripped everyone yesterday in the matter of run-getting, being not out 161 when stumps were drawn. Fine as his cricket was, however, he might have been out twice before he had made 30 runs, Jephson letting him off at cover-slip and Leveson-Gower at cover-point. When the day's cricket ended it was mentioned in the pavilion as an extraordinary fact that while 478 runs were being scored, the wicket-keeper did not have a chance either of stumping or making a catch – a compliment to the excellence of the batting and the truth of the ground.

Friday

Some interesting records were set up at the Oval yesterday, when the Yorkshire batsmen continued to make light of the Surrey attack. In raising their overnight score of 478 for four wickets to 704, the visiting county made the highest total ever compiled against Surrey bowling, while the overnight not-outs, Wainwright and Hirst, distinguished themselves by heading their previous best individual scores. This pair, who on Thursday had carried all before them, were not separated until the fifth wicket had produced 340 runs in three hours and a half – a remarkable rate of scoring to be so long maintained. There was a splendid attendance, when, at twenty-five minutes to twelve, Wainwright (161) and Hirst (84) were opposed by Lockwood and Richardson. Neither batsman seemed in difficulties with the bowling, and Wainwright quickly passed his previous best score of 171 against Middlesex, at Lord's, while the 500 appeared shortly afterwards, the innings having then lasted for five hours and forty minutes. With a drive for 4 off Lockwood, Hirst sent his 100 up, a double change in Brockwell and Jephson then being tried. When 188, Wainwright should have been taken off Brockwell at the wicket, and with Hayward bowling for Jephson the sixth century was hoisted, the last hundred having occupied 80 minutes. Meanwhile Hirst had emulated Wainwright by making his highest score in first-class cricket, reaching 150 after a stay of three hours and five minutes. Not until the board showed 642 was a separation effected, Wainwright then being taken by Hayward at third man for a brilliant contribution of 228. In all, Wainwright was batting for five hours and a half, and during his long stay he only gave two real chances, one at 9 and the second at 188. The famous all-round cricketer was seen quite at his best, his chief hits being thirty-four 4's, five 3's, and twenty 2's. Hirst did not long survive, for in lashing out at Richardson he was bowled at 650. His 186 was compiled without blemish in three hours and forty minutes, and throughout he played the bowling with the utmost ease. His hits included thirty-one 4's, two 3's, and eleven 2's. Ernest Smith shaped very uncomfortably before being sent back for 8, and his dismissal was due to a finely-judged catch by Jephson at long-off. At the luncheon interval Lord Hawke and Haigh were associated, the score then standing at 667 for seven wickets.

Richardson bowled with marked success on resuming, taking the last three wickets, and causing the venture to close for the huge total of 704. In all the innings lasted for eight hours and twenty minutes, and in addition to the total being the highest ever recorded against Surrey, it was the second highest ever compiled at the Oval. The Surrey bowling calls for little comment, the bulk of the wickets falling to Richardson, who, however, like the others, proved very expensive.

With an enormous task before them, Surrey opened their initial venture at twenty minutes to four with Brockwell and Pretty. The bowlers were Rhodes and Ernest Smith, and the last-named met with conspicuous success, causing Pretty to hit his wicket at 23, and getting Hayes caught in the slips at 29. Abel and Brockwell played carefully, but shortly after the 50 had been recorded in fifty-five minutes, Brockwell was also taken in the slips by Mitchell. Three for 58 was the state of the score when Hayward joined Abel, but a steady improvement set in, the batsmen gradually getting the upper hand by dint of cautious methods. The 100 was passed in a little under two hours, the bulk of the scoring being accomplished by Hayward. Abel was exceedingly slow until some loose balls by Wainwright gave him an opportunity to hit. With

Hayward (front left) and Abel (right)

Smith on for Wainwright, Hayward's 50 was recorded, but subsequently the pace slackened, while the fielding was close and keen. This stand was of the utmost value to Surrey, and before the close of the partnership had yielded 111. The total then stood at 169 for three wickets, Hayward being 75 not out and Abel 42. When 63 Hayward was apparently bowled by Haigh, but the umpire ruled in his favour, while at 71 Tunnicliffe gave him a life in the slips, the bowler being Smith.

Saturday

What was in all senses a remarkable match terminated at the Oval on Saturday in a draw. Some 14,000 people witnessed the closing stages, and they will have good cause to remember the astonishing performance of the famous pair of professionals, Hayward and Abel. All but forty minutes of Saturday's play was confined to the batting of these two men, who had practically saved Surrey on the previous evening by adding 111 to the score at a critical time. They became associated when the total stood at 58 for three wickets, and actually added 448 runs in six hours, thus eclipsing the fine stand for 340, by Wainwright and Hirst, in the Yorkshire innings of 704. The annals of cricket can point to scarcely anything so unique as the match under notice, for in practically three full days' play only one innings was actually completed, 1,255 runs

being scored for the loss of but seventeen wickets. It was something indeed for Surrey to come out of the ordeal so well, in the face of a day and a half in the field under a scorching sun and Yorkshire's huge total of over 700. In all, Abel was batting for seven hours and a quarter for 193, during which time the total was increased by 500, while Hayward occupied six and a half hours in the compilation of 273, scoring at times with much greater freedom than his partner. That both men gave chances under such circumstances goes without saying, and doubtless the game was greatly affected by the peculiar incident on Friday evening, when Hayward was alleged to have been bowled by Haigh with his score at 83. Apparently the umpire was in doubt, and the batsmen benefited thereby. He was badly missed by Tunnicliffe at slip when 71, but gave no further chance until 254, Pretty, who was fielding temporarily for Lord Hawke, missing him at mid-on. True, there were a few other faulty strokes, and Hayward narrowly missed being taken in the slips when he sent his first hundred up, after a stay of two hours and three-quarters. Abel gave two chances – at 102 and 179 – but throughout exhibited magnificent defence and patience. The first of the pair to leave was Hayward, who at twenty minutes past five, with the total at 506, was taken at the wicket off Jackson. Six hours and a half had he occupied the wickets, and his 273 contained forty-three 4's, four 3's, and fifteen 2's.

Curiously enough, both he and Abel reached their 2,000 runs for the season during this notable partnership, incidents which the delighted crowd did not fail to appreciate. Abel did not long survive Hayward, being sent back by a very smart catch at point by Smith.

All were sorry that Abel failed to record his 200, but he only fell seven short of the coveted number, after giving a wonderful display for a cricketer approaching his fortieth year. Few men of even much younger age could exhibit a greater amount of stamina than the little player who is unquestionably the idol of Surrey's Saturday afternoon crowds. In Abel's great innings of 193 were included twenty-eight 4's, five 3's, and fifteen 2's. Jackson secured two further wickets before stumps were drawn at six o'clock, with the Surrey total at 551 for seven wickets. Lockwood was out to a splendid catch in the long-field by Stedman, who was fielding as substitute. England's chances for today's test match were probably not enhanced by the hard work many of her representatives had to undergo in the game concluded on Saturday, but it should be stated that Rhodes rested the greater part of the day, being slightly indisposed. His place in the field was ably taken by Lees Whitehead. Throughout the match the fielding left little room for complaint, and Hunter distinguished himself by not giving away a single bye during the eight hours and a quarter Surrey were batting. A collection on the ground for Abel and Hayward realised £72 14s. The partnership between

Abel and Hayward was the second best on record in first-class cricket, coming next to the 554 of Brown and Tunnicliffe, recorded at Chesterfield last season. Score:

YORKSHIRE

F. S. Jackson, c Richardson, b Brockwell 18	E. Smith, c Jephson, b Lockwood 8
Tunnicliffe, c Hayes, b Richardson 50	S. Haigh, not out 24
Denton, c Pretty, b Brockwell 47	Lord Hawke, b Richardson 13
F. Mitchell, b Jephson 87	Rhodes, b Richardson 8
Wainwright, c Hayward, b Lockwood 228	Hunter, b Richardson 0
Hirst, b Richardson 186	B 25, l b 7, w 2, n b 1 35
	Total 704

SURREY

Brockwell, c Mitchell, b Smith 29	D. L. A. Jephson, c Tunnicliffe b Jackson 23
H. C. Pretty, hit wicket, b Smith ... 15	Lockwood, c sub, b Jackson 4
Hayes, c Mitchell, b Smith 6	K. J. Key, not out 4
Abel, c Smith, b Jackson 193	W 2, n b 2 4
Hayward, c Hunter, b Jackson 273	Total (7 wickets) 551

H. G. Leveson-Gower, Richardson (T.), and Stedman did not bat.

YORKSHIRE – First Innings

	O	M	R	W		O	M	R	W
Lockwood	38	9	146	2	Jephson	25	1	97	1
Richardson	53.1	15	152	5	Abel	10	2	42	0
Brockwell	49	12	144	2	Pretty	4	1	15	0
Hayward	14	4	56	0	Hayes	4	0	17	0

Lockwood and Richardson each bowled a wide, and Hayward a no-ball.

SURREY – First Innings

	O	M	R	W		O	M	R	W
Rhodes	28	11	51	0	Wainwright	31	7	100	0
Smith	55	16	141	3	Haigh	31	8	61	0
Jackson	47.2	15	101	4	Denton	6	0	25	0
Hirst	22	5	63	0	Tunnicliffe	2	0	5	0

Hirst and Rhodes each delivered a no-ball, and Jackson and Wainwright each bowled a wide.

Umpires – Titchmarsh and White.

15: *Sussex v Surrey*
HOVE, 19–21 JULY 1900

C. B. Fry (1872–1956) was the personification of the gifted amateur of the golden age. In cricketing literature he is, more often than not, likened to a Greek god in his sporting abilities. Wisden called him 'the greatest all-rounder of his or any generation'. Lest it be thought that this was taking matters too far, it should be noted that he was the world record long-jumper, played in an F.A. Cup final, and England never lost when he captained them at cricket. Moreover, in the early 1920s he was offered the throne of Albania, then newly independent from the Turks. Fry was Ranjitsinhji's deputy in the League of Nations (Ranji batted, as it were, for India) and had to deliver a speech on Albania written by Ranji. So impressed was the Albanian legation by his support for their country that they, having been told that the ideal king would be 'an English

country gentleman with £10,000 a year' felt Fry was their man. He turned the offer down, claiming that he could not afford it, but Ranji had offered to finance him should he have wanted to be King Charles I of the Albanians. Instead, Fry continued his career as a cricket writer and commandant of a training ship on the Hamble, for which he had been awarded the even greater dignity of the honorary rank of captain in the Royal Naval Reserve.

This match was the second of five occasions upon which Fry scored two hundred in a match; and it was the first example in first-class cricket of a batsman making a century and a double century in a match. In a first-class career that lasted from 1892 to 1921 he scored 30,886 runs at an average of 50, including 94 centuries, and took 166 wickets at 29 each. He played 26 times for England.

17: Essex v Sussex
LEYTON, 30 JUNE–2 JULY 1902

Prince Ranjitsinhji (1872–1933) was one of the most glittering figures of the golden age, and with C.B. Fry (see game 15) provided for Sussex one of the most attractive batting combinations in cricket history. 'Ranji', as he was universally known, joined Sussex in 1895 after a moderate career at Cambridge, and played regularly for the county until returning to India after the 1904 season; he played sporadically after that, in 1908, 1912 and (though he had by then lost an eye in a shooting accident) 1920. In 1899 he became the first batsman to score 3,000 runs in a season, and repeated the feat in spectacular fashion the following year, scoring 3,065 runs from just 40 innings at an average of 87. He made 24,692 runs at an average of 56 in his short career, including 72 centuries (14 of them double centuries). His 285 not out against Somerset in 1901 was a record for the county that stood until his nephew, Prince Duleepsinhji, scored 333 in 1930 (see game 46). His stand of 344 with Newham for the seventh wicket not only saved Sussex from rout; it was a world record for that wicket. It has only since been surpassed once, by Atkinson and Depeiza for the West Indies against Australia in 1954–55. During his innings Ranji injured his leg, and had to withdraw from the imminent test match against Darling's Australians at Sheffield (the only test ever played at Bramall Lane). Fry, who had been dropped for making a pair in the previous test, was called up to replace him.

William Newham (1860–1944) played for Sussex as an amateur from 1881 until 1905, and once for England. He made 14,657 runs in his career at an average of 24, and was at various times captain, secretary and manager of the Sussex club.

Leyton, Monday

A remarkable day's cricket was witnessed at Leyton yesterday in the opening of the match between Essex and Sussex. Going in first, Sussex for a time fared very badly indeed, six wickets actually going down for 92. A total of less than 200 seemed in store for them, but once more the endless possibilities of the game were illustrated. The Essex eleven were kept in the field for the remainder of the afternoon and did not succeed in getting down another wicket. Ranjitsinhji, who had gone in fourth wicket down at 82, was joined by Newham, and the pair successfully resisted all endeavours to part them. As the result of four hours' batting they added 332 runs, the score at the close of the day standing at 424. Such an astonishing change in the fortunes of a game has rarely been witnessed, and a different story would have had to be told had only Russell stumped Ranjitsinhji when that batsman was 27. It was a bad blunder and a very heavy price has had to be paid for it. When 176 the Indian was missed at the wicket, but that mistake mattered little, all the mischief having then been done. Apart from those two chances, Ranjitsinhji played delightful cricket, hard square cuts and drives being the chief features of his play. He reached his 100 in two hours, and in making his 184 he only took four hours and a quarter. From 123 he was handicapped by a strain in the right calf and had to have a man to run for him. Ranjitsinhji's 184 is already the highest individual innings scored in first-class cricket this season, just beating R. A. Duff's 182 made last week at Bradford. Newham was three hours and a quarter in completing his 100, but in the last three-quarters of an hour he added 46 runs. Newham played a thoroughly sound game, so complete being his mastery over the ball that he hardly made a bad stroke. He had not made 100 for his county since his 107 against Cambridge University at Brighton in 1897. The weather was fine, and there was a fair attendance.

Tuesday

Ranjitsinhji and Newham only made the trifling addition of 12 runs to their great stand at Leyton yesterday. Their partnership for the seventh Sussex wicket extended over four hours and twenty minutes, and produced 344 runs. Newham, who was the first to leave, was cut to a simple catch at short square leg, after in the same over giving a chance of stumping. That was the only blemish in his innings, which was of a sedate though thoroughly sound description. His 153 included ten 4's, seven 3's, and eighteen 2's. Ranjitsinhji continued to play bright cricket, advancing his score from 184 to 230, and was then extremely well caught at long on. Eighth out at 503, he was in while 415 runs were put on, his stay at the wickets extending over five hours and twenty minutes. As has been previously stated, he should have been stumped at 27, and was missed at the wicket when 176, but these were the only real faults in a superb display. It was noticeable that he made a goodly proportion of his runs in front of the wicket, and only occasionally played the ball off his legs. His chief figures were twenty-six 4's,

47

nine 3's, and seventeen 2's. Ranjitsinhji again had a man to run for him, but he was far less lame than on Monday evening, and later was able to field at point. With the four outstanding wickets adding 96 runs, the Sussex total reached 520, having taken six hours and three-quarters to compile. Essex only had an hour and three-quarters' batting, heavy rain at a quarter to four putting an end to play for the day. In the time at their disposal Essex scored 101 runs, and lost two wickets. Fane made some capital hits, and McGahey played with more vigour than usual with him. After two early escapes from being caught, Carpenter settled down to very cautious tactics.

Wednesday

What would have happened at Leyton yesterday had the sun shone brightly can only be surmised, but Essex would certainly have been hard pressed to save the match. Happily for them the sky remained overcast all day, and the wicket, which had been drenched by the rain of the previous evening, was too soft to give the bowlers any assistance. Indeed, it was so wet that it was nearly twelve o'clock before the game could be resumed, and the pitch drying slowly and quietly under the influence of the wind never became at all difficult. Still, the Essex men had a thankless task before them, and they emerged from it with every credit. Against their opponents' big total of 520 they had on Tuesday scored 101 for two wickets, and they had therefore to stay in all day to avoid defeat. The early play was such as to cause them grave anxiety, for in less than an hour four more wickets went down. At that point, however, McGahey, to whom much of the credit of saving the match was due, found a steady partner in Russell, the pair staying together for an hour and forty minutes, and adding 104 runs. Their partnership was ended by an unwise attempt on the part of McGahey to score a fourth run. It was a little curious that McGahey should have taken such a risk, as all through his admirable innings he displayed praiseworthy caution. In second wicket down at 57, he was seventh out at 243, and during a stay at the wickets extending over three hours he did not make a mistake. His chief hits were eleven 4's, seven 3's, and three 2's. After McGahey left the innings was finished off somewhat rapidly, the side being all out for 266. Still, they had kept in until a quarter to four, and had fairly broken the back of their task. Following on, Essex soon lost Carpenter, and then Fane and Sewell hit with such freedom as to put on 169 runs in an hour and three-quarters. Sewell, who missed his 100 through faulty judgment, made a number of splendid drives, his score including eleven 4's, but he might have been stumped when only a single, and was missed in the deep field when 54. Fane played capital cricket, not giving any chance. With the dismissal of Sewell the stumps were finally pulled up and the game left drawn, Essex, with eight

wickets in hand, wanting 67 runs to avert an innings' defeat. Ranjitsinhji having departed for Sheffield and Marlow having an injured hand, Sussex had two substitutes all day and late in the afternoon Fry left the ground to proceed to Sheffield. Score:

SUSSEX

C. B. Fry, c Kortright, b Young 15	G. Brann, b McGahey 0
Vine, c Russell, b Young 12	W. Newham, c Carpenter,
Killick, c Kortright, b McGahey ... 30	b Mead 153
Relf, b Mead 9	Tate, c Russell, b Mead 5
Marlow, c Russell, b Young 10	Butt, not out 29
K. S. Ranjitsinhji, c Sewell,	Cordingley, b McGahey 3
b McGahey 230	B 18, l b 2, w 2, n b 2 24
	Total 520

ESSEX

F. L. Fane, c Butt, b Tate 31	not out 69
Carpenter, c sub, b Tate 35	c Cordingley, b Tate 16
Sewell, c Relf, b Tate 10	c Cordingley, b Brann 99
C McGahey, run out 104	
C. J. Kortright, c sub, b Tate 9	
Buckenham, c Cordingly, b Tate 1	
G Tosetti, run out 0	
Russell, c sub, b Relf 47	
Reeves, l b w, b Tate 6	
Young, not out 3	
Mead, c Butt, b Relf 2	
B 10, l b 6, n b 2 18	B 2, l b 1 3
Total 266	Total (2 wickets) 187

SUSSEX – First Innings

	O	M	R	W		O	M	R	W
Mead	17	5	129	3	Buckenham	7	1	30	0
Young	41	7	131	3	Kortright	4	0	23	0
McGahey	31.1	8	57	4	Sewell	9	1	7	0
Tosetti	19	3	51	0	Reeves	8	0	48	0
Carpenter	2	0	7	0					

Young bowled one wide and two no-balls and Buckenham one wide.

ESSEX – First Innings

	O	M	R	W		O	M	R	W
Tate	51	14	96	6	Vine	11	1	35	0
Relf	19.1	6	65	2	Cordingley	12	3	30	0
Killick	16	8	22	0					

Tate and Killick each bowled one no-ball.

Second Innings

	O	M	R	W		O	M	R	W
Tate	18	7	42	1	Killick	8	0	48	0
Relf	12	4	22	0	Brann	8	0	51	1
Cordingley	5	0	21	0					

Prince Ranjitsinhji

18: Sussex v Gloucestershire
HOVE, 1–3 JUNE 1903

A commentary in *The Daily Telegraph* after the first day of this match described Jessop as 'surpassing himself'; a quite literal use of the term, as Jessop scored the fastest double century in first-class cricket, and established a record that would not be beaten for 80 years. The commentary said that 'the Brighton ground, in fine weather, is perhaps the most flattering in England to a big hitter, but allowing for the perfect wicket and the rather easy boundaries on the Pavilion side, Jessop's feat was an astounding one.' Moreover, at this time the ball had to be hit out of the ground, and not merely over the ropes, to score six. The commentary continues: 'Indeed, we wonder we should question whether anyone else could have done it. The score is the highest he has ever played in a first-class match, beating by 53 runs his wonderful innings at Lord's for the Rest of England against Yorkshire at the end of the season of 1901.'

Gloucestershire had split with W.G. Grace in 1899, and the Grand Old Man had formed the London County Cricket Club. In the last two seasons Gloucestershire had languished at 14th in the table, one from the bottom, the worst performances in the club's history. *The Daily Telegraph* commented of Jessop that 'it would, indeed, be difficult to recall another case in which the success of a county team depended so much on the efforts of one man . . . it is a mere truism to say that he is one of the greatest personalities in the cricket field at the present day. There has never been a batsman who could so rapidly turn the fortunes of a match.' Unfortunately, when Jessop failed Gloucestershire would crumble, and not until Hammond's prime would they again enjoy consistent success.

Brighton, Monday

Gilbert Jessop yesterday, at Brighton, put together the highest innings he has ever made during his career in first-class cricket. Going in when Gloucestershire had lost three wickets for 94, he found his side with every prospect of being cheaply dismissed, when shortly after the luncheon interval there were five wickets down for 129. Then, however, he found an invaluable partner in Board, and, hitting away in most brilliant and daring fashion, he, during a stay of rather less than three hours, actually scored 286 out of 355 – a performance which, considering the pace of the run-getting and the extent of the score, must be quite unprecedented. Two years ago at Lord's, when Jessop played his highest innings until that of yesterday, he scored 233 in two hours and a half, but 286 in less than three hours must be regarded as a far greater achievement. Despite the tremendous rate at which he scored and the risks he ran, the only mistake – so far as could be seen – he made was a sharp chance to Marlow at mid-on when 98. He took seventy minutes to get his first 100, but doubled his score in another 50 minutes. His grand innings, which included forty-one 4's, seven 3's, and twenty-nine 2's, was only closed by a one-handed catch in the deep field by Ranjitsinhji. Board, who deserved great praise for the restraint he imposed upon himself, assisted his captain to put on 320 runs for the sixth wicket in two hours and a half. He enjoyed some share of good fortune, but for all that his 71 was a capital performance. He was at the wickets for two hours and fifty minutes, and hit eight 4's, being seventh out at 473. After Brownlee's dismissal at 129 Gloucestershire added 351 runs, and only lost four more wickets. Glorious weather prevailed and a big company of spectators assembled at the Hove ground.

Tuesday

Most unfortunately for Sussex, who on Monday had fielded out all day, rain fell yesterday morning at Brighton, not only delaying the resumption of the game with Gloucestershire until after one o'clock, but rendering the wicket soft and slow to begin with, and afterwards – under the influence of bright sunshine – extremely difficult. Under such altered conditions, Sussex naturally failed to score anything like as heavily as their opponents had done, and left off last evening wanting 131 more runs to escape a follow-on with only one wicket to fall. The Gloucestershire innings, in which, thanks to Jessop's superb hitting, 480 had been scored for nine wickets, was finished off for the addition of 2 runs. Killick, who did not go on to bowl until absurdly late, dismissed four batsmen in nine overs at a cost of only 17 runs. At the start of the Sussex innings the wicket remained fairly easy, and Fry and Vine made fine use of their opportunities, putting on 83 runs before lunch and afterwards raising the score to 120 before the first wicket fell. Fry was then well caught at extra deep-mid-off. He had played a brilliant game for an hour and forty minutes, making most of his 83 runs by powerful drives and square cuts, the latter stroke being one which only a couple of years ago he scarcely attempted at all. When 78 he trod on the stumps, but had finished his stroke, and was starting to run, so did not lose his wicket. So pronounced a change came over the game subsequently that although the total had reached 120, with no one out, there were four wickets down for 181, and ought to have been five, Smith being missed directly he went in. The bowlers contrived to hold the upper hand, batsmen having to fight very hard for their runs. Smith was given a second life, and after Butt and Cox had failed he altered his game so completely that 42 runs were soon added for the eighth wicket. Pleasant weather prevailed and a large company assembled at the Hove ground.

Wednesday

Last week at Manchester, Ranjitsinhji, with a score of 105, gave conclusive evidence of being in first-rate form this season, and yesterday at Brighton, he played another great innings and was mainly instrumental in saving Sussex from defeat. The position from which Sussex started in the morning was a very thankless one, as in face of Gloucestershire's big total of 482 they had on Tuesday on a pitch damaged by rain lost nine wickets for 202. Happily for the side, Marlow and Tate, the overnight not-outs, offered a stubborn resistance to the bowling and in the course of rather more than an hour put on 64 runs, thus carrying the score to 266. This left Sussex 216 behind and they were, of course, compelled to follow on, the second innings beginning at one o'clock. The start was disastrous, Fry being bowled off his pads in the first over and Vine leg before wicket in the second. These two wickets were lost for ten runs, the position at once becoming critical. However, Killick and Ranjitsinhji stayed together and though they never mastered the bowling they carried the total to 62 and were still not out at lunch time. After the interval, 15 runs were added and then Killick left, the third wicket falling at 77. At this point Rolf joined Ranjitsinhji and in the course of an hour and twenty-five minutes the two batsmen put on 100 runs, the partnership making defeat highly improbable. Still, when Rolf was bowled for an invaluable 50 and Smith went in Sussex were thirty runs behind with two hours remaining for play. So far Ranjitsinhji had kept himself under restraint, but feeling that there was nothing more to fear he changed his plan and played with far greater freedom. With the stroke which completed his hundred – obtained in just three hours – he wiped off the arrears, and then he and Smith hit away in magnificent form. They added in all 139 to the score in an hour and a half, and were still together when at six o'clock – a draw being inevitable – the match was given up. So greatly had the position changed that Sussex at the finish were 109 runs ahead with six wickets in hand. Ranjitsinhji's only real mistake during a stay of four hours was a chance at square leg when he had made 109. He hit twenty-three 4's, four 3's, and twelve 2's. Score:

GLOUCESTERSHIRE

S. A. P. Kitcat, b Cox 36	Board, b Killick 71
Wrathall, c Butt, b Relf 0	Huggins, c Butt, b Killick 9
Hale, c Marlow, b Vine 42	Nott, c Tate, b Cox 8
Langdon, c and b Cox 13	Dennett, l b w, b Killick 1
G. L. Jessop, c Ranjitsinhji,	Roberts, not out 0
b Killick 286	B 1, l b 10, w 5 16
L. D. Brownlee, b Cox 0	Total 482

SUSSEX

C. B. Fry, c Jessop, b Dennett 83	b Roberts 6
Vine, b Huggins 29	l b w, b Dennett 4
Killick, c Hale, b Dennett 10	c Dennett, b Brownlee 33
K. S. Ranjitsinhji, b Huggins 0	not out 162
Relf, c Board, b Huggins 7	b Kitcat 50
C. L. A. Smith, c Jessop,	not out 54
b Dennett 34	
Butt, c Hale, b Dennett 4	
Cox, b Huggins 0	
Marlow, c Roberts, b Jessop 46	
Bland, c Dennett, b Roberts 4	
Tate, not out 29	
B 9, l b 9, w 1, n-b 1 20	B 12, l b 1, n-b 1, w 2 16
Total 266	Total (4 wickets) 325

GLOUCESTERSHIRE

	O	M	R	W		O	M	R	W
Relf	22	8	65	1	Vine	21	6	80	1
Tate	24	8	100	0	Marlow	5	1	31	0
Bland	17	7	44	0	Killick	9	3	17	4
Cox	25.5	2	129	4					

Cox bowled four and Relf one wide.

SUSSEX – First Innings

	O	M	R	W		O	M	R	W
Roberts	23	8	35	1	Nott	8	1	24	0
Huggins	32	13	76	4	Jessop	7.3	4	18	1
Dennett	45	18	93	4					

Roberts bowled one no-ball and Dennett one wide.

Second Innings

	O	M	R	W		O	M	R	W
Roberts	14	3	30	1	Brownlee	21	5	75	1
Dennett	22	8	50	1	Nott	4	0	26	0
Huggins	18	10	27	0	Kitcat	5	2	17	1
Jessop	6	1	31	0	Langdon	9	1	53	0

Dennett and Langdon each bowled a wide, and Roberts one no-ball.

19: Derbyshire v Essex
CHESTERFIELD, 18–20 JULY 1904

It is a signal achievement to score 343 not out in a total of 597 and yet be on the side that loses the match; indeed, no loser has ever scored more. For this reason, rather than having made the highest score ever for Essex (a record that still stands), or for having hit more boundaries (68) in an innings than ever before or since, is Percy Perrin's feat remembered. This season was Essex's worst since joining the Championship, and with performances such as this it is little wonder that they ended the season one from bottom. Derbyshire's feat was unprecedented in first-class cricket.

The game was a masterpiece of attacking cricket, and exemplifies the gulf between the different approaches then and now. On the first day Derbyshire bowled nearly 140 overs – 23 an hour – despite the punishment Essex were handing out, and it is not hard to see how, with such an attitude, they were able to come back from apparent oblivion. Perrin (1876–1945) played for Essex until 1928, scoring 29,709 runs at an average of 35. The highest proportion of boundaries in this innings may partly be accounted for by Perrin's legendary immobility, which marked him down as perhaps the worst fieldsman in England. He never played for England, but in 1939 became the chairman of the selectors. Charles Ollivierre (1876–1949), who made the best score of his career and won the match for Derbyshire, was from Jamaica. He toured England with the first West Indian side in 1900 and stayed on to qualify for Derbyshire, for whom he played for seven seasons, before being forced to retire with eye trouble. He settled in the West Riding, and between the wars coached schoolboy cricketers in Holland.

Chesterfield, Monday

Percy Perrin yesterday, at Chesterfield, succeeded in putting together the highest score of the season. Going in when Essex had lost one wicket for 12, he withstood the Derbyshire bowling for five hours, and left off 295 not out, thus beating Hayes' 273 not out – also against Derbyshire – by 22 runs. From the first he displayed a perfect mastery over the bowling, and scored at a great pace, playing such faultless cricket that it was

not until he had made 152 that he gave a chance, Bestwick then dropping an easy catch at mid-on. As the afternoon advanced he naturally tired under the great heat, and he might on several occasions have been taken in the long field, but for all that his performance was one of exceptional brilliancy. As Essex at the drawing of stumps had still two wickets to fall Perrin should have an excellent chance of reaching 300 to-day. Fane, playing faultless cricket, assisted to put on 120 for the second wicket in seventy minutes, and with Perrin and Gillingham together 126 were obtained for the fourth wicket. Then came the one brief spell of success for Derbyshire, Warren in one over dismissing Sewell and Reeves. It was in this over, too, that Perrin should have been out for 152. Keigwin stayed while 69 runs were scored, and Perrin and Douglas hit up 130 in an hour and a quarter. It will be noticed that the day's cricket yielded more than 500 runs.

Tuesday

At Chesterfield yesterday Perrin succeeded in raising his overnight score of 295 against Derbyshire to 343, and was still not out when the Essex innings closed for 597. In so doing he put together the fifth highest individual innings ever recorded in first-class cricket, just beating the 338 which W. W. Read made for Surrey against Oxford University in 1888.

Perrin, who added 48 to his score yesterday in fifty minutes, was altogether at the wickets five hours and three-quarters. His placing on the leg-side and his driving were as nearly perfection as possible, and if missed more than once late on Monday afternoon, he did not make his first mistake until he had scored more than 150. His wonderful innings was made up by sixty-eight 4's, three 3's, eleven 2's, and thirty-four singles.

Undismayed by the huge total they had to face, Derbyshire went in to bat, and gave a display which compared by no means unfavourably with that of their opponents, hitting up between a quarter to one and the drawing of stumps 446 for the loss of four batsmen, and thus at the finish having six wickets to go down, and wanting only 2 runs to escape a follow-on. Ollivierre and Wright set their colleagues a brilliant example by scoring 101 in an hour and forty minutes – a record for the first wicket in Derbyshire cricket. Then with Ollivierre and Storer together, 128 were added in an hour and a quarter, and none of the Derbyshire batsmen failed. Wright batted in excellent form, but the play of Ollivierre overshadowed everything else. The West Indian played magnificent cricket for three hours and three quarters, and hit up 229 out of 378

Percy Perrin, Essex's highest scorer

before he was third man out. He scored with delightful freedom all round the wicket, and included in his score were a 5, thirty-seven 4's, five 3's, and five 1's. His innings is the highest he has ever put together, and second highest ever played for Derbyshire. Up to the drawing of stumps last evening the match had produced 1,043 runs for fourteen wickets, so it is quite possible it may establish a fresh record in the way of an aggregate for first-class cricket in England by beating the 1,492 scored in the game between Worcestershire and Oxford University ten days ago. It may be recalled that it was at Chesterfield, six years ago, that J. T. Brown and Tunnicliffe put on 554 runs for the first Yorkshire wicket, Brown making 300 and Tunnicliffe 243.

Wednesday

In beating Essex by nine wickets, at Chesterfield, yesterday, the Derbyshire team accomplished what, in its way, was the most phenomenal performance ever recorded at the game of cricket. They went in on Tuesday against a total of 597, succeeded yesterday in getting to within 40 of that number, then dismissed Essex in an hour and fifty minutes for 97, and finally hit off the 147 runs necessary to give them a victory in an hour and twenty minutes for the loss of only one wicket. Such an achievement is quite without parallel. The nearest approach to it occurred in the ever-memorable Test match between Stoddart's first Team and Australia, at Sydney, in December 1894, when the Englishmen, after fielding out a first innings of 586, snatched an astonishing victory by 10 runs. On that occasion, however, the game ran into the sixth day, the Englishmen enjoyed the benefit of a follow-on, and when, at the close of the fifth day, Australia, with eight wickets in hand, wanted only 64 to win, drenching rain during the night, followed by bright sunshine, reduced the wicket to such a state that Peel and Briggs were almost unplayable. In the match which finished yesterday, Derbyshire did all their magnificent work in three days, had no follow-on to tire out the Essex bowlers, and were helped by no rain. Thus their performance must be regarded as distinctly more wonderful than that of Stoddart's team. Another instance of a side winning after fielding out a first innings of over 500 occurred at Adelaide in March last year, Lord Hawke's team, captained by P. F. Warner, making 553 at their first attempt, and being beaten by 97 runs. In that contest, however, the follow-on led to the Englishmen fielding out for 758 runs.

At the drawing of stumps on Tuesday, Derbyshire had scored 446 for the loss of only four batsmen. Yesterday the innings terminated rather quietly, the six outstanding wickets going down for the addition of 102 runs, and the innings being all over for 548. Cadman played very well, but received indifferent support. Like their opponents, Derbyshire took about six hours to put their big total together.

Leading by 49, Essex had three-quarters of an hour's batting before lunch, and although the wicket had certainly worn to some extent, there appeared not the slightest chance of anything but a draw. So finely, however, did Bestwick and Warren bowl, however, that six batsmen were actually dismissed before the interval for 27 runs. Subsequently, Sewell and Douglas made a great effort to save their side, and put on 57 in fifty minutes, but, with Gillingham unable to bat, owing to an attack of lumbago, the innings was all over for 97. Warren took four wickets for 42, Bestwick three for 34, and just at the finish Curgenven dismissed two batsmen very cheaply.

Derbyshire had two hours and five minutes in which to get 147. They lost Wright at 11, but afterwards always looked like accomplishing the task. Buckenham and Reeves were nothing like so difficult as Bestwick and Warren had been, and Ollivierre and Storer batting with the utmost freedom and confidence, the runs were actually obtained in an hour and twenty minutes, Derbyshire gaining their glorious victory with three-quarters of an hour to spare. Ollivierre, who had hard luck in not being able to get another hundred, again played brilliant and faultless cricket, and scored 321 runs in the match for once out. He yesterday hit fifteen 4's. Derbyshire had never previously won a home match with Essex, and their brilliant triumph naturally aroused immense enthusiasm among the 3,000 people present. It may be recalled that Derbyshire this season beat Essex at Leyton, after being 122 behind on the first innings. Score:

Essex

F. L. Fane, l b w, b Curganven	63	b Warren	2
Carpenter, b Bestwick	5	c Warren, b Bestwick	2
P. Perrin, not out	343	c and b Warren	8
C. McGahey, b Bestwick	32	c Cadman, b Bestwick	5
Rev. F. H. Oldingham, c and b Warren	43	absent, ill	0
Sewell, b Warren	10	c Cadman, b Curgenven	41
Reeves, b Warren	0	b Bestwick	0
F. P. Kelgwin, l b w, b Ashcroft	14	c Needham, b Warren	0
J. W. H. T. Douglas, b Ollivierre	47	not out	27
E. Russell, c Humphries, b Cadman	23	b Curgenven	0
Buckenham, l b w, b Bestwick	3	b Warren	8
B 2, l b 5, w 3, n-b 4	14	W 2, n b 2	4
Total	597	Total	97

Derbyshire

L. G. Wright, c Fane, b Reeves	68	c. Carpenter, b Buckenham	1
C. A. Ollivierre, b Reeves	229	not out	92
Storer, b Buckenham	44	not out	48
E. M. Ashcroft, b Sewell	34		
Needham, b Reeves	47		
G. Curgenven, b Buckingham	31		
Morton, b Reeves	16		
Warren, b Douglas	18		
Cadman, c Douglas, b Reeves	34		
Humphries, not out	2		
Bestwick, l b w, b Douglas	0		
B 6, l b 18, w 1	25	B 4, l b 3, w 1, n b 1	8
Total	548	Total (1 wicket)	149

Essex – First Innings

	O	M	R	W		O	M	R	W
Warren	29	3	148	2	Ashcroft	7	1	38	1
Bestwick	42.1	8	160	3	Morton	8	1	39	0
Cadman	22	3	65	1	Wright	4	0	15	0
Storer	7	0	41	0	Ollivierre	3	0	15	1
Curgenven	16	1	67	1					

Warren bowled two wides and one no-ball, Wright one wide, Bestwick two no-balls, and Morton one no-ball.

Second Innings

	O	M	R	W		O	M	R	W
Bestwick	16	14	34	3	Cadman	2	0	10	0
Warren	16.1	5	42	4	Curgenven	5	2	7	2

Bestwick and Warren each bowled a wide, and Warren a no-ball.

Derbyshire – First Innings

	O	M	R	W		O	M	R	W
Buckenham	43	5	176	2	Douglas	15.3	1	54	2
Kelgwin	7	1	36	0	McGahey	11	2	34	0
Reeves	51	7	192	5	Sewell	7	0	31	1

Buckenham bowled a wide.

Second Innings

	O	M	R	W		O	M	R	W
Buckenham	13	0	78	1	Douglas	2	0	14	0
Reeves	13	1	43	0	McGahey	2	1	6	0

Buckenham bowled a wide and Douglas a no-ball.

Umpires – W. Wright and S. Brown.

Last year: Essex, 220 and 282 (innings declared closed); Derbyshire, 139 and 131. Essex won by 232 runs.

20: *Surrey v Essex*
THE OVAL, 4–6 MAY 1905

I t is scarcely surprising, in retrospect, that Jack Hobbs (1882–1963) should have made a century in his first Championship match for Surrey; and it was a happy irony that he should do so against a county that turned him down as a professional. Hobbs, like his colleague Hayward, was a Cambridge lad, the son of a college groundsman. He learned his cricket on Parker's Piece, not far from the University ground at

Fenner's. Essex, his nearest first-class county, did not like the look of him, so he went to the Oval, and played for Surrey until 1934. He was 'The Master', the greatest batsman of his age, blessed with a technique that suggested he had more time than anyone else to play the ball. No cricketer has ever scored more runs than his 61,237 (average 50.65), nor more centuries than his 197, and none, probably, ever will. He played

61 times for England, and for his country and his county was part of four of the most famous opening partnerships in cricket history: with Hayward and Sandham for Surrey (with the latter he still holds the county's first wicket record); and with Rhodes and Sutcliffe for England. There has never been a finer first pair than Hobbs and Sutcliffe; 11 times they put on more than 100 for their country; yet it was with Rhodes, at Melbourne in 1911–12, that Hobbs put on the 323 that remains a record in England-Australia tests. Hobbs was knighted in the 1953 Coronation honours.

Walter Lees (1875–1924), whose ten wickets undid Essex, was Surrey's leading bowler of the time, and played on five occasions for England. When he retired in 1911 he had taken 1,402 wickets at 21 each. F.L. Fane (1875–1960), the Essex captain, later captained England against Australia and South Africa.

The Oval, Thursday

Had the weather only been genial, the cricket at the Oval yesterday, in the opening of the Surrey and Essex match would have been attractive to watch. The game is always the more interesting when batsmen have to fight hard for their runs and scores rule low, but though the bowlers held the upper hand and the struggle for supremacy was very close, the day's play fell somewhat flat. It was difficult to feel at all enthusiastic with a grey sky and a north-east wind blowing. The time occupied by cricket was a trifle over five hours, and considerable progress was made, an innings on each side being completed. Both elevens were at the wickets about the same length of time, Surrey being put out for 138, and Essex for 123. In gaining first innings Surrey undoubtedly obtained an advantage. At the outset the wicket, which owing to rain in the night was soft, played fairly well for a time, but after a while the bowlers were able to get on some spin, and the ball occasionally rose rather awkwardly. Still, the smallness of the scores may be more properly attributed to lack of practice on the part of the batsmen than the difficulties of the pitch or any special excellence in the bowling. Had the Essex men only held their catches they would probably have got rid of Surrey for less than 100. Taking advantage of some loose bowling by Young, Hayward and Hobbs scored 28 in the first twenty minutes, and altogether put up 56 in just over an hour for the first wicket. Hobbs, who obtained most of his runs on the on-side, was twice missed, the first occasion being when he was 12, and though he made some good strokes, Hayward was occasionally in difficulties. Holland who was the top scorer with 31, gave a sharp chance shortly after going in, and was let off in the long field in the over in which

Walter Lees

he was dismissed, but he nevertheless played capital cricket. Watching the ball closely, he rarely allowed a fair chance of scoring to escape him, being particularly strong on the off-side. Before lunch Reeves bowled very well, and after the interval Buckenham did a neat piece of work, taking three wickets for 13 runs. After losing their captain without a run, the Essex batsmen fought steadily all along the line, seven of them reaching double figures. Freeman obtained his runs in good style, and he and McGahey put on 30 for the third wicket, that being the most profitable stand. Reeves hit out pluckily, scoring his 17 in four strokes, and the brothers Russell also made useful little scores. One or two blemishes apart, the Surrey men ably supported their bowlers, and Stedman was in good form behind the wicket, having a hand in the dismissal of five batsmen.

Friday

Though the wind was still in a cold quarter, cricket at the Oval yesterday was conducted under more enjoyable conditions than on Thursday, the sun shining brilliantly all day. The ground was much faster, and as a consequence runs were obtained much more readily. On the opening day an innings on each side had been completed for an aggregate of 261, while yesterday in well under six hours 495 runs were scored, and only thirteen wickets went down. Surrey, who held the trifling lead of 15, began their second innings first thing, and were not disposed of until nearly a quarter to five, putting together, in four hours and twenty minutes, the handsome total of 383. The outstanding feature of the day's play was an extremely well-played innings by Hobbs, the latest addition to the Surrey ranks. Last week, against the Gentlemen of England, Hobbs gave evidence of being a batsman of more than ordinary ability, and yesterday he fully confirmed the good impression that had been formed of his powers. Going in first, he scored 50 out of 90 in eighty minutes, 101 out of 170 in two hours, and when an hour later he was caught at deep square leg, he had made 155 out of 249, being the fourth man out. Though scoring at this brisk rate, Hobbs made singularly few mistakes. Early in his innings he was within an ace of being bowled, but he did not give anything approaching a chance until 90, when he was missed at the wicket. Directly afterwards he might possibly have been caught from a return, but the ball went rather wide to Young. These, however, were only small blemishes in a most attractive display, which was marked by skilful placing of the ball on the leg and on-side. He was somewhat favoured by the bowlers for his favourite strokes, and he made the most of his opportunities, turning the ball time after time with delightful precision. The Essex captain was slow to realise the strong point of Hobbs' batting, and it was not until quite late that he put on a man on the leg side. Had he done so earlier there is no doubt that a good many runs would have been saved. Hobbs made some good cuts and off-drives, but his chief power lay on the other side of the wicket. Included in his 155 were three 5's (two of them strokes through the slips and one a straight drive), and nineteen 4's. Hayward, who was bowled by a ball that went with Young's arm, helped to put on 81 for the first partnership, but Hobbs received his chief assistance from Baker, the two men punishing the bowling with such severity as to add 175 runs in an hour and forty minutes. When only 6, Baker was let off in the slips, but afterwards he played very well, hitting nine 4's. The sixth wicket fell at 283, and then in forty minutes Lord Dalmeny and Nice put on 83 runs. The latter forced the game in a spirited manner, twice scoring 16 in an over, and altogether sending the ball to the boundary twelve times. Set 299 runs to get to win, Essex began badly by losing Carpenter and Perrin for 22 runs, but Fane and McGahey made a plucky effort to improve matters, carrying the score to 109. Fane gave a bright display, scoring all round the wicket, and hitting ten 4's. When the stumps were drawn for the day Essex had three wickets down for 112, and thus still require 287.

Saturday

As the overnight position of the game suggested would be the case, Surrey won the match at the Oval on Saturday very comfortably, beating Essex by 185 runs. Set the heavy task of 399 runs to get to win, Essex had lost three of their best batsmen for 112, and no reasonable doubt could be felt as to the result. The last real hope that the Essex men might have entertained disappeared when at 124, McGahey, who had batted very steadily on Friday evening, was bowled by a good ball. Young, who had been sent in late overnight, left at the same total, and Edward Russell should also have gone at that point. Holland, however, dropped an easy catch in the slips, and an hour and a quarter elapsed before that batsman was dismissed. Russell, however, did little more than play a purely defensive game. Freeman again batted in nice fashion, making thee or four good drives and two neat strokes on the left side. In forty minutes Freeman hit up 32 out of 37, his score including seven 4's. Buckenham made a few hits and Reeves batted with some spirit. The end, however, was reached by twenty minutes past one, the seven wickets only adding 101 runs, and the side being all out for 213. While keeping wicket on Friday T. Russell had the misfortune to split the top of his left thumb, but he nevertheless batted. Lees again took five wickets, and in the match had the excellent record of ten for 134. Score:

SURREY

Hayward, b Reeves	24	b Young	24
Hobbs, c Young, b Trelim	28	c Reeves, b McGahey	155
Hayes, c Carpenter, b Reeves	9	c Carpenter, b Tremlin	1
Baker, c McGahey, b Reeves	2	run out	53
Holland, c Buckenham, b Reeves	31	c F. Russell, b Tremlin	5
Lees, st T. Russell, b Reeves	13	b Tremlin	5
Nice, c Carpenter, b Buckenham	5	c Freeman, b Buckingham	66
Lord Dalmeny, b Buckenham	9	l b w, b Reeves	38
Stedman, c t. Russell, b Buckenham	7	b Carpenter	9
N. A. Knox, b Buckenham	4	c Freeman, b Reeves	3
Smith, not out	0	not out	3
B 21 b 4	6	B 16, l b 4, n-b 1	21
Total	138	Total	383

ESSEX

F. L. Fane, c Hayward, b Lees	0	b Lees	66
Carpenter, c Stedman, b Lees	12	b Knox	2
P. Perrin, c Smith, b Knox	10	b Lees	7
C. McGahey, l b w, b Lees	16	b Knox	32
Freeman, b Nice	21	b Lees	32
Russell (E.), c Stedman, b Lees	11	b Lees	14
Buckenham, c Smith, b Nice	2	c Stedman, b Nice	16
Reeves, st Stedman, b Lees	17	c Hobbs, b Nice	23
Tremlin, st Stedman, b Nice	0	b Nice	0
Russell (T.), not out	16	not out	2
Young, c Stedman, b Knox	9	c Hayes, b Lees	9
B	9	B 7, l b 2, n-b 1	10
Total	123	Total	213

SURREY – First Innings

	O	M	R	W		O	M	R	W
Young	5	0	26	0	Buckenham	18.1	8	34	4
Reeves	25	8	57	5	Tremlin	9	5	15	1

Second Innings

	O	M	R	W		O	M	R	W
Buckenham	18	2	51	4	Tremlin	23	3	78	3
Reeves	26.3	6	110	2	Perrin	4	0	22	0
McGahey	12	3	42	1	Carpenter	2	1	4	1
Young	11	1	55	1					

ESSEX – First Innings

	O	M	R	W		O	M	R	W
Knox	10.2	2	29	2	Nice	16	5	38	3
Lees	26	9	47	5					

Second Innings

	O	M	R	W		O	M	R	W
Knox	22	12	49	2	Hayes	4	0	21	0
Lees	20	7	87	5		10.2	1	46	3

Umpires – W. Marlow and J. E. West.

21: Middlesex v Sussex
LORD'S, 25–27 MAY 1905

Fielding a team composed almost entirely of amateurs, Middlesex look the incarnation of what we are told to assume of the 'golden age' of cricket before the Great War. This was Bosanquet's match, in which he became the first man ever to score two centuries in a match and take more than ten wickets. The Middlesex side is studded with famous names. Of A.E. Trott's tragic life we shall hear later (see game 24). P.F. 'Plum' Warner (1873–1963) was central to the English game for 60 years, as captain of England and Middlesex, President and a Trustee of the MCC, a test selector, cricket correspondent of *The Morning Post* and founder of *The Cricketer*. He scored 29,028 runs at an average of 36 in his career. J.T. Hearne (1867–1944) played for Middlesex from 1888 to 1923 and was one of the finest medium-pace bowlers in the country. He took 3,061 wickets at nearly 18 in his long career, a haul exceeded by only three other bowlers in the game's history.

B.J.T. Bosanquet (1877–1936) is perhaps best remembered for inventing the 'googly', or 'bosie', as it was named after him; an off-break bowled with the same action as a leg-break. This season was the last in which he shone as a bowler, but his batting continued to improve to the extent that he topped the averages in 1908, the last season in which he played regularly. He was a considerable all-round sportsman, being a fine ice-hockey player, and having played billiards for Oxford; indeed, it was on a billiard table, playing 'twisti-twosti' with a tennis ball, that he had the idea of the googly. In his career he made 11,696 runs at an average of 33, and took 629 wickets at 24 each. He played seven times for England, without conspicuous success.

Lord's, Thursday

Against the very ordinary Sussex bowling Middlesex did nothing exceptional to bat for the whole of yesterday at Lord's, and they were somewhat fortunate to score so many as 309. During one partnership only did the batting obtain the mastery, the fortune of the game going against the fielding side. If never appearing formidable, the bowling did not become slack, and though the ground work was slovenly at times, no catch was missed. False hits, and several were made, always went wide of the fieldsmen, and the bowlers often beat the bat with balls that passed very close to the stumps. Altogether, in fact, Sussex could consider themselves unlucky to be kept out for five hours and a quarter; but really they did fairly well to prevent the home team from putting together a larger total, and for the most part it was a hard struggle for runs.

By far the best batting was that of Bosanquet, who almost from the moment he went in scored with a freedom none of his colleagues approached. Warner and E. A. Beldam took nearly as many minutes to get 50 for the first wicket, both playing nicely, but finding very few balls to punish. When 24, Warner went forward to Goldie's first ball and must have been easily caught if the bowler could have checked his run in time. Otherwise Warner's innings of 49 was sound, and it was ended by a brilliant catch at point, Goldie taking a hard cut low with the right hand, and though rolling over retaining his hold of the ball. When Warner left, third out at 94, the result of an hour and a half's cricket, Bosanquet joined Field, and for an hour and three-quarters played almost perfectly. If occasionally Bosanquet did not send the ball quite in the direction intended his false strokes were few and never open to serious criticism. Invariably keeping the ball on the ground, he drove to the off and cut with superb strength, and his leg glances and sweeping hits in the same direction showed absolute precision in timing. Completing 50 in rather less than an hour Bosanquet scored still more freely afterwards, and altogether made 103 out of 149. His figures included eleven 4's, six 3's, and ten 2's.

In striking contrast to his brilliant partner Field played a stubborn, careful game. Field, who was in the Cambridge Eleven of 1894, and appeared at full back in England's Rugby football team about the same period, has not had much experience of first-class cricket in recent years; but if short of practice he did Middlesex splendid service yesterday by his patient and sound defence. Never tempted to hit except at a loose ball on the leg side, Field, who went in second wicket down at 66 at ten minutes past one, carried out his bat when the innings closed at twenty-five minutes past six. Taking two hours and a quarter over his 50, he was altogether batting four hours and ten minutes for 107. Limited as his means of scoring were almost entirely to the out, Field played in rather unattractive style, but his value could not be over-estimated. He gave no chances, and hit thirteen 4's, three 3's, and five 2's. Despite the long partnership for the fourth wicket seven men were out for 248, but following a slow half-hour, in which Wyatt and Field put on 23, Trott hit up 20 out of 26, and

in the slips, Crawford running in more than a yard and taking the ball close to the ground. At this point the position looked quite desperate, Yorkshire, with only three wickets to fall and Rothery partially disabled, still wanting nine runs to save the single innings defeat. However, with Haigh in things improved.

Hirst, who had gone in for a few minutes to have a slight injury attended to, a ball from Crawford having taken the skin off one of his knuckles, scored for only the second time in about fifty minutes. We should question whether he has ever before taken such a long time to get two singles. Soon after this he should have been run out, but, luckily for him, May failed to gather a very awkward return. Runs now came rather fast, both batsmen hitting vigorously. Haigh, however, also escaped being run out. Knox, who was never off for long, separated the batsmen just before luncheon, Haigh hitting across a ball that sent the middle stump flying. The total at the interval was 241 for eight wickets, Yorkshire being forty runs ahead and Hirst not out 46.

All hope of avoiding defeat had practically disappeared, but Yorkshire did not go down without a last struggle, Hawke, after luncheon, staying in with Hirst for nearly seventy minutes. He was content to get 8 of the 51 runs put on, his one object being to give Hirst as good a chance as possible. His innings, so much more valuable than it looks on paper, was ended by a catch at slip, the ball going to Hayes off Strudwick's gloves. Hirst all this time played in his best form, and missed few opportunities of scoring. He seemed certain to take out his bat, but a break-back from Lees beat him, Yorkshire's innings coming to an end just after four o'clock for 297. Altogether Hirst was batting for about three hours and a quarter. No one could have tried harder to save a lost game or played with greater pluck. Though hurt three or four times during his innings, he never for a moment lost his confidence. The great feature of his play was the certainty with which he pulled fast balls round to square-leg, his timing being a marvel of accuracy. Now and then he was in difficulties, and once May got past him with a fast yorker, but for the most part he was master of the bowling. His chief hits were eleven 4's.

Despite the disadvantage under which he laboured, Knox took six wickets for 105 runs. He could not get up the same pace as on Thursday, and was, as a matter of fact, slower than May. Still, he was far more alarming, the ball getting up to such a dangerous height. Taking in all ten wickets for 181 runs, he did far more than anyone else to win the match. The way in which he stuck to his work, despite his lameness, spoke volume for his pluck and stamina. We believe he was suffering a good deal from shin soreness, this being no doubt the price he pays in dry weather for the long run and great exertion involved in his tremendous speed. It struck us that Dalmeny leaned rather too heavily on Saturday on his fast bowlers. He took Crawford off when that bowler was keeping Hirst to

a rigidly defensive game and wickets were falling at the other end, and seemed very loth to put on Lees. When at last Lees got a fair chance he finished the innings by taking Hawke's and Hirst's wickets. On Thursday Dalmeny managed his bowling with the nicest judgment, making every change at exactly the right moment.

The closing stage of the match need not be described at any length. Going on to bowl so soon after his long innings Hirst was not fresh enough to be at all deadly, and neither Jackson nor Haigh presented much difficulty. Hayward and Hobbs went in first, and put on runs quite readily till at 39 Hobbs skyed a ball and was caught by Hunter fully a dozen yards from the wicket. With Hayes in, 50 went up when the innings had been in progress barely three-quarters of an hour, and the remaining runs were obtained at a great pace, the hitting being very clean and brilliant. Hayward's batting, as in his first innings, approached perfection. So far as we noticed, he was never in any way at fault.

YORKSHIRE

Rhodes, c Hearne, b Knox	15	b May	53
Rothery, c Stradwick, b Lees	13	not out	2
Denton, c Crawford, b Lees	4	c Holland, b Knox	12
Hon. F. S. Jackson, c Stradwick, b Knox	10	c Hayes, b Knox	20
Hirst, c Goatly, b Lees	0	b Lees	87
Tunnicliffe, c Crawford, b Lees	60	c Hayes, b May	53
T. L. Taylor, c Holland, b Crawford	26	l b w, b Knox	5
		c Crawford, b Knox	7
Wilkinson (W. H.), c Stradwick, b Lees	10	b Knox	15
Haigh, c May, b Knox	27	c Hayes, b Lees	8
Lord Hawke, c and b Knox	0	c Holland, b Knox	6
Hunter, not out	0		
B 11, l-b 5, w 4, n-b 1	21	B 10, l-b 11, w 1, n-b 7	29
Total	186	Total	297

SURREY

Hayward, c Tunnicliffe, b Hirst	76	not out	44
Hobbs, l b w, b Haigh	34	c Hunter, b Haigh	22
Hayes, c Tunnicliffe, b Jackson	53	not out	28
Goatly, c Hunter, b Hirst	8		
J. N. Crawford, run out	51		
Holland, c Tunnicliffe, b Jackson	10		
Lord Dalmeny, b Haigh	40		
Lees, c and b Jackson	41		
P. R. May, c Rothery, b Rhodes	32		
Stadwick, c and b Rhodes	3		
N. A. Knox, not out	16		
B 14, l-b 8, n-b 1	23	B 1, l-b 1, w 1	3
Total	387	Total (1 wicket)	97

YORKSHIRE – First Innings

	O	M	R	W		O	M	R	W
Lees	23	6	61	5	May	2	0	7	0
Knox	22	6	76	4	Crawford	9	2	21	1

Knox bowled four wides and one no-ball.

Second Innings

	O	M	R	W		O	M	R	W
Lees	17.3	5	42	2	May	27	2	105	2
Knox	34	3	105	6	Crawford	16	9	16	0

Knox bowled one no-ball and May one wide and six no-balls.

SURREY – First Innings

	O	M	R	W		O	M	R	W
Hirst	26	8	53	2	Haigh	24	1	96	2
Jackson	31	5	98	3	Wilkinson	10	1	40	0
Rhodes	19.1	3	77	2					

Hirst bowled one no-ball.

Second Innings

	O	M	R	W		O	M	R	W
Hirst	5	1	10	0	Wilkinson	6	0	18	0
Jackson	5	1	21	0	Rhodes	2	0	10	0
Haigh	8.4	0	35	1					

Haigh bowled a wide.

Umpires – C. Richardson and Marlow.

23: Somerset v Yorkshire
BATH, 27–29 AUGUST 1906

George Hirst (1871–1954) was the greatest all-rounder of his day. This season was his best. He achieved the unique feat (it remains unique, and is never likely to be beaten) of taking 200 wickets and scoring 2,000 runs in a season (to be exact, 2,385 runs and 208 wickets). This match symbolises the power of his all-round abilities: he is the only man in the history of the game to score a hundred in each innings and take five wickets in each of his opponents'. He played regularly for Yorkshire from 1891 until 1921, and occasionally thereafter until 1929, while he was coach at Eton. In his career he scored 36,356 runs at an average of 34, including 60 centuries. His highest score, 341 against Leicestershire at Leicester in 1905, remains the highest for Yorkshire. With his left-arm bowling he took 2,742 wickets at 19 each. He performed the 'double' 14 times (twice scoring over 2,000 runs) and scored more than 1,000 runs in a season 19 times; his 11 consecutive doubles is a record. He played 24 times for England but, despite his excellence at county level, he did not excel in tests. In 1922 Wisden said of him: 'In purely county cricket Hirst was perhaps the greatest match-winning professional cricketer yet produced . . . Hirst was a cricketing genius.' He developed the 'swerve', a technique of making the ball move about deceptively that provided him with many of his wickets.

In making his second century of this match Hirst passed his 2,000 for the season. After the second day of the match, before his five second innings wickets, Hirst needed just 10 wickets for his 'double double'. He had achieved his first 'double' in just 16 matches, the only cricketer ever to complete it before the end of June.

Bath, Monday

After their defeat in the sensational match at Bristol, Yorkshire entered upon their last fixture in the county championship yesterday at Bath. Fortunate in winning the toss, they stayed in all the afternoon, scoring 347 for the loss of eight wickets in rather less than five hours. In making such an admirable start they were mainly indebted to three of their most reliable batsmen – Rhodes, Denton, and Hirst – and for a long time they looked like doing still better. Before lunch the batting was quite brilliant, 168 runs being scored for three wickets. Braund got rid of Tunnicliffe at 24, but Denton – missed from a sharp chance at short leg by Mordaunt before scoring – and Rhodes punished the bowling so freely as to add 102 in fifty-five minutes. Second out, Rhodes hit very cleanly on the off-side, and in his 64, obtained out of 126 in eighty minutes, were nine 4's. Denton, who left at 162, caught at the wicket, was in just as long as Rhodes, and, after his early escape, played in quite his best form; he cut brilliantly, and there were eight 4's in his 67. By steady bowling and close fielding, Somerset kept down the rate of scoring after lunch, but Hirst played another splendid innings – his fifth of a hundred this season. He went in when Denton was out, and was sixth to be dismissed at 318, having scored 111 out of 157 in two hours and thirty-five minutes. Getting a large number of runs by pulls and drives, he always seemed master of the bowling, never being seriously at fault, but he did not find many opportunities to cut. He hit a dozen 4's in an admirable innings, which gave the cricket its chief feature. Hirst had a very careful partner in Taylor, the four wickets adding 64, and Rudston stayed an hour and a quarter, while 83 runs were obtained, the bowling during this time being specially difficult to score from. An interval for tea was taken with only four men out for 285, and on resuming four wickets fell for 62 runs in seventy minutes, Braund getting three of them cheaply. Suffering from a strain, Woods could not play, and Lionel Palairet, appearing for the first time this season, captained Somerset. Fine though somewhat oppressive weather prevailed, and there was a fairly large company.

Tuesday

Going all in favour of Yorkshire, yesterday's cricket at Bath was chiefly remarkable for the all-round cricket of Hirst and Rhodes. The two famous players bowled admirably early in the day, and were afterwards associated in a wonderful display of hitting. Yorkshire had secured a lead of 243 on the first innings, and as no special reason existed for making Somerset follow-on, Ernest Smith let his side bat again. With nothing to risk, the batsmen forced the game, and after Tunnicliffe had helped to score 78 in three-quarters of an hour, Hirst went in to try and complete his 2,000 runs. Not only did he succeed in this, but he and Rhodes actually put on 202 runs in an hour and a quarter without being separated. Brilliant in the extreme, the batting was scarcely marred by an error of any kind.

Hirst made his first 52 in thirty-five minutes, thus reaching his 2,000, and he went on to gain the distinction of scoring two hundreds in a match for the first time in his career, following up his 111 in the first innings with 117 (not out). Only one Yorkshireman had previously accomplished this feat – namely, Denton, at Trent Bridge in June. Hirst took 66 minutes to get his 100, while Rhodes was occupied half an hour longer over his. When 93 Hirst was almost caught in the long field by Johnson, who only just reached the ball, and split one of his fingers in attempting to hold it. This was the only semblance of a chance either batsmen gave. After they had mastered the regular bowlers the cricket could scarcely be regarded seriously, Palairet and Martyn going on and keeping wicket to each other without gloves.

Leading as they did by 523 runs, Yorkshire will most likely close their innings this morning, and it is interesting to mention that Rhodes hit eighteen 4's in his 115 and Hirst twenty-two 4's in his 117.

Cricket of a totally different character took place before this terrible hitting, Yorkshire losing the last two wickets in their first innings for an addition of 21 to the overnight score of 347 and then Somerset being dismissed in two hours and forty minutes for 125. In eighty minutes before lunch three wickets fell for 62 and a similar period on resuming sufficed to finish off the innings for 53 more runs. Johnson and Braund put on 44 for the third partnership, and the 100 went up with five wickets in hand, but then came an astonishing collapse. Hirst bowled particularly well, and after the interval took five wickets for 35 runs. He altogether took six for 70 – his day's work being quite astounding – and Rhodes helped materially in Somerset's cheap dismissal by getting rid of three men for 28. Palairet stayed nearly an hour, some of his strokes on the off side showing all his old grace of style, but he found no one to help him stop the inglorious breakdown.

George Hirst with ball and bat

With the weather again fine, there was another good company of people to see the remarkable cricket.

Wednesday

Yorkshire beat Somerset at Bath yesterday by 389 runs, thus finishing up their county matches for the season with the easiest of victories. Thanks to the brilliant hitting of Hirst and Rhodes, a lead of 523 had been obtained on Tuesday, and, as might have been expected, the innings was declared closed yesterday morning without any loss of time. Somerset, had, of course, nothing to hope for but a draw. Not for a moment did they look like saving the match, being all out in a little over two hours for a paltry total of 134. Though the bowling against them was extremely good, they ought to have made many more runs, the pitch being quite unimpaired. Johnson and Lewis were got rid of in Hirst's second over with the score at 9, and from this bad start there was no recovery. Braund and Phillips did not give much trouble, and four wickets were down for 40. After this Palairet and Martyn tried hard to put a decent appearance on a lost game, and succeeded in adding 47 while they were together, Martyn having the satisfaction of completing his 1,000 runs for the season. Palairet played in perfect style for an hour and a quarter, making some brilliant hits on the offside, but he was out sixth at 90. Robson and Poynts put on 31 for the seventh wicket, and then the match quickly came to an end the last few batsmen failing utterly. Hirst, after taking five wickets and making his record for the whole game eleven wickets for 115 runs gave way to Haigh, who finished off the innings in remarkable fashion. He obtained four wickets, and of the 11 runs scored from him, Lee made 5 in one big hit. Score:

YORKSHIRE

Rhodes, c Johnson, b Bailey	64	not out	115
Tunnicliffe, c and b Braund	4	c, Braund, b Bailey	38
Denton, c Martyn, b Braund	67	Hirst, not out	117
T. L. Taylor, c Poynts, b Mordaunt	41		
Hirst, c and b Mordaunt	111		
Rudston, c Poynts, b Braund	21		
E. Smith, c Mordaunt, b Braund	34		
Haigh, b Braund	1		
Myer, l b w, b Braund	6		
Hunter, b Mordaunt	8		
Ringrose, not out	2		
B 7, w 1, n-b 1	9	B 2, l-b 6, w 2	10
Total	368	Total (1 wkt dec)	280

SOMERSET

P. R. Johnson, b Rhodes	29	b Hirst	5
H. Martyn, b Ringcross	2	c Rhodes, b Hirst	23
Lewis, b Hirst	3	b Hirst	0
Braund, b Hirst	28	b Ringrose	12
L. C. H. Palairet, b Hirst	31	c Hunter, b Hirst	42
F. A. Phillips, l b w, b Rhodes	2	b Hirst	2
Robson, c Hunter, b Hirst	3	b Haigh	26
H. S. Poynts, c Hirst, b Rhodes	14	b Haigh	10
F. M. Lee, not out	6	not out	6
O. C. Mordaunt, b Hirst	3	l b w, b Haigh	0
Bailey, b Hirst	0	b Haigh	2
B 3, l b 1	4	B 2, l-b 1, w 1, n-b 2	6
Total	125	Total	134

YORKSHIRE – First Innings

	O	M	R	W		O	M	R	W
Braund	38.3	3	125	6	Robson	14	2	37	0
Lewis	11	3	43	0	Mordaunt	36	10	71	3
Bailey	19	2	83	1					

Bailey bowled 1 wide and Robson 1 no-ball.

Second Innings

	O	M	R	W		O	M	R	W
Mordaunt	9	0	54	0	Robson	4	0	39	0
Braund	6	0	44	0	Phillips	2	0	19	0
Bailey	10	2	36	1	Palairet	2	0	9	0
Lewis	10	2	52	0	Martyn	2	0	17	0

Lewis and Palairet each bowled a wide.

SOMERSET – First Innings

	O	M	R	W		O	M	R	W
Hirst	26	3	70	6	Rhodes	14	4	28	3
Ringrose	12	5	21	1	Haigh	1	0	2	0

Second Innings

	O	M	R	W		O	M	R	W
Hirst	15	2	45	5	Rhodes	10	1	34	0
Ringrose	9	1	38	1	Haigh	5	1	11	4

Ringcross bowled one wide and two no-balls.
Umpires – W. A. J. West and A. Millward.

24: Middlesex v Somerset
LORD'S, 20–22 MAY 1907

The most glorious feats Albert Edwin Trott (1873–1914) ever accomplished in his career were to cause his undoing. In 1899, playing for the MCC against the Australian tourists, he hit Noble for six clean over the pavilion at Lord's, the only time in history the feat had been achieved. It was said subsequently of Trott that his batting went to pieces too often because he was striving to repeat it. Then, having chosen this match against Somerset for his benefit, he performed a feat without equal in cricket before or since; he took two hat-

tricks in an innings – one of them part of four wickets in four balls – and brought his match to a close so early on the final day that he lost a fortune in takings. Trott, after playing his last match in 1911, fell into penury, suffered from mental illness, and eventually shot himself. At a time when many ex-cricketers seemed to end their lives in grief, Trott's story was nonetheless one of exceptional tragedy.

He had always been a highly-strung character. He had been a successful Australian test cricketer in the Nineties, but when he failed to be picked to tour England in a side captained by his brother, he emigrated there, joined the Lord's ground-staff, and set on his revenge. He was an extraordinarily successful all-rounder, scoring 1,000 runs and taking 200 wickets in his second and third seasons for Middlesex, and playing for England. Known as 'Alberto', he made 10,696 runs in his career at an average of 19, and took 1,674 wickets at 21 each. His astonishing feat of bowling came during a bleak patch in his career, making it all the more remarkable; though the Somerset batting, with the exception of Palairet and Braund, was truly mediocre.

Lord's, Monday

The weather was not kind yesterday to Albert Trott's benefit match at Lord's. A bitter wind made the cricket before luncheon quite a penance to those looking on, and even the players themselves could hardly have found much pleasure in the game. Later in the day a steady rain set in, and nothing was done from ten minutes to four until five o'clock. As the wind dropped after the rain the temperature became bearable, but altogether a less genial Whit Monday has not often been experienced. Considering what had to be contended against, the match proved quite as strong an attraction as could have been expected, 7,044 people paying at the gates. It is safe to say that on a reasonably pleasant day the crowd would have been more than twice as large. Middlesex won the toss, and staying in during the whole time available for play, completed their innings for 286. At one time a much bigger score seemed in prospect, 150 going up with only three men out, but just when the prospect looked brightest, three wickets fell in quick succession.

Warner and Tarrant opened the innings, and gave their side a capital start, scoring 89 together in an hour and twenty minutes. Forsaking the methods he adopted at the start of the match with Hampshire, Tarrant carried caution to an extreme, being at the wickets fully half an hour before he made his first run. Warner, on the other hand, though not at his best, did not miss many opportunities. Lewis and Bailey started the bowling, and the first change came at 59, Bailey giving way to Braund. A wicket should have fallen in Braund's second over, Warner, with his score at 30, giving a chance of stumping. Fifty went up after three-quarters of an hour's play, the game so far having been somewhat uneventful. Mordaunt was tried for Lewis at 64, and this change proved successful, at 89 Warner, in trying to sweep a straight ball round to square-leg, being bowled. George Beldam began in a way that promised success, but after staying till the score had reached 117 he got right in front of the stumps to turn a ball from Mordaunt, and was out leg-before-wicket. At lunch-time the total was 130 for two wickets,

Tarrant having made 52 and Bosanquet 7.

In the first over after resuming Tarrant was caught in the slips. At the wickets for nearly two hours, he played a good game from the moment he began to hit. Some of the best cricket of the day was seen while Bosanquet and Littlejohn were together. Bosanquet made two splendid hits past cover-point to the boundary off Lewis, and scored freely on both sides of the wicket from Mordaunt. He seemed nicely set for a long innings, when at 163 he was caught at slip, the ball going straight into Johnson's hands. Other misfortunes soon followed, Trott and Milton being bowled by Lewis without giving any trouble. With six wickets down for 171 the advantage of having gone in first did not amount to much. However, MacGregor stayed with Littlejohn, and things began to look better. Success last week had no doubt given Littlejohn plenty of confidence. He played extremely well, scoring several times in the most skilful way on the leg-side, and getting a large majority of the runs. MacGregor did not start too well, and had a narrow escape of being caught at slip. When the rain came on the total had been carried to 215.

There was no more play for an hour and a quarter, and before he could settle down again Littlejohn was caught at slip. His was, perhaps, the best hitting in the innings. For some time after the rain the bowling came along easily enough, and of this state of things Murrell took full advantage, taking every chance of scoring. More than once at the beginning of his innings the ball did not go where he intended, but he soon improved, and hit away freely. MacGregor also scored with some freedom, and in half an hour over 50 runs were put on. Mordaunt, who had bowled unchanged at the pavilion end since the score stood at 64, gave way to Robson at 272, and the change quickly got rid of Murrell. The partnership for the eighth wicket placed Middlesex in quite a flattering position. MacGregor left at 283, and Mignon being soon bowled, the innings closed at five minutes past six for 286.

Everyone expected to see Somerset go in for ten minutes batting, but with the light bad and rain threatening, stumps were pulled up.

Tuesday

Though still cold and unseasonable, the weather was not nearly so bad at Lord's, yesterday, as it had been on Monday, and, thankful for small mercies, the people present – a fair number, but not nearly so many as one could have wished – quite enjoyed the cricket.

Going in yesterday, Somerset had to face a total of 286. They stayed at the wickets until just after half-past three and scored 236, thus finishing up fifty runs behind. Their innings was a curiously uneven one, the batting going all to pieces after quite a big score had seemed in prospect. The start was unfortunate, Palairet being out when only twelve runs had been obtained, but Braund and Johnson put on 119 for the second wicket. Early in this long partnership Middlesex committed blunders in the field for which they had to pay a high price. Johnson might have been caught in the slips when he had made 13 and again – a more difficult catch – when 21, and Braund gave a sharp chance, also in the slips, with his score at 28. After these escapes both batsmen showed capital cricket, Johnson playing in a very free, attractive style, and Braund combining hard hitting with his always watchful defence. While the score was rising at a rapid rate MacGregor was somewhat capricious in the management of the bowling, only keeping Trott on for five overs and not trying Tarrant at all till the total had reached 113. When at last he was given a chance Tarrant soon separated the batsmen, fairly beating Johnson at 131. In the meantime Bosanquet had bowled in two styles, first medium pace and then his usual slows. Johnson was batting for about an hour and a half for 57, his hits including half-a-dozen 4's. Braund did not stay much longer, being caught at the wicket at 137. Poynts was leg before wicket at 154, but Lewis and Woods hit away vigorously and at lunch time Somerset stood in a flattering position, the score being 194 with only four men out.

After the interval the game underwent a sudden change, as without the addition of a run Lewis was brilliantly caught at slip, at the second attempt, and Woods taken at long-off. Robson and Lee made some fine hits, Robson punishing Mignon for three 4's in one over, but after Hearne had gone on and bowled Lee the innings was quickly concluded. In forty minutes after lunch the last six wickets went down for 42 runs, Tarrant bowling six overs, two maidens, for 15 runs, and four wickets. Bailey, the last man, was out to a beautiful catch by Littlejohn at mid-off.

The advantage with which Middlesex opened their second innings was soon discounted, as with the score at 20 Warner and Beldam were out to successive balls from Lewis. Bosanquet improved matters a little, but, as on Monday, he lost his wicket just when he had begun to look dangerous, Bailey going on and bowling him at 54. Not long after this Lewis left the field, and Somerset for the rest of the afternoon felt the need of his bowling. Tarrant and Littlejohn put quite a good appearance on the game for their side, carrying the score to 110, at which point Tarrant fell to a catch at slip. He was in his most cautious mood yesterday, taking fully an hour and a quarter to get 28 runs, but his defence kept the batting together at a critical time. In strong contrast to his play was the freedom of Littlejohn, who in an hour hit up 52 out of 93, showing the brightest cricket in the innings. Milton, whose introduction to the Middlesex eleven has so far been marked by nothing but disaster, failed once more, but Trott and MacGregor hit well, and gave the bowlers a lot of trouble. At one point there seemed little likelihood of the Middlesex innings ending before the call of time, but the last three wickets went down very quickly.

Wednesday

Those who were at Lord's yesterday – they formed a crowd of very modest dimensions – saw some startling cricket, Albert Trott finishing off his benefit match with a truly astonishing piece of bowling, and gaining for Middlesex a victory by 166 runs. Doing the 'hat trick' twice in one innings, he accomplished a feat which, to the best of our knowledge, is without precedent in first-class cricket. In matters of this kind, it is well to speak with reserve, bowling records not having always been preserved in such detail as could be wished. To begin with, Trott took four wickets with four successive balls, and he wound up by getting the last three wickets with three successive balls. His average – seven wickets for 20 runs – has, of course, often been beaten, but the double 'hat trick' in the same innings makes the performance, we believe,

Trott: a tragic end

unique. The pitch was rather the worse for wear, it being possible to get a good deal of break on the ball, and the batting at the close was feeble to a degree, but that Trott bowled very finely can scarcely be questioned. No doubt he has on many occasions bowled quite as well without meeting with anything like the same success, but that is just the luck of the game.

Needless to say, the few spectators gave Trott a very hearty reception as he walked back to the dressing-room. The ball used will, it is understood, be mounted and suitably inscribed. Owing to the unseasonable weather the match as a benefit fell very far short of expectation, but that could not be helped. Judging from what he did yesterday, and his excellent work in other matches at Lord's, it does not seem too much to expect that Trott will this season regain the position among bowlers that he held in his best years. Success at cricket is a great stimulus.

Wanting 264 runs, the Somerset eleven probably did not expect to win yesterday, but the opening of the innings was so encouraging as to give every promise of a good finish. Palairet and Braund went in and scored 56 together, Palairet losing his wicket just when he seemed set. Johnson, on whom much depended, never settled down, and was caught in the slips at 74. Then came the collapse, Lewis, Poynts, Woods, and Robson going down before Trott's bowling in four balls. Lewis was leg-before-wicket, and Woods played on, the other two being clean bowled. With seven men out for 77, the match was as good as over, and, in a very bad light, Trott's second hat trick brought about the end with startling suddenness. Mordaunt was out to a simple catch at mid-off, Wickham was bowled, and Bailey, lifting the ball tamely, was caught at mid-on. In this way the innings closed for 97. Braund saw all ten wickets fall, taking out his bat for 28. Apart from one chance, he played exceedingly well. Though quite overshadowed by Trott yesterday, Tarrant had a big share in winning the game for Middlesex, scoring 52 and 28, and taking in all nine wickets for 82 runs. Score:

MIDDLESEX

P. F. Warner, b Mordaunt 46	b Lewis 11
Tarrant, c Lee, b Lewis 52	c Palairet, b Mordaunt 28
G. W. Beldam, l b w, b Mordaunt .. 12	l b w, b Lewis 0
B. J. T. Bosanquet, c Johnson, b Mordaunt 32	b Bailey 29
F. S. Littlejohn, c Braund, b Lewis 44	b Mordaunt 52
Trott (A. E.), b Lewis 1	c Wickham, b Robson 35
H. A. Milton, b Lewis 3	b Mordaunt 0
G. MacGregor, c Woods, b Bailey 39	c Poynts, b Robson 39
Murrell, b Robson 33	c and b Braund 9
Hearne (J. T.), not out 3	not out 4
Mignon, b Bailey 1	c Wickham, b Braund 0
B 15, l-b 4, n-b 1 20	B 3, l-b 2, n-b 1 6
Total 286	Total 213

SOMERSET

L. C. H. Palairet, c MacGregor, b Mignon 6	c Bosanquet, b Tarrant 35
Braund, c MacGregor, b Bosanquet 59	not out 28
P. R. Johnson, b Tarrant 57	c Trott, b Tarrant 14
Lewis, c Tarrant, b Mignon 31	l b w, b Trott 1
E. S. M. Poynts, l b w, b Tarrant 9	b Trott 0
S. M. J. Woods, c Bosanquet, b Tarrant 17	b Trott 0
Robson, not out 20	c Trott, b Trott 7
F. M. Lee, b Hearne 18	c Mignon, b Trott 4
O. C. Mordaunt, c Beldam, b Tarrant 1	b Trott 0
Rev. A. P. Wickham, c Trott, b Tarrant 0	c Mignon, b Trott 0
Bailey, c Littlejohn, b Tarrant 3	
L-b 14, w 1 15	B 4, l-b 4 8
Total 236	Total 97

MIDDLESEX – First Innings

	O	M	R	W		O	M	R	W
Lewis	32	14	88	4	Mordaunt	30	6	97	3
Bailey	16	5	33	2	Robson	7	1	15	1
Braund	13	1	33	0					

Lewis bowled one no-ball.

Second Innings

	O	M	R	W		O	M	R	W
Lewis	7	2	17	2	Mordaunt	15	1	47	3
Bailey	16	3	58	1	Robson	6	2	30	3
Braund	13.4	1	55	2					

Lewis bowled one no-ball.

SOMERSET – First Innings

	O	M	R	W		O	M	R	W
Beldam	4	1	15	0	Hearne	8	1	22	1
Mignon	24	6	88	2	Bosanquet	8	0	39	1
Trott	5	1	10	0	Tarrant	15	4	47	6

Beldam bowled one wide.

Second Innings

	O	M	R	W		O	M	R	W
Beldam	3	1	10	0	Mignon	5	1	24	0
Tarrant	14	4	35	3	Trott	8	2	20	7

Umpires – Marlow and S. Brown.

25: *Northamptonshire v Kent*
NORTHAMPTON, 30 MAY–1 JUNE 1907

Northamptonshire had only joined the County Championship in 1905, the sixteenth and penultimate team to do so (Glamorgan, the last, joined in 1921). They had come 13th and 11th in their first two seasons, but would plunge to 15th in 1907. This thrashing by Kent would not be their worst humiliation of the season – that is recorded in the next section. It did, though, provide Colin Blythe with the finest match figures (17–48) then obtained in a first-class match, just bettering the 17–50 taken by Turner for the Australian tourists against England XI in 1888. Just W.G. Grace had ever taken 17 wickets in a championship match before, and that in 1877. Only Laker's 19–90 at Manchester in 1956 has exceeded Blythe's achievement, which remains the best in county cricket. Blythe took all his in a day, and on a 'sticky' wicket, demonstrating how lethal he was in a rain-affected match.

Blythe (1879–1917) was perhaps the finest slow left-arm bowler of the 'golden age'. In 16 seasons for Kent he took 2,503 wickets at under 17 each. Given the lengthy careers of slow bowlers in those days, he might have taken more wickets even than Wilfred Rhodes' 4,187, had he not been killed in action at Passchendaele in 1917. He topped the bowling averages in his last three seasons, 1912–14, taking his 178 wickets at only 12.26 each in 1912. His 10–30 in the first innings of this match was the best performance of his career, though he took nine wickets in an innings on five other occasions, 16 in a match once and 15 three times. He played 19 times for England in the first decade of the century, his appearances being limited at the height of his career because of increasing incidence of epilepsy.

Northampton, Thursday

Cricket at Northampton was seriously interfered with by rain yesterday, the match being in progress for only about three hours. In that time, however, Kent made excellent use of their opportunities, and when play was abandoned for the day shortly after half-past four they were in a strong position, having scored 212 runs for the loss of only four wickets. In an hour and a quarter's batting before the interval they obtained 90 runs for the loss of Woolley, who was bowled at 64. Hardinge, who opened the innings with him, stayed till 136 had been scored, the second partnership thus yielding 71 runs. Hardinge was fortunate in being twice missed at mid-off when 12 and 43 respectively, but otherwise no fault could be found with his batting during the two hours he was at the wickets. After the departure came some dashing cricket by Hutchings, who was not out 49 at the close. Except that Dillon is included in place of Munds, Kent are represented by the team that gained such a brilliant victory over Derbyshire at Chesterfield.

Friday

No play took place at Northampton yesterday, the rain, which caused an early abandonment on Thursday, continuing throughout the night and lasting until nearly two o'clock yesterday afternoon. The prospects then looked to be brighter, but soon after three a heavy thunderstorm put all hope of cricket out of the question.

Saturday

Thanks to some remarkable bowling by Blythe Kent forced a victory in brilliant style at Northampton on Saturday, beating Northamptonshire by an innings and 155 runs. Blythe took all ten wickets in the Northamptonshire first innings, and came out with a record for the match of seventeen wickets for 48 runs. The game ended at half-past four, but Kent only just

Colin Blythe

won in time, for no sooner had the players left the field than rain fell heavily. When play was resumed in the morning there did not seem much chance of a definite result. Having scored only 212 runs Kent could not well declare, and after the rain of Thursday and Friday the pitch was expected to be soft and dead. However, the remaining Kent batsmen hit out fearlessly, and the six outstanding wickets added 42 runs.

Then, on going in, Northamptonshire gave a deplorable display. So helpless were the batsmen against the bowling of Blythe that the first seven wickets fell for 4 runs – two of them extras. The eighth should have gone down at the same total, but Vials was missed by Blythe. Profiting by this escape, Vials hit pluckily, and the innings was carried over the luncheon interval, the score in the end reaching 60. Blythe took the leg wickets at a cost of only 3 runs apiece. Following on 194 behind. Northamptonshire fared even worse than before, the whole side being dismissed in an hour and a quarter for the miserable total of 39. There was no excuse for the feeble resistance offered in the first innings, but when the team went in a second time the wicket was appreciably faster, and the ball came off the ground at a great pace. Score:

KENT

Woolley, b Driffield	26	Huish, not out	19
Hardings, c Cox, East	73	Fairservice, b East	9
Seymour, b Wells	37	Blythe, c Vials, b Driffield	6
K. L. Hutchings, b Driffield	52	Fielder, b East	1
A. P. Day, c Kingston, b East	23	B 2, l-b 1, n-b 1	4
E. W. Dillon, b East	4		
Humphreys, c Pool, b Driffield	0	Total	254

NORTHAMPTONSHIRE

Buswell, st Huish, b Blythe	0	c. Woolley, b Blythe	7
Cox, st Huish, b Blythe	0	st Huish, b Blythe	12
C. J. T. Pool, c Fielder, b Blythe	0	st Huish, b Blythe	5
W. H. Kingston, l b w, b Blythe	2	l b w, b Blythe	0
G. J. Thompson, b Blythe	0	c Hardings, b Blythe	1
East, c Huish, b Blythe	0	c Huish, b Fairservice	0
E. M. Crosse, c Fairservice, b Blythe	0	c Hardings, b Blythe	2
A. R. Thompson, c Seymour, b Blythe	10	c Humphreys, b Blythe	7
G. A. T. Vials, not out	33	b Fairservice	1
Wells, c Humphreys, b Blythe	0	b Humphreys	0
L. T. Driffield, b Blythe	12	not out	1
B 1, l-b 2	3	b	3
Total	60	Total	39

KENT – First Innings

	O	M	R	W		O	M	R	W
G. J. Thompson	15	1	76	0	Driffield	22	9	50	4
East	33.2	6	77	5	Cox	5	1	13	0
Wells	6	1	34	1					

Thompson bowled a no-ball.

NORTHAMPTONSHIRE – First Innings

	O	M	R	W		O	M	R	W
Blythe	16	7	30	10	Fielder	3	0	10	0
Fairservice	12	5	17	0					

Second Innings

	O	M	R	W		O	M	R	W
Blythe	15.1	7	18	7	Humphreys	6	3	3	1
Fairservice	9	3	15	2					

Umpires – Attewell and Dench.

26: *Gloucestershire v Northamptonshire*
GLOUCESTER, 10–12 JUNE 1907

Much of Northamptonshire's difficulty in 1907 could be attributed to the weather: that summer is still regarded as one of the wettest in history. Blythe's match (see game 25) was cut in half by rain. Only just over five hours' play was possible in this match, yet 37 wickets fell in that time; and had the last day not been completely obliterated by the weather Gloucestershire would, presumably, have bowled out the visitors well short of the 137 they needed to win: almost a dozen times what they had managed in their first innings. Their total of 12 remains the lowest recorded in a first-class match in the world; and now that wickets are covered it will be hard to beat, though Surrey came perilously close against Essex in 1983 (see game 93).

Playing for Gloucestershire in this bowler's match was Charlie Parker, whose career as a bowler was to be so successful that his tally of wickets would be exceeded only by Rhodes and Freeman; yet he was unsuccessful in this game.

His fellow slow left-arm bowler, George Dennett (1879–1937), with whom he operated in harness for over 20 years, took 15 wickets for 21 runs, and but for the weather would probably have beaten Blythe's record, as he was proving unplayable on this rain-affected uncovered wicket. To this day, no-one has ever taken 15 wickets in a match so cheaply. Dennett took 2,151 wickets in his career at just under 20 each. Although Northamptonshire were very much a low-grade side, they included at least one cricketer of distinction. George Thompson (1877–1943) was a fine all-rounder, and the first Northants man to play for England; in his career, which a war wound ended, he took 1,591 wickets at under 19 each.

Gloucester, Monday

Owing to a succession of heavy storms, cricket at Gloucester yesterday was restricted to fifty minutes. In that time Gloucestershire met with nothing but disaster, losing four batsmen for 20 runs. Thompson bowled exceedingly well on a wicket which rendered run-getting a by no means easy task, the ball coming along at varying paces.

Tuesday

It will be small consolation to the Northamptonshire eleven to know that in getting out for 12 runs at Gloucester, yesterday, they added something to cricket history. Their score is the lowest ever obtained in county matches, and ties with the smallest on record in first-class cricket of any kind – Oxford University's 12, at Oxford, in May, 1877. The bowlers in the innings thirty years ago were Rylott – still a member of the M.C.C.'s ground staff at Lord's – and the late Fred Morley. It was Morley who did the chief mischief, his record of seven wickets for 6 runs being no less remarkable than Dennett's yesterday. Oxford batted one man short, A. J. Webbe, who was captain of the eleven in 1877 and 1878, being absent. Oxford did not collapse in anything like the same way as Northamptonshire, their innings lasting nearly two hours. Morley bowled twenty-two overs and Rylott twenty-one overs and two balls. The rule then was four balls to the over, so that Morley delivered eighty-eight balls and Rylott eighty-six. Yesterday Dennett bowled only thirty-six balls, and Jessop thirty-three – a striking contrast.

On a pitch that gave the bowlers great assistance, some startling cricket was seen at Gloucester yesterday. Rain during the night was followed by bright sunshine, and in the first hour's cricket Gloucestershire, who had overnight scored 20 for the loss of four wickets, were dismissed for another 40 runs. The pitch was at the worst when Northamptonshire went in, and, bowling unchanged, Dennett and Jessop dismissed the whole side in forty minutes for 12 runs. This is the smallest total on record for a first-class inter-county match, the previous lowest being 13 by Notts against Yorkshire at Trent Bridge in 1901. Dennett, making the ball turn in an extraordinary way, was almost unplayable. Six runs were scored from him before he got a wicket, but for the remainder of the innings only 3 runs were obtained from his bowling.

While he dismissed eight batsmen, Jessop also bowled splendidly, keeping such a fine length that in sending down 33 balls he had only 3 runs scored off him.

Dennett's good work did not end in Northamptonshire's first innings, as, after Gloucestershire, on going in for the second time, had been got rid of for 88, he obtained seven more wickets, at a cost of 11 runs. He accomplished the 'hat trick' in dismissing Hawtin, Beasley, and Buswell with successive balls, and should have had four wickets in four balls, Wrathall dropping a catch offered by East. During the day Dennett took fifteen wickets for 20 runs, and no bowler could possibly have made better use of the assistance given by the state of the wicket. When play ceased for the day Northamptonshire, with three wickets to fall, required 97 runs to win.

Wednesday

The renewal of the wet weather at Gloucester yesterday was a great misfortune for Gloucestershire, for they apparently had victory well in hand at the drawing of stumps overnight. Then it will be remembered, Northants still required 97. However, they were saved from defeat by the heavy rain in the night, which left the wicket so completely saturated that a resumption at the usual time was out of the question. Afterwards there was a further downpour, and the match was consequently abandoned. Dennett's bowling was, of course, the feature of what cricket was possible. Score:

GLOUCESTERSHIRE

Wrathall, b Thompson	4	b Thompson ... 7
E. Barnett, l b w, b Thompson	3	b East ... 0
Board, b Thompson	3	l b w, b Thompson ... 5
M.. G. Salter, c Buswell, b East	3	c and b East ... 3
G. I. Jessop, b East	22	c Hawtin, b East ... 24
R. T. H. Mackenzie, b East	0	c King, b East ... 21
Langdon, b East	4	l b w, b Thompson ... 4
Huggins, c Crosse, b East	8	c Buswell, b East ... 3
Spry, l b w, b Thompson	6	b East ... 4
Parker, not out	2	not out ... 8
Dennett, c Pool, b Thompson	0	b East ... 0
B 2, l b 3	5	B ... 9
Total	60	Total ... 88

NORTHAMPTONSHIRE

E. M. Crosse, c Board, b Dennett	4	c and b Dennett ... 0
Cox, l b w, b Dennett	2	c Barnett, b Dennett ... 12
C. J. T. Pool, c Spry, b Dennett	4	st Board, b Dennett ... 9
Buswell, st Board, b Dennett	1	c Langdon, b Dennett ... 0
L. T. Driffield, b Dennett	0	not out ... 5
G. J. Thompson, b Dennett	0	l b w, b Dennett ... 8
R. W. R. Hawtin, l b w, b Dennett	0	l b w, b Dennett ... 2
East, st Board, b Dennett	0	b Dennett ... 0
R. N. Beasley, b Jessop	1	not out ... 1
S. King, not out	0	
Wells, c Parker, b Jessop	0	B 2, l-b 1 ... 3
Total	12	Total (7 wkts.) ... 40

GLOUCESTERSHIRE – First Innings

	O	M	R	W		O	M	R	W
Thompson	16.5	7	29	5	East	16	5	26	5

Second Innings

	O	M	R	W		O	M	R	W
Thompson	15	2	43	3	East	14.2	4	36	7

NORTHAMPTONSHIRE – First Innings

	O	M	R	W		O	M	R	W
Dennett	6	1	9	8	Jessop	5.3	4	3	2

Second Innings

	O	M	R	W		O	M	R	W
Dennett	15	8	12	7	Parker	5	2	5	0
Jessop	10	3	20	0					

Umpires – A. Millward and J. E. West.

Northamptonshire side of 1907

27: Worcestershire v Kent
STOURBRIDGE, 5–7 JULY 1909

The years immediately before the Great War brought consistent triumph to Kent. They won four Championships between 1906 and 1913, one of them in this season. Their innings defeat of Worcestershire came thanks to Woolley, then in only his fourth season and with his days as England's most celebrated all-rounder still ahead of him, and to Fielder, a fast bowler. Their partnership of 235 for the last wicket secured Kent not just a first innings lead, but one that enabled them to win by an innings (thanks also to Blythe) with a quarter of an hour to spare. The partnership was then the highest in the world for the last wicket, and has only been passed twice since; it remains the highest in the Championship.

Frank Woolley (1887–1978) scored more runs than any batsman in the game's history except Hobbs: 58,969 at an average of 41, including 145 centuries. He also took 2,066 wickets at under 20, figures that leave him with few, if any, rivals as an all-rounder; and if that was not enough, he took more catches (1,018) than any other cricketer. He scored 1,000 runs in the season 28 times, a feat equalled only by Grace, did the 'double' in eight seasons, four times taking more than 200 wickets – the only player to have done this so often. He also played 64 tests between 1909 and 1934. Arthur Fielder (1877–1949) was Kent's principal fast bowler until the Great War. His 186 wickets in 1906 had been central to Kent's first Championship title, and it was in that year that he took all ten wickets for the Players against the Gentlemen at Lord's. His century in this game was the only one of his career.

Stourbridge, Monday

Worcestershire – the first team this season to lower the colours of Yorkshire, Kent, and Middlesex – entered yesterday, at Stourbridge, upon their return engagement with Kent, and, occupying the wickets for the whole of the day, put together a total of 360. Pearsons, ninth out at 345, in making 161, put together his highest score for Worcestershire. His innings, which extended over three hours and three-quarters, was a magnificent display, practically faultless, and including twenty-three 4's, four 3's and eight 2's. His forcing strokes were particularly good.

Tuesday

Kent had to face a total of 360, at Stourbridge, yesterday, but they played up so finely that at the end of the afternoon they were 79 runs ahead with a wicket to fall. The performance was the more remarkable as the innings opened in a disastrous way. Burns, who is often dangerous for a few overs, clean bowled Dillon with his fourth ball, and bowled Seymour after that batsman had made one hit to the boundary.

Thenceforward, however, everything went well for Kent. Hutchings scored 61 in an hour. In addition to three 6's, he hit seven 4's. Humphreys stayed in for two hours. Hardinge hit up 30 in forty minutes. Troughton batted fairly well for an hour and three-quarters, and Huish was also seen to advantage. The

A. Fielder bowling

A. FIELDER (KENT)

Mockford
Tonbridge

most successful batting, however, came in the close. Woolley was joined by Fielder, the last man and the two batsmen, without being separated, put on 119 runs. Woolley has so far scored 136 in three hours and a quarter. When he had made 19 he had to retire for a time, owing to a severe blow in the face.

Wednesday

Batting for Kent against Worcestershire, at Stourbridge yesterday, Woolley and Fielder put on no fewer than 235 runs for the last wicket, and in so doing beat the record established at Lord's ten years ago, when R. W. Nicholls and W. Roche, for Middlesex against Kent, obtained 230 runs for the last wicket. The two batsmen came together on Tuesday afternoon, when Kent, going in against a total of 360, had nine wickets down, for 328, and during the last hour they increased the total to 422 before the drawing of stumps, so that when they proceeded with the Kent innings yesterday their partnership had already produced 119 runs, Woolley being 136 and Fielder 67.

At once both Woolley and Fielder settled down again to a brilliant, punishing game, and in an hour and twenty minutes, before the dismissal of Woolley brought the innings to an end, added another 115 runs, their full partnership yielding 235 runs in two hours and twenty minutes. Despite the tremendous pace at which they scored, the two Kent batsmen played cricket of the highest order. Fielder had never before approached anything like a hundred in a county match, his biggest previous innings for Kent being 39. He gave nothing like a chance in his 112 not out, and hit fourteen 4's, two 3's and nine 2's.

Woolley in putting together 235, also succeeded in making the highest score of his career, his previous best being 153 against Northamptonshire at Gravesend. He was at the wickets for four hours and three-quarters, and his hits included a 6, twenty-four 4's, a 3,

and eleven 2's. Altogether, the Kent innings which reached the formidable total of 555, extended over six hours and fifty-five minutes.

Irrespective of the record stand for the last wicket, the match was a memorable one, inasmuch as Kent, having to face a score of 360, proved victorious in a single innings. Worcestershire, on going in for the second time, were 195 runs in arrear, and speedily found themselves in a desperate plight. Just at six o'clock the last wicket went down for 162, and with only a quarter of an hour to spare Kent scored a famous triumph by an innings and 23 runs. Score:

WORCESTERSHIRE

H. G. Bache, b Fielder	22	b Blythe	10
Bowley, l b w, b Fielder	37	c Huish, b Blythe	1
Pearson, c Huish, b Fairservice	161	b Blythe	43
H. K. Foster, run out	4	c Seymour, b Blythe	8
Arnold, c Seymour, b Fairservice	1	b Blythe	12
Cuffe, b Blythe	57	b Fielder	1
M. K. Foster, C Huish, b Fielder	15	c Huish, b Fielder	30
W. B. Burns, c Seymour,		c Dillon, b Blythe	3
b Woolley	14	c Hutchings, b Blythe	19
Turner, c Seymour, b Woolley	6	c Huish, b Fielder	5
W. Taylor, not out	13	not out	8
Gankrodger, b Fairservice	10		
B 5, l-b 9, n-b 6	20	B 10, l-b 1, w 1, n-b 10	22
Total	360	Total	162

KENT

R. W. Dillon, b Burns	0	Fairservice, b Cuffe	1
Humphreys, c Burns, b Cuffe	37	L. H. W. Croughton, b Taylor	46
Seymour, b Burns	4	Huish, b Taylor	23
K. L. Hutchings, c Taylor, b Cuffe	61	Fielder, not out	112
Woolley, c H. K. Foster,		B 34, l-b 14, w 8	56
b Arnold	185		
Harding, l b w, b Arnold	30	Total	555

WORCESTERSHIRE – First Innings

	O	M	R	W		O	M	R	W
Fielder	26	4	95	3	Fairservice	29.3	6	103	3
Blythe	20	3	67	1	Woolley	23	5	75	2

Second Innings

	O	M	R	W		O	M	R	W
Fielder	25	7	67	3	Fairservice	6	1	19	0
Blythe	24.5	10	44	7	Woolley	6	3	10	0

KENT – First Innings

	O	M	R	W		O	M	R	W
Burns	20	1	87	2	Arnold	21	5	61	2
Cuffe	50	10	157	3	Taylor	20	0	93	3
Pearson	14	0	82	0	Turner	3	0	19	0

Taylor bowled four wides and Arnold bowled four wides.
Umpires – J. West and Mason.

28: Derbyshire v Warwickshire
BLACKWELL, 19–21 JUNE 1910

The 'golden age' of cricket was nothing of the sort for Derbyshire. Between 1899 and 1914 they never managed better than tenth in the Championship, and four times were bottom: they would only just avoid that fate this year. Warwickshire were also enjoying a poor run, having been 12th in each of the previous two seasons. They would decline to 14th this year, though would shock the sporting world by winning the title the following year. However,

these two mediocre sides produced a remarkable game at the Blackwell colliery ground, when Derbyshire were saved from seemingly inevitable defeat by a ninth wicket stand of 283 between Warren and John Chapman, the Derbyshire captain. Their stand, made in just three hours despite the pressure of possible defeat, remains a world record for this wicket.

Warwickshire's initial supremacy was thanks to Crowther Charlesworth (1875–1953), a

went in, there was a reasonable amount of time at their disposal. The opening of their innings gave promise of their ultimate victory, but such are the vagaries of cricket that before the end was reached Sussex were in danger of being beaten, Notts nearly pulling the match out of the fire. Robert Relf and Vine gave their side a brilliant start, the former being in quite a happy mood. In seventy-five minutes the pair put up 112 runs, Relf contributing 71 by delightful cricket and hitting nine 4's.

Then came a sudden and decisive change in the swing of the pendulum. The score had only been advanced to 139 when Heygate, Vine and Albert Relf were dismissed. Vine was batting for an hour and three quarters, and after Robert Relf left was very quiet, taking a long time to make his last nine runs. Further misfortunes overtook the side, Cox and Tudor failing, and Sussex, with six men out for 148, were not only behind the clock, but with the worst of the match. When Leach joined Killick 89 runs were wanted, with seventy-five minutes, and against the steady bowling of John Gunn and Riley, who were splendidly backed up by the field, the batsmen found run-getting a matter of difficulty.

So slowly did Killick and Leach score, that it became evident that their best game was to endeavour to play out time, and they were partners for an hour, putting on 50 runs. Leach left first, and quickly was followed by Killick. Ten minutes were left when the eighth wicket fell, but, as it happened, Smith and Vincett stayed together until half-past six. At the close Sussex, with only two wickets, were 24 runs short of the number required to win. So as the upshot of a magnificent game, in which the fortunes varied in a startling way, Sussex by their lead on the first innings gain three points and Notts one. Score:

Notts

A. O. Jones, b Cox	57	b Leach 0
Iremonger, c and b A. E. Relf	0	c Tudor, b Killick 83
G. Gunn, st Butt, b Cox	90	st Butt, b R. Relf 66
Hardstaff, b Cox	8	c Butt, b A. E. Relf 7
J. Gunn, c R. Relf, b Killick	33	b R. Relf 19
Payton, c Heygate, b Killick	20	l b w, b A. E. Relf 0
Whysall, b Killick	1	c Butt, b A. E. Relf 3
Lee, c and b Killick	10	c Cox, b Leach 26
Alletson, c Killick, b A. E. Relf	7	c Smith, b Cox 189
Oates, not out	3	b Leach 1
Riley, c Smith, b Killick	3	not out 10
B 5, n-b 1	6	B 3, l-b 2, w 2, n-b 1 8
Total	238	Total 412

Sussex

R. Relf, b Jones	42	c Oates, b Jones 71
Vine, b Jones	77	c Payton, b Riley 54
R. B. Heygate, c Lee, b Iremonger	32	b J. Gunn 13
Cox, c Alletson, b Riley	37	st Oates, b Riley 5
A. E. Relf, c and b Jones	4	c Oates, b Riley 0
C. I. Tudor, c Oates, b Riley	23	b J. Gunn 4
Killick, c Hardstaff, b Lee	81	c Lee, b Riley 21
Leach, b Lee	52	b J. Gunn 31
C. L. A. Smith, not out	33	not out 12
Vincett, c Iremonger, b Lee	9	not out 1
Butt, b Riley	13	
B 4, l-b 3, w 1, n-b 3	11	N-b 1
Total	414	Total (8 wkts.) 213

Notts – First Innings

	O	M	R	W		O	M	R	W
A. E. Relf	19	5	40	2	R. Relf	11	0	36	0
Leach	11	2	53	0	Cox	25	4	58	3
Vincett	4	0	31	0	Killick	10.2	4	14	5

Cox bowled one no-ball.

Second Innings

	O	M	R	W		O	M	R	W
Leach	19	2	91	3	Cox	9.4	2	27	1
A. E. Relf	33	13	92	3	R. Relf	19	6	39	2
Killick	20	2	130	1	Vincett	3	1	25	0

Vincett bowled two wides, and Leach one no-ball.

Sussex – First Innings

	O	M	R	W		O	M	R	W
Iremonger	34	7	97	1	Jones	22	2	69	3
Riley	29.4	5	102	3	Alletson	1	0	3	0
J. Gunn	29	2	87	0	Lee	14	1	45	3

Jones bowled one wide and J. Gunn bowled three no-balls.

Second Innings

	O	M	R	W		O	M	R	W
Iremonger	14	2	34	0	Jones	5	1	24	1
Riley	33	9	82	4	J. Gunn	25	9	41	3
Lee	4	0	31	0					

J. Gunn bowled one no-ball.
Umpires – Wood and White.

30: *Yorkshire v Leicestershire*
BRADFORD, 12–14 JUNE 1911

Only W.G. Grace has matched C.J.B. Wood's feat of carrying his bat through 17 completed innings in first-class cricket. No-one, though, had ever carried his bat in both innings of the same match and scored a century in each, with the strain of being on the field for the duration of the match. For Wood to have done so against the mighty Yorkshire attack that included Rhodes and Hirst added lustre to this already magnificent achievement. Wood's defensive effort could not save his side from defeat, but that was a common story in a season when Leicestershire finished one from the bottom of the Championship.

Wood (1875–1960), who was later to captain his county, played for Leicestershire from 1896 to 1923, for his first season only as a professional, and then as an amateur. He was by far his county's most successful batsman of the age, making more than 1,000 runs in a season 12 times and 2,000 once, in 1901. He made 23,879 runs in his career at an average of 31. He was also a gifted soccer player, and briefly during his retirement was the Leicestershire secretary. Yorkshire owed much to Wilfred Rhodes (1877–1973), who had begun his career as a bowler, but within a few years had risen up the order for both his county and his country to open the innings, and his all round talent led him to do the 'double' 16 times, a record that will probably never be beaten, like his feat of taking 100 wickets in a season 23 times. He took 4,187 wickets at just under 17 each, making him the leading wicket-taker of all time; and scored 39,802 runs at an average of almost 31, with a top score of 267 not out. He played 58 times for England, scoring 2,325 runs and taking 127 wickets in tests.

Bradford, Monday

Gaining first innings at Bradford yesterday, Leicestershire, after a poor start, succeeded in putting together a total of 302. In achieving this result they were greatly indebted to Cecil Wood, who played a remarkably patient innings. He went in first and took out his bat, being in for four and a half hours. It may be remarked that he accomplished a similar feat against Northamptonshire last week. Though he only scored 107, his innings was simply invaluable to the side.

Though the wicket was in good order, Leicestershire at the outset looked like making a poor score, two wickets falling for 29. However, by lunch time Wood and Lord had carried the score to 110, their partnership for the third wicket altogether producing 97 in just over an hour and a half. Four men were out for 133, but from that point Wood found several good partners. Coe, though he strained his leg and had a man to run for him, scored 49 out of 71 in an hour. Mounteney played a useful innings, and Shipman, by brilliant hitting, made 38 out of 43, obtaining eight 4's.

Booth was punished for 19 in one over – four 4's and a 3. Shield also brought off some excellent hits, and after the slow play at the opening of the innings, the game was quite interesting. During his long stay Wood gave no chances. He maintained a strong defence from first to last, always playing with a perfectly straight bat. During the last half an hour he was in he only scored 7 runs. His chief hits were eight 4's, two 3's, and twelve 2's.

Yorkshire had forty minutes' batting at the close of the day, and Rhodes and Wilson scored 29 without loss. With R. J. Radcliffe unable to get away, Yorkshire have a purely professional eleven, and Hirst is captain.

Tuesday

In the match at Bradford yesterday the Yorkshire eleven gave a splendid all-round display, and at one point it was quite on the cards they might win before the drawing of stumps. Going in against a deficit of 25, Leicestershire collapsed before some fine bowling by Hirst. Then Wood, who, as in the first innings, had set up a strong defence, found a brilliant partner in Mounteney, and at the close Leicestershire, with four wickets in hand, were 169 runs on.

Overnight Yorkshire had scored 29 in their first innings without loss, and though Wilson was out with 9 added, they steadily gained the upper hand. Rhodes played an extremely valuable innings, exhibiting great steadiness. Fourth out at 179, he was at the wickets for two and a half hours, making runs freely after completing his 50. When 75 he received a life at the hands of Whitehead at slip, but he made no other mistake. He hit six 4's. Excellent as was the batting of Rhodes, the best innings was that of Booth. By splendid cricket he scored 71 out of 100 in an hour and a quarter. Hitting cleanly in all directions, he obtained seven 4's. Haigh hit with capital vigour for half an hour, and was unlucky in being thrown out by Knight. Altogether Yorkshire were batting for four hours and three-quarters.

Some rain had fallen in the early morning, but the pitch did not seen to be affected. Leicestershire made a most deplorable start in their second innings, losing half of their batsmen in an hour for 46. Up to that point Hirst had taken four wickets for 27. Then Mounteney joined Wood and began hitting with fine vigour, reaching his 50 out of 80 in forty minutes. Wood, who always seemed comfortable with the bowling, completed his 50 out of 118 in two hours.

At length Mounteney was out in attempting a big hit to reach three figures. His hitting was splendid, and in an hour and twenty minutes he scored 96 out of the 147 added for the sixth wicket. He did not give a chance, and hit two 6's and twelve 4's. Wood has so far batted for nearly two hours, and looks like again carrying his bat through the innings.

Wednesday

C. J. B. Wood, the Leicestershire cricketer, accomplished a wonderful batting performance in the match which ended at Bradford yesterday in a victory for Yorkshire over Leicestershire by five wickets. In the first innings of Leicestershire he had carried his bat right through for 107, and yesterday, when the second innings of the visitors came to a conclusion, he was again not out with 117 runs to his credit. Thus, he not only scored two separate hundreds in the same match – no mean achievement in itself – but on each occasion carried his bat right through the innings.

In being not out each time, Wood established a record in first-class cricket, for although D. R. A. Gebra, the Australian who formed one of the team which visited this country six years ago, scored 148 not out and 100 not out at Freemantle in the following season for South Australia against Western Australia, a game against Western Australia could not be fairly regarded as a first-class fixture. Wood, batting with wonderful patience, was altogether at the wickets for eight hours and forty minutes, and, of course, in the field during the whole of the seventeen hours the match was in progress. This tremendous strain, of being in the field for the whole of a match was, it may be recalled, undergone by W. G. Grace when in his 47th year. The contest between Kent and Gloucestershire took place at Gravesend, and W. G. not only scored 267 in the first innings, when he was last man out, but when Gloucestershire went in with 104 to win, scored 73 not out.

Wood's unprecedented feat notwithstanding, Yorkshire won easily enough, but considering that Leicestershire, with half their men out, were only 21 runs to the good, the Midland county made a splendid fight. Thanks to Wood and Mounteney, Leicestershire entered upon the concluding stage of the contest 169 runs ahead with four wickets to hand. Unhappily, Coe, having strained his leg badly, could not bat, nevertheless, the visitors kept Yorkshire in the field for an hour and three quarters, and the three wickets produced 102 runs. Wood's defence was as perfect as ever. At the wickets for four hours and ten minutes, he gave no semblance of a chance, and he hit twelve 4's, two 3's, and nine 2's.

Yorkshire were set 272 to get in just under three hours and a half, and went for the runs in such determined fashion that they accomplished their task with three-quarters of an hour to spare. Wilson was bowled at 20, but then Denton hit away so brilliantly that the success of the home side was always probable. Rhodes scored 38 out of 81 in rather less than an hour,

Wilfred Rhodes – one of the great all-rounders

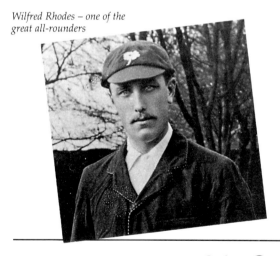

and Drake assisted Denton to put on 57 in twenty-five minutes. Denton made his first 50 in fifty-five minutes, completed his 100 in an hour and three-quarters, and altogether scored 137 not out in two hours and twenty-five minutes. He gave no actual chance, and hit three 6's – on one occasion sending the ball over the football stand – one 5, and sixteen 4's. Certainly he gave a delightful display, but it must be stated that both the bowling and fielding of Leicestershire were only of moderate quality. Score:

LEICESTERSHIRE

C. J. B. Wood, not out	107	not out	117
Knight, c Dolphin, b Hirst	12	b Hirst	14
Whitehead, c Dolphin, b Hirst	5	c Booth, b Hirst	2
Lord, c Hirst, b Booth	43	b Hirst	4
King, b Hirst	2	b Drake	1
Coe, c Hirst, b Rhodes	49	absent hurt	0
F. M. Joyce, b Haigh	0	b Hirst	5
Mounteney, c Booth, b Hirst	21	c Denton, b Rhodes	96
Shipman, c Wilson, b Rhodes	38	c Turner, b Haigh	29
J. Shields, c Dolphin, b Rhodes	20	c Hirst, b Hayes	6
Brown, not out	4	b Hirst	8
B 7, l-b 1	8	L-b 13, n-b 1	14
Total	309	Total	296

YORKSHIRE

Rhodes, c Whitehead, b Joyce	92	c Wood, b King	38
Wilson, b Shipham	21	b Joyce	16
Denton, c sub., b Brown	27	not out	137
Drake, c Whitehead, b Joyce	19	c sub., b Shipman	25
Hirst, c sub., b Joyce	20	b Shipman	10
Booth, c King, b Joyce	71	c Shields, b Joyce	18
Turner, c Mounteney, b Brown	12	not out	16
Oldroyd, c sub., b Whitehead	17		
Haigh, run out	39		
Dolphin, b Shipman	1		
Bayes, not out	5		
B 4, l-b 6	10	B 9, l-b 1, w 1, n-b 1	12
Total	334	Total (5 wkts.)	272

LEICESTERSHIRE – First Innings

	O	M	R	W		O	M	R	W
Hirst	29	7	77	4	Haigh	9	2	22	1
Booth	24	6	65	1	Rhodes	16.3	3	47	3
Bayes	11	2	50	0	Drake	10	1	40	0

Second Innings

	O	M	R	W		O	M	R	W
Hirst	29.2	8	68	5	Rhodes	12	2	58	1
Booth	13	1	50	0	Bayes	7	0	29	1
Drake	16	5	37	1	Haigh	15	3	40	1

Booth bowled one no-ball.

YORKSHIRE – First Innings

	O	M	R	W		O	M	R	W
Shipman	22	3	63	2	Joyce	20	1	70	4
King	15	1	50	0	Lord	1	0	1	0
Brown	16	1	64	2	Wood	13	1	39	0
Whitehead	10.4	0	37	1					

Second Innings

	O	M	R	W		O	M	R	W
Shipman	16	0	93	2	Brown	4.2	0	26	0
Joyce	13	2	48	2	Whitehead	5	0	29	0
King	6	0	41	1	Lord	2	1	1	0
Wood	3	0	22	0					

Shipman bowled one no-ball and Joyce one wide.
Umpires – Bagshaw and Flowers.

31: Surrey v Kent
THE OVAL, 21–23 AUGUST 1911

Surrey and Kent were two of the finest teams in England before the Great War, and this was a sensible choice for Herbert

Strudwick, the Surrey wicket-keeper, for his benefit match. Strudwick had to endure a double irony. After one of the hottest summers in history, the weather chose the days of his benefit match to provide the first rain in weeks, although the crowds eventually packed in to the Oval and made it a financial success. And although Surrey eventually won a thrilling victory, it was the performance of the other wicket-keeper, Huish, that dominated the match.

Never before, or since, had a wicket-keeper stumped nine men in a match, though Pooley, the Surrey wicketkeeper whose world record of 12 dismissals in a match has been equalled twice but never beaten, had stumped eight Kent batsmen in 1878. Huish (1869–1957) kept wicket for Kent from 1895 to 1914, beginning a tradition of long-serving keepers for that county that was to followed by Ames, Evans and Knott. He made 1,310 dismissals in his career. The beneficiary, Strudwick (1880–1970), was in his day the most prolific wicketkeeper of all time, with 1,497 dismissals (1,242 caught, 255 stumped), a record that was not passed for half a century. Strudwick played 28 times for England. W.C. 'Razor' Smith (1877–1946), who destroyed Kent (but was put in the shade by Woolley) was a regular off-spinner with Surrey from 1900 until the War, taking 1,077 wickets at under 18 each. In the previous season he had taken 247 at just 13 each.

The Oval, Monday

Strudwick, for whose benefit the Surrey and Kent match at the Oval is being played, was unlucky in the weather yesterday; for, after weeks of uninterrupted sunshine, the rain came at last, and it was a quarter-past four before a start could be made. The home captain won the toss, but to bat first in the circumstances was a doubtful advantage. However, more rain was a distinct probability when Bird had to make up his mind, and he certainly chose the lesser of two evils. The play that followed was interesting and somewhat surprising too. The wicket was certainly very slow; but the sun did not come out, and it gave the spectator the impression of not being specially difficult. One imagined, at any rate, that it would be too slow to suit Carr's bowling. We were soon undeceived, for the famous googly bowler beat the Surrey batsmen one after another.

Hayward was the first to go, superbly caught in the long field by Prest, who had to race hard to reach the ball. Then Hayes was taken at cover-point from a mishit. Ducat and Hobbs were both stumped, and, with Bush making Carr's fifth victim, half the side were

out for 67 runs. Bird was the next to be beaten. He had made a magnificent hit for 8 at Blythe's expense, but in trying to repeat it he failed. Campbell put his legs in front of the wicket when a straight ball was bowled, and Kirk was added to the list of those who found the Carr-Huish combination too much for them.

Eight wickets had fallen for 84 runs when Strudwick and Hitch became associated. They did a little useful hitting for a time, though it was noticed that Hitch was rather tempting fate by playing Carr's bowling with his legs. With the total 111 he paid the penalty for doing so. Smith came in to bat, but before another ball could be bowled the game was stopped on account of the dark. The rain screens were at once brought out and placed in position in expectation of the threatened storm. There had been thunder and lightning for some few minutes when that happened. There was no further cricket.

The feature of the short day's play was, of course, the extremely effective bowling of Carr. He did not at once find his length, and, indeed, when Hayward and Hobbs began the Surrey innings there was not much to suggest his subsequent success. But the longer he bowled the better he bowled. Two special methods of dealing with him were eminently unsuccessful – namely, dashing in to hit and staying at home with the leg in front of the wicket. Carr puzzled practically all his opponents, and he was, if anything, a little unlucky not to do better still. A catch was missed from his bowling, and two or three times he delivered balls which beat the bat and missed the wicket. At the other end Blythe bowled steadily, but without getting the Surrey batsmen into difficulties.

Tuesday

Although the weather all day was dismal and threatening, and there was no play till after lunch, a huge crowd patronised the Oval yesterday afternoon; and, if no more rain falls, Strudwick's benefit match may yet prove to be a financial success. Overnight Surrey had scored 111 runs for the loss of nine wickets, and when the game was continued at a quarter to three it was seen that the wicket was slow and easy.

Strudwick and Smith at once proceeded to make the very most of their opportunities. They timed the ball well, they made no mistakes, and they hit with such excellent judgment that the last wicket partnership proved to be the best of all. Thirty-four runs were made in half an hour, and then a good catch by Hubble in the deep field brought the innings to a close.

At twenty minutes to four A. P. Day and Humphreys began the Kent batting, and very early a good ball from Smith beat the amateur. Then followed a little sound batting by Humphreys and Seymour ere the latter was caught at deep extra cover. On Woolley joining Humphreys the play became more forcible, and the score was 68 when Smith (who by that time looked to be making the ball do more than at the beginning of the innings) defeated the left-hander.

A few minutes later Bird got Humphreys out cleverly. He was fielding second slip, but he moved up close to the wicket, and he was only some three yards from the batsman when he made a smart catch. Humphreys' useful innings was not faultless, for twice was he reprieved at mid-off. One of those catches was a very difficult one, but the other was missed because of a mistake which is not often made in a match of importance. Two men tried for the catch and collided.

When once Smith had begun to give trouble he continued to do so, and in quick succession he caused Hutchings and Hubble to make weak strokes which were fatal to them. Huish was his next victim. He put his leg in front of a straight ball, and Carr did likewise with the total 92. It was then five minutes past six. The light had been bad for a couple of hours, but just at this time from the ordinary spectator's point of view, it looked to have got, if anything, rather better. The public, therefore, were surprised when the umpire agreed to stop the game. They were disappointed, too, for, so far, there has only been rather less than five hours' actual cricket in the match.

Wednesday

After a great finish Surrey beat Kent at the Oval yesterday afternoon by 9 runs. The end came a little after half-past four, and it was a brilliant catch in the slips by Smith which brought to a close some four hours of most exciting play. Then the huge crowd surged across the ground, and there was enthusiastic cheering in front of the pavilion. Up to the very last it was anybody's game, and all the afternoon its fortunes fluctuated in surprising fashion.

To Smith Surrey are mainly indebted for their victory; but, destructive as he again proved, Smith did not accomplish the great bowling performance of the last day of the match. The honour of doing that fell to Woolley, who, tried at a time when his opponents looked to have established a strong winning lead, actually took seven wickets for 9 runs.

When play was stopped on Tuesday evening on account of bad light Kent, with a couple of wickets in hand, were 52 runs to the bad. They reduced that deficit to one of 38, and at a quarter-past twelve the really exciting play began. The friends of Surrey hoped to see Hayward and Hobbs hit while the wicket still felt the effects of the heavy roller, but they were disappointed, for the googly bowler got them both out almost at once, and things were looking very bad again for Surrey when Ducat went in to bat.

Ducat immediately altered the whole aspect of the game, and played fine cricket with excellent judgment. Anything punishable he punished in no uncertain fashion, and he ran legitimate risks while maintaining a sound defence. Hayes stayed with him, and, with eight wickets in hand, Surrey were between 80 and 90

runs to the good. Such was the state of affairs when Hutchings substituted Woolley for Carr.

Immediately some amazing cricket was seen, Woolley, as has been said, taking seven wickets for 9 runs. The pitch, of course, was difficult, and, Woolley, it goes without saying, bowled extremely well. At the other end Blythe checked the run-getting, but Woolley succeeded in doing what Blythe very seldom did – he made the batsmen play at the pitch of the ball. And when they did so they made every conceivable mistake. Often they failed to get the bat on to the ball at all, and Huish, crouching behind the stumps, reaped an even richer harvest than when he took his first crop. Judicious hitting such as Ducat indulged in no doubt was wanted, but the batting display given against Woolley's bowling was quite unworthy of the men who gave it.

So once again the fortunes of war reversed, and Kent were only required to get in their second innings 102 runs to win the match. That the runs would want a lot of getting was the general verdict when the final stage of the contest began. But at once came another surprise. No doubt under the influence of the heavy roller, the pitch, when A. P. Day and Humphreys faced the bowling of Smith and Kirk, was not quite so awkward as it was when Woolley accomplished his wonderful performance.

Still, even the optimists were surprised when they saw how strongly, how accurately, and how confidently Day and Humphreys set to work. The ball was met with the middle of the bat, and was sent spinning along the ground to the boundary. What might have happened one can perhaps guess had not the deservedly successful batsmen become too venturesome in running. They tried to steal a single, but the active Strudwick was just too active for them. With a capital shot he threw the wicket down, and the umpire's decision was against Humphreys.

Nothing went right with Kent afterwards. The effects of the roller wore off, and Smith began to make things very awkward for the batsmen. However, as at the other end Kirk was again ineffective, Bird decided to let Hayes keep the run-getting down, and to leave the wicket-taking to Smith. That policy paid so well that at the fall of the seventh wicket the Kent total was only 60. Suddenly, however, fortune once more seemed to favour the visitors, for Hubble and D. W. Carr, by solid and careful batting, in which the getting of singles was a feature, caused the Surrey crowd much anxiety.

Slowly but surely the score rose, and Smith for once did not come to the rescue. Twenty-two runs had been added, and the situation was becoming desperate, when Bird again requisitioned the service of Kirk. The left-hander rose to the occasion in fine style, and rapidly got the three remaining wickets.

There were several extraordinary incidents in the game. Huish stumped as many as nine men; while the two wicketkeepers claimed no fewer than fourteen victims. On twenty occasions – for the catch which brought the match to an end was appealed against – was the decision of the umpire against the batsman. But, in spite of the rather weak batting which was seen, the match was a thoroughly enjoyable one; and as there was again a capital attendance yesterday, Strudwick should do – as he deserves to do – extremely well. Score:

Huish – nine stumpings

SURREY

Hayward, c Prest, b Carr	7	st Huish, b Carr	5
Hobbs, st Huish, b Carr	17	c Hutchings, b Carr	2
Hayes, c Blythe, b Carr	3	b Woolley	12
Ducat, st Huish, b Carr	12	c Seymour, b Woolley	34
Major H. S. Bush, st Huish, b Carr	12	st Huish, b Woolley	0
M. C. Bird, b Blythe	17	st Huish, b Woolley	4
L. P. F. Campbell, l b w, b Carr	1	st Huish, b Woolley	0
Strudwick, c Hubble, b Blythe	25	b Woolley	1
E. C. Kirk, st Huish, b Carr	2	st Huish, b Blythe	0
Hitch, l b w, b Carr	17	c Huish, b Woolley	2
Smith (W. C.), not out	20	not out	0
B 6, l-b 3, n-b 3	12	L-b 2, w 1	3
Total	145	Total	63

KENT

A. P. Day, b Smith	3	c Strudwick, b Smith	19
Humphreys, c Bird, b Smith	30	run out	17
Seymour, c Hitch, b Kirk	12	c Strudwick, b Hayes	10
Woolley, b Smith	22	st Strudwick, b Smith	8
K. L. Hutchings, c and b Smith	7	b Smith	0
H. E. W. Prest, c Campbell, b Kirk	18	c Hayes, b Smith	4
Jubble, c and b Smith	2	c and b Kirk	15
Huish, l b w, b Smith	4	l b w, b Smith	1
D. W. Carr, l b w, b Smith	0	not out	12
Blythe, st Strudwick, b Smith	1	b Kirk	6
Fielder, not out	3	c Smith, b Kirk	0
L-b 3, n-b 2	5		
Total	107	Total	92

SURREY – First Innings

	O	M	R	W		O	M	R	W
Blythe	25.2	7	66	2	Carr	25	4	67	8

Second Innings

	O	M	R	W		O	M	R	W
Blythe	13	4	19	1	Woolley	6.3	3	9	7
Carr	7	0	32	2					

Carr bowled one wide.

KENT – First Innings

	O	M	R	W		O	M	R	W
Smith	31	16	31	8	Kirk	30.5	9	71	2

Kirk bowled two no-balls.

Second Innings

	O	M	R	W		O	M	R	W
Smith	20	10	33	5	Hayes	11	1	26	1
Kirk	8.4	1	33	3					

Umpires – Moss and J. E. West

32: *Lancashire v Yorkshire*
LIVERPOOL, 10–12 JULY 1913

This is one of only two county matches in this book that was not played in the Championship (for the other, see game 6). To mark a progress around Lancashire by King George V, a special first-class match between the county and its historic rival was arranged at Liverpool, in addition to the two Championship matches they would also play that season. It merits inclusion because of the prodigious bowling performance of Harry Dean, the Lancashire left-arm fast bowler, whose armoury included a difficult fast spinner. His 17 for 91 in the match remains the best bowling ever for Lancashire, and was only the sixth time 17 wickets had been taken by the same bowler in a county match. Dean (1884–1957) played for the

county from 1906 to 1921, taking 1,301 wickets at 18 each. Although regarded as one of the country's leading quick bowlers he played just three times for England, during the ill-fated triangular series of 1912, where his 11 wickets cost only 14 each. He took 100 wickets in a season eight times.

Three Tyldesleys were playing for Lancashire. Six players of that surname represented Lancashire between 1895 and 1936; Ernest and John, playing in this match, were brothers; and three brothers of William would also represent the county. All six appeared at some time in 1914; William (b. 1887) was killed in action in 1918. John (1873–1930) was a leading test batsman, playing 31 times for England. In his career he made 37,897 runs at an average of 41, including 86 centuries. Ernest (1889–1962) played just 14 tests, but in a career lasting from 1909 to 1936 made 38,874 runs at an average of 45, including 102 centuries, overtaking his brother as the most prolific batsman in the county's history.

Liverpool, Thursday

The additional match to the Bank Holiday fixtures arranged by the two Northern counties was begun at Liverpool yesterday under somewhat unfavourable conditions, play being limited to three hours and thirty-five minutes, during which Yorkshire completed an innings for 177.

So much rain fell during the night that the captains agreed to take an early lunch and start afterwards, but the ground recovered more rapidly than expected, and it was possible to commence earlier. As a consequence Lancashire took the field without Dean, who had left the ground, presuming, of course, that cricket would not take place until after two o'clock.

As it happened, Dean's bowling proved the feature of the cricket. Called upon after the interval, Dean actually took nine wickets for 62 runs. His length was remarkably accurate, and he got on an appreciable amount of spin. He owed a lot to the smart fielding of his colleagues, and altogether Lancashire gave a very smart display, which was enjoyed by about 3,000 spectators.

Seeing that the sun did not shine until late in the afternoon, the pitch assisted bowlers more than anticipated. It was always difficult to hit with much power on the dead turf, and but for Rhodes the visitors would have made poor use of their opportunity on winning the toss. Going in first, and being eighth to leave at 121, Rhodes played his usual watchful game, and so sound was his defence that he stayed for two hours and fifty minutes. He obtained only 8 runs during the last fifty-five minutes, and altogether hit no more than three 4's, his batting throughout being marked by great restraint. The first partnership produced 34, and Booth was in while 32 were scored.

After Rhodes's dismissal Birtles did valuable service, and he received capital help, Dolphin assisting to add 36 in twenty minutes – the best stand of the day – while Bayes hit up 13 of the last 20 runs. This free cricket gave Yorkshire a much better total than seemed probable, and one that will not easily be exceeded. Except for the absence of Sir A. W. White and Drake (injured), both counties are at full strength.

Friday

Batsmen had an unhappy experience on the Aigburth ground at Liverpool yesterday, hot sunshine following the rain giving the bowlers an opportunity that was not missed. In the course of little more than four hours and

a half's cricket twenty-four wickets went down for an aggregate of 236 runs, the bowlers being masters of the situation until late in the afternoon, when Lancashire commenced the task of getting 159 to win in the last innings of the game. At the close of play Lancashire had lost four wickets for 71 runs, having fared badly again just at the finish, and thus require another 88 for victory.

Among several bowling successes, the work of Dean, the Lancashire left-hander, stood out by itself. On Thursday Dean had taken nine wickets for 62 runs, and yesterday, in Yorkshire's second innings, he secured eight for 29, so having the remarkable record of seventeen wickets at a cost of only 91 runs. The feat of taking seventeen wickets has only been accomplished on seven other occasions in modern cricket. One other Lancashire bowler has been equally successful in a match, Walter Brearley dismissing seventeen Somerset batsmen at Manchester in 1905. Yesterday's honours with the ball were shared with Dean by Rhodes, with five wickets for 7 runs each, and Kilner, with three for 8.

The day's play started with Lancashire going in against a total of 177, and an hour and three-quarter's cricket resulted in Yorkshire gaining the invaluable lead of 85 runs. While so many batsmen failed against Rhodes and Kilner, Makepeace played magnificently to score 48 out of a total of 92. Going in first and being last to leave, he invariably met the ball with the middle of his bat, and was so sound in his defence that he made no real mistake. His hits included four 4's.

In their turn, Yorkshire found the pitch extremely difficult, and, out in an hour and a half for 73, fared even worse than their opponents. They lost their first three wickets for 8, and Booth was let off in the field before he obtained one of his 13 runs. Lancashire later

Dean – 17 wickets

missed another catch offered by Holmes when 2. Birtles, with 14 not out, proved the top scorer of the innings, and he certainly played the best cricket. Going in when seven wickets were down for 40 runs, he stayed forty minutes. At the end of the day Hornby batted splendidly for his 32 not out, and John Tyldesley brought off some fine hits. The game has no bearing on the championship, being an extra fixture arranged in connection with the King's visit to Lancashire.

Saturday

At Aigburth, Liverpool, the extra match arranged this season between Yorkshire and Lancashire ended early on Saturday in a well-deserved and totally unexpected victory for the home county by three wickets, Lancashire's triumph being an accomplished fact at half-past one. Overnight they had four men out in the fourth innings for 71 runs, and required another 88 to win on a pitch that, always difficult, appeared likely to be at its worst for the final stage.

Some showers in the night and morning probably eased it slightly, and to that, added to the fact that the Yorkshire bowlers scarcely did themselves justice on turf that should have suited them to a nicety, the home county owed their victory. Hornby played a great innings, and his stand with McLeod, which yielded 57 in three-quarters of an hour, practically settled matters. The old Cambridge man played extremely well, but he, Hornby (bowled by a yorker at 141), and Heap were all dismissed before Whitehead made the stroke which won Lancashire the match. Hornby was in for two hours and ten minutes, batting skilfully the whole time, and never making the slightest mistake. He hit eight 4's, four 3's, and five 2's.

YORKSHIRE

Rhodes, l b w, b Dean	58	c Huddleston, b Dean	0
Wilson, c E. Tyldesley, b Dean	10	b Huddleston	1
Denton, c Whitehead, b Dean	8	b Dean	2
Kilner, l b w, b Dean	0	l b w, b Huddleston	8
Booth, c Whitehead, b Dean	12	l b w, b Dean	13
Hirst, c W. Tyldesley, b Dean	15	c E. Tyldesley, b Dean	2
H. C. Stanley, c and b Huddleston	3	b Dean	7
Holmes, c Boddington, b Kilner	5	l b w, b Dean	8
Birtles, not out	27	not out	14
Dolphin, c Huddleston, b Dean	14	l b w, b Dean	6
Bayes, b Dean	13	b Dean	0
B 9, l-b 1, n-b 2	12	B 10, l-b 1, n-b 1	12
Total	177	Total	73

LANCASHIRE

A. H. Hornby, b Hirst	1	b Hirst	68
Makepeace, c Dolphin, b Bayes	48	b Kilner	8
J. T. Tyldesley, c Dolphin, b Bayes	3	c Hirst, b Rhodes	22
W. Tyldesley, st Dolphin, b Rhodes	11	c Rhodes, b Hirst	0
E. Tyldesley, c Holmes, b Rhodes	7	l b w, b Rhodes	3
K. G. McLeod, c Denton, b Rhodes	12	b Bayes	30
Heap, b Kilner	3	c Birtles, b Rhodes	13
Whitehead, c Birtles, b Rhodes	1	not out	
R. A. Boddington, c Dolphin, b Kilner	0	not out	0
Huddleston, c Bayes, b Rhodes	0	Did not bat	
Dean, not out	1		
B 4, n-b 1	5	B 6, n-b 1	7
Total	92	Total (7 wkts.)	159

YORKSHIRE – First Innings

	O	M	R	W		O	M	R	W
Huddleston	32	10	66	1	Dean	31.1	6	62	9
Heap	23	9	37	0					

Second Innings

	O	M	R	W		O	M	R	W
Dean	16.3	4	29	8	Huddleston	9	3	13	2
Heap	7	2	19	0					

LANCASHIRE – First Innings

	O	M	R	W		O	M	R	W
Bayes	7	0	26	1	Rhodes	11	2	35	5
Hirst	12	6	18	1	Kilner	5.4	2	8	3

Hirst bowled one no-ball.

Second Innings

	O	M	R	W		O	M	R	W
Hirst	21	6	42	2	Booth	2	0	12	0
Kilner	11	0	45	1	Bayes	5	1	10	1
Rhodes	16.4	5	43	3					

Bayes bowled one no-ball.
Umpires – Butt and Carlin

33: Worcestershire v Warwickshire
DUDLEY, 1–3 JUNE 1914

When Worcestershire and Warwickshire met on Whit Monday for their local derby, the assassination of Franz Ferdinand, which sparked the Great War, was four weeks away, but the 'golden age' showed no sign of ending. Frank Foster (1889–1958) had captained his county since 1911, when he inspired them to the Championship. He was a fine all-rounder. This was one of two seasons in which he performed the 'double' (the other was 1911). In his short career he made 6,548 runs at an average of 26, and took 718 wickets at 21 each: he played in 11 tests. His 305 not out, made at over a run a minute, remains the highest score for Warwickshire, and 645 for 7 is their second highest total. During the war Foster had a motorcycle accident, which ended his career. Frank Field (1874–1934) in this match turned in the most astonishing bowling performance of his life to win the game for Warwickshire, taking the last six wickets for two runs with only one scoring stroke off him in 8.4 overs.

Considering the carnage that intervened before first-class cricket resumed in 1919, the Worcestershire side was fortunate. Nine of those on the card for this match would play for the

Oval in 1924 he took four wickets in four balls, and took 795 wickets at 26 each in his career from 1919 to 1931. The other Surrey centurion, Andrew Ducat (1886–1942) was one of Surrey's main batsmen from 1906 to 1931, scoring 23,373 runs at an average of 39. He was a leading footballer, captaining the victorious Aston Villa side in the 1920 FA Cup final. He died of heart failure while batting at Lord's in a wartime match.

Northampton, Wednesday

The visit of Surrey for the last match of the season at Northampton attracted a large crowd, who enjoyed some good cricket in which the home side showed to considerable advantage against their powerful visitors, who brought in C. T. A. Wilkinson, J. H. Lockton, and Shepherd for Miles Howell, G. M. Reay, and Harrison, of the side who beat Yorkshire. Northants recovered from a bad start, Adams being out to Rushby's third ball with 3 scored, and Haywood falling to a catch in the slips at 24 before Woolley and Hawtin steadily pulled the game round, adding in all 81.

Walden, who went in at the fall of the third wicket, was the ninth to leave, having made 128 out of 183 in two hours and a quarter. He hit with splendid power, and though some of his strokes were faulty he gave no actual chance. Among his figures were twenty-four 4's. This is Walden's best score in first-class cricket, his previous highest being two innings of 111 each – one against Lancashire in 1914, and the other against Sussex this year. Surrey had a few minutes' batting in a defective light and lost Hobbs for 12 runs. Two appeals were made against the light, and the second being successful, stumps were drawn at twenty-five minutes past six.

Thursday

Giving a remarkable display of hitting, the Surrey batsmen established a fresh record for the season at Northampton yesterday, scoring 619 for five wickets soon after the tea interval, and so exceeding by three runs the total at which Hampshire declared a few hours earlier. Fine weather and an easy wicket were all in favour of the batsmen, but still, as Hobbs had been dismissed for 12 runs overnight, the visitors achieved a remarkable performance in scoring 607 runs for four more wickets. For a long time runs came at a sedate pace, but after lunch the Northamptonshire bowlers came in for terrific punishment. Sandham and Wilkinson, the not out batsmen, took the total to 97 before Wilkinson, who had given two sharp chances, was bowled by Woolley. Sandham, who completed 50 in an hour, continued playing admirably, and he made 92 out of 160 in an hour and three-quarters before giving mid-on a catch. He did not make a mistake in

his excellent innings, and hit eleven fours.

A brilliant stand was made by Peach and Ducat for the fifth wicket. The total stood at 213 at lunch time, and afterwards the bowling was hit all over the field. Peach, who completed his 50 in an hour, doubled his score in forty minutes, having the satisfaction of scoring his first hundred for Surrey. Ducat, hitting still more freely, took five minutes less over his hundred, and so remarkable was the hitting that 200 runs were actually put on in an hour and a half, and the partnership altogether realised 288 in two hours and a quarter before a catch at the wicket dismissed Ducat, who had as his share 149. Freely as he hit, Ducat did not make a serious mistake, and among his strokes were nineteen fours and three threes. With Fender in the previous remarkable hitting was eclipsed. The amateur should have been caught at cover-point by Freeman when

Percy Fender – the fastest 100 ever

two, and for this bad mistake the home side had to pay a heavy cost.

Peach and Fender hit with such astonishing freedom that they put on 171 runs in forty-two minutes. Fender actually made his 100 in thirty-five minutes, which must approach a record in important cricket, if, indeed, his performance has ever been surpassed, and it exceeds a memorable 100 by Jessop at Harrogate in forty minutes. Fender hit five 6's, sixteen 4's, and a 3. Apart from a chance to cover point when two and a difficult one in the long field when 34, he did nothing wrong in his 113. Peach went on to complete 200, and then the closure was applied with the score 619 for five wickets, the brilliant partnership being unbroken. Peach did not give a chance during three hours and ten minutes, though always scoring at a great rate. He hit twenty-six 4's.

Friday

At half-past six yesterday evening Surrey won the match at Northampton by eight wickets. Remarkable for wonderful hitting throughout, the match creates a new record, the aggregate runs scored, 1,475 for the loss of 27 wickets, being larger than obtained in any previous inter-county match. Surrey wanted 118 runs for victory, and they got them in 80 minutes. Hobbs made 54 out of 93, being bowled by a ball which came from leg and hit the off stump. He lost Sandham at 24, but the result was never in doubt, as play could have gone on for another half-hour if necessary. Hitch, it may be mentioned, took his hundredth wicket. Score:

NORTHAMPTONSHIRE

W. Adams, b Rushby	3	c Hobbs, b Fender ... 31
A. P. R. Hawtin, c and b Fender	34	b Rushby ... 5
Haywood, c sub, b Hitch	15	c Peach, b Fender ... 96
C. N. Woolley, c Wilkinson, b Fender	58	lbw, b Hitch ... 42
Walden, c Hitch, b Lockton	128	b Rushby ... 63
S. G. H. Humphrey, b Ducat	24	b Hitch ... 31
Wells, c Strudwick, b Hitch	4	c Rushby, b Shepherd ... 71
R. O. Eaven, b Ducat	4	lbw, b Shepherd ... 28
Murdin, b Shepherd	15	c Strudwick, b Shepherd ... 4
Thomas, not out	8	c Ducat, b Hitch ... 30
Bellamy, c Hitch, b Fender	11	not out ... 13
Extras (l-b 2)	2	Extras (B 9, l-b 6, n b 1) ... 16
Total	306	Total ... 430

SURREY

Hobbs, c Bellamy, b Murdin	3	b Walden ... 54
Sandham, c Hawtin, b Woolley	92	b Thomas ... 6
C. T. A. Wilkinson, b Woolley	43	
Shepherd, c Bellamy, b Woolley	9	not out ... 42
H. A. Peach, not out	200	
A. Ducat, c Bellamy, b Thomas	149	not out ... 11
P. G. H. Fender, not out	113	
Extras (B 9, l-b 1)	10	Extras ... 7
Total (5 wkts.)*	619	Total (2 wkts) ... 120

* Innings declared closed.
Hitch, J. H. Lockton, Strudwick, and Rushby did not bat.

NORTHAMPTONSHIRE – First Innings

	O	M	R	W		O	M	R	W
Hitch	24	6	90	2	Shepherd	6	1	17	1
Rushby	25	10	66	1	Fender	21.5	1	69	3
Lockton	20	5	53	1	Ducat	9	4	9	2

Second Innings

	O	M	R	W		O	M	R	W
Hitch	28.2	2	137	3	Ducat	8	1	23	0
Rushby	27	5	68	2	Shepherd	13	5	27	0
Fender	29	1	118	2	Peach	4	2	7	0
Lockton	10	0	34	0					

Fender bowled one no-ball.

SURREY – First Innings

	O	M	R	W		O	M	R	W
Wells	31	6	133	0	Woolley	26	3	116	3
Murdin	22.4	0	162	1	Humphrey	4	0	36	0
Thomas	23	0	142	1	Haywood	4	0	20	0

Second Innings

	O	M	R	W		O	M	R	W
Murdin	9	1	37	0	Woolley	9.3	2	26	0
Thomas	14	3	24	1	Walden	4	0	26	1

Umpires – Moss and Russell

36: *Warwickshire v Hampshire*
BIRMINGHAM, 14–16 JUNE 1922

This was one of the most astonishing games in the history of first-class cricket. For a side to be bowled out for 15 and win by 155 runs is an almost unimaginable achievement, and one without close parallel. At that time only two sides had ever been bowled out more cheaply in the Championship, and Warwickshire, 208 ahead on first innings, had no cause to expect anything other than victory, which seemed assured when Hampshire were still 31 behind with only four second-innings wickets to fall. There is a story, which may be apocryphal, that Calthorpe, the Warwickshire captain, was asked by his committee to delay taking the new ball in order to prolong the game well beyond lunch on the second day, that more entertainment might be provided. W.G. Quaife, the veteran leg-spinner, therefore bowled all afternoon while Hampshire piled up the runs, to end the day 267 ahead.

Hampshire's victory was a team effort in every sense, led by their captain, Lionel (later Lord) Tennyson (1889–1951), grandson of the poet, who captained them for the first 15 seasons after the war, and whose decision to put the home side in paid off in the end. George Brown (1887–1964) was one of the finest all rounders of the time, though he played in only seven tests, all between 1921 and 1923: as well as 25,649 runs and 626 wickets in his career he also kept wicket for his county and for England. His partner in the match-winning stand of 177,

Lord Tennyson with police escort

Livsey (1893–1978) was if anything more heroic, making the highest score of his career (without giving a chance) coming in at 10, and then sharing in a stand of 70 for the last wicket.

Birmingham, Wednesday

Sensational cricket took place at Birmingham in the opening of the match between Warwickshire and Hampshire, for after Warwickshire had put together a total of 223, Howell and Calthorpe bowled with such deadly effect that in half an hour they dismissed Hampshire for the ridiculously small total of 15. Mead, Tennyson, and Shirley were the only batsmen to score, getting 11 between them, the remaining runs being four byes.

Howell, who was very fast on a pitch that helped bowlers, took six wickets for 7 runs, and Calthorpe four for 4. Three Hampshire men were out before a run had been scored; half the wickets were down for 5, and the eighth man left at 10. Mead then scored a single, and four byes followed before Livsey and Boyes, the last two batsmen, were disposed of by Howell.

Tennyson himself will probably never forget the experience, as on winning the toss for Hampshire earlier in the day he put his opponents in to bat. Smith scored 24 out of 36 before being second out, but with Santall and Calthorpe hitting magnificently Warwickshire had 166 on the board before the fourth wicket fell. These two men put on 122 runs in eighty minutes, Calthorpe having three 6's and eight 4's as his chief strokes. Santall hit a 6 and eleven 4's, batting two hours and ten minutes for a splendid 84. The later batsmen, however, failed, and the total of 223 was a poor one considering what the score was with only four wickets down.

Following on 208 behind, Hampshire gave a much better display at their second attempt, and before play ceased they made 98 for the loss of three wickets, so that with seven men to be got rid of they are still 110 to the bad.

Thursday

Hampshire, who on Wednesday at Birmingham had collapsed in such sensational fashion against the bowling of Howell and Calthorpe, made what was in the circumstances a remarkably fine recovery in their match with Warwickshire. Brown took chief honours with a three-figure innings of considerable merit. Batting four hours and three-quarters, he made his 172 out of 324, hitting eighteen 4's, four 3's, and fourteen 2's. When play ceased Hampshire led by 267 runs.

Friday

An altogether wonderful match at Birmingham ended yesterday afternoon in a victory for Hampshire by 155 runs. It is of interest to go over the ground briefly of what occurred on the first two days. Tennyson, it may be recalled, put Warwickshire in after winning the toss and, having scored 223, they got rid of the Hampshire eleven for the paltry total of 15. From that point Hampshire made such a marvellous recovery that when play ceased on the second evening they had pulled the game completely round, having scored 475 for nine wickets. Such a transformation has rarely, if ever, been seen in first-class cricket. Hampshire proceeded with the good work yesterday, another 46 runs being added before the innings closed.

Livsey carried out his bat for 110, an innings which was without blemish, occupying three hours and a quarter, including ten 4's, seven 3's, and eight 2's. This was the first time Livsey had played a three-figure innings for his country, and much of the credit of the victory is due to him, for he helped Brown to add 177 on Thursday for the ninth wicket, while his partnership with Boyes altogether realised 70 runs.

So Warwickshire, despite their sensational bowling successes on the opening afternoon, found themselves left with no fewer than 314 runs to get to win. It can be said at once that after the fall of the second wicket at 77 they never looked like making anything of a fight of it. Bates had been dismissed with only 2 scored, but then Smith and Calthorpe added 75. With Newman going on for Boyes at 77, the issue was soon placed beyond all doubt. Without addition Calthorpe was bowled, and following Smith's dismissal

at 85 Newman got rid of Santall and Waddy with consecutive deliveries. The Quaifes stayed together a little while, but by twenty minutes past four Warwickshire were out for 158, and a memorable match was all over. Score:

WARWICKSHIRE

Bates, c Shirley, b Newman	3	c Mead, b Kennedy	1
Smith, c Mead, b Newman	24	c Shirley, b Kennedy	41
F. R. Santall, c McIntyre, b Boyes	84	b Newman	0
W. G. Quaife, b Newman	1	not out	40
Hon. F. S. G. Calthorpe, c Boyes, b Kennedy	70	b Newman	30
Rev. E. F. Waddy, c Mead, b Boyes	0	b Newman	0
B. W. Quaife, b Boyes	0	c and b Kennedy	7
Fox, b Kennedy	4	b Kennedy	0
J. Smart, b Newman	20	b Newman	3
C. Smart, c Mead, b Boyes	14	c and b Boyes	15
H. Howell, not out	1	c Kennedy, b Newman	11
Extras (l-b 2)	2	Extras (B 6, l-b 4)	10
Total	223	Total	158

HAMPSHIRE

Bowell, b Howell	0	c Howell, b W. G. Quaife	45
Kennedy, c Smith, b Howell	0	b Calthorpe	7
H. L. V. Day, b Calthorpe	0	c Bates, b W. G. Quaife	15
Mead, not out	6	b Howell	24
Hon. L. H. Tennyson, c Calthorpe, b Howell	4	c C. Smart, b Calthorpe	45
Brown, b Howell	0	b C. Smart	172
Newman, c C. Smart, b Howell	0	c and b W. G. Quaife	12
W. R. Shirley, c J. Smart, b Calthorpe	1	lbw, b Fox	30
A. S. McIntyre, lbw, b Calthorpe	0	lbw, b Howell	0
Livsey, b Howell	0	not out	110
Boyes, lbw, b Howell	0	b Howell	29
Extras (B 4)	4	Extras (B 14, l-b 11, w 1, n b 1)	27
Total	15	Total	521

WARWICKSHIRE – First Innings

	O	M	R	W		O	M	R	W
Kennedy	24	7	74	2	Boyes	16	5	56	4
Newman	12.3	0	70	4	Shirley	3	0	21	0

Second Innings

	O	M	R	W		O	M	R	W
Kennedy	26	12	47	4	Boyes	11	4	34	1
Newman	26.3	12	53	5	Brown	5	0	14	0

HAMPSHIRE – First Innings

	O	M	R	W		O	M	R	W
Howell	4.5	2	7	6	Calthorpe	4	3	4	4

Second Innings

	O	M	R	W		O	M	R	W
Howell	63	10	156	3	J. Smart	13	2	37	0
Calthorpe	33	7	97	2	Santall	5	0	15	0
W. G. Quaife	49	8	154	3	C. Smart	1	0	5	1
Fox	7	0	30	1					

Calthorpe bowled one wide and Howell one no-ball.
Umpires – Atfield and R. Brown

37: *Somerset v Surrey*
BATH, 5–8 MAY 1923

In this match, which resulted in a breathtaking victory for Surrey, Hobbs scored the hundredth century of his career. At the time only two other cricketers, W.G. Grace and Tom Hayward, had accomplished this feat, and in the next two years Hobbs was to overtake both of them, equalling and then overhauling Grace's 126 centuries with a century in each innings of

the match that Surrey played against Somerset at Taunton in August 1925. Colonel Philip Trevor, *The Daily Telegraph's* cricket correspondent, told readers in a commentary that Hobbs' hundredth hundred had come in his 817th innings, at the end of which he had scored 34,534 runs. His last 11 years before he retired, aged 52, in 1934 were to bring him another 27,000 runs and 97 centuries, an overwhelming achievement during years when most players would have already retired.

Hobbs had made 70 of his centuries for Surrey, seven for England, 11 for the MCC, five for representative teams and seven for the Players against the Gentlemen. He had reached this goal at the age of 41 despite losing four summers to the war, and almost the whole of 1921 to illness. He was established as England's batsman. Since first playing for England in 1907 he had never missed a test except through injury or sickness.

In addition to Hobbs' epic achievement, the match was remarkable for Somerset's destruction of Surrey on the first day, and Surrey's fight back to allow Fender's daring declaration. Fender's bowling was crucial to the victory. Ernest Robson (1870–1924) had been a mainstay of Somerset's bowling since the mid-1890s. He was still bowling his medium pace to great effect at the age of 53, as Surrey found in the first innings. He was to die suddenly a year later after an operation.

Bath, Saturday

The Surrey team had a very dreary experience on Saturday in the opening stage of their match with Somerset at Bath. So wet did the weather prove that not until half-past five could play be attempted, and then, after three overs had been sent down, a thunderstorm bursting over the ground put an end to matters. Hobbs and Sandham, who came out to start the Surrey batting, did not score from either Robson or J. C. White, so the game was left at nought for no wicket. Surrey are making one change from the side that met Glamorgan, Thain standing down in favour of Harrison.

Monday

With the solitary exception of Ducat, the Surrey batsmen failed in extraordinary fashion against Somerset at Bath yesterday. So difficult did they find run-getting against Ernest Robson and J. C. White that, although they kept the home team in the field for two hours and fifty minutes, their total amounted to no more than 91. Ducat carrying his bat out for 52 and five leg-byes being registered, the united efforts of the other ten members of the Surrey eleven produced only 34 runs. Disasters began at once, for on Hobbs and Sandham proceeding with the innings in which nothing had been scored during the three overs to which play was restricted on Saturday, a further maiden was sent down, and then a brilliant catch low down at cover-point by Daniell, who fell over in taking the ball, disposed of Hobbs, the first wicket thus going

down without a run.

Other misfortunes speedily befell the visiting side, Sandham and Shepherd both leaving with the score at 7. Hitch succeeded in making a couple of good drives, but at 23 a ball from White beat him completely, and one run later a one-handed catch in the slips at the second attempt sent back Fender. Ducat and Harrison offered a stubborn opposition for forty minutes, but the former had a narrow escape from being caught by Daniell, and the score had only been increased by 17 when Harrison, hitting out at White, skied the ball back to the bowler. With Abel promptly bowled there were actually seven wickets down for 42, the interval arriving with the total at 48. On resuming Peach kept up his end while Ducat brought off some good strokes, and in all 32 runs had been added in little more than half an hour when Robson got Peach leg-before. Ducat continued to do well, but in turn Strudwick and Lowe were also leg-before, and the innings closed for 91. Going in first wicket down, Ducat at the close was not out 52. If lucky in escaping dismissal on one or two occasions, he played a great game and saved his side from what, had he failed, must have been an utter collapse. His hits included two 4's and six 3's. Backed up by brilliant fielding, Robson and White, even allowing for the assistance they received from the state of the ground, accomplished a big performance. White took four wickets for 27 and Robson, who completed his 52nd year last week, disposed of six batsmen for 59.

Having disposed of their opponents so cheaply, Somerset set to work in resolute fashion to increase their advantage. A fine catch with one hand at mid-on by Harrison sent back Johnson at 15, but MacBryan and Young carried the score to 37 before the latter was leg-before, and at the end of three-quarters of an hour's batting the home side, with 50 on the board and only two men out, stood in a very strong position. At that point, however, Lowe got rid of MacBryan, and Considine failed, but by the tea interval Lyon and Daniell had raised the score to 68. Afterwards Lyon hit hard, and with a very powerful stroke that lifted the ball on to the scorers' tent he placed Somerset ahead. He and Daniell put on 45 for the fifth wicket. Sixth out at 108, Lyon, who showed by far the brightest cricket

Jack Hobbs – the master

of the day, made his runs in three quarters of an hour with one 6 and four 4's as his chief strokes. Afterwards the home batting rather lacked enterprise, but with Jones, of Chard, a young left-handed batsman, keeping up his wicket for more than half an hour, the Somerset total reached 140. Lowe began by taking three wickets for 19, but subsequently the batsmen played him with much care, and his analysis came out at four wickets for 51. Surrey fielded very smartly, the catches by which Harrison disposed of Johnson and Ducat got rid of Daniell being particularly good.

Forty-nine runs in arrear on the first innings, Surrey at their second attempt scored 23 runs for the loss of Sandham, and so left off 26 behind with nine wickets to fall.

Tuesday

It was under most anxious conditions that Hobbs accomplished his notable feat yesterday. So badly had Surrey batted on the previous day that Somerset secured a lead of 49, and Surrey at their second attempt had, before the drawing of stumps on Monday, lost Sandham and scored only 23 runs. Thus on the game being proceeded with the visitors were still 26 runs in arrear. The early play suggested that Surrey might come badly to grief, for without any addition to the over-night total Ducat, who on the previous day had saved the side from utter collapse, was run out through a brilliant piece of fielding on the part of Hunt, who threw down the wicket. Despite the position of the game and this warning that no liberties could be taken with the Somerset fielding, Hobbs and Shepherd, when they had been together a little while, attempted a sharp single and promptly paid the penalty, a smart return by Considine resulting in the loss of Shepherd's wicket at 36. For the moment the Surrey batsmen seemed to have quite lost their heads, as, with Fender in, Hobbs, starting for a run which his captain would not have, must have been out if MacBryan had not blundered. The total had been advanced to only 45 when Robson got Fender leg before, Surrey at this point, with four men out, being still 4 runs in arrear.

However, when the outlook for Surrey was extremely gloomy, Hobbs found an invaluable partner in Hitch. The two batsmen soon settled down to a confident and effective game, and despite the early disasters, Hobbs reached his 50 in two hours, while at lunch time the score had been advanced to 121, Hobbs being 56 and Hitch 43. On resuming Hitch completed his 50 after batting an hour and a quarter, but with the total at 153 a catch at the wicket disposed of him. The partnership, which extended over ninety-five minutes, had yielded 121 runs. Hitch's resolute innings of 67 included ten 4's. Joined by Harrison, Hobbs went on batting in masterly fashion, and reached his 100 in three hours and five minutes, having registered his second 50 runs in sixty-five minutes. When 112 Hobbs was let off at silly point by Daniell, who in that position

had caught him so brilliantly on Monday. A little later, with the total at 216 for five wickets and Hobbs not out 116, Fender, at twenty minutes past three, declared the Surrey innings closed. At the wickets three hours and a half, Hobbs had three 6's and eleven 4's in his splendid innings.

No small risk of defeat was Fender taking in declaring when he did, for, set with no more than 168 to win, Somerset had plenty of time in which to accomplish the task. Still, as under the regulations which now govern the championship the side behind on the first innings is as badly off as a side actually defeated, the Surrey captain had good cause for his declaration. Far from well did Somerset start. At the tea interval three wickets had fallen for 44. Considine and Daniell made a gallant effort for the home side, putting on 48 for the fourth wicket in forty minutes, but half the side were out for 99. Then followed some capital batting by Lyon, and as long as he remained Somerset possessed a fair chance of victory. In a rather indifferent light, however, few of the other batsmen achieved much success, and with play extended beyond half-past six in order to arrive at a definite issue, the Somerset innings closed for 157, Surrey thus gaining a sensational victory by 10 runs. Score:

SURREY

Batsman		R			R
Hobbs, c Daniel, b Robson		0	not out		116
Sandham, b Robson		0	lbw, b White		4
Ducat, not out		52	run out		0
Shepherd, lbw, b White		4	run out		8
Hitch, b White		9	c Lyon, b Robson		67
P. G. H. Fender, c Young, b Robson		0	lbw, b Robson		5
Harrison, c and b White		9	not out		10
Abel, b Robson		1			
Peach, lbw, b Robson		9			
Strudwick, lbw, b Robson		0			
Lowe, lbw, b White		2			
Extras		5	Extras		6
Total		91	Total (5 wkts)*		216

* Innings declared closed.

SOMERSET

Batsman		R			R
P. R. Johnson, c Harrison, b Lowe		11	b Fender		13
J. C. W. MacBryan, c Abel, b Lowe		22	hit wicket, b Lowe		11
Young, b Lowe		15	c Abel, b Lowe		5
S. G. U. Considine, b Fender		1	hit wicket, b Fender		19
J. Daniell, c Ducat, b Fender		13	c Lowe, b Peach		23
M. D. Lyon, b Peach		39	b Fender		26
Jones, c Shepherd, b Abel		14	run out		3
J. C. White, c Fender, b Lowe		10	c Strudwick, b Peach		0
Hunt, lbw, b Abel		2	b Fender		19
C. A. Winter, b Abel		3	not out		9
Robson, not out		0	c Strudwick, b Peach		7
Extras		10	Extras		22
Total		140	Total		157

SURREY – First Innings

	O	M	R	W		O	M	R	W
Robson	33	12	59	6	Hunt	2	2	0	0
White	30.3	16	27	4					

Second Innings

	O	M	R	W		O	M	R	W
Robson	34	10	87	2	Hunt	9	2	17	0
White	32	7	101	1	Winter	3	0	5	0

SOMERSET – First Innings

	O	M	R	W		O	M	R	W
Hitch	4	1	13	0	Peach	8	3	13	1
Lowe	20.2	3	51	4	Abel	6	3	6	3
Fender	19	8	47	2					

Second Innings

	O	M	R	W		O	M	R	W
Hitch	4	0	15	0	Fender	29	8	61	4
Peach	25.1	9	39	3	Lowe	13	6	20	2

38: Gloucestershire v Middlesex
BRISTOL, 23–26 AUGUST 1924

Gloucestershire enjoyed their best season for 26 years in 1924, finishing sixth in the table. Middlesex were to be runners-up, so Gloucestershire's victory over them, after being bowled out for 31, was to become even more significant. Despite Hammond's marvellous innings the real hero was Charlie Parker, the slow-left arm bowler, who had joined Gloucestershire 21 years earlier and was to enjoy his best season the following year, taking 222 wickets at 15 each. Here he took the hat-trick in each innings, the first time it had been performed twice in a championship match since Trott's match in 1907 (see game 24). Altogether Parker took six hat-tricks in his career, a number exceeded by only one other bowler, Doug Wright. Parker (1882–1959) retired in 1935 with 3,278 wickets to his credit, a total exceeded only by two of his great contemporaries, 'Tich' Freeman and Wilfred Rhodes. So burdened was England with talent at that time that Parker played only one test match, at the age of 39 against Warwick Armstrong's Australians.

Middlesex were still a side in which amateurs predominated, though they were highly talented ones. One of them, Nigel Haig (1887–1966), had been principally responsible for Gloucestershire's collapse on the wet Saturday, taking 6 for 11 in 12 overs. Haig, a nephew of Lord Harris, was a regular player in the Middlesex side from 1912 to 1934, and he appeared five times for England during the 1920s. Though mainly a medium-pace bowler he performed the 'double' three times, scoring 15,220 runs and taking 1,117 wickets at 27 each in his career. He eventually captained Middlesex, and was an all-rounder in the true Edwardian sense, being a brilliant golfer, tennis and squash player.

Charlie Parker

Bristol, Saturday

So startling did the cricket prove at Bristol on Saturday that although the day's play was cut short by nearly two hours, both Gloucestershire and Middlesex concluded an innings. The visiting county secured a lead of 43 runs, and that advantage should prove of the utmost value. On a drying pitch batsmen had a very sorry time, and the twenty wickets that fell produced an aggregate of only 105 runs. Bowlers obtained remarkable figures, Durston and Haig being unchanged, while getting Gloucestershire out, and Parker having the Middlesex batsmen in great difficulties. Haig, in the course of twelve overs had only 11 runs hit from him, at which cost he took six wickets, the other four falling to Durston for 18. Parker had an even more sensational record, as his performance of seven for 30 included the hat trick. Twice this season, the first being against Surrey at the Oval, and four times in all has the Gloucestershire left-hander dismissed three batsmen with successive balls.

Monday

A wonderful innings by Hammond not only helped to retrieve another wretched start, but placed Gloucestershire in a good position in their match with Middlesex, at Bristol, yesterday. Dismissed for 31 on Saturday, and losing two wickets at their second attempt for only 12 runs, the home county seemed in a hopeless plight, but Hammond, who can rarely have played with such skill and judgment on a bad pitch, scored freely, and obtained such a mastery over the attack that not until late in his innings did he make the slightest mistake. After Gloucestershire's early disasters he found many useful partners, and Middlesex, so far from following up the advantage gained, had in the end a difficult task.

When Hammond had been at the wickets five minutes short of two hours he completed a faultless 100 out of 160. He and Robinson added 71 in sixty-five minutes for the seventh partnership, the 200 being sent up just before the Gloucestershire captain was caught. With Parker in, Hammond gave his first chance, at 137, but that was only a small blemish in a great innings. In forty minutes the ninth pair scored 51, the ninth wicket falling at 264. With the total standing at 294 for nine, Gloucestershire declared their innings closed, to give Middlesex an hour's batting before the close.

Undefeated, Hammond was at the wickets for three hours and fifty-five minutes, and hit one six and twenty-one 4's. Thanks almost entirely to his effort Middlesex were set the task of getting 252 runs to win. Of that number the visiting county scored 46 for one wicket before the end, so that they still require 206. Dales batted with marked skill in the closing stages.

Tuesday

Wonderful Gloucestershire! At Bristol yesterday, after a match of astonishing fluctuations, they beat Middlesex by 61 runs. No better or more startling performance has any of the counties achieved in this especially wet season; not even Lancashire's victory over Yorkshire at Leeds in June was more remarkable than yesterday's triumph of the West country cricketers. To appreciate the full merit of their success against Middlesex it is necessary that the match should be taken from its inception. Nigel Haig, making the ball do all manner of capers, played havoc with the Gloucestershire batting on Saturday.

It was Parker who again did all the mischief; for the second time in the game, and for the fifth occasion in his career he performed the 'hat-trick,' dismissing Mann, Guise, and Haig with successive balls. And he did this when his fielders were given to missing catches. His total bag was fourteen wickets for 131. We have to go back twelve years ago to find a double 'hat-trick'; then J. T. Matthews, the Australian, against the South Africans at Manchester, performed the feat.

There is, of course, on record Albert Trott's four wickets with four balls and three wickets with three balls in his benefit match against Somerset. But Parker, who, during the present campaign, has got rid of 184 batsmen for an average of 13.51, has accomplished many notable deeds. In 1921 against Somerset at Bristol he took all ten wickets, and in his benefit match with Yorkshire two years ago – again at Bristol – he upset the wickets five times with successive balls (the fifth was a no-ball). Parker, who, as a young man, played golf, came into the Gloucestershire eleven nineteen years ago, and was one of England's bowlers in the Test match at Manchester in 1921.

Middlesex began yesterday faced with a task of getting 206 runs to win with nine wickets standing. Lee was let off when 14, but Middlesex had lost four good men for an addition of 48 to the overnight total of 46 for one wicket; and had the fielding been better, they would have fared even more disastrously. Dropped catches threatened to keep victory from Gloucestershire; but then Parker, having defeated the hard-hitting Mann, brought about a memorable finish. Score:

GLOUCESTERSHIRE

Dipper, c Dales, b Haig	6	c Durston, b Haig 7
F. J. Seabrook c Murrell, b Haig	7	b Durston 4
Hammond, c Hearne, b Haig	5	not out 174
B. H. Lyon, c Durston, b Haig	4	c Hendren, b Hearns 42
Smith, b Durston	3	lbw, b Hearne 2
F. G. Rogers, c Dales, b Haig	0	b Hearne 0
Bloodworth, not out	1	run out 9
Lt.-Col. D. C. Robinson, b Durston	0	c Lee, b Haig 24
Mills, c Murrell, b Durston	0	b Allen 5
Parker, b Durston	0	c Dales, b Haig 13
Dennett, b Haig	3	not out 5
Extras (l-b 1, n b 1)	2	Extras (B 6, l-b 1, n b 4) 11
Total	**31**	**Total (9 wkts dec.)** **294**

MIDDLESEX

H. L. Dales, c Dipper, b Hammond	7	lbw, b Mills 42
Lee, c Lyon, b Parker	21	b Hammond 21
J. W. Hearne, c Rogers, b Parker	6	c Hammond, b Parker 6
Hendren, c Hammond, b Parker	5	lbw, b Parker 23
R. H. Twining, c Lyon, b Parker	1	b Mills 8
G. O. Allen, c Dennett, b Parker	0	c and b Parker 31
F. T. Mann, st Smith, b Parker	0	c Lyon, b Parker 22
J. L. Guise, c Lyon, b Hammond	22	c Dennett, b Parker 0
N. Haig, b Mills	8	lbw, b Parker 0
Murrell, c Hammond, b Parker	2	b Parker 22
Durston, not out	0	not out 3
Extras (B 1, n b 1)	2	Extras (B 2, l-b 8, n b 2) 12
Total	**74**	**Total** **190**

GLOUCESTERSHIRE – First Innings

	O	M	R	W		O	M	R	W
Haig	12	7	11	6	Durston	11	4	18	4

Durston bowled one no-ball.

Second Innings

	O	M	R	W		O	M	R	W
Haig	33	2	95	3	Hearne	21	1	75	3
Durston	16	3	61	1	Lee	5	1	9	0
Allen	9.2	1	26	1	Murrell	4	0	17	0

Durston bowled three no-balls and Hearne one no-ball.

MIDDLESEX – First Innings

	O	M	R	W		O	M	R	W
Hammond	9	2	27	2	Mills	2	0	15	1
Parker	10.1	3	30	7					

Parker bowled one no-ball.

Second Innings

	O	M	R	W		O	M	R	W
Parker	31.1	5	101	7	Mills	15	4	45	2
Hammond	13	8	22	1	Dennett	8	4	10	0

Parker bowled two no-balls.

Umpires – Phillips and Reeves

39: Lancashire v Somerset
MANCHESTER, 21 MAY 1925

It was noted earlier that on four occasions Lancashire have beaten Somerset in a day (see game 3). This was the third of them, and *The Daily Telegraph's* correspondent points out that Somerset made quite a habit of this against other counties. In this and the following six seasons Somerset would never come higher than 13th in the Championship, their side still reliant on amateurs of low ability. Lancashire, on the other hand, were enjoying their finest run since the 1890s. Although they would manage only to come third this year they would win the title in four out of the next five seasons, coming second in the other year.

McDonald (1891–1937), who disposed of Somerset in the morning and made the highest score of the Lancashire first innings, was probably the greatest fast bowler of his day. A Tasmanian who also played for Victoria, he had toured England with Armstrong's Australians in 1921 and had been the outstanding bowler of a touring side that ranks with Bradman's team of 1948 as perhaps the finest in history. McDonald had originally planned to play league cricket for Nelson, something the editor of Wisden said he found 'very distasteful' because 'I object strongly to the importation of Australian players'. Expressing a sentiment that would be heard at deafening volume half a century later, Wisden went on: 'Clubs with money to spend should encourage native talent and not buy cricketers of established reputation'. Nonetheless, McDonald qualified to play for Lancashire from 1924 to 1931, taking more than 100 wickets in all but one of those seasons. This season was his best, when he took 205 wickets at 18.66 each. Settling in Lancashire, he was killed in a car crash there aged only 46.

McDonald – the greatest fast bowler of his day

Manchester, Thursday

The wicket at Old Trafford having been damaged so much by rain on Wednesday, it was found necessary to prepare another before the match could be commenced. In an hour and thirty-five minutes before lunch Somerset were dismissed for 74. Five wickets fell for 15, but Bligh and Earle put on 46, Earle hitting two 6's and five 4's. Macdonald, in taking half the wickets at a cost of 24 runs, kept a splendid length. Lancashire lost four wickets for 32, but with the seventh wicket falling at 71, R. Tyldesley and Macdonald hit out, and in twenty minutes added 44. The innings closed for 130. White, who made the ball turn appreciably, took five wickets for 67.

Facing a deficit of 56, Somerset collapsed badly, and in an hour and twenty minutes the side were out for 73, and Lancashire were left with only 18 runs to get to win. These were hit off for the loss of one wicket. Parkin, taking six wickets for 44, secured during the day eight wickets for 78, and R. Tyldesley five for 26.

As no play took place on Wednesday owing to rain, the match was begun and finished in a day. The last time this occurred in a first-class match in England was when Kent played Sussex at Tonbridge in 1919. It is of particular interest to note that this is the fifth occasion upon which Somerset have been concerned in a similar occurrence, and singularly enough three of these matches have been against Lancashire at Old Trafford. The first in 1892, the second in 1894, and the third yesterday. In 1894 also their match with Yorkshire at Huddersfield was over in one day, and in 1899 the game between Middlesex and Somerset at Lord's ended in a day. Score:

SOMERSET

A. E. S. Rippon, c Hopwood b Parkin	0	lbw, b R. Tyledesley	15
Young, b Macdonald	2	c Parkin, b Macdonald	6
A. F. Bligh, b H. Tyldesley	20	lbw, b Parkin	3
Hunt, c Watson, b Macdonald	0	b Parkin	1
P. R. Johnson, c R. Tyldesley, b Parkin	0	lbw, b Parkin	6
J. C. White, c Duckworth, b Macdonald	2	c Parkin, b R. Tyldesley	2
G. F. Earle, c K. Tyldesley, b R. Tyldesley	43	c E. Tyldesley, b Parkin	0
J. Daniell, lbw, b R. Tyldesley	1	c Sharp, b Parkin	20
C. C. Case, b Macdonald	3	b Parkin	5
M. L. Hambling, not out	0	c Parkin, b R. Tyldesley	10
M. L. Hill, b Macdonald	0	not out	0
Extras (B 1, n b 2)	3	Extras (B 4, l-b 1)	5
Total	74	Total	73

LANCASHIRE

Makepeace, c Hambling, b White	11	c Daniel, b White	5
Hallows, c Earle, b Hunt	12	not out	4
E. Tyldesley, c Daniell, b Hunt	8	not out	11
Watson, c and b White	1		
J. R. Barnes, run out	26		
J. Sharp, b Hunt	8		
Hopwood, c and b White	1		
R. Tyldesley, c Daniel, b White	27		
Duckworth, c Earle, b White	0		
Macdonald, not out	35		
Parkin, c Rippon, b Hunt	1		
Total	130	Total (1 wkt)	20

SOMERSET – First Innings

	O	M	R	W		O	M	R	W
Parkin	11	4	34	2	R. Tyldesley	5	2	13	3
Macdonald	15.3	6	24	5					

Macdonald bowled two no-balls.

Second Innings

	O	M	R	W		O	M	R	W
Parkin	13	3	44	6	R. Tyldesley	6	2	13	3
Macdonald	6	2	11	1					

LANCASHIRE – First Innings

	O	M	R	W		O	M	R	W
Hunt	29	9	63	4	White	28	11	67	5

Second Innings

	O	M	R	W		O	M	R	W
Hunt	3.1	2	8	0	White	3	1	12	1

Umpires – Buswell and Denton

40: Nottinghamshire v Middlesex
NOTTINGHAM, 20–23 JUNE 1925

'An unparalleled feat' read the headline on the report of the third day's play in this match, a statement needed to correct the headline 'Middlesex losing' that had appeared the previous day. No county side had ever made so huge a score – 502 – in the fourth innings to win a match, and only three other sides had ever matched the feat anywhere in the world. Middlesex's achievement has never been beaten in the County Championship; the closest a side has come was when Sussex made 428–5 to beat Northamptonshire at Kettering in 1939. The highest a side had ever made to win a Championship match before was 404–5 by Lancashire against Hampshire at Southampton in 1910.

Nottinghamshire set so hard a target thanks to three batsmen. Whysall (1887–1930) played four tests for England and between 1910 and 1930 made 21,592 runs at an average of 39. He died while still at his peak, from blood poisoning after injuring himself falling over on a dance floor. A.W. Carr (1893–1963) would captain England against Australia the following year and captained his county from 1919 to 1934: he was sacked from the latter in a controversy about bodyline bowling, one of the leading exponents, Larwood, being a Nottinghamshire player. During 1925, his best season with the bat, he hit the then record number of 48 sixes. Payton

(1882–1943) scored 22,132 runs at an average of 34 between 1905 and 1931. Hendren (see game 57) won the match for Middlesex. His first partner, Bruce (1885–1957), succeeded to the title of Lord Aberdare, and played just 62 games for Middlesex over 21 years. Mann (1888–1964), was the Middlesex captain from 1921 to 1928 and captained MCC and England on the tour of South Africa in 1922–23.

Nottingham, Saturday

Saturday was bowlers' day at Trent Bridge, and in the match between Notts and Middlesex twenty wickets went down for an aggregate of 294 runs, Notts leading on the first innings by forty. The failure of batsmen – only two on each side made over twenty runs apiece – was the more unaccountable, as the pitch to all appearances seemed entirely in favour of run-getting. Payton, however, played a really splendid innings, the only blemish in an admirable display being a difficult chance to deep square leg when he had made seventy.

Middlesex could do no more than score 137. Barratt took five wickets for less than nine runs apiece.

Monday

Vastly different in character was the cricket at Trent Bridge yesterday from that seen on Saturday afternoon, when twenty wickets went down for 294. Notts, with a lead of 40 runs, hit the previously successful Middlesex bowlers to all parts of the field. Both Carr and Payton made centuries, and Whysall, in an hour and three-quarters, scored 82. The Notts second innings, with the total at 461 for nine wickets down, was closed, Payton taking out his bat for 126.

Middlesex, left with 502 runs to win, have lost three wickets for 60.

Tuesday

The possibilities of cricket seem endless. Middlesex, having to make no fewer than 502 to win, obtained them for the loss of six batsmen, and gained a brilliant and astonishing victory over Notts by four wickets. Such a performance is without parallel in county cricket. Indeed in first-class matches there are only three other instances of a side getting over 500 in the last innings.

That Middlesex should have accomplished their task with four wickets to spare was the more remarkable as overnight they had lost three good batsmen for 60 runs, while a fourth was dismissed first thing yesterday morning for the addition of 6. Then came a splendid partnership by Hendren and Bruce, the latter of whom made 103 out of 154 put on in ninety-five minutes, but with six men out shortly before lunch for 231 the position certainly did not favour Middlesex.

At that point, however, Hendren was joined by his captain, and the two men, establishing a complete mastery over a varied attack, stayed together until

Arthur Carr

twenty minutes to six, and, by adding 271 in three hours and a quarter, hit off the balance without being separated.

The hero of the day was undoubtedly Hendren, who for the third time in a fortnight – in the course of which he has scored no fewer than 869 runs – put together an innings of over 200. Altogether he was five hours and a quarter at the wickets, hitting two 5's and nineteen 4's in his truly wonderful 206 not out. As far as could be seen the only mistake he made was at 161, when he gave a very difficult chance directly after the tea interval to short-slip. From start to finish his timing of the ball was as near perfection as possible, and in making his runs he brought into use a variety of skilful strokes in which drives and hits to leg predominated. It is of interest to note that his other scores of over 200 during the period mentioned above were 234 against Worcestershire and 240 against Kent, while in between them he scored 142 in the match with Lancashire at Lord's.

Notts had to pay a big price for mistakes in the field. Bruce, who drove superbly to hit a 6 and fifteen 4's, was twice missed before reaching 40, but an even more expensive blunder occurred later, Mann being let off at backward point when he had made only 4. Apart from that Mann played a very fine innings indeed. Leaving most of the scoring to Hendren, and seeing a possibility of bringing off a 100 to 1 chance, he refrained from taking any risks. He neglected few opportunities, however, of scoring off loose balls, and in the course of his innings, which included fifteen 4's, he made many powerful drives and splendid hits to leg. As some indication of the pace at which runs were scored throughout the innings it is only necessary to observe that Middlesex obtained their 502 in six hours and a quarter.

NOTTS

Lilley, lbw, b Haig	12	c Kidd, b Hearne ... 34
Whysall, b Haig	11	lbw, b Stevens ... 82
Walker, c Hendren, b North	25	c Stevens, b Durston ... 6
A. W. Carr, b Haig	4	c Kidd, b Hearne ... 123
Payton, c North, b Durston	78	not out ... 126
Flint, lbw, b Durston	0	b North ... 8
S. H. Staples, c Hendren, b North	3	b Stevens ... 19
Richmond, b Durston	1	c Lee, b Stevens ... 8
Barratt, c Stevens, b North	1	b North ... 16
Matthews, b Durston	7	c Durston, b Stevens ... 10
Larwood, not out	5	not out ... 8
Extras (B 12, l-b 8)	20	Extras (B 13, l-b 8) ... 21
Total	167	Total (9 wkts) ... 461

MIDDLESEX

G. T. S. Stevens, run out	18	lbw, b Matthews ... 28
Lee, c Whysall, b Barratt	0	b Flint ... 19
J. W. Hearne, c Carr, b Barratt	16	c Matthews, b Barratt ... 5
Hendren, c Flint, b Staples	10	not out ... 206
Hon. C. N. Bruce, c Payton, b Staples	21	c Payton, b Staples ... 103
K. L. Kidd, b Barratt	28	b Matthews ... 7
F. T. Mann, c Barratt, b Staples	6	not out ... 101
N. Haig, c Whysall, b Staples	18	
Murrell, b Barratt	0	
North, c Matthews, b Barratt	6	c Flint, b Matthews ... 3
Durston, not out	2	
Extras (l-b 2)	2	Extras (B 14, l-b 7, w 5, n b 4) .. 30
Total	127	Total (6 wkts) ... 502

Notts – First Innings

	O	M	R	W		O	M	R	W
Haig	14	3	37	3	Stevens	5	1	16	0
Durston	18.1	7	46	4	North	10	1	40	3
Hearne	5	2	8	0					

Second Innings

	O	M	R	W		O	M	R	W
Haig	25	4	86	0	Hearne	20	4	68	2
Durston	22	5	76	1	Stevens	19	2	83	4
North	26	4	127	2					

Middlesex – First Innings

	O	M	R	W		O	M	R	W
Barratt	19.4	2	44	5	Larwood	12	5	23	0
Matthews	5	1	25	0	Staples	15	3	33	4

Second Innings

	O	M	R	W		O	M	R	W
Barratt	28	3	87	1	Flint	18	2	60	1
Staples	31	5	109	1	Larwood	24	4	76	0
Matthews	23	2	97	3	Richmond	14.5	3	43	0

Matthews bowled four wides and two no-balls; Staples one wide, and Richmond two no-balls.

41: *Lancashire v Yorkshire*
MANCHESTER, 31 JULY–3 AUGUST 1926

Much of the reputation that the Roses Match has for being a dour contest, more concerned with the grinding down of opponents and avoiding defeat at all costs than chasing victory, stems from the half-century before the Second World War, when Lancashire and Yorkshire were apparently permanently in contention for the Championship. This was the hundredth time that the two sides had met. In 1926 Lancashire won the title and Yorkshire were runners-up; no wonder 76,617 people packed into Old Trafford over the bank holiday weekend, forming the third highest attendance ever at a county match. What grim, unrelenting cricket they saw: Lancashire, passing 500 for the first time against Yorkshire, batted until the middle of the afternoon on the second day to reach it. They scored their runs off 196 overs, barely two-and-a-half an over. Yorkshire's 352 took more than nine hours, or 179 overs, less than two an over; and these performances from sides that contained the finest batsmen in England.

Joseph Makepeace (1881–1952) played for Lancashire from 1906 to 1930, and played four times for England on their disastrous tour of

Australia in 1920–21. His best season was 1926, when he scored 2,340 runs at an average of nearly 49. In his career he scored 25,745 runs at an average of 36.15, including 43 centuries.
He played football for Everton and for England, and from his retirement almost until his death was the Lancashire coach. Edgar Oldroyd (1888–1964) recovered from his injury, if not from his mode of dismissal. He played for Yorkshire from 1910 to 1931, scoring 15,929 runs at an average of 35.16, including 38 centuries.

Manchester, Saturday

The return match between Lancashire and Yorkshire – the 100th meeting of the two counties – drew a crowd of 22,000 people to Old Trafford, and at the end of the day Lancashire had made 297 for two wickets. Before the luncheon interval Makepeace and Hallows scored 74 together, and in all they put on 84 for the first wicket in 100 minutes. Then came a long partnership between Makepeace and E. Tyldesley, and three hours and a quarter elapsed before the Yorkshire bowlers met with any further success. Makepeace was cautious in the extreme, and when at last he completed his 100 out of 210 he had been batting for four hours and five minutes. Altogether he was at the wickets for four hours and fifty minutes. His partnership with Tyldesley produced 169 runs – the second best stand made against Yorkshire this season.

Monday

The attendance at Old Trafford yesterday constitutes a record for any county fixture, 38,600 people paying

for admission and the total number of spectators being estimated at 45,000. Lancashire reached a total of 500 for the first time against Yorkshire, and declared nine runs later, with nine wickets down. Not out 90 on Saturday, Ernest Tyldesley made his eighth 100; he batted altogether five hours, and his 139 included a 6 and twelve 4's. Watson batted in painstaking fashion for three and a half hours, and was out when needing eight to complete his second 100 of the season. Rhodes had the remarkable figures of seven wickets for 116 runs, to prove that in bowling he is still a force to be reckoned with.

When Yorkshire commenced batting, about two hours, fifty minutes remained for cricket. Holmes and Sutcliffe made light of the bowling, and for the thirty-fifth time they sent up the 100 together. No real chance had been given by either batsman when stumps were drawn without Lancashire gaining any success, and Yorkshire, with all their wickets intact, are within 326 of the home county's total.

Tuesday

Reduced to a struggle for a lead on the first innings, the match at Old Trafford ended in favour of Lancashire, who obtained three points from the champions. When the Yorkshire innings of just over nine hours closed for 352, giving the home county an advantage of 157, the spectators cheered as though Lancashire had won the match instead of drawing it. On Monday York-

Ernest Tyldesley

shire's opening batsmen scored 183 together, in reply to the Lancashire total of 509 for nine wickets, declared. The pitch remained in good order, and when Sutcliffe left the stand had realised 199 in three hours, ten minutes.

There followed an incident that altered the whole course of the cricket. Oldroyd, when facing Macdonald, was struck on the head by the ball and was carried off the field unconscious. He was taken to Manchester Infirmary, suffering from haemorrhage. It was noticed that a bail had fallen and Oldroyd was adjudged out, after a consultation between the umpires. Leyland joined Holmes, and Yorkshire concentrated upon playing out time, the former scoring only ten runs in an hour. Holmes played a remarkable innings. When he was caught at mid on, with 17 runs added to the luncheon interval total, he had been at the crease five and a half hours without making one false stroke, though he had two escapes of being run out. His 143 included two 6's and 16 4's. Kilner left at 300, and the turning point of the match came when Watson bowled at 319, and took two wickets with following balls. Score:

LANCASHIRE

Makepeace, b Rhodes	126	
Hallows, lbw, b Robinson	41	
E. Tyldesley, st Dolphin, b Rhoes	139	
Watson, c Dolphin, b Kilner	92	
Iddon, c Dolphin, b Rhodes	15	
Macdonald, c Leyland, b Rhodes	19	
R. Tyldesley, c Oldroyd, b Rhodes	2	
Taylor, c and b Rhodes	3	
Sibbles, b Rhodes	6	
L. Green, not out	30	
Duckworth, not out	9	
Extras (B 8, l-b 14, w 1, n b 4)	27	
Total (9 wkts dec.)	*509	

* Innings declared closed.

YORKSHIRE

Holmes, c Hallows, b Macdonald	143	
Sutcliffe, lbw, b R. Tyldesley	89	
Oldroyd, hit wkt, b Macdonald	12	
Leyland, b Sibbles	31	
Kilner, c Iddon, b Macdonald	17	
Rhodes, c Duckworth, b Watson	12	
Robinson, lbw, b Iddon	12	
Macaulay, c Iddon, b Watson	0	
Waddington, c Iddon, b Watson	17	
Maj. A. W. Lupton, b Iddon	0	
Dolphin, not out	4	
Extras (B 11, l-b 3, w 1)	15	
Total	352	

LANCASHIRE – First Innings

	O	M	R	W		O	M	R	W
Robinson	41	10	80	1	Kilner	47	15	90	1
Macaulay	34	4	94	0	Rhodes	42	7	116	7
Waddington	28	2	86	0	Oldroyd	4	0	16	0

Kilner bowled one wide and Waddington four no-balls.

YORKSHIRE – First Innings

	O	M	R	W		O	M	R	W
Macdonald	49	11	154	3	Watson	17	9	16	3
Sibbles	47	18	72	1	Iddon	21	10	35	2
R. Tyldesley	45	22	60	1					

Tyldesley bowled one wide.

Umpires – Parris and Buswell

42: *Middlesex v Surrey*
LORD'S, 28–31 AUGUST 1926

Hobbs' 316 not out remains the highest score ever made at 'Headquarters'. It contributed to a resounding victory for Surrey in this keenly-fought fixture, and helped the county to finish fifth – one place above their rivals – in the Championship, then drawing to its close for the season. Hobbs' regular opening partner for Surrey – and occasionally for England – at this time was Andrew Sandham (1890–1982), who, but for being overshadowed by Hobbs for most of the time he played for Surrey, would no doubt be better remembered as one of the greatest batsmen of his generation. Sandham played for Surrey from 1911 to 1937, and in his career made 41,284 runs at an average of 45. He is one of only four Englishmen to have made a treble century in a test (325 not out against the West Indies in 1929–30). He and Hobbs put on 100 for the first wicket 63 times, of which this was one, and together they still hold the Surrey first-wicket record of 428, against Oxford University in 1926. When his days as a player were over he was first coach, and then scorer for Surrey, until finally retiring at the age of 80.

Hobbs' other main support in this match was Douglas Jardine (1900–1958), still best remembered as captain of MCC's side to Australia in 1932–33, the 'Bodyline' series. History has been so busy heaping obloquy on Jardine, caricatured in his Oxford Harlequin cap, for his alleged infamy in seeking to beat the Australians by unfair means that it has largely overlooked what an excellent bat he was. He made his highest aggregate of runs this season, 1,473 at 46, but in the next two seasons averaged 91 and 87. In his career he made nearly 14,848 runs at an average of 47. Averaging 48 in tests, he was in the highest rank.

Lord's, Saturday
By Colonel Philip Trevor CBE.

Hobbs batted all day at Lord's on Saturday, and was still undefeated (256 not out) when stumps were drawn at a quarter to seven. For five hours and thirty-five minutes he kept a large crowd enthralled. Hobbs owed nothing either to situation or circumstance. Surrey are out of the running in the race for the County Championship, so are Middlesex. Those who watched

Hobbs forgot the match, and the rivalry of the two neighbouring counties, content to see the greatest batsman of the age, batting hour after hour, as they knew no one but he could bat.

His innings was not merely faultless: it was flawless. Middlesex had seven bowlers, and not one of them bowled badly. On the other hand, not one of them gave Hobbs a moment's uneasiness or caused him to make an uncertain stroke. I have seen Hobbs play a few hundred innings in the course of the last twenty-one years, but I do not call to mind another case of a very long innings of his in which his bat was so much 'all middle and no edge' as it was on Saturday.

Hobbs, partnered by Sandham, went to the wickets at noon, and for eighteen minutes not a run came from the bat. In time he settled down, and by lunch the score was 84 – Hobbs 39, Sandham 42: and Sandham it was who got his 50 first. When Sandham had scored 52 he gave a technical chance at the wicket off Haig's bowling, and the stroke gave him a couple of runs. The ball was turned so much and so sharply as to make it practically uncatchable. I mention the incident merely because this was the only catch 'missed' all day. Very rarely have I seen batting during an entire day's play which was so devoid of blemish. And, as that was so, my congratulations are offered to the Middlesex eleven for their undismayed bowling and their tireless fielding.

Hobbs was quite up to Hobbs standard, and in the making of one particular stroke he was at his absolute best – the pull stroke. This is at once the easiest and the most difficult and intriguing of strokes a batsman can make. No one brings it off with more certainty and greater force than the local blacksmith on the village green. Still, at my age, I will field forward short leg to that worthy with complacency. He will only use it when a long hop is bowled, and I shall have time to get out of the way. But no English batsman pulls the ball just short of a good length like Hobbs does.

I imagine Surrey will do a bit more batting this morning, and they may just as well. In that case Hobbs may break the Lord's record – held by Holmes – of 315 not out. To do that he needs 60 runs. The Hobbs-Jardine partnership has already produced 202 runs. D. R. Jardine never struggles to get into the limelight, and is apt to go unobserved in consequence, for he is the reverse of dramatic. On Saturday we were all looking at Hobbs, and it was only when stumps were drawn that we seemed to understand that Jardine had made 72 runs without doing anything wrong.

Monday

Hobbs broke the Lord's record yesterday morning. On Saturday evening when stumps were drawn he had scored 256. It took him eighty minutes when the game went on again to get the 60 runs necessary to beat Holmes's score of 315 not out, made for Yorkshire against Middlesex last season.

Douglas Jardine – in Harlequin cap

The display given by Hobbs was superb from first to last. It was not merely chanceless, but without blemish of any kind. For exactly seven hours he kept us enthralled, and it is fitting that the greatest batsman of the age should hold the batting record at the historic head-quarters of the game. Hobbs started very slowly. For all that he got his runs at an average rate of 45 an hour. His was a great display, but it has its pathetic side. There is scarcely a record left for him to beat. D. R. Jardine, who joined him with the total 258, also played a three-figure innings – and a very good one, too. With his score 92 Jardine was rather badly missed off Powell's bowling at cover point, but that was his only mistake. Directly Hobbs had broken record the Surrey innings was declared closed, and at one o'clock Middlesex began their uphill task.

They made a bad start, losing Stevens and Allen for 37 runs. The left-hander, Dales, however, playing his free game with success, hit the ball well and hard. Things began to look a little better for the batting side until Jardine was put on to bowl. He at once clean bowled Dales, and a little later he caused Mann to give a very easy catch to mid-off. Enthoven paid the penalty of attempting a short run to cover-point. Hobbs dashed in, gathered the ball, and threw the wicket down. Haig was out to a fine catch at the wicket, and then there was a profitable partnership between Hendren and Lee. Lee was rather worried by Fenley's bowling, but he stuck it out, and 93 runs had been added when once again an attempt was made to take a liberty with Hobbs, who made another unerring shot at the wicket and Lee had to go.

Hobbs made in all four shots at the wicket and hit

it every time. When Hendren had scored 98 he again attempted a short run to cover-point. He just sprinted home as Hobbs made the bails fly. It was a desperately near thing. On the fourth occasion the batsman had dashed back in time to save himself. I doubt if there has ever been a fieldsman who was the equal of Hobbs at doing this sort of thing, and he is equally good at throwing at either wicket. It was not quite one of Hendren's best innings. He gave the bowler a catch when he had scored 58; and once Fender morally bowled him out with about the best ball I have seen bowled this season. Its pace – it was a very fast one – was cleverly masked. It was a perfect length; it broke in about four to five inches, and almost scraped the bail. Incidentally it went for four byes. Fender rapidly finished off the innings, which came to an end at twenty-five minutes past six. Hendren carried out his bat. Following on in a minority of 304, Middlesex had four minutes' batting before stumps were drawn.

Tuesday

Surrey beat Middlesex very easily at Lord's yesterday by an innings and 63 runs, the end coming at a quarter-past four. Middlesex never looked like saving the game. They had scored one run and had all their wickets in hand when the day's play began, and it was always practically certain that they would lose. Stevens, always most to be relied on when things are bad for his side, played a good and plucky innings, while Mann, Hendren, and Lee each got a few runs.

For winning outright Surrey had to thank their fieldsmen. No catches were missed, and four very good ones were made. In this respect Fenley greatly distinguished himself. He was fielding at mid-off when he made both catches. Hendren hit the ball a full blow to the fieldsman's left side, and Fenley made light of that one. Later Murrell hit a skyer, and falling back

Fenley took the ball high over his head with his right hand.

Jardine's catch at forward short-leg, by which he got rid of Allen, was a very hot one. Jardine is about the most intrepid of the fieldsmen who are wont to lie in wait at forward short-leg or silly mid-on. Strudwick, standing back to the fast bowling of Holmes, brought off a capital catch when he got rid of Lee, jumping smartly to leg and taking a ball which had been turned a great deal.

SURREY

Hobbs, not out	316		A. Jeacocks, run out	26
Sandham, c Hendren, b Haig	58		P. G. H. Fender, not out	1
Ducat, b Durston	41		Extras (B 12, l-b 7)	19
Shepherd, c and b Stevens	15			
D. R. Jardine, c and b Powell	103		Total (5 wkts dec)	*579

* Innings declared closed.
E. R. T. Holmes, Peach, Strudwick, and Fenley did not bat.

MIDDLESEX

G. T. S. Stevens, c Strudwick, b Holmes	2	c Fender, b Peach	63
H. L. Dales, b Jardine	52	c Fender, b Holmes	4
G. O. Allen, c Shepherd, b Peach	21	c Jardine, b Fenley	17
Hendren, not out	101	c Fenley, b Jardine	37
H. J. Enthoven, run out	1	b Fenley	5
F. T. Mann, c Peach, b Jardine	3	not out	37
N. Haig, c Strudwick, b Fender	12	c Shepherd, b Fender	18
Lee, run out	42	c Strudwick, b Holmes	31
Murrell, c Peach, B Fenley	20	c Fenley, b Peach	7
Durston, b Fender	0	b Holmes	1
Powell, c and b Fender	0	c Strudwick, b Holmes	4
Extras (B 15, l-b 6)	21	Extras (B 11, l-b 3, w 2, n b 1)	17
Total	275	Total	241

SURREY – First Innings

	O	M	R	W		O	M	R	W
Haig	37	7	118	1	Lee	8	1	44	0
Durston	31	12	69	1	Powell	27	4	109	1
Allen	19	3	88	0	Enthoven	10	1	37	0
Stevens	22.3	1	95	1					

MIDDLESEX – First Innings

	O	M	R	W		O	M	R	W
Holmes	14	2	41	1	Fender	23	5	76	3
Peach	18	7	26	1	Shepherd	9	5	22	0
Fenley	24	4	76	1	Jardine	8	2	13	2

Second Innings

	O	M	R	W		O	M	R	W
Holmes	15.4	2	49	4	Fender	14	2	38	1
Peach	23	5	41	2	Shepherd	8	3	12	0
Fenley	23	4	66	2	Jardine	6	1	18	1

Holmes bowled one wide and Fender one wide and one no-ball.
Umpires – Burrows and Chidgey

43: Gloucestershire v Surrey
CHELTENHAM, 15–17 AUGUST 1928

I t was said of Wally Hammond: 'He did not walk to the wicket; he strode.' Hammond was indeed the towering presence of inter-war English cricket; one of its greatest batsmen, he was also an effective bowler and probably the finest fieldsman in the game. Seldom can a cricketer have dominated a game, or won it so single-handedly, as Hammond did this one. Against one of the finest sides in the Championship, Hammond not only scored a century in each innings (the second of seven

occasions on which he did this, a feat exceeded only by Zaheer Abbas), and took ten catches in the match (the only time this has ever been done, let alone by a man scoring two centuries), but he also opened the bowling in the first innings. In Gloucestershire's next match, against Worcestershire, he took 16 wickets.

Hammond (1903–1965) is still generally reckoned to be the finest all-rounder in the game's history. Largely thanks to him Gloucestershire were enjoying the first of four seasons of relative prosperity; they would come fifth in 1928, their best season since 1898, fourth in 1929, and would be runners-up in 1930 and 1931 before slumping to 13th. At this stage a professional, he would in 1938 become an amateur and captain his county and his country. For eight successive seasons he topped the batting averages; he made 36 scores of 200 or more, just one fewer than Bradman and 14 more than his next closest rival, Hendren. Hammond played 85 times for England, and in his first-class career (which stretched from 1920 to 1951) he made 50,551 runs at an average of 56, took 732 wickets and 819 catches. He scored 167 centuries scoring his hundredth just 12 years after his first.

Cheltenham, Wednesday

Hammond played a masterly innings for Gloucestershire against Surrey at Cheltenham yesterday, and thanks largely to his efforts the Western county came off much better than at one time seemed likely.

Gloucestershire fared so badly as to lose five wickets for 141 by lunch-time. Up to that point Hammond had made 95. Altogether he scored 139 out of 199 in two hours and forty minutes, hitting three 6's and eighteen 4's, twelve of which were fine off-drives.

Following the departure of Barnett, Smith and Green made the one effective stand of the innings, putting on 51 runs in forty minutes. Smith showed much of his old form in obtaining 56 in an hour and fifty-five minutes. Thanks to a useful stand for the last wicket, Gloucestershire in the end put together a total of 304, their innings having lasted four hours and thirty-five minutes.

Going in at twenty minutes past five, Surrey lost Sandham with only 8 runs on the board, and Ducat was out at 40, but runs came well on Shepherd joining Hobbs, and Surrey finished the day 219 behind, with eight wickets in hand.

Thursday

Although Hobbs put together a characteristic score of 96 and Shepherd and P. G. H. Fender each made over 50, the batting of the rest of the Surrey eleven at Cheltenham was extremely moderate, and when an innings had been completed on each side Gloucestershire found themselves 37 runs in front.

Parker and Hammond bowled very well, and after Shepherd had been got rid of at 120 and Hobbs was out in the last over before lunch, only Fender offered any resistance. Fender, who went in at the fall of the fifth wicket at 174, found a little difficulty in timing the ball, but when he had settled down there seemed a likelihood of a stand until a clever catch at short leg ended

Hobbs's admirable display. The famous Surrey batsman scored his 96 out of 224 – the sixth partnership having realised 50 runs – in three hours and ten minutes, and hit eight 4's.

With wickets falling quickly afterwards, Fender tried hard to force the pace, hitting six 4's in scoring 55 runs in eighty-five minutes. Altogether the Surrey innings lasted four hours. Parker accomplished splendid work in taking six wickets, and Hammond in the course of the innings brought off four catches in the slips.

Batting a second time Gloucestershire lost Sinfield at 55. Hammond did not attack the bowling in the same confident style as in the first innings, and it took him ninety minutes to complete his 50. Still, he was not out at the close when Gloucestershire, with four men out for 156, held a lead of 193 runs. Lyon, who went in

Wally Hammond: 'He did not walk to the wicket, he strode'

after Dipper left at 79, hit up 27 out of 52 added for the third wicket by him and Hammond.

Friday

Hammond, the brilliant all-round cricketer, enjoyed a personal triumph in the match at Cheltenham against Surrey, which ended in a substantial victory for Gloucestershire by 189 runs.

Not out 64 overnight, Hammond carried his score to 143, having previously scored 139 in the first innings, a feat he accomplished against Surrey in the match at the Oval last season. In addition he brought off six splendid catches, and as he had already made four and taken one wicket in the first innings, he had a hand in the dismissal of eleven Surrey men.

Another Gloucestershire player who contributed largely to the success of his side was Parker, who proved so difficult to play that he took seven wickets yesterday for just over 12 runs apiece, and had a record for the game of thirteen for 197 runs, his best performance of the year.

Hammond gave one chance when 125, but otherwise his cricket was free from fault, and in a very fine display, which lasted for three hours and twenty-five minutes, he hit a 6 and twelve 4's. The Gloucestershire innings was declared closed during the luncheon interval, when nine men were out for 319, Surrey, with four hours left for cricket, being set to get 357 to win.

With Hobbs and Sandham out for 13, Surrey were soon struggling for runs. Ducat and Fender offered some resistance, Ducat hitting seven 4's, while towards the end Garland-Wells brought off some fine drives, three of which were 6's. Parker, backed up by magnificent fielding never lost his length, and Surrey were all out for 167. Score:

GLOUCESTERSHIRE

Dipper, c and b G. Wells	7	c and b Peach	41
Sinfield, b Peach	0	lbw, b Shepherd	22
Hammond, c Shepherd, b Peach	139	c Gregory, b Fenley	143
B. H. Lyon, c and b Fender	6	c Hobbs, b Shepherd	27
F. J. Seabrook, c Gregory, b Fender	0		
W. L. Neale, c Ducat, b G. Wells	10	b Fender	5
Smith, c Fender, b Shepherd	56	b Shepherd	0
C. J. Barnett, c G. Wells, b Peach	0	c Ducat, b Fenley	45
Capt. M. A. Green, c Sandham, b Fenley	37	not out	21
Parker, c Brooks, b Fender	19	c Shepherd, b Fenley	11
Mills, not out	7	b Shepherd	2
B 12, l-b 10, n-b 1	23	B	2
Total	**304**	**Total (9 wkts dec.)**	**319**

SURREY

Hobbs, c Seabrook, b Hammond	96	c Smith, b Parker	2
Sandham, c Smith, b Sinfield	0	c Hammond, b Sinfield	10
Ducat, c Dipper, b Parker	6	c Hammond, b Parker	55
Shepherd, c Barnett, b Parker	52	c Hammond, b Parker	17
Barling, c Hammond, b Parker	4	c Hammond, b Parker	2
Gregory, c Hammond, b Parker	7	c Hammond, b Parker	3
P. G. H. Fender, c Hammond, b Sinfield	55	c Hammond, b Parker	20
H. M. Garland-Wells, c Hammond, b Parker	6	st Smith, b Sinfield	49
Peach, b Mills	5	c Smith, b Parker	1
Brooks, lbw, b Parker	2	run out	0
Fenley, not out	0	not out	0
B 27, l-b 7	34	B 1, l-b 7	8
Total	**267**	**Total**	**167**

GLOUCESTERSHIRE – First Innings

	O	M	R	W		O	M	R	W
Fender	24.3	10	57	3	Garland-Wells	22	5	65	2
Peach	27	6	68	3	Gregory	2	0	4	0
Fenley	12	2	44	1	Shepherd	15	4	43	1

Peach bowled one no-ball.

Second Innings

	O	M	R	W		O	M	R	W
Fender	25	6	55	1	Garland-Wells	14	3	34	0
Peach	26	9	71	1	Shepherd	32.4	5	74	4
Fenley	18	2	83	3					

SURREY – First Innings

	O	M	R	W		O	M	R	W
Hammond	22	3	71	1	Parker	38.4	6	117	6
Sinfield	9	4	10	2	Mills	24	11	35	1

Second Innings

	O	M	R	W		O	M	R	W
Sinfield	27	9	59	2	Mills	6	0	20	0
Parker	32	10	80	7					

Umpires – Bestwick and Young

44: Middlesex v Lancashire
LORD'S, 15–18 JUNE 1929

Perhaps the most striking feature of G.O. 'Gubby' Allen's career, as with many distinguished amateurs of this period, is how excellently he played with so little match practice. The major difference made by the Great War to the amateur game – and it was, ultimately, to be its death – was the need of a greater number of amateurs to earn a living, whereas many of them had once survived on unearned income. Allen (1902–1989) was a stockbroker whose first-class career stretched from 1921 to 1954, and yet in all that time he played just 265 first-class matches. His 788 wickets came at 22 each, and he was a far from bad batsman, making 9,232 runs at an average of 28.

His feat of taking all ten Lancashire wickets in the first innings of this match is still the only time it has been accomplished at Lord's. It is the best bowling ever for Middlesex. Allen won a blue in two seasons at Cambridge, but made the University side only after being picked for Middlesex to play against them, and taking 6 for 13. He played 25 tests, touring Australia on the 'Bodyline' trip and being the only fast bowler to stand up to Jardine and refuse to bowl leg-theory.

He captained the next tour of Australia, in 1936–37, winning the first two tests but losing the series. Allen served as a Colonel in the intelligence corps during the war, once being arrested by the Home Guard as a suspected German spy. He became more famous for his behind-the-scenes role in the last 35 years of his long life than he had been as a cricketer: he was for six years chairman of the selectors, for 12 years treasurer of MCC and its President in 1963–64; as such he had profound influence over the modern game, and was knighted in 1986 for his services to cricket.

Lord's, Saturday
By B. Bennison

G. O. Allen, at Lord's on Saturday, for Middlesex against Lancashire, the champion county, had the rare distinction of taking all ten wickets, eight clean bowled, the last four with five balls without a run being scored from him. And a crowd of some 8,000 people, as he spread-eagled the stumps of Hodgson, Liverpool's footballer, to finish the innings, rose to him as one man; they cheered the old Cantab loud and long. Herewith his analysis:

O	M	R	W
25.3 ...	10 ...	40 ...	10

It was immediately after the tea interval that Allen, bowling his fastest and with a nice appreciation for length, ran riot, six wickets falling for 26, and Lancashire, who had scored 215 for four, were all out for 241. We saw Hallows in company with Watson for twenty-five minutes, the two scarce, so it seemed, having a nodding acquaintance with enterprise, though no demon lurked in the bowling until the advent of Allen, and then Hallows, in trying to turn him to leg, had his off stump disturbed. Thereafter Watson, and in a lesser degree Tyldesley, suggested that even mild speculation was foreign to their nature.

MONUMENTAL PATIENCE

Watson 'sat on the splice' as if that were the special and only mission of his cricketing life. Not even long hops and half-volleys – and several were served up to him – could induce him to uncurl himself: he was all for operating behind a cast-iron defence which he built around him. And so he took five minutes longer than two hours to make 47. His innings was one of monumental patience: that is all that may be said of it. He had the satisfaction, however, of seeing the hundred hoisted; but it was the batting of Tyldesley after Watson's departure, and the suddenly acquired deadliness of Allen – the rest of the Middlesex bowling, by comparison, was transparently moderate – that made the cricket really worth while.

Tyldesley took some time to discover himself: there was good and substantial reason why he should exercise every care, for Iddon, to whom we looked to produce a certain amount of liveliness, was bowled all over the place before he had troubled the scorers. But from the moment he was joined by the little-known Hopwood he was the great batsman, sound, polished, confident, masterful, if never unusually free. Slow, indeed, he was in building up his first 50 – two hours and five minutes – but he never smacked of stodginess; Tyldesley could never do that. And when, after making his second half-century in a little more than an hour, he was bowled leg stump by Allen, he claimed 102 out of 192.

There was but one false stroke in his most excellent performance: he hit nine 4's and seven 3's. Had it not been for Hopwood, who helped Tyldesley to increase the total by 113, there would be nothing left to say about the batting of Lancashire; Allen was supreme.

Middlesex in their reply have begun none too well; they have lost three wickets for 34 to McDonald and Richard Tyldesley.

Monday

The outstanding feature of yesterday's cricket in the match between Middlesex and Lancashire was a brilliant innings of 124 by Lee, who, helped generously by his captain, Nigel Haig, saved his county from a collapse. As the game now stands, Lancashire are 145 ahead, with three men out in their second innings.

Lancashire, when McDonald, not now I fear the great bowler he was during his earlier association with English cricket, bowled Robins with a 'squatter,' seemed assured of a commanding lead, for then Middlesex had six wickets down for 71. Allen, Saturday's hero, was the first batsman to capitulate – clean bowled he was in an attempt to drive Richard Tyldesley, who proceeded immediately to get Lord Aberdare stumped by Farrimond, a Bolton youth, as efficient, so North-country folk will have it, as Duckworth, England's keeper.

It was Lee, primarily, who was responsible for preventing something perilously near to a complete Middlesex collapse. He stayed three hours and a half to score 124 out of a total of 218, and it was Nigel Haig who was his best and most dependable partner. Save that they paid the respect demanded by Richard Tyldesley, who ever required the most careful watching, Lee, notably, and Haig exposed the Lancashire attack as one of moderate quality, at times severely plain and ordinary. Haig had the good fortune to escape being caught when 21, and he remained to score 40. Then, fittingly enough, McDonald claimed him as his victim.

Lancashire began the second innings at 3.40, and, as on Saturday, with Hallows and Watson. In twenty-seven minutes, when Watson was bowled by Haig, they had made 13. And when Ernest Tyldesley joined forces with Hallows the voice of the 'barracker' was heard. There was neither excuse nor place for this most obnoxious person; neither Haig nor Allen, who began the bowling, invited or deserved punishment. If Hallows or Tyldesley had attempted to take liberties they would most probably have paid the extreme penalty: they would certainly have been condemned for their rashness. Besides, in the circumstances, they were not inexcusably slow: as a matter of fact, when tea was taken Lancashire had scored 42 for the loss of Watson's wicket, in an hour. Things considered, not bad going.

Hallows, after the adjournment, dared to jump out to Robins, and he saw his off bail dislodged, and when Tyldesley was caught by Durston, and three wickets were down for 74, Lancashire had all the appearance of riding for a fall, for, truth to tell, they are

not without a decided tail – such as Hallows, Watson and Tyldesley out, and oftener than not I fear it would be comparatively easy for the other side. However, Iddon and Hopwood, despite many bowling changes, played out time.

Tuesday

The match at Lord's between Middlesex and Lancashire was drawn, the home county, left 324 to win, having scored 170 for five wickets when stumps were drawn at six o'clock. It was a game of many fluctuations, and will long be remembered because of the personal triumphs won by members of each team – the rare bowling feat by G. O. Allen, who took all the Lancashire wickets in the first innings; two separate hundreds by Lee, and three-figure scores by Ernest Tyldesley and Hopwood.

First Middlesex appeared to be definitely on top; it was left to Hopwood and Richard Tyldesley to rescue Lancashire, for after Iddon had played brightly to score 43, and Halliday left after taking seventy minutes to score 11, Farrimond was brilliantly caught by Robins in the slips, one-handed, low down; Eckersley was bowled without opening his account, and Lancashire had seven men out and led by no more than 226.

Then it was that Hopwood and Richard Tyldesley altered the position entirely. When the luncheon interval had come they had raised the total to 258, Hopwood by skilful, brilliant batting all round the wicket, and Tyldesley, after groping his way to settledness, by hitting with gusto, especially after the resumption. Six times did Tyldesley thump the ball to the boundary before he struck across at Durston, designedly, I suspect, for I was sure he had had enough, and was bowled. Then he had rattled up 53, a priceless as well as a heroic contribution. His partnership with Hopwood, which lasted forty-five minutes, produced 87. With the dismissal of McDonald at 310 and nine wickets down, Eckersley applied the closure, so that Hopwood carried out his bat for 106, as near perfect as any innings could well be. His was a thoughtful, a scholarly exposition of batting, chanceless. His stay was a long one – three hours and twenty minutes – but Hopwood was never dull.

Middlesex were left to get 324 runs to make in three hours and a quarter of actual play, or at the rate of 100 an hour. A prodigious task, but Lee and Guise, against the bowling of McDonald and Hodgson, began in such an enterprising way that they made fifty in exactly thirty minutes. Lee simply raced along with the

Gubby Allen

keenest possible relish for the short pitched balls, which McDonald frequently sent down; and Hodgson, too, he treated severely. And with Guise also all for hustling the odds were that Middlesex would carry the day. Sixty-two had been knocked up and then Watson, in his first over, got Guise caught at the wicket by Farrimond. Haig filled the breach, but he had only scored a single when he was out lbw to Richard Tyldesley, Lancashire's best bowler undoubtedly, who had been called up at 64.

Lord Aberdare had the unenviable distinction of making a second duck; and it must be said that he courted disaster by the manner in which he struck across at a ball from Watson, who shortly afterwards caused Hearne to be given out leg before, a fate which he suffered in his first innings. With four wickets down for 73 Lancashire may be said to have turned the tide in their favour entirely, but it happened that Lee, when 50, was missed by Iddon in the neighbourhood of the boundary, and the pendulum took to swinging the other way. For Lee found in Allen a rare and efficient partner, and in an hour the two added 62. And when Allen fell to make way for Robins, Lee, like the old Cantab, withstood all the wiles of the several bowlers employed by the Lancashire captain.

Except for the chance he offered when he had half completed his second century Lee made no mistake during the two hours and three-quarters he was at the wickets to score 105 not out. The only Lancashire bowler who gave him the least trouble, apparently, was Richard Tyldesley, who could not have bowled better either in the matter of length, variety, or cunning, but who, I thought, was hardly made the most of by his captain. Lancashire, however, were no doubt well satisfied with the points they took by virtue of their first innings lead. Score:

LANCASHIRE

Hallows, b Allen	12	b Robins	22
Watson, b Allen	47	b Haig	6
Tyldesley, (E.), b Allen	102	c Durston, b Robins	31
Iddon, b Allen	0	c Lee, b Robins	43
Hopwood, c Price, b Allen	48	not out	106
Halliday, b Allen	0	lbw, b Allen	11
Farrimond, b Allen	6	c Robins, b Haig	0
P. T. Eckersley, not out	8	b Haig	0
Tyldesley (R), b Allen	0	b Durston	53
McDonald, st Price, b Allen	1	c Hearne, b Durston	8
Hodgson, b Allen	0		
B 11, l-b 3, n-b 1	17	B 23, l-b 6, n-b 1	30
Total	241	Total (9 wkts dec.)	310

MIDDLESEX

Lee, b Hodgson	124	not out	105
J. J. Guise, b McDonald	3	c Farrimond, b Watson	19
Hearne, lbw, b Tyldesley (R.)	10	lbw, b Watson	1
Price, b Tyldesley (R.)	3		
G. O. Allen, b Tyldesley (R.)	5	c Halliday, b Watson	29
Lord Aberdare, c Farrimond, b Tyldesley (R.)	0	b Watson	0
R. W. V. Robins, b McDonald	1	not out	12
N. Haig, b McDonald	40	lbw, b Tyldesley (R.)	1
Hulme, h w, b Tyldesley (R.)	20		
Durston, c and b McDonald	20		
I. A. R. Peebles, not out	0		
l-b 1, w 1	2	B 2, l-b 1	3
Total	228	Total (5 wkts)	170

LANCASHIRE – First Innings

	O	M	R	W		O	M	R	W
Haig	29	8	48	0	Peebles	12	2	26	0
Durston	10	3	17	0	Hearne	8	1	28	0
Allen	25.3	10	40	10	Guise	5	1	11	0
Robins	22	1	54	0					

Allen bowled one no-ball.

Second Innings

	O	M	R	W		O	M	R	W
Haig	28	6	70	3	Durston	10	2	16	2
Allen	28	10	65	1	Robins	31	1	93	3
Peebles	10	2	22	0	Hearne	5	0	14	0

Peebles bowled one no-ball.

MIDDLESEX – First Innings

	O	M	R	W		O	M	R	W
McDonald	26.2	1	108	4	Hopwood	11	3	17	0
Hodgson	15	0	53	1	Watson	7	6	8	0
Tyldesley (R.)	21	6	40	5					

Hodgson bowled one wide.

Second Innings

	O	M	R	W		O	M	R	W
McDonald	14	1	42	0	Watson	15	4	37	4
Hodgson	3	0	22	0	Tyldesley (R.)	13	5	13	1
Hopwood	3	0	16	0	Iddon	10	1	37	0

Umpires – Stone and Benwell

45: *Sussex v Kent*
HASTINGS, 10–13 AUGUST 1929

Prince Duleepsinhji – or 'Smith' as he became known – was the most exciting cricketer from the Indian sub-continent since his uncle, Ranji, had also played for Sussex a generation earlier. Duleep (1905–1959) had distinguished himself while still a schoolboy at Cheltenham in the early 1920s, and made his debut for Sussex in 1924. He won a blue in three of his four years at Cambridge, and played 12 times for England, routing Australia in 1929–30. Duleep's career lasted only eight seasons, being truncated by tuberculosis; he missed a year at

Cambridge when he almost died from it, and he was to die of a heart attack at the relatively early age of 54. Yet in his short playing career he accomplished perhaps more than anyone has ever done in so little time. He scored 15,485 runs at an average of 50, including 50 centuries, and averaged 59 for England. Had illness not handicapped him, he might have become the greatest batsman of the inter-war years.

His century and double century in this match against Kent was only the fifth time such a feat had been accomplished, and the match itself (thanks largely to the speed with which Duleep made his runs) was one of the highest-scoring in English cricket and the second highest then recorded in the Championship. The high over rates at the time also helped make this an exciting game, with 385 being bowled in the match, or 130 a day. For Kent, C.H. Knott (1901–1988), a former blue, played 104 times for the county over 19 seasons, his appearances being restricted by his work as a schoolmaster at Tonbridge. Among the fine cricketers that he produced from that school was Colin Cowdrey, the Kent and England captain.

Prince Duleepsinhji

Hastings, Saturday

Sussex, beaten in an innings when they met Kent at Maidstone last month, gave a very different display in the return match at Hastings on Saturday, when they ran up a total of 428 in four hours and forty minutes.

Some 8,000 people saw remarkable cricket, and especially before the luncheon interval, when Sussex actually scored 201 runs for four wickets. Bowley left with three runs on the board, but, on Duleepsinhji joining Harold Gilligan, such a mastery was obtained over the attack that 121 runs came in fifty-five minutes, the total being carried from 52 to 104 in a quarter of an hour.

Duleepsinhji, playing in his very best form, scored 115 in a hundred minutes, and, despite his fierce hitting, made nothing like a mistake. He drove with power, hit to leg and cut with the utmost certainty, and, in addition to lifting Freeman over the ring for six, claimed fourteen fours in a truly admirable display.

Gilligan, with two sixes and five fours, also played finely, and afterwards Langridge and Wensley continued to punish the Kent bowlers, seven of whom were tried before the tea interval. Wensley obtained 61 out of 97 in fifty minutes, nine of his strokes reaching the boundary, and Langridge, batting for nearly two hours and a half, hit six fours and had two strokes increased to five by overthrows.

R. L. Holdsworth, the old Oxford Blue, out of county cricket for two years until last week, showed much of his old skill in scoring 69 not out, and was credited with no fewer than nine fours after batting for an hour and three-quarters.

Considering the size of the score and the fierce hitting, Freeman did uncommonly well to take six wickets at a cost of 131 runs.

Kent lost Bryan with 19 scored, but Hardinge and Woolley played soundly, and were still together at the drawing of stumps, the visitors leaving off 383 behind with nine wickets to fall.

Unfortunately for Kent, they will have to bat a man short. A. P. F. Chapman, who took over the captaincy of the side, had the misfortune to fall while fielding after 22 runs were scored, and, as it happened, injured his left knee so badly as to be compelled to retire from the match. It is thought he will be out of the game for ten days.

Monday

Although they had to bat a man short owing to A. P. F. Chapman being injured, Kent yesterday at Hastings got within 30 runs of the Sussex score of 428.

Kent owed a great deal to Knott, who put together his first 100 of the season and remained unbeaten with 140 to his credit. Despite good batting by Woolley, who stayed for over 100 minutes for 58, which included seven 4's, Kent, who on Saturday scored 40 for one wicket, had five men out for 129 when Knott joined Ashdown, and in the early part of his innings the amateur was none too comfortable.

Following the dismissal of Ashdown, caught at the wicket after batting admirably for two hours, Knott and Wright made runs at a splendid pace, and the amateur, after giving a chance of stumping when 94, reached his 100 in two hours.

Sussex began their second innings by losing Gilligan at 8, while Bowley left at 75. Duleepsinhji, as on Saturday, made light of the Kent bowling, and reaching 50 in under an hour doubled his score in half an hour, reaching his second 100 of the match with a glorious straight drive for 6 off Woolley.

In two hours 200 runs were on the board, and at the drawing of stumps Sussex had made 215 for three wickets in two hours and ten minutes. Duleepsinhji, batting faultlessly for just over two hours, remained unbeaten with 149 to his credit, having hit a 6 and twenty-one 4's. He and Langridge put on 85 in forty minutes. Thus at the close Sussex were 245 runs on with seven wickets to fall.

112

Tuesday

The match at Hastings, which produced an aggregate of 1,451 runs for thirty-six wickets, ended yesterday in Sussex beating Kent by 167. Only once before has a greater number of runs been obtained in a county championship match – that between Surrey and Northamptonshire at Northampton in 1920, in which 1,475 were scored for twenty-seven wickets.

Glorious weather made the annual Festival the most successful ever held at Hastings, and yesterday another large company saw more superb hitting by Duleepsinhji, who, having scored 149 overnight, added 97 in seventy minutes before falling to a catch at long on. He did not play quite so well as on Saturday, or Monday, giving two hard catches but, for the most part, he was master of the Kent bowling, and, batting altogether for three hours and a quarter, hit no fewer than five 6's and thirty-one 4's.

Driving and strokes to leg were the outstanding features in a wonderfully fine display of free batting. Sussex having carried their total of 215 for three wickets to 381 for eight were able to declare soon after half-past twelve, 166 runs having been added in ninety minutes, and thus Kent were set the tremendous task of getting 412 in three hours and forty minutes.

Any hopes that the visitors might have of saving the game – victory, with Chapman still absent, could scarcely come into their calculations – were destroyed when Hardinge and Woolley both left to slip catches with 20 on the board, and soon after luncheon Kent had four men out for 66. There followed a most plucky partnership between Ames and Todd, who, without being rash, attacked the bowling with such success as to put on 128 in seventy-five minutes, but after the tea interval Tate, with the new ball, clean bowled Ames, and Wright fell to a beautiful catch low down off the next delivery. Kent's four outstanding wickets went down in less than half an hour, and shortly before five o'clock the innings closed for 244.

Ames, who batted for two hours and a quarter, gave one very difficult chance when 56, but otherwise played very well indeed, hitting two 6's and sixteen 4's. Tate, taking seven wickets for 58 runs, made his record for the whole match 13 for 194.

Duleepsinhji's feat of scoring 115 and 246 is all the more noteworthy by reason of the fact that only on four previous occasions in first-class cricket has a player made a score of 100 in one innings and over 200 in another. Score:

SUSSEX

Bowley, b Ashdown	3	lbw, b Freeman	30
A. H. H. Gilligan, c Hardinge, b Freeman	56	c Ashdown, b Wright	4
K. S. Duleepsinhji, c Bryan, b Marriott	115	c sub, b Freeman	246
Cook, c Wright, b Freeman	7		
Langridge (James), lbw, b Woolley	80	c Ames, b Ashdown	32
Wensley, c Marriott, b Freeman	61	c Ashdown, b Freeman	33
R. L. Holdsworth, not out	69	lbw, b Marriott	8
Tate, c Ames, b Freeman	5	b Marriott	9
G. S. Grimston, b Freeman	4	b Marriott	6
Cornford, b Marriott	6	not out	6
Hollingdale, b Freeman	3		
B 13, l-b 5, n-b 1	19	B 5, l-b 2	7
Total	428	Total (8 wkts dec.)	381

KENT

Hardinge, b Tate	22	c Duleepsinhji, b Tate	5
J. L. Bryan, c Duleepsinhji, b Tate	3	c Hollingdale, b Tate	17
Woolley, c Hollingdale, b Tate	58	c Duleepsinhji, b Tate	4
Ames, c Duleepsinhji, b Cook	14	b Tate	118
Ashdown, c Cornford, b Tate	63	b Tate	21
Todd, c Wensley, b Hollingdale	6	c sub, b Wensley	43
C. H. Knott, not out	140	not out	26
Wright, c Duleepsinhji, b Wensley	69	c Duleepsinhji, b Tate	0
Freeman, b Tate	0	c Gilligan, b Wensley	0
C. S. Marriott, c Cornford, b Tate	0	c Langridge, b Tate	3
A. P. F. Chapman, absent hurt	0	absent hurt	0
B 6, l-b 15, n-b 2	23	B 5, l-b 1, n-b 1	7
Total	398	Total	244

SUSSEX – First Innings

	O	M	R	W		O	M	R	W
Wright	16	2	61	0	Woolley	16	3	40	1
Ashdown	15	5	62	1	Hardinge	7	1	21	0
Freeman	32.1	3	131	6	Todd	2	0	3	0
Marriott	17	1	91	2					

Woolley bowled one no-ball.

Second Innings

	O	M	R	W		O	M	R	W
Ashdown	19	1	97	1	Marriott	15.2	2	69	3
Wright	18	1	73	1	Woolley	6	0	29	0
Freeman	23	4	106	3					

KENT – First Innings

	O	M	R	W		O	M	R	W
Tate	41	5	136	6	Langridge	8	3	36	0
Wensley	30	6	80	1	Bowley	8	0	37	0
Cook	11	4	30	1	Grimston	9	1	24	0
Hollingdale	9	1	32	1					

Wensley and Hollingdale each bowled one no-ball.

Second Innings

	O	M	R	W		O	M	R	W
Tate	23.3	6	58	7	Grimston	2	0	20	0
Wensley	23	3	85	2	Langridge	5	0	34	0
Bowley	5	0	16	0	Hollingdale	10	4	24	0

Wensley bowled one no-ball.

Umpires – Day and Hardstaff

46: *Sussex v Northamptonshire*
HOVE, 7–9 MAY 1930

This, if anything, was an even greater batting performance by Duleep. His 333 remains the highest score ever made for Sussex, beating a record held by his uncle, Ranji. His treble century was only the 16th made in the Championship and was the fifth highest score. In making his runs in five and a half hours on the first day, Duleep became only the second man (after Frank Foster) to make 300 in a day in the Championship, and his 333 is still the highest score made in the competition in a day. Admittedly, Northamptonshire were easy pickings. In 1930 they came bottom of the Championship, a position they were to fill on seven occasions during the Thirties. With the exception of V.W.C. Jupp (1891–1960), their captain and club secretary, they had no-one of outstanding ability in the side; and Jupp failed in this match. He had earlier played for Sussex and, though batting at four, was principally a medium-pace bowler. He took 1,658 wickets at 23 in his career, but also made 23,296 runs at an average of 30, and did the 'double' in ten consecutive seasons.

If anyone had a better match than Duleep it was Maurice 'Chubby' Tate, who not only scored a century but demolished Northamptonshire in their second innings. In a career that lasted from 1912 to 1937 Tate (1895–1956) took 2,784 wickets at an average of 18, and made 21,717 runs at an average of 25, with a top score of 203. He achieved the 'double' in eight seasons, in three of them taking over 200 wickets to match his 1,000 runs. Ten years into his first-class career he changed his bowling style from off-spinners to medium-pace, and it was in this mode that he had his great success. He played 39 times for England.

Brighton, Wednesday

Sussex started badly in their first home match of the season yesterday at Brighton, losing two wickets for 30 runs, but Duleepsinhji, always master of the bowling, completely changed the aspect of the game with a truly great innings, so that the home side at the tea interval were in a very strong position.

On a rather soft pitch Sussex began by losing Bowley with only 1 run on the board, while at the end of forty-five minutes Parks (J.) fell to a slip catch, the score then being 30. The Northamptonshire bowlers, however, came in for severe punishment afterwards.

Duleepsinhji, scoring all round the wicket with delightful ease, reached 51 out of 73 in little over an hour, and he and Cook, the latter mainly content to defend while the brilliant amateur made runs, had put on 77 in sixty-five minutes for the third wicket, when a great catch sent back the professional.

Clark bowled at a fine pace after luncheon, causing Langridge to give a chance at slip with 7 runs added, and keeping even Duleepsinhji quiet for a time, but, having played himself in again, Duleepsinhji, who was wonderfully quick off his feet and timed the ball with the utmost sureness, drove on either side of the wicket with power, and completed 100 out of 141 in two hours and twenty minutes.

Langridge left at 182, the stand for the fourth wicket having realised 75 in eighty minutes. Then Duleepsinhji, whose batting was marked by some glorious square cuts, got his third 50 in under an hour.

The Northamptonshire bowling was never loose, and the visitors gave little away in the field, but, with the pitch playing very easily, they had a rather thankless task.

It took Duleepsinhji just over four hours to complete 200 out of 293. Tate also hit finely all round the wicket, and the Northamptonshire bowlers were mastered. Duleepsinhji went on to beat his previous highest score – 254 not out for Cambridge against Middlesex, three years ago – and, later, the record individual score ever made for Sussex – 285 not out by his uncle, K. S. Ranjitsinhji, against Somerset at Taunton in 1901. He completed his third 100 in five hours and a quarter.

Meanwhile Tate, hitting at everything, reached his 100 in ninety-five minutes, and, when bowled with the total at 490, the professional had helped to add 255 in an hour and three-quarters. Tate hit two 6's and ten 4's.

Duleepsinhji, batting without mistake of any kind for five hours and a half, was eventually stumped when going well down the pitch, the total then being 514. His great innings of 333 included one 6 and thirty-four 4's.

Thursday

Northamptonshire were engaged in a desperately uphill game against Sussex at Brighton yesterday. The home team, thanks to the brilliant batting of Duleepsinhji and Tate on Wednesday, declared at the overnight total of 521 for seven wickets – made in five hours and three-quarters – and so left their opponents needing 372 to escape the follow-on.

Whatever chance Northamptonshire might have had of accomplishing this was lost during the first hour. J. Parks dismissed Bakewell at 28, and then Wensley, changing ends, bowled Woolley with the total at 32, and, with the next ball, caused Jupp to be taken in the slips. Thereafter the Northamptonshire batsmen were almost entirely confined to defence.

Bellamy was by no means comfortable against J. Parks, but he managed to stay in, and, in partnership with Timms, increased the total by 38 runs in about an hour. After the first wicket fell Tate did not bowl again before luncheon, which was taken with Northamptonshire's score standing at 84 for four wickets.

Two quick successes rewarded the home county when the game was resumed, J. Parks with his second delivery sending back Matthews before a run had been added, and Bellamy, having kept up his end for over ninety minutes, being clean bowled at 102.

Liddell, hitting out with confidence, did something to improve the visitors' position, and after the seventh wicket fell Cox and Thomas engaged in the best partnership of the day, these two adding 62 in fifty minutes.

Maurice Tate

Tate, resuming for the first time since noon, got rid of Cox, who had batted well for over half an hour.

The innings, having lasted four hours, closed for 187, and Northamptonshire had to follow on 334 behind. Another disastrous start was made when the visitors went in again at twenty minutes to five, Bakewell being sent back with 13 runs on the board and Woolley leaving at the same total.

Tate, getting a lot of nip off the pitch, bowled with great effect, and when the fifth wicket fell in fifty minutes with the score at 45, he had taken four of them at a cost of 22 runs. Bellamy, as in the first innings, batted with great steadiness, and Liddell, missed at point when 6, stayed with him until the total had been carried to 97. At the close, however, Northamptonshire, with six men out for 106, were in a hopeless position, 228 runs still being needed to save an innings defeat.

Friday

Just under forty minutes' cricket proved sufficient for Sussex yesterday at Brighton to defeat Northamptonshire in overwhelming fashion by an innings and 209 runs.

The brilliant all-round form of the home county had such a result almost inevitable at the drawing of stumps on Thursday, Northamptonshire, following on 334 behind, having lost six men for 106. Yesterday morning the four outstanding wickets fell for an addition of 19 runs.

Bellamy, as in the first innings, again batted with pluck and skill, and, in at the fall of the third wicket on

Thursday evening, he was last to leave yesterday, his innings of 35, marked by clean driving, lasting for ninety-five minutes. He lost Cox without addition to the overnight score: Thomas was bowled by a 'trimmer,' and the innings, having lasted in all for two hours and twenty minutes, closed for 125.

Tate, cleverly nursed by his captain, bowled with great life as the pitch became faster, and came out with the splendid figures of seven wickets for 45 runs. Cornford was at his best behind the stumps, and, generally, the work of the Sussex men reached a high level. Score:

SUSSEX

Bowley, c Bellamy, b Thomas	1
Parks (J.), c Liddell, b Thomas	9
K. S. Duleepsinhji, st Bellamy, b Matthews	333
Cook, c Liddell, b Clark	19
Langridge (James), b Cox	17
Parks (H.), b Clark	11
Tate, b Partridge	111
A. H. H. Gilligan, not out	8
Wensley, not out	0
L-b 6, n-b 6	12
Total (7 wkts. dec.)	**521**

Hollingdale and Cornford did not bat.

NORTHAMPTONSHIRE

Woolley, b Wensley	18	c Duleepsinhji, b Wensley	4
Bakewell, lbw, b Parks (J.)	12	b Tate	7
Timms (J. W.), c Parks (J.), b Langridge	19	lbw, b Tate	20
V. W. C. Jupp, c Duleepsinhji, b Wensley	0	lbw, b Tate	11
Bellamy, b Wensley	21	c Cornford, b Tate	35
Matthews, lbw, b Parks (J.)	13	c Duleepsinhji, b Tate	0
Liddell, c Gilligan, b Bowley	18	c Cook, b Tate	28
Cox, lbw, b Tate	40	c Cornford, b Cook	4
Thomas, lbw, b Wensley	29	b Hollingdale	11
Partridge, not out	3	b Tate	2
Clark, b Tate	1	not out	0
B 9, l-b 4	13	B 2, l-b 1	3
Total	**187**	**Total**	**125**

SUSSEX – First Innings

	O	M	R	W		O	M	R	W
Clark	27	1	75	2	Jupp	20	3	92	0
Thomas	29	11	69	2	Cox	11	2	50	1
Partridge	12	0	80	1	Liddell	2	0	16	0
Matthews	22	2	101	1	Timms	3	0	26	0

Clark bowled five no-balls and Matthews one no-ball.

NORTHAMPTONSHIRE – First Innings

	O	M	R	W		O	M	R	W
Tate	9.5	1	18	2	Langridge	14	7	21	1
Wensley	28	10	45	4	Hollingdale	10	2	21	0
Parks (J.)	22	11	37	2	Bowley	13	2	32	1

Second Innings

	O	M	R	W		O	M	R	W
Tate	20.2	3	45	7	Bowley	4	2	6	0
Wensley	14	5	41	1	Hollingdale	8	3	14	1
Parks (J.)	2	0	12	0	Cook	1	0	4	1

Umpires – Toone and Chester

47: *Warwickshire v Nottinghamshire*
BIRMINGHAM, 22–24 JULY 1931

The two George Gunns, senior and junior, are the only father and son to score centuries in the same innings. The elder Gunn (1879–1958) was part of a dynasty of Nottinghamshire cricketers that included his brother and uncle as well as his son. Between 1902 and 1932, he made 35,208 runs at an average

of 36. Although regarded as the greatest Notts batsman, he played just 15 times for England, and only once at home; yet he averaged 40 in tests. He acquired a reputation as an unnecessarily defensive batsman, which counted against him. His son (1905–1957) played for Nottinghamshire from 1928 until 1950, though was never in the same class as his father, making 10,026 runs in his career at an average of under 30, and his 281 wickets costing over 35 each.

In this dour match, where each wicket fell at a cost of over 100 runs and not even the first innings were completed, Carr, the Nottinghamshire captain, was reduced to bowling underarm. Croom (1896–1946), Warwickshire's most successful batsman, played nearly 400 times for the county between 1922 and 1939, scoring 17,692 runs at an average of 31. This was his best season, in which he made 1,584 runs at an average of almost 39. Bates (1895–1971), the son of the Edgbaston groundsman, played for the county from 1913 to 1935, making 19,380 runs at an average of 28. The Rev. John Parsons (1890–1981), one of the county's best bats, had been a professional before the Great War. Commissioned during it, he won the Military Cross and played as an amateur on his return; then turned professional for five seasons; and finally was ordained, and reverted to amateur status. He had the rare distinction of playing on both sides in Gentlemen v Players matches.

Birmingham, Wednesday

Still very weak in bowling, Notts had a very disheartening experience yesterday, Warwickshire running up the huge total of 394 for three wickets.

The home county, who included the Rev. J. H. Parsons for D. G. Foster, made full use of their chance of batting first on a firm pitch, and by tea-time they scored 271 runs for only one wicket.

Croom and Kemp-Welch put on 158 for the opening partnership in two hours and twenty-five minutes. Kemp-Welch batted extremely well, but chief honours rested with Croom, whose run of success in recent engagements has been one of the features of county cricket. He reached 100 out of 185 in three hours. This was his sixth century of the season and his third consecutive three-figure innings.

After Kemp-Welch had left, Bates batted in enterprising fashion. Croom, who in the thirties had two escapes, enjoyed further good fortune, when he was missed by A. Staples at slip. Bates later scored with freedom, his driving being especially good. Croom was caught at slip at 332, the partnership having realised 174 runs in two and a half hours. In his admirable innings Croom hit sixteen 4's.

Thursday

Warwickshire took their total to 511 for three wickets before they declared against Notts at Birmingham yesterday, but it does not look as if the visitors will be defeated, as they are batting so carefully that they have lost only one wicket and have scored 163 runs.

Against a mediocre attack the Rev. J. H. Parsons and Kilner, the overnight not-outs, made runs easily at the start. There was one slight delay owing to a shower, and later on A. W. Carr, the Notts captain, went on with lobs. This type of bowling had not been seen on the Edgbaston ground since the days of G. H. Simpson-Hayward, the Worcestershire amateur. In five overs Carr was hit for 31 runs. In all the fourth partnership realised 164 runs in rather less than two hours, and Warwickshire batted seven hours and ten minutes for their total.

Kilner was in for nearly two hours, hitting twelve 4's, while Parsons, batting for two hours and ten minutes, sent the ball nine times to the boundary.

Notts required 363 to avoid the follow-on, G. Gunn and Keeton scarcely attempting to score except when perfectly safe to do so.

The opening stand realised 123 runs before Keeton was caught at slip. He had batted for three hours and ten minutes, and he hit only five 4's. Gunn remained to the end.

Croom, who batted so well on Wednesday, did not field, as he was suffering from an attack of muscular rheumatism in the right shoulder.

Friday

A remarkable scoring match at Birmingham ended in a draw yesterday, but the closing stages were not without interest, for Notts made a great and successful

Gunn – father and son

attempt to gain the major points for a lead on the first innings. The game went on a little longer to enable G. V. Gunn, who batted so well at an important period, to complete his first 100 in first-class cricket.

Gunn and Harris followed up the fine work of the earlier Notts batsmen with an unbroken partnership of 138, which gave Notts the lead.

Notts began the day with 163 runs on the board, and only one man out, but they were still 348 runs behind. Walker helped George Gunn to add 83 runs, and then Gunn and Carr put on 61 before Gunn left. He hit thirteen 4's in his century, which stood out as a wonderful testimony to the fitness and ability of a man now in his 53rd year. It was quite a point of interest that father and son should in the same innings have each put together scores of three-figures. In the match no fewer than 1,032 runs were scored for the loss of only 10 wickets. Score:

WARWICKSHIRE

G. D. Kemp-Welch, c & b Harris ... 60	Kilner, not out 81
Croom, c Staples, b Oates 159	B 10, l-b 9, w 1, n-b 2 22
Bates, c Lilley, b Oates 105	
Rev. J. H. Parsons, not out 84	Total (3 wkts dec.) 511

R. E. S. Wyatt, Santall, Smart, Sanders, Mayer, and Paine did not bat.

NOTTS

Gunn (G.), c Paine, b Santall 183	Staples (A.), c Mayer, b Wyatt 8
Keeton, c Sanders, b Paine 72	Lilley, b Paine 30
Walker, b Mayer 29	Gunn (G. V.) not out 100
A. W. Carr, c Parsons, b Sanders .. 38	Harris, not out 41
Payton, lbw, b Wyatt 6	B 10, l-b 3, w 1 14
	Total (7 wkts) 521

Oates and Barratt did not bat.

WARWICKSHIRE – First Innings

	O	M	R	W		O	M	R	W
Barratt	35	6	76	0	Gunn (G. V.)	34	4	115	0
Carr	16	2	71	0	Gunn (G.)	8	1	39	0
Harris	33	5	99	1	Oates	28	3	89	2

NOTTS – First Innings

	O	M	R	W		O	M	R	W
Mayer	46	18	106	1	Santall	24	4	72	1
Wyatt	51	12	134	2	Parsons	4	2	5	0
Paine	74	24	125	2	Bates	1	0	3	0
Sanders	34	11	62	1					

48: *Essex v Yorkshire*
LEYTON, 15–17 JUNE 1932

Percy Holmes and Herbert Sutcliffe formed the most famous county opening partnership of the inter-war years. Their 555 for the first wicket was the highest then made for any wicket in first-class cricket, beating by one run Brown and Tunnicliffe's record, also for Yorkshire, against Derbyshire in 1898. It remained a first wicket record until 1976–77, when it was overtaken in Pakistan by Waheed Mirza and Mansoor Akhtar, who put on 561 for the Karachi Whites against Quetta. Their achievement prompted the editor of Wisden to write furiously about the dubious nature of high-scoring records being made in Pakistan, since some teams there were being accorded first-class status when they had no right to it. So easily were Essex overcome by Yorkshire, the reigning and future champions, that the same might have been said about them. Perhaps the most comic feature, though, was that once Sutcliffe had thrown away his wicket (having passed the old record) it seemed that he and Holmes had not passed it at all: an uncredited no-ball was 'found' on close inspection of the scorebook but, despite our correspondent's insistence that this was so, the Essex captain, Gray, later admitted to agreeing to its 'discovery'; so, really, the record was not broken at all.

Sutcliffe (1894–1978) scored 50,138 runs at an average of 52, in a career that lasted from 1919 to 1945. He played 54 times for England, scoring 4,555 runs at an average of 61, a magnificent record. His 313 was the only 300 of his career, in which he made 149 centuries. He and Holmes put on 100 for the first wicket 74 times. Holmes (1886–1971) hit two 300s in a career that lasted from 1913 to 1933, made 30,573 runs at an average of 42, and played seven times for England.

Leyton, Wednesday
By White Willow

Under the flaming skies at Leyton yesterday, Yorkshire's opening batsmen, Holmes and Sutcliffe, were kings of the match from morn till evening, the Essex bowlers and fieldsmen being their abject slaves in a bondage that is not yet ended. Opening the innings for their side, these famous partners put on 423 runs, of which Sutcliffe has scored 231 and Holmes 180, and they were still invincible at the close of play.

As the sun went down the sky Holmes and Sutcliffe nearly crowned their magnificent achievement by creating a world's first-wicket record, but this remains a possibility in store for to-day. Their monarchy has become so absolute that it seems as if only a revolution will end it – or else a captain's order to hit, or an early declaration.

Holmes and Sutcliffe – one of history's most famous partnerships

They might already have broken the record if they had not dealt mercifully between lunch and tea with an attack that was then at a standstill, helpless and without hope of anything except that one or the other would get himself out. A feat which was also missed through that 60-an-hour run-getting, instead of about twice the rate, is the completion of Sutcliffe's 1,000 for the season. He needed only 14 when stumps were drawn.

That no more than 124 runs were scored in two hours after luncheon, on a pitch that resembled a slab of marble, caused a slight barracking among a crowd that were otherwise grateful and generous. At the end of the morning 113 were on the board, Sutcliffe being 61 and Holmes 50, but the moderate pace of this pre-lunch period may be explained by the fact that the batsmen were playing themselves in, and perhaps a little more cautiously, because Holmes had been missed behind the wicket off a fast ball from Nichols when he was only 3.

This lost chance, which was all the more unfortunate because Sheffield was one of the few Essex men who maintained a high standard in the field throughout a wearying day, is already a tragic blunder. Neither batsman tempted fate apart from that, but they could not have been so sober after lunch only for that reason.

At 3 o'clock, when the 150 went up, Sutcliffe was travelling through the 80's, and Holmes was in the 60's, and yet it was more than half an hour later, after he had batted three hours and a quarter, that Sutcliffe reached his century – his 97th – out of 195, and Holmes took half-an-hour longer, the score then being 219.

Holmes used fewer strokes than his partner, so that it was not surprising to find Sutcliffe leaving him behind after tea, when Yorkshire were 237. During the third and last of the day's two-hour spells Sutcliffe hit delightfully, and increased his total by 110, while Holmes made 71. So far Sutcliffe has scored a 6 and twenty-one 4's, and Holmes sixteen 4's.

Essex marshalled every possible bowler against them – eight altogether – but although the flight of the ball was made slightly puzzling by a refreshing breeze, and Nichols worked like a galley-oarsman, only Smith gave an impression of other than mediocrity. Within two days the Essex attack has had such

punishment at the hands of Surrey and Yorkshire that 732 runs, including four centuries, have been scored by the batsmen without the consolation of a single wicket.

Thursday

Unique and thrilling deeds have made the match between Essex and Yorkshire unforgettable. Yesterday at Leyton the expected happened, and Holmes and Sutcliffe, continuing their great partnership, created a world's first-wicket record in circumstances which led to a sensation off the field of play. And then, facing a score of 555, at which Yorkshire declared with only one wicket down, Essex caused a further sensation by collapsing in a fashion that means inevitable defeat.

Nothing but a breakdown in the weather can save them, and that appears improbable. Splendid bowling by Bowes was succeeded by a deadly seven overs from Verity, during which he took five wickets for 8 runs, and Essex were all out for 78. Following on 477 behind, they showed rather more courage, and at the close had scored 92 for five. To-day they require 385 to save defeat by an innings.

Prodigious figures! But they have arisen almost inevitably out of a prodigious game that took its place in cricket history at one o'clock exactly. For an hour and a half in the morning Holmes and Sutcliffe had gathered runs majestically, the previous night's total of 483 being carried into the fifth hundred in fifty minutes. Before that, of course, Sutcliffe had completed his 1,000 runs for the season.

Sutcliffe has also broken his personal batting record of 255 – made, curiously, against the same county at Southend eight years ago. Thus when he reached 300 it was for the first time in his career. Finally, to the accompaniment of enthusiastic applause, Sutcliffe hit Eastman twice to the boundary in the same over – he made thirty-three 4's in all, and Holmes twenty – and the immortal names of Brown and Tunnicliffe – Yorkshiremen again – were relegated to second place in the annals of first-wicket partnerships after standing supreme for 34 years.

Now came that off-the-field sensation. Sutcliffe had, straightway and a little prematurely thrown away his wicket by playing on to Eastman with a very casual stroke indeed, whereupon the Yorkshire innings was declared at 555 for one. But as Holmes and Sutcliffe stood in front of the score-board waiting to be photographed, the figures were altered to 554!

The crowd had flocked excitedly across the pitch, and they loudly demanded that the record-breaking score should be restored. Eventually this was done, an overlooked no-ball explaining the disparity between score books and score board. Later on I was permitted an inspection of the score books, and there is no doubt about the no-ball having been registered when it occurred – in Daer's thirtieth over.

By sheer mischance, however, the scorers had omitted to place their customary distinguishing mark above the entry of the seven-ball over, and their reckoning and checking did not include it. It was on a research that the omission was rectified. Let this statement of the case dispose for once and all of any lurking suspicion that Holmes and Sutcliffe are not really entitled to the great honour.

All afternoon telegrams of congratulation to the day's heroes poured into the ground, one of the earliest being from Lord Tennyson, the Hampshire captain. At first the messengers were allowed on to the field, but when they threatened to become a procession the telegrams were heaped up in the Yorkshire dressing-room instead, and opened at the close of play.

And Holmes and Sutcliffe deserved every one of them. Theirs had been a magnificent feat in all ways, especially of endurance, for Holmes is 45 and Sutcliffe 38, whereas Brown and Tunnicliffe were 29 and 32 respectively.

What a contrast of riches and poverty there was when Essex began their reply a few minutes before lunch! One wicket for no runs, with Crawley clean bowled by Bowes! No wonder the batsmen who came next, already without heart, were easy victims first to Bowes' pace off the fiery pitch and then to Verity's superbly-flighted bowling into the wind. At 19, 19, 48, 59, 60, 66, 72, 74, 78 ten wickets toppled, Nichols, O'Connor, and Eastman scoring 61 between them.

Verity's success, those who deny him the ability to 'flight' the ball will be interested to note, was all gained in the air. He opened with three maidens and two wickets for no runs. When Essex followed on it was Bowes who chiefly worked the havoc – and he was barracked for making the ball fly.

Leyland had to retire through a painful knock on the knee when fielding against Crawley's refreshingly hard hitting, but he hopes to be fit for the Test trial on Saturday.

Friday

Yorkshire needed only one more achievement to crown their epoch-making conquest at Leyton yesterday, that of victory itself, and this they had gained by one o'clock, Essex being overwhelmingly defeated by an innings and 313 runs.

There was naturally no fight left in the losers, and Bowes and Verity found them easy prey, with the exception of Nichols. This right-armed bowler and left-handed batsman played a really stylish innings, just as he had done in the first knock, and he remained unbeaten at the end, after a resistance that lasted three hours and forty minutes. Once he had the audacity to hit a no-ball off Bowes for 6, and altogether he scored six well-placed 4's.

Continuing the Essex second innings at 92 for five, with Bray, Nichols saw his captain stumped off Verity at 128 and Taylor caught in the slips off the same bowler at 148. By that time Essex were in a hopeless situation, but Nichols had the consolation of passing his 50 – the only one scored for the side all through the match – after two hours, and soon afterwards the innings ended.

Bowes took the last two wickets, making the ball fly high, as he had done on the previous day. He has incurred much criticism thereby, but unjustly, for a bowler of pace has a perfect right to exploit a fiery turf in that fashion as long as he does not aim at the batsman's body, and Bowes would scorn to do such a thing.

Verity's flighting of the ball won him the very fine figures for the match of ten wickets for 53 runs, and thus he had a good share in a great triumph for his county, one which, following that over Kent in the first part of the week, may well prove to be the start of an all-conquering march to the championship. Score:

YORKSHIRE

Holmes, not out	224	
Sutcliffe, b Eastman	313	B 13, 1-b 3, n-b 2 18
		Total (1 wkt dec.) 555

A. Mitchell, M. Leyland, W. Barber, A. B. Sellars, A. Wood, A. C. Rhodes, G. G. Macaulay, H. Verity, and W. E. Bowes did not bat.

ESSEX

L. G. Crawley, b Bowes	0	c Sutcliffe, b Bowes	27
Pope, c Rhodes, b Bowes	6	c Mitchell, b Bowes	9
O'Connor, b Bowes	20	c Rhodes, b Bowes	7
Cutmore, lbw, b Bowes	0	b Verity	1
Nichols, b Verity	25	not out	59
Eastman, c Sutcliffe, b Macaulay	16	c Barber, b Verity	19
C. Bray, c and b Verity	1	st Wood, b Verity	6
Taylor, c Macaulay, b Verity	5	c Macaulay, b Verity	13
Sheffield, c and b Verity	0	c Sutcliffe, b Verity	5
A. G. Daer, c and b Verity	0	c Mitchell, b Bowes	0
Smith (P.), not out	2	c Rhodes, b Bowes	0
B	3	B 15, 1-b 1, n-b 2 18
Total 78		Total 164

YORKSHIRE – First Innings

	O	M	R	W		O	M	R	W
Nichols	31	4	105	0	Eastman	22.4	2	97	1
Daer	40	5	106	0	Crawley	3	0	7	0
Smith	46	10	128	0	Taylor	4	0	14	0
O'Connor	23	5	73	0	Bray	1	0	7	0

ESSEX – First Innings

	O	M	R	W		O	M	R	W
Bowes	12	1	38	4	Macaulay	7.1	2	14	1
Rhodes	10	5	15	0	Verity	7	3	8	5

Second Innings

	O	M	R	W		O	M	R	W
Bowes	23.4	5	47	5	Verity	30	12	45	5
Rhodes	9	5	23	0	Macaulay	16	5	31	0

49: Kent v Warwickshire
FOLKESTONE, 29 JUNE–1 JULY 1932

'Tich' Freeman (1888–1965) was the most prolific bowler of the inter-war years. He is the only man to take 300 wickets in a season, taking 304 at 18 each in 1928. He played virtually non-stop that summer, in 37 first-class matches, which helped him rather, though it was still a phenomenal striking-rate. As Wisden records, 'In four consecutive seasons (1928–1931) A.P. Freeman took 1,122 wickets, and in eight consecutive seasons (1928–1935) 2,090 wickets. In each of these seasons he took over 200 wickets.' In a career lasting from 1914 to 1936 he took 3,776 wickets at 18.42, with only Wilfred Rhodes ahead of him, and 17 times took 100 wickets in a season. He played just 12 tests, and none at all during his prime years of county cricket. He twice took 17 wickets in a match, this being the second time, the first being for Kent against Sussex at Hove in 1922, where he got them more cheaply (for 67 runs). Nine times in all he took 15 wickets or more in a match and in the previous season, 1931, he did this three times (he only managed it twice in 1932). He took all ten wickets in an innings three times, and nine wickets five times.

Kent, enormously strong in batting as well as bowling, were enjoying a good run in the Championship. 1932 was the second of three consecutive seasons in which they came third. Warwickshire were far from a bad side but were only spared complete humiliation by Wyatt, their captain. Bob Wyatt (b. 1901) was one of the finest amateur batsmen of the period. He played for Warwickshire from 1923 to 1939, and then enjoyed six seasons after the war with Worcestershire, whom he also captained. He made over 39,405 runs at an average of 40 during his career, including 85 centuries, and played 40 times for England, whom he also led.

Folkestone, Wednesday

There is really nothing for it after to-day's breathless happenings but to christen this Folkestone Festival afresh. It is Freeman's feast, and is rapidly becoming the Folkestone fiasco. For the second time in a week and the fourth time in the four matches of two summers, the game looks like being won and lost, or virtually so, on the second day, twenty-three wickets having fallen to-day for 350 runs.

Kent were all out by three p.m., and so were Warwickshire by 5.15. Kent led on the first innings by 45, and they have increased their lead by 47 for the loss of three batsmen in the second innings. The issue appears an open one still, but not to those who understand the state of the wicket, which is the villain of the piece. It is a mixture of marl and chalk, and in a few hours it became crumbling dust – a spin bowler's paradise; in other words, Freeman's paradise.

The badly handicapped Midlanders will work a little miracle if they avoid defeat. There is no knowing what record of brevity for a first-class fixture would have been set up if Woolley had not covered himself with the glory that escaped him in the Test match. He, and Wyatt later on, were the only batsmen who made substantial scores, and his delectable bat flashed out with 92 runs before lunch, including thirteen 4's and a mighty 6.

This innings may prove to be a vital factor in the result, for after lunch, when the score was 150 for four, what a change came over the scene! The scene-shifters to begin with were Mayer and Foster, who is playing his first match this season. In fewer than ten overs six wickets fell on that hot turf for 24 runs.

In 40 minutes after lunch Mayer took three wickets for 5 runs in five overs, and Foster three for 19 in 4.3 overs. Their success, however, was ironic. Had they known it, they were merely preparing the way for Freeman's spin bowling by pounding the pitch into powder.

The little Kent wonder continued his deadly triumph of Monday as though he had never paused in it. The Warwickshire batsmen were utterly bewildered and helpless immediately, and Wyatt struggled vainly to stop the collapse after coming in when wickets had fallen at 23 and 28. Bates scored 14 in a desperate over off Ashdown, and was beaten by Freeman at 48.

Then Wyatt, looking very grim, hit 12 off one over from Hardinge, and a 6 off the next into the marquee occupied by the Brotherhood of Cheerful Sparrows, slightly injuring one of them. Nobody scored off Freeman, and he got the fourth wicket at 86, and becoming really irresistible after tea took five of the remaining six wickets in half an hour for 4 runs in four overs, of which two were maidens! Altogether his figures were:

19 overs, 7 maidens, 31 runs, 8 wickets

This astonishing man has already had 21 victims at the festival. In the circumstances Wyatt's undefeated stand of 85 minutes was splendid.

Leading by 45, Kent batted again at 5.30, but although they did well in adding three more victims to the day's holocaust, they must have envied Kent their Freeman.

Thursday

The climax of the 'Freeman festival' came at 5.15 this evening, when Kent's mighty atom among bowlers won for his county their fourth successive victory by taking his seventeenth wicket in the match and his thirtieth in four days during the Folkestone Cricket Week.

Warwickshire, apart from Wyatt, their captain, have been his helpless victims from start to finish, and they were beaten by 74 runs. This is the second time in his career that Freeman has captured seventeen wickets in one match, a world record equalled by others, but never outdone.

The condition of the Folkestone pitch, to which I referred yesterday, and which is being characterised by the players and other principals as absurd, must not be allowed to detract from Freeman's achievement. Nevertheless, it has to be noted that an inquest was held out in the middle after play ended, as well it might be. For all to-morrow, like Tuesday, will be left idle, involving a heavy financial loss for the week.

The match would have been over still earlier if the pitch had not turned itself for some hours into a hindrance to Freeman instead of a help. The spin on that grotesque patch of powdered chalk became so exaggerated that Freeman had difficulty in adapting himself to it, and while he was doing so Warwickshire's fight for runs proved steadily fruitful.

Kent had again batted poorly against fast bowling, and Hardinge's not out innings, lasting two hours and ten minutes, stood out splendidly. Chiefly through him the Southern side finished their second innings 214 ahead, Foster and Mayer sharing the honours with him.

Warwickshire scored nearly 50 for one wicket down in their second innings, but the ball was baffling the bat as well as the bowler, and at 49 the second wicket fell, and then Freeman seemed to have taken the measure of the pitch and got three quick wickets at 49, 55 and 58.

STAND FOR WARWICK

Santall and Wyatt, however, added 46 in 25 minutes, bringing Warwickshire within a not impossible distance of victory, the hundred going up for only five wickets. Then Freeman, with the triumphant cunning of a magician, pitched his delivery nearly a yard outside Santall's leg stump, and the batsman, thinking himself safe, attempted a huge agricultural mow; missed, and was dismayed to hear the stumps rattling from a ball that crept right round his legs. Nothing could stop Freeman after that, and the five last wickets

fell to him at 104, 108, 114, 126 and 140.

Wyatt was then one short of his second 50 in the match. He had batted two really great fighting innings, and he takes his place next to Freeman as an outstanding figure in Kent's eighth victory of the season. Score:

KENT

A. M. Crawley, b Foster	5	lbw, b Mayer	2
Ashdown, c Santall, b Foster	30	b Foster	5
Woolley, c Wyatt, b Mayer	92	c Foster, b Mayer	25
Ames, c Croom, b Mayer	12	lbw, b Foster	16
Hardinge, c Kilner, b Mayer	18	not out	66
A. P. F. Chapman, c Kilner, b Mayer	3	c Smart, b Mayer	1
I. Akers-Douglas, b Mayer	1	c Smart, b Foster	20
B. H. Valentine, c Wyatt, b Foster	3	c Wyatt, b Foster	3
Todd, b Foster	2	c Roberts, b Foster	13
Watt, not out	1	b Foster	4
Freeman, b Foster	4	b Mayer	4
W 1, n-b 2	3	B 2, 1-b 8	10
Total	**174**	**Total**	**169**

WARWICKSHIRE

G. D. Kemp-Welch, run out	9	st Ames, b Freeman	3
Croom, lbw, b Freeman	12	lbw, b Freeman	28
Bates, st Ames, b Freeman	18	c Valentine, b Watt	14
R. E. S. Wyatt, not out	59	not out	49
Rev. J. H. Parsons, c Ashdown, b Freeman	11	c Hardinge, b Freeman	1
Kilner, lbw, b Freeman	13	lbw, b Freeman	1
Santall, st Ames, b Freeman	1	b Freeman	21
Roberts, st Ames, b Freeman	0	c Ashdown, b Freeman	0
Smart, st Ames, b Freeman	1	b Freeman	6
D. G. Foster, b Freeman	0	b Freeman	6
Mayer, c Ames, b Watt	0	lbw, b Freeman	3
B 4, 1-b 1	5	B 3, 1-b 3, n-b 2	8
Total	**129**	**Total**	**140**

KENT – First Innings

	O	M	R	W		O	M	R	W
Mayer	13	2	25	5	Roberts	3	0	28	0
Foster	18.3	1	81	5	Santall	3	0	14	0
Wyatt	5	1	23	0					

Second Innings

	O	M	R	W		O	M	R	W
Mayer	21.2	4	48	4	Wyatt	5	0	15	0
Foster	24	5	82	6	Croom	3	0	9	0
Santall	5	2	5	0					

WARWICKSHIRE – First Innings

	O	M	R	W		O	M	R	W
Ashdown	14	3	63	0	Hardinge	2	0	19	0
Freeman	19	7	31	8	Watt	3.3	1	11	1

Second Innings

	O	M	R	W		O	M	R	W
Watt	23	3	71	1	Freeman	22.4	5	61	9

'Tich' Freeman

50: Yorkshire v Nottinghamshire
LEEDS, 9–12 JULY 1932

Hedley Verity (1905–1943) was England's premier slow left-arm bowler in the 1930s, taking over the role at Yorkshire from Wilfred Rhodes. In a career that lasted just only from 1930 to 1939, he took 1,956 wickets at under 15 each. In nine seasons he took over 100 wickets, and three times over 200, in a decade that produced some of the most prolific batsmen and batting cricket has ever seen. He twice took all ten in an innings, though no-one in the history of the first-class game has ever taken all ten so cheaply as Verity did in this match against Nottinghamshire, at just a run each. He comfortably beat the existing record, of 10–18 by George Geary for Leicestershire against Glamorgan in 1929. Five times Verity took 15 wickets in a match (and the following year would take 17–91 against Essex at Leyton, his county's first appearance there since Holmes and Sutcliffe's 555 partnership), and this was the second time he had taken all ten: the previous

Hedley Verity

summer he had taken 10–36 against Glamorgan. On seven other occasions he took nine wickets in an innings. The hat-trick Verity took in this match was the first of two in his career. He remained at the peak of his profession until the war came. Commissioned into the Green Howards, he was killed in action by a sniper in Sicily in 1943, cricket's most tragic loss of the war.

Harold Larwood (b. 1904) and Bill Voce (1909–1984) were the leading opening bowling partnership of the era, and both proved the legend that when Nottinghamshire wanted a fast bowler it went to a colliery and whistled down the pit. Both Larwood, who took 1,427 wickets at under 18, and Voce, who took 1,558 wickets at 23 in their careers, were central figures in the 'Bodyline' crisis of the next winter.

Leeds, Saturday

Notts batted all day at Leeds, where, after losing five wickets for 67, they recovered splendidly, to score 234.

Notts profited from mistakes in the field. Shipston was let off before he had scored, Keeton was missed when 4, and later Gunn should have been stumped.

Keeton, first to leave at 15, played a ball on to his wicket without removing the bails, but one of them, the umpires discovered, on close examination, had been dislodged from its groove, and Keeton was accordingly given out. Carr stayed half an hour without scoring, and A. Staples took twenty minutes over three runs. Walker batted two hours and a quarter for his 36.

Harris and G. V. Gunn pulled the game round somewhat in a sixth partnership that realised 53 in seventy minutes, and Gunn and Lilley added 39. Gunn was given a life at 25.

The partnership of the innings, however, was that between Lilley and Larwood, who put on 74 in 85 minutes, Larwood hitting a 6 off Verity, and four 4's. Larwood was top scorer with 48.

Then, in two overs, Leyland dismissed Larwood, Voce, and S. Staples without conceding a run, and by 6.15 Notts were all out.

Monday

With the exception of Holmes and Barber, who shared in a valuable third-wicket partnership, the Yorkshire batsmen, replying to the total of 234 put together by Notts on Saturday, collapsed against the bowling of

Larwood and Voce at Leeds. When a thunderstorm broke over the ground at 3.55, the champions, with only one wicket to fall, were still 71 behind.

The third ball of the day began Yorkshire's downfall, Sutcliffe giving a catch to third slip before he had scored. Mitchell, after a confident start, was hit on the back of the hand by a rising ball from Larwood, and had to retire. Leyland failing, two wickets were down for 37.

Holmes, making some pretty late cuts off Larwood, scored readily, reaching his 50 in ninety minutes. But after lunch, when 12,000 people were present, Holmes had his leg stump knocked out of the ground with the score at 122. Holmes had seven 4's in his 65, and he and Barber put on 85 together.

With one run added, both Sellers and Barber were out, Mitchell then returning to continue his innings, but at 126 rain caused an interruption of a quarter of an hour. Two runs had been scored afterwards when Wood left; Rhodes put up a simple catch to short leg seven later; at 152 Verity was bowled, and Mitchell a little later was run out. The light deteriorated, and with the total at 163 for nine wickets the players left the field – just in time to avoid a drenching.

Larwood bowled magnificently following the luncheon interval, in one spell dismissing three batsmen for three runs.

Tuesday

An amazing bowling performance, never before achieved in first-class cricket, was accomplished by Verity, of Yorkshire, at Leeds yesterday.

Verity took all ten Notts wickets, including the hat trick, for ten runs.

This great achievement enabled Yorkshire to gain an unexpected victory, which takes them to the head of the championship table.

Sixteen maidens in under twenty overs! And never was so great an effort made at such a timely moment, for it justified a bold declaration by the Yorkshire captain, bringing victory to a side which in the morning seemed to have no chance of success.

Overnight Notts had scored 234, and Larwood and Voce between them had dismissed nine Yorkshiremen for 163 – which left them still 71 behind with only a wicket to fall.

Yesterday morning the pitch was still affected by the rain which had curtailed play on Monday, and, the start being delayed until 12.30, Sellers decided to stake everything on the ability of his bowlers. May the success of his gamble be linked with Verity's triumph as an inspiration to captains.

Notts were all out for 67 and then Sutcliffe and Holmes confounded the prophets by knocking off the 139 runs needed for victory with a freedom that added to the wonder of Verity's achievement. True, the wicket had recovered, but a sudden metamorphosis is inconceivable.

Furthermore, when Notts started their second innings, Keeton and Shipston scored steadily, and by lunch-time had obtained 38 without being parted. Up to that point neither batsman had appeared to be in the slightest trouble. Yet in seventy minutes after the interval the side were out for the addition of 29 runs.

The first wicket pair increased their stand to 44 when Keeton fell to a catch at slip. With three runs added Shipston was taken at the wicket, and Carr quickly put up a catch in the long field.

At 63, Verity, getting rid of Walker, Harris, and Gunn with consecutive balls, achieved the hat-trick; with the last two balls of his next over he sent back A. Staples and Larwood, and ended the innings by dismissing Voce and S. Staples with the third and fourth balls of the following over. In his last two overs and four balls Verity took seven wickets for three runs.

Holmes and Sutcliffe hit off the runs in little more than an hour and a half. Holmes hit nine 4's and Sutcliffe four in their 72nd opening partnership of three figures.

This is the second successive season that Verity has taken all ten wickets in an innings, a sequence equalled by only one other player – Freeman, of Kent, whose record is three seasons running. Last year Verity skittled out Warwickshire on the same ground for 36 runs. Score:

NOTTS

Keeton, b Rhodes	9	c Macaulay, b Verity ... 21
Shipston, b Macaulay	8	c Wood, b Verity ... 21
Walker, c Barber, b Bowes	36	c Macaulay, b Verity ... 11
A. W. Carr, c Barber, b Verity	0	c Barber, b Verity ... 0
Staples (A.), b Macaulay	3	c Macaulay, b Verity ... 7
Harris, lbw, b Leyland	35	c Holmes, b Verity ... 0
Gunn (G. V.), b Verity	31	lbw, b Verity ... 0
Lilley, not out	46	not out ... 3
Larwood, b Leyland	48	c Sutcliffe, b Verity ... 0
Voce, b Leyland	0	c Holmes, b Verity ... 0
Staples (S. J.), b Leyland	0	st Wood, b Verity ... 0
B 8, l-b 6, w 2, n-b 2	18	B 3, n-b 1 ... 4
Total	234	Total ... 67

YORKSHIRE

Holmes, b Larwood	65	not out ... 77
Sutcliffe, c Voce, b Larwood	0	not out ... 54
Mitchell, run out	24	
Leyland, b Voce	5	
Barber, c and b Larwood	34	
A. B. Sellers, b Staples (A.)	0	
Wood, b Larwood	1	
Rhodes, c Staples, b Voce	3	
Verity, b Larwood	12	
Macaulay, not out	8	
Bowes, not out	1	
B 5, l-b 5	10	B 4, l-b 4 ... 8
Total (9 wkts dec.)	163	Total (no wkt.) ... 139

NOTTS – First Innings

	O	M	R	W		O	M	R	W
Bowes	31	9	55	1	Macaulay	24	10	34	2
Rhodes	28	8	49	1	Leyland	8.2	3	14	4
Verity	41	13	64	2					

Second Innings

	O	M	R	W		O	M	R	W
Bowes	5	0	19	0	Verity	19.4	16	10	10
Macaulay	23	9	34	0					

YORKSHIRE – First Innings

	O	M	R	W		O	M	R	W
Larwood	22	4	73	5	Staples (S. J.)	7	2	8	0
Voce	22	2	52	0	Staples (A.)	11	3	20	1

Second Innings

	O	M	R	W		O	M	R	W
Larwood	3	0	14	0	Staples (A.)	6	1	25	0
Staples (S. J.)	18.4	5	37	0	Harris	3	0	12	0
Voce	10	0	43	0					

51: Sussex v Middlesex
HOVE, 5–8 AUGUST 1933

The 490 scored for the first wicket by Bowley and Langridge remains a Sussex record for any wicket, and is still the third highest made for any wicket for any match in England. Ted Bowley (1890–1974) was in his last full season for Sussex (he would turn out for them in a handful of games in 1934), for whom he had first played in 1912. In his career he made 28,378 runs at an average of 35, and was also a distinguished bowler, taking 741 wickets at 26 each, and once taking nine wickets in an innings. It was as a batsman that he was picked five times to play for England, 15 times exceeding 1,000 runs in a season. His 283 in this match was the highest score of his career. He spent almost a quarter of a century as coach at Winchester after his retirement.

His partner, John Langridge, was the younger of two brothers who between them played over 1,250 matches for Sussex from the mid-1920s to the mid-1950s. John (b. 1910) made 34,380 runs in his career at an average of 37, 11 times scoring over 2,000 in a season and exceeding 1,000 in a further six, yet he never played in a test. He had, though, been chosen for the MCC side that would have toured India in 1939–40 had war not broken out. After his retirement he became one of England's leading umpires. His elder brother James (1906–1966), who finally bowled Sussex to victory, did represent England in eight tests. He was a fine all-rounder, making 31,716 runs at an average of 35 in his career, and taking 1,530 wickets at 22 each. This was one of six seasons in the 1930s that he performed the 'double'. In 1950 he became the first professional to captain the county, and after his retirement he became the county coach.

Hove, Saturday

BY OUR SPECIAL REPRESENTATIVE

There was some remarkable cricket at Hove, where Bowley and John Langridge (batting for almost the whole day) scored 490 runs for the Sussex first wicket against Middlesex.

This achievement broke two records for the county. The highest first-wicket total previously stood at 368 and the highest total score for any wicket was 385.

Bowley, who is in his 44th year, passed his previous highest score of 280, and it is a mournful reflection that this great player will after this season be no longer available for his county.

He was batting for a little over six hours for his 283, and his innings included two 6's, one 5 and twenty-three 4's. Langridge also surpassed his former record of 142, and during his innings hit sixteen 4's.

From the very first the Middlesex bowling was mastered, with Bowley scoring at a rapid rate. He reached 50 out of 82 in the first hour, and had he not continually been deprived of the bowling would most certainly have attained his 100 before lunch.

As it was, he succeeded about fifteen minutes after the interval, and the proportion was restored when he reached his second century before the tea interval.

All the bowling, on a wicket that seemed cruelly insensitive, was uniformly innocuous. Nevinson, in between some rather expensive intervals, gave moments of discomfort, and Haig slaved with great industry for long profitless periods. Allen, who owing to injury had been rested, was conscripted at 98, but neither his fiery onslaught nor the new ball bought any relief, and by the tea interval Bowley and Langridge had raised the total to 355.

The 400 was sent up after five hours' play, and just as it was becoming more and more likely that the pair would exceed the world record of 555 scored by Holmes and Sutcliffe last season, Sims got Langridge lbw. There was irony in his downfall, for it happened at three minutes after 6.30, the normal hour of closure, and had it not been arranged to play till seven the pair would have resumed to-day with the record in sight.

As it was, Sussex lost two more wickets in the extra half-hour, and when stumps were drawn their score was 512 for three wickets. Middlesex showed commendable endurance. Their bowling was soon mastered, but their spin never. Hulme, above all, was absolutely tireless; his work on the boundary must have saved 40 runs.

Monday

Middlesex, dismissed for 290 in reply to the Sussex score of 512 for three declared, had to follow-on at Hove. They lost four second innings wickets for 92 before the close, and, still 130 behind, would appear to be in imminent danger of defeat.

It was a disappointing day, relieved only by a good 79 by Hendren. It was not Hendren at his best, otherwise he would not have offered a chance behind the wicket at 46. But after a somewhat tremulous opening he batted with courage and decision. At 69 he had scored 2,000 runs for the season, and altogether he hit eight boundaries during a stay of two and three-quarter hours.

The scoring was slow when the innings opened, and it came as no surprise when Tate bowled Lee with a classic break-back. Price followed shortly afterwards, and Hearne had never appeared to sight the ball clearly when he was out lbw with the score at 54.

Hendren and Allen, however, stayed together for a diverting partnership of 56, and their association looked full of fruitful promise until Tate, coming on for a second spell, had the amateur caught behind the wicket. With Hendren out at 177, five valuable wickets had fallen, and Middlesex had lost ground which they could ill afford.

Not even Haig's dare-devil fury could reclaim the position – he made a rapid 41 before sending a lofty valedictory drive into Cook's hands — and, despite a gallant stand of 57 for the ninth wicket between Sims and Watkins, Middlesex ended their innings 222 behind.

When Sussex forced the follow-on Tate resumed the attack in a sensational manner. With his second ball and before a run had been scored he shattered Lee's wicket; Hearne, usually so dependable in an emergency, journeyed to the wicket only to return immediately, having been dismissed first ball, lbw, and with only five runs on the board Price fell a victim to Tate.

The Sussex bowler at this stage had the remarkable analysis of three wickets for one run, but Hendren and Allen were not to be intimidated, and, by means of some discreet defensive play dispelled any fears of an abrupt finish. Hendren, it is true, left at 45, but Allen with a complete disregard for his injured ribs hit out with vigour.

Tuesday

Ninety minutes' play at Hove yesterday gave Sussex their fourteenth victory of the season. Middlesex, who had followed on 222 behind, could only raise their overnight total of 92 for four to 157, so that they were defeated by an innings and 65 runs.

Tate, after his remarkable performance of the previous evening, took only one more wicket. It was James Langridge who completed the visitors' downfall with some excellent bowling.

His cleverly flighted spinners, assisted by the dexterity of Cornford behind the stumps, were more than Middlesex could manage.

Allen resisted all the bowling for 2½ hours to score his 80, but it was mainly pure resistance, with rarely a hint of aggression. At 54 his score was unmoved for almost half an hour, and indeed for almost the whole of the morning it was a kind of spider-and-the-fly contest, with Allen proof against Langridge's every tempting blandishment.

Not until he had seen Enthoven, Haig and Sims fall victims to Langridge's guile, did Allen appear to sense defeat, and then for a fast desperate fifteen minutes he hit with almost vindictive relish.

As was inevitable he, too, fell to Langridge, bowled after running half-way up the pitch to meet the ball – a noble death for a very gallant fighter. His innings included eight 4's. He had come in with the score at 5 and was last man out. Score:

SUSSEX

Bowley, c Hulme, b Lee	283	Langridge (Jas.), not out	10
Langridge (John), lbw, b Sims	195	B 6, l-b 11	17
Parks (J.), C Enthoven, b Sims	5		
Cook, not out	2	Total (3 wkts. dec.)	512

MIDDLESEX

	First Innings		Second Innings
Lee, b Tate	10	b Tate	0
Price, c Langridge (John), b Parks (J)	15	b Tate	4
Hearne, lbw, b Wensley	12	lbw, b Tate	0
Hendren, b Wensley	79	b Cornford (J.)	17
G.O. Allen, c Cornford (W.), b Tate	23	b Langridge (Jas.)	80
Hulme, st Cornford (W.), b Langridge (Jas.)	19	c Cornford (J.) b Tate	35
H.J. Enthoven, lbw, b Langridge (Jas.)	8	st Cornford (W.), b Langridge (Jas.)	4
N. Haig, c Cook, b Langridge (Jas.)	41	b Langridge (Jas.)	2
Sims, not out	36	st Cornford (W.) b Langridge (Jas.)	0
Watkins, run out	25	c Scott, b Langridge (Jas.)	1
J.H. Nevinson, b Tate	0	not out	0
B 8, l-b 12 n-b 2	22	L-b	14
Total	290	Total	157

SUSSEX – First Innings

	O	M	R	W		O	M	R	W
Nevinson	25	4	84	0	Hearne	10	0	53	0
Hulme	8	1	33	0	Haig	20	1	63	0
Sims	31	2	122	2	Allen	7	1	8	0
Enthoven	13	2	42	0	Lee	27	2	90	1

MIDDLESEX – First Innings

	O	M	R	W		O	M	R	W
Tate	28	10	41	3	Langridge (Jas.)	30	10	68	3
Cornford (J.)	20	4	61	0	Wensley	26	6	53	2
Parks (J.)	10	1	25	1	Bowley	5	0	20	0

Second Innings

	O	M	R	W		O	M	R	W
Tate	15	5	20	4	Cornford (J.)	16	6	34	1
Langridge (Jas.)	20.3	7	33	5	Bowley	2	0	14	0
					Wensley	17	2	42	0

Langridge and Bowley after their record stand

52: *Essex v Kent*

BRENTWOOD, 30 MAY–1 JUNE 1934

Essex enjoyed a reasonably successful run in the Championship during the 1930s, twice finishing in the top four and usually managing to be around the middle of the table. Kent, although they included more high-quality players, were only marginally more successful. Their superiority over their neighbours was not, though, so marked as this rout might suggest. The wicket at Brentwood had been prepared with liberal supplies of dung, making the smell the main handicap to those playing on it. It was absolutely dead as far as the bowlers were concerned, which goes much of the way to explaining how Kent could so quickly score 803 for 4, their highest ever, and the fourth highest total made in the Championship.

Bill Ashdown (1898–1979) was the only man to have played first-class cricket before the First and after the Second World Wars, having played in a first-class match against Oxford University when only 15 years old in 1914, and ending his career in 1947. He is one of only four players – the others being J.T. Brown, W.R. Hammond and Percy Holmes – to make more than one treble century in county cricket; he made 305 not out the following year against Derbyshire at Dover. In his career he scored 22,589 runs at an average of 31. Les Ames (1905–1990) was perhaps the finest wicketkeeper-batsman of all time. He played for Kent from 1926 to 1951, scoring 37,248 runs at an average of 43, including 102 centuries, and played 47 times for England. He made over 1,000 runs in a season 17 times and in the previous season, 1933, had scored 3,058 at an average of 59. His total of 128 dismissals in 1929 remains a record for a season, and in his career he made 1,121, despite not keeping wicket after the war. His 418 stumpings are the most by any wicketkeeper.

Brentwood, Wednesday

Six hours' flawless batting by Ashdown brought the Kent player 307 runs without defeat against Essex, at Brentwood. And finding their inspiration in Ashdown, Woolley and Ames came along with centuries for Kent to finish the day with 623 on the board and eight wickets still standing!

Kent's total is two runs better than their previous highest score – also against Essex at Tonbridge in 1922 – and Ashdown passed his previous best when he had made 179. Among Ashdown's figures were a six (four from an overthrow) and forty 4's.

During the last 100 minutes he and Ames, who is not out 106, put on 201.

Ashdown and Woolley played brilliant cricket, putting on 352 in three hours and five minutes for the second wicket. This fell only 46 runs short of the record for a second stand which has stood for 44 years; the late Arthur Shrewsbury and William Gunn made 398 between them for Notts against Sussex at Trent Bridge in 1890.

Batting without a mistake, Ashdown reached his 100 in 2 hours 20 minutes, and doubled his score in a further hour and a half. Like Woolley, who completed his century in a hundred minutes, he scored chiefly by means of drives, but both men hit all round the wicket with power and skill.

Woolley was bowled in playing back at 422. He had made 172 and his figures included a six and twenty-one 4's. Missed by Cutmore when 2, he had two more pieces of good fortune, being let off in following overs by P. Smith.

Ames gave a chance when 30, and for this, too, a heavy price had to be paid, the Kent wicket-keeper driving so hard as to reach 100 out of 165 in eighty minutes. So far the wicket-keeper has hit a 6 and fourteen 4's.

Thursday

Although Kent eventually scored 803 runs for four declared at Brentwood, Essex are making such a brave show – they finished with 366 on the board, with three wickets in hand – that they may save the game to-day, even though they need 288 to save the follow-on.

Kent did not declare at their overnight score of 623, but batted for another 65 minutes to put on 180 runs for the loss of two more batsmen.

Their total of 803, for which they batted seven hours, has only twice been exceeded in English cricket – in 1896 by Yorkshire (887 v. Warwickshire) and in 1899 by Surrey (811 v. Somerset) – but no other score of over 800 for only four wickets has been made in any country.

Ashdown stayed to be third out at 667. He gave nothing like a chance during his innings of six hours and a quarter, and among the figures of his 332 were a 6 and forty-five 4's.

Ames, with whom Ashdown put on 245 in two

hours for the third wicket, completed his 200 in fifty minutes longer time. Besides a 6, Ames had twenty-nine 4's in his 202 not out.

Bowling analyses made remarkable reading, only six maiden overs being sent down throughout an innings in which Sheffield conceded no more than eight byes.

When Essex went in Pope batted carefully, but he never neglected an opportunity to punish loose deliveries. He and Pearce, though often compelled to defend, put on 156 in 2 hours and 40 minutes for the second stand.

Pope reached his first three-figure score of the season, off-driving finely. Second out at 231, he hit a 5 and nine 4's during 3 hours and 20 minutes at the crease.

Later O'Connor and Cutmore shared in a stand that yielded 74 in half an hour. O'Connor reached 50 in three-quarters of an hour, but he took another fifty minutes over his next 30 runs.

Friday

Kent easily beat Essex at Brentwood by an innings with 192 runs to spare, thus gaining revenge for the reverse by two wickets that they suffered at Gravesend. Essex scored 408 – O'Connor hit the fifth century of the match – but had to follow on 395 behind.

The last day's cricket was in contrast to that of the first two. Whereas only eleven wickets fell for an aggregate of 1,169 runs in the first two days play, thirteen went down yesterday while 245 were scored!

Freeman and Wright were the Kent match-winners, and between them they took all but one of the wickets yesterday. Freeman, in obtaining six for 60, made his full record eleven for 176. Score:

KENT v. ESSEX
BRENTWOOD
May 31st. 1934
W. ASHDOWN 332
L. E. AMES 202 not out
F. E. WOOLLEY 172

The end of the Kent innings

KENT

Ashdown, c Ashton, b Nichols ... 332	I. D. K. Fleming, not out 42
Fagg, lbw, b Smith (R) 31	B 8, w 4, n-b 1 13
Woolley, b Ashton, ... 172	
Ames, not out 202	Total (4 wkts dec.) 803
Watt, c Smith (R.), b Ashton 11	

Todd, B. H. Valentine, A. P. F. Chapman, Wright and Freeman did not bat.

ESSEX

Eastman, c Chapman, b Wright 52	c Woolley, b Freeman 4
Pope, c Woolley, b Valentine 100	c Ames, b Wright 11
T.N. Pearce, c Ames, b Valentine .. 79	c Woolley, b Freeman 17
O'Connor, not out 105	lbw, b Freeman 25
Nichols, c Valentine, b Wright 3	lbw, b Wright 20
Cutmore, c Ames, b Watt 30	c Fleming, b Wright 0
C.T. Ashton, st Ames, b Freeman . 11	not out 71
Taylor, st Ames, b Freeman 1	st Ames, b Freeman 1
Smith (P.), c Woolley, b Freeman .. 11	c Ashdown, b Freeman 0
Sheffield, c Woolley, b Freeman 0	c Watts, b Ashdown 31
Smith (R.), b Freeman 0	st Ames, b Freeman 1
B 7, l-b 8, n-b 1 16	B14, l-b 8 22
Total 408	Total 203

KENTS – First Innings

	O	M	R	W		O	M	R	W
Nichols	20	1	93	1	O'Connor	16.2	0	83	0
Smith (R.)	22	1	115	1	Cutmore	12	0	63	0
Ashton	31	2	185	2	Taylor	7	0	36	0
Smith (P.)	36	2	208	0	Pope	2	0	7	0

Nichols, Smith (R.), O'Connor and Taylor each bowled one wide and Ashton one no ball.

ESSEX – First Innings

	O	M	R	W		O	M	R	W
Watt	23	4	85	1	Todd	6	0	11	0
Ashdown	6	2	22	0	Woolley	7	2	10	0
Freeman	50.5	15	116	5	Valentine	9	2	31	2
Wright	38	9	117	2					

Second Innings

	O	M	R	W		O	M	R	W
Watt	9	0	20	0	Wright	27	12	59	3
Valentine	5	2	16	0	Woolley	5	0	26	0
Freeman	34.2	13	60	6	Ashdown	1	1	0	1

53: Surrey v Kent
THE OVAL, 27–30 JULY 1935

This was Andrew Sandham's benefit match, used by the immensely strong Kent batting side of the period to inflict a severe defeat on Surrey. Both sides were passing through one of the least inspiring periods in their history, as Kent would finish 10th in the Championship this summer and Surrey 11th. Woolley, at the age of 47, played one of the most thrilling innings of his career on the Saturday, his double century coming in under two and three-quarter hours out of 305 runs scored while he was at the wicket. The Surrey bowling, which was the side's weak link, had failed to penetrate, and only Alf Gover (b. 1908) had any real success, at huge cost. Gover took 1,555 wickets in his career between 1928 and 1947, twice taking over 200 in a season, and was regarded as one of the best fast bowlers of the time; yet he played only four tests for England.

Surrey's only really successful batsman, other than the beneficiary himself, was Tom Barling (b. 1906). Barling played for the county from 1927 to 1948, scoring 19,209 runs at an average of 35, and having his best season in 1946, immediately after the war, when he made over 2,000 runs at an average of 44. Charles Marriott (1895–1966), who helped Freeman bowl Surrey out, was another of Kent's schoolmaster-cricketers, teaching at Dulwich. A Cambridge blue who began his cricketing career by playing three seasons for his native county, Lancashire, he was able only to play in late July and August, and in a first-class career of 159 matches between 1919 and 1938 he took 711 wickets at 20 each. He played just one test, in which he took 11 for 96 against the West Indies in 1933.

The Oval, Saturday

Wonderful Woolley! The crowd at the Oval – over 15,000 spectators were there to give Sandham's benefit match a splendid send-off – watched the tall Kent left-hander take toll of the Surrey bowling in his most majestic manner.

For over three hours Woolley went on in his own grand way to crack on 229 runs. It was an innings studded with four 6's and thirty 4's – and one magnificent hit sent the ball soaring out of the ground, on to the tram lines and then, first bounce, into a nearby garden!

Here is Woolley's time schedule: 52 in 28 minutes, 100 in 80 minutes, 150 in 125 minutes, 200 in 160 minutes and 229 in three hours five minutes. But mere figures can convey nothing of the easeful grace with which the Kent batsman met the harassed – but always hopeful – Surrey attack.

Woolley's brilliance overshadowed the workmanlike hundred built up in 190 minutes by Fagg. As it was, Fagg, getting sixteen 4's, shared in two century stands: he put on 136 with Ashdown – their fourth big opening stand this season – and helped Woolley add 133 in 70 minutes. And of that second partnership Woolley made 87.

After Ames had left at 297 – he is completely out of luck these days – there was still a third three-figure partnership. Yet Todd was so completely overshadowed by Woolley's hurricane hitting, that of the 106 runs added in an hour Todd's share was 38.

The Surrey bowlers had another gruelling time against Valentine, who took 35 minutes to score 71 out of 91. Valentine got 42 of his runs by nine strokes – three 6's and six 4's.

Finally, the crowd had the rare sight of Sandham taking a turn with the ball. And Sandham claimed A.P.F. Chapman's wicket after the Kent captain had scored a couple of runs.

Monday

Forced to follow-on, needing 289 runs to save the innings defeat, Surrey put on 78 for the loss of Gregory before the close of their game with Kent at the Oval.

Sandham, whose benefit match it is, batted pluckily to score 59 of the runs raised in Surrey's second venture. He hit all round the wicket, and so far has eight 4's among his figures. If he can reproduce his form to-day, Sandham may yet rescue Surrey.

Chapman declared the Kent innings at Saturday's total of 579 for eight wickets, and though Sandham, Gregory and Barling all batted well, Surrey's first innings closed at 290.

After taking pains to play himself in, Sandham cut and drove splendidly while scoring 47 out of 81 for the opening partnership. The first three Surrey batsmen were lbw victims to Freeman, and when Gregory went, third out, he actually put his right leg to the ball.

Never in a hurry, Gregory was content to take runs when the right ball came along. Batting two hours 40 minutes, he obtained his 62 out of 154, and hit four 4's.

Surrey's bad patch came between lunch and tea, five wickets falling to Marriott and Freeman for 110.

Both Fishlock and Garland-Wells went to splendid catches, and a grand bit of stumping by Ames got rid of Holmes. Another brilliant piece of stumping – wide on the leg side – got Barling's valuable wicket.

Going in second wicket down at 83, Barling was eighth to leave at 238. He made his 87 out of 155 in two and a half hours and sent the ball to the boundary 10 times.

Brooks drove hard and in partnership with Watts scored 30 out of 52 for the ninth wicket in half an hour.

Marriott bowled without a break between lunch and tea, and, keeping a superb length, sent down 24 overs, of which five were maidens, to take two wickets for 45. Altogether he took four for 81, while Freeman captured half the Surrey wickets for 99. Both the Kent slow bowlers relied on length and flight for their success.

When Surrey went in again just before half-past five, Gregory – taking 35 minutes to collect eight – was snapped at the wicket at 43, but Sandham went on to give a delightfully free display of batting.

Tuesday

At one time at the Oval yesterday Kent's policy of making Surrey follow-on looked like failing.

About three o'clock Surrey had cleared the heavy arrears of 280 with half their wickets in hand, but

Andrew Sandham

afterwards the batting broke down, and Kent, set to get 80 to win, obtained the runs without loss, and won by 10 wickets.

Interest in Sandham's benefit was maintained throughout, and during the three days 20,971 paid for admission.

Sandham failed by 7 to reach his century, but Barling put together his first three-figure score of the season.

Surrey were faced with the task of avoiding the innings defeat, 211 in arrears with nine wickets to fall. When Squires was caught at slip they had 102 on the board and only two men out, but runs seemed hard to get when Sandham left.

Chapman, the Kent captain, did not take his place in the field until after noon. His first move was to put Todd on to bowl, and off the left-hander's third ball Chapman caught Sandham in the gully.

Seldom has Sandham shown more enterprise. He cut, drove and hit to leg in most attractive fashion, taking only an hour and 50 minutes over his 93, made out of 145, and among his figures were twelve 4's.

Fishlock, completing his 1,000 runs for the first time in his career, hit six 4's in scoring 35 in 40 minutes. Barling completely overshadowed Holmes, the Surrey captain scoring only 28 out of the 70 put on for the fifth wicket in an hour.

Barling was ninth out at 364. He scored his 113 out of 262 by drives, pulls and cuts, his best strokes being twelve 4's.

Ashdown and Fagg took only 42 minutes to knock off the 80 runs. Ashdown, who hit seven 4's, completed his 50 in making the winning hit. Score:

KENT

	First Innings		Second Innings
Ashdown, c Gregory, b Gover	61	not out	50
Fagg, c Fishlock, b Watts	111	not out	28
Woolley, b Brown	229		
Ames, b Gover	12		
Todd, lbw, b Holmes	38		
Sunnucks, not out	33		
B. H. Valentine, c Barling, b Gover	71		
A. P. F. Chapman, c Watts, b Sandham	2		
Watt, b Gover	2		
B 7, l-b 6, w 4, n-b 3	20	n-b 2	2
Total (8 wkts. dec.)	579	Total (0 wkt.)	80

Freeman and C. S. Marriott did not bat.

SURREY

	First Innings		Second Innings
Sandham, lbw, b Freeman	47	c Chapman, b Todd	93
Gregory, lbw, b Freeman	62	c Ames, b Marriott	8
Squires, lbw, b Freeman	1	c Woolley, b Freeman	16
Barling, c Ames, b Watt	87	c Watt, b Marriott	113
Fishlock, c Chapman, b Marriott	1	c Ashdown, b Freeman	35
E.R.T. Holmes, st Ames, b Freeman	6	c Ames, b Freeman	28
H.M. Garland-Wells, c Fagg, b Freeman	0	c Valentine, b Watt	40
F.R. Brown, c Ashdown, b Marriott	16	run out	2
Watts, not out	24	lbw, b Marriott	6
Brooks, st Ames, b Marriott	30	not out	4
Gover, lbw, b Marriott	0	st Ames, b Freeman	4
B 11, l-b 5	16	B11, l-b 8	19
Total	290	Total	368

KENT – First Innings

	O	M	R	W		O	M	R	W
Gover	29.4	4	144	4	Gregory	14	4	65	0
Watts	18	1	97	1	G. Wells	3	0	11	0
Brown	25	4	135	1	Squires	2	0	13	0
Holmes	17	2	86	1	Sandham	2	0	8	1

Holmes bowled four wides and Gover three no-balls.

Second Innings

	O	M	R	W		O	M	R	W
Gover	8.1	1	33	0	Brown	6	0	27	0
Watts	2	0	18	0					

SURREY – First Innings

	O	M	R	W		O	M	R	W
Watt	17	4	37	1	Freeman	30	5	99	5
Todd	23	3	57	0	Marriott	37	8	81	4

Second Innings

	O	M	R	W		O	M	R	W
Watt	12	1	38	1	Freeman	46	8	137	4
Todd	12	1	39	1	Marriott	41	7	135	4

54: *Gloucestershire v Nottinghamshire*
GLOUCESTER, 29 AUGUST– 1 SEPTEMBER 1936

Wally Hammond scored more runs – 1,281 – in August 1936 than any batsman had ever scored in a calendar month, and the record has only been surpassed once, by Len Hutton's 1,294 in June 1949. Hammond scored a quarter of that total in this innings against Nottinghamshire, the third of his four treble centuries and the highest score he made in the Championship. He was only one short of equalling W.G. Grace's record score for the county, made in 1876. Coming at the close of the Championship race this was an important match for both sides. After their victory

Gloucestershire finished fourth in the table, and Nottinghamshire fifth.

Gloucestershire's leading bowler of the period was Tom Goddard (1900–1966), who led the destruction of Nottinghamshire on the first afternoon of this match. He played for the county from 1922 to 1952, first of all as a fast bowler, at which he had no success, and left the county in 1927 to work on the MCC staff. However, he learned to bowl off-spinners so well while at Lord's that Gloucestershire were persuaded to take him back. His first season with them as a slow bowler, 1929, brought him more wickets

(184) than he had taken his whole previous career. By the time he finally retired he had taken 2,979 wickets at under 20 each, 16 times exceeding 100 in a season and four times passing 200 – the last when he was 46 years old. He did the hat-trick six times and took all ten wickets in an innings against Worcester at Cheltenham in 1937. On eight other occasions he took nine in an innings and seven times more than 15 in a match.

Gloucester, Saturday

Although without Sinfield, who has fractured a thumb, Gloucestershire put out Nottinghamshire for 200 in Goddard's benefit match at Gloucester, and finished 93 behind with seven wickets in hand. Nottinghamshire started so badly that they had four men out for 66, but then Hardstaff and Staples put on 76. Voce took the first two Goucestershire wickets for 23, but Hammond and Haynes put on 52 for the third wicket, and Hammond is unbeaten.

Monday

Hammond scored 317 runs against Nottinghamshire at Gloucester yesterday and made his aggregate for August 1,281. This beats the record of the month, set up by W. G. Grace – also of Gloucestershire – 60 years ago.

Hammond batted for six hours and a half, hit three 6s and 34 4s, and completed his last 100 runs in 80 minutes. It was his highest score in England, his previous best being 302 not out against Glamorgan, at Bristol in 1934, and is only 19 less than the best of his career – 336, a Test record, against New Zealand, at Auckland, in 1932.

Hammond played defensively at the start of the day, and with his score 111 he nearly played-on. Voce and Butler bowled admirably, and were splendidly supported by the fieldsmen. It was not until three hours had gone that a wicket fell, and then Neale was taken in the slips. Hammond had other useful partners in Crapp and Hopkins, and the total reached 485. Nottinghamshire, 285 behind, scored 22 in their second innings without losing a wicket.

Tuesday

Hammond, who scored 317 against Nottinghamshire at Gloucester on Monday, was unable to play yesterday. He has a badly bruised instep, and may not take part in the Folkestone festival today.

Goddard was also hurt, and Barnett, Cranfield and Stephens bowled splendidly to dismiss Notts for 245. Gloucestershire won by an innings and 70 runs.

The first four Nottinghamshire wickets went down for 64, but Harris and Staples had a sound stand, which yielded 71 in as many minutes. Harris revealed

Tom Goddard

excellent defence in staying two hours and 20 minutes for 50.

No sooner had Staples reached his 50 in 95 minutes than he, like Harris, fell to a good catch, so that seven men were out for 166. Voce and Wheat hit freely, but the end was not long delayed. Score:

NOTTINGHAMSHIRE

Keeton, b Stephens 35	lbw, b Cranfield 20
Harris, b Hammond 6	c sub, b Stephens 50
Walker, c Barnett, b Goddard 6	b Cranfield 9
Hardstaff, c Hopkins, b Stephens . 46	b Cranfield 0
Gunn, b Goddard 5	b Goddard 12
Staples, c Goddard, b Cranfield 58	c Allen, b Cranfield 52
G.F.H. Heane, c Page,	c Barnett, b Stephens 18
b Cranfield 11	b Barnett 23
Voce, b Cranfield 25	c Stephens, b Barnett 0
Woodhead, not out 6	c Page, b Barnett 24
Wheat, c Stephens, b Goddard 1	not out 3
Butler, lbw, b Goddard 0	B 3, l-b 1 4
L-b 1	
	Total 215
Total 200	

GLOUCESTERSHIRE

Barnett, b Voce 2	D.A.C. Page, lbw, b Heane 8
Haynes, c Staples, b Voce 18	Stephens, b Voce 0
B.O. Allen, c Staples, b Butler 18	Goddard, b Heane 1
Hammond, b Woodhead 317	Hopkins, not out 25
Neale, c Heane, b Butler 66	Cranfield, c Wheat, b Staples 0
Crapp, c Woodhead, b Gunn 22	B 6, l-b 1, n-b 1 8
	Total 485

NOTTINGHAMSHIRE – First Innings

	O	M	R	W		O	M	R	W
Hammond	7	0	21	1	Stephens	11	0	27	2
Barnett	13	3	51	0	Cranfield	23	6	51	3
Goddard	28.1	9	49	4					

Second Innings

	O	M	R	W		O	M	R	W
Barnett	11.3	2	25	3	Goddard	25	6	71	1
Stephens	8	1	32	2	Haynes	6	1	12	0
Cranfield	33	11	71	4					

GLOUCESTERSHIRE – First Innings

	O	M	R	W		O	M	R	W
Voce	31	2	117	3	Staples	17.1	2	69	1
Butler	31	5	79	2	Gunn	19	3	53	1
Woodhead	24	3	86	1	Heane	28	5	73	2

Voce bowled one no-ball.

55: Leicestershire v Glamorgan
LEICESTER, 19–21 MAY 1937

Leicestershire and Glamorgan were two of the weakest counties in the Championship during the 1930s. In the ten seasons before the war Glamorgan only once finished higher than 11th – in this season, when they came 7th after finishing 16th in 1936 (as they did again in 1938). Leicestershire were usually in the bottom three, and they finished 16th in 1937. Glamorgan's success in 1937 was thanks principally to Emrys Davies (1904–1975), their leading player. His opening stand of 274 with Dyson was a county record, and his achievement of a hat-trick and a hundred in the same match had only happened three times before in the Championship.

Davies, a leading all-rounder of this era, never played for England: he was one of those picked for MCC's Indian tour of 1939–40 that was aborted because of the war. He played for Glamorgan from 1924 to 1954, scoring 26,566 runs at an average of 28, and taking 903 wickets at 29 each. His best season was this one: in 1937 he scored 2,012 runs averaging 40, and took 103 wickets at 23, the only Glamorgan player ever to do this 'double'. His opening partner, Arnold Dyson (1905–1978), made 305 consecutive appearances for Glamorgan in the Championship, and with Davies put on 100 for the first wicket 22 times; the pair of them helped transform Glamorgan into a championship-winning side in 1948. Turnbull, the other centurion, was killed in action in Normandy in 1944, having made 17,544 runs in his career at an average of 30. He played 9 tests, and was a Welsh rugby international. The Leicestershire captain and centurion, 'Stewie' Dempster, (1903–1974) was one of New Zealand's greatest batsmen, scoring 12,145 runs in his career at an average of 45.

Emrys Davies

Leicester, Wednesday

Congratulations to Emrys Davies and Arnold Dyson, the Glamorgan opening batsmen, on scoring 274 for Glamorgan's first wicket against Leicestershire at Leicester yesterday.

It is a record for a Glamorgan first-innings partnership; the biggest stand of the season, so far; the first time both Glamorgan opening batsmen have scored a century in the same innings.

A six-wickets victory over the New Zealanders gave Glamorgan confidence. Winning the toss added to it. By the end of the day they had built up a commanding position.

Davies and Dyson did not master the Leicester bowling easily. Davies snicked a ball from Smith dangerously near Armstrong, at second slip, early in his innings, and when he had made 41 he gave a stumping chance off Astill – the way he eventually fell.

Davies drove, pulled and hit to leg strongly, and Dyson, who batted without a mistake for his second century of the season, was particularly strong on the leg-side, through he, too, drove the occasional loose ball.

The curious part about this splendid partnership was that, having taken up the greater part of the day – four hours and 20 minutes – it was broken with the last ball of one over, when Davies was dismissed, and with the first ball of the next Dyson followed him to the pavilion. Davies hit 14 fours and Dyson 10.

Both found the left-hand spinners of Bowley difficult to score off, and in one spell the Leicester bowler had only 17 runs hit off him in 15 overs, but each scored freely off Prentice, brought on as one of the many changes.

Glamorgan's position was strong enough to encourage bold batting, but neither Dai Davies nor Duckfield could withstand Bowley's left-arm spinners and the total changed from 274 for one wicket to 299 for four.

Then Turnbull found in Smart a partner who could force the game properly and the two batsmen punished the tired bowling to the extent of 71 runs; 140 runs were added in the last hour.

Turnbull, at his best in driving and pulling, reached 53 in an hour and hit three 6's and eight 4's. He is not out 81.

Thursday

Glamorgan set Leicestershire the formidable task of scoring 320 to avoid a follow-on at Leicester. They were in an impregnable postion overnight, with 410 runs on the board and half their wickets in hand, and batted for another 40 minutes.

M.J. Turnbull, 81 not out overnight, completed his first century of the summer, and, being the third batsman in the innings to reach three figures, set up another Glamorgan record. He secored 54 out of 59 added yesterday and his 135 out of 195, in two hours and 20 minutes, included four 6's and 13 4's.

In the Glamorgan innings, which lasted six hours and 40 minutes, Corrall, the Leicestershire wicket-keeper, did not give away a bye.

Barry and Prentice gave Leicestershire a good start by scoring 52 in 70 minutes, but both left at the same total. Berry being splendidly taken by Dai Davies at deep square leg and Prentice caught close to the wicket on the onside.

The third partnership realised 62, when Dempster chopped a ball on to his stumps and, with the aid of smart fielding, Emrys Davies caused such a breakdown that by tea six men were out for 147, and the innings closed at 164, Leicester following-on.

Friday

Glamorgan gained their second win in the county championship when trouncing Leicestershire by an innings and 49 runs at Leicester.

Emrys Davies was the outstanding player of the match, being top scorer with a sparkling innings of 139 and bringing off a bowling hat-trick in Leicester's second innings.

Davies, who scored a thousand runs and took a hundred wickets two seasons ago, played a big part in the Leicester collapse which set in at the end of the Armstrong-Dempster partnership. He got Geary and Bowley caught in the slips from the last two balls of one over, and had Smith lbw from the first ball of his next.

Leicestershire resumed yesterday needing 253 to avoid an innings defeat. Two valuable wickets – those of Berry and Prentice – had fallen, but the position was improved in the stand between Armstrong and Dempster.

This partnership added 155 runs in three hours and raised Leicester's hopes. Armstrong, taking few risks, scored mainly on the leg side, but Dempster hit freely all round the wicket.

Dempster made 102, his first century of the season, in three hours and a half, and hit 11 boundaries.

With the break-up of this partnership Leicester's resistance cracked, the last six wickets falling for 39 runs. Geary attempted some big hitting, but did not stay long, being one of Davies' hat-trick victims.

GLAMORGAN

Dyson, c Dempster, b Bowley	126	Duckfield, lbw (n), b Bowley	1
Davies (E.), st Corrall, b Astill	139	Smart, c Berry, b Bowley	33
M.J. Turnbull, c Berry, b Astill	135	Brierley, run out	10
Davies (D.), c Armstrong,		Jones (E.C.), not out	3
b Bowley	13	L-b 8, n-b 1	9
		Total (7 w., dec.)	469

J.C. Clay, Mercer and W.D. Hughes did not bat.

LEICESTERSHIRE

Berry, c Davies (D.), b Smart	24	lbw, b Clay	22
Prentice, c Turnbull, b Smart	23	c Turnbull, b Mercer	6
Armstrong, c Smart, b Jones	44	c Brierley, b Jones	73
C.S. Dempster, b Davies (E.)	35	c & b Mercer	102
Graham, b Clay	4	run out	3
Riley, c Davies (D.), b Davies (E.)	0	lbw, b Clay	9
Geary, c Davies (D.), b Davies (E.)	6	c Smart, b Davies (E.)	13
Astill, b Jones	11	not out	7
Bowley, b Davies (E.)	0	c Davies (D.), b Davies (E.)	0
Smith, c Mercer, b Jones	8	lbw, b Davies (E.)	1
Corrall, not out	0	c Dyson, b Jones	1
B 2, l-b 7	9	B18, l-b 1	19
Total	164	Total	256

GLAMORGAN – First Innings

	O	M	R	W		O	M	R	W
Smith	44	11	115	0	Astill	26.3	6	82	2
Geary	38	3	90	0	Prentice	4	0	15	0
Bowley	48	8	155	4	Armstrong	2	0	3	0

LEICESTERSHIRE – First Innings

	O	M	R	W		O	M	R	W
Mercer	8	1	15	0	Smart	11	1	36	2
Hughes	11	3	16	0	Clay	18	6	30	1
Jones	15.3	7	31	3	Davies (E.)	18	6	27	4

Second Innings

	O	M	R	W		O	M	R	W
Mercer	27	4	53	2	Clay	23	4	55	2
Hughes	4	0	18	0	Davies (E.)	22	8	31	3
Jones	27	7	63	2	Davies (D.)	5	2	5	0
Smart	6	0	12	0					

56: Sussex v Lancashire
HOVE, 28–30 JULY 1937

Just how favourable the wickets of the 1930s were to batsmen is clear from the fact that of the 33 treble centuries made in the Championship since 1890, 11 of them – a third – were made between 1930 and 1939. On the day that Eddie Paynter took 322 off Sussex, then the second largest number of runs scored in the Championship in a day (after Duleep's 333 in 1930: see game 46), the Hampshire amateur Richard Moore was taking 316 off Warwickshire at Bournemouth. Lancashire's 640 remains the second largest number of runs ever scored by one side in a day in the Championship, just behind Surrey's 645 against Hampshire in 1909. It was made from 138 overs, a rate that seems astonishing today but was quite usual at the time.

Paynter (1901–1979) came to first-class cricket late, not securing a regular place in the Lancashire side until 1931, when he was 30 and about to make his England debut. His career was effectively ended by the war, so was relatively short. In that time he scored 20,075 runs at an average of 42, and in the 20 tests he played for England he made 1,540 runs at an average of 59, putting him in the highest rank. Even more remarkable was his average against the strong Australian side of the thirties: in seven tests it was over 84. This season, 1937, was his best, as he made 2,904 runs at an average of 54. In addition to his treble century he made six double centuries, two of them for England. George Cox (1911–1985), the Sussex centurion, was a member of the side from 1931 to 1960, scoring 22,949 runs at an average of 33, including 50 hundreds. He was one of the most popular cricketers of his age, with a reputation as a match-winner: not, though, on this occasion.

Hove, Wednesday
By Thomas Moult

A mammoth bonfire of runs was lit here to-day by Lancashire against Sussex. They scored 640 for eight wickets, the season's highest total, and three of the batsmen who fed the mid-summer blaze heaped up 522 between them.

Easily the biggest share of these was Paynter's record-making and record-shaking 322, that flashed from his bat so swiftly that he nearly added a new speed achievement to the remarkable figures contributed during the afternoon to cricket history.

Lancashire's diminutive left-hander, who had come straight from the Test match at Manchester, filled the day with a brilliant glow, especially the morning hours, when his batsmanship was fresh and untired. He hit 100 before lunch, and he and Washbrook, who opened the innings together, put on 175 – Paynter 108 – in the two hours before the interval.

They went on to 268 before the first wicket fell. Washbrook was caught at mid-on low down by Harry Parks. He had batted delightfully; his understanding with Paynter as they ran between the wickets was thrilling to watch. A perfect partnership indeed, and the large crowd were roused to as much enthusiasm as if the achievement had been by their own batsmen.

Another fine stand, this time realising 271, and completed at a significantly similar rate of about two hours and a quarter, followed the dismissal of Iddon, second out at 275. Oldfield was now Paynter's partner, and he, too, batted at his best.

His stamina, however, appeared to give out as he approached three figures, and he stopped short at 92, caught behind the wicket, five runs after Paynter's own huge knock was brought to an end at 546.

Paynter got himself out – he ran down the pitch to James Parks and was leg-before. He had been sending the spectators into the happiest mood even after he turned 300 by cracking the ball all over the field, and, weary though he was, his bat still made the lovely clear music that comes when the ball hits the middle every time.

Out of the welter and confusion of arithmetical facts created by Paynter quite an important number must be selected for special emphasis. He made his first 100 out of 162 in less than two hours; he completed 200 out of 345 in 205 minutes, 300 out of 513 in 290 minutes, and his remaining 22 out of 33 were scored in 10 minutes – 300 minutes altogether. He hit three 6's and 39 4's.

Now for Paynter's record-breaking. In addition to the feat of scoring 100 before lunch for the second time this season and reaching three figures for the fifth time, Paynter beat his own previous top score of 266, also made this season, and he passed Hutton's 271, the record individual total of the summer.

His 322 is the highest ever made by a Lancashire professional, and he beat the highest score against Sussex, made by Victor Trumper in 1899. He just failed to equal Duleepsinhji's 333 on the Hove ground in 1930, and he also failed to reach the highest ever made by a professional batsman – 'Bobby' Abel's 357 at the Oval 47 years ago.

Thursday

A splendid fight by Sussex against the monstrous handicap of Lancashire's first innings total has lasted the livelong day, and will continue here to-morrow; but it looks like ending vainly. They reached a total of 340 after Lancashire had declared at their overnight score of 640 for eight wickets, and, 300 behind, followed on and made 112 for the loss of John Langridge and James Parks.

The pitch is already slightly worn, and needing 183 to avoid an innings defeat, Sussex are threatened with their second setback of the season.

Sussex faced insuperable odds very pluckily, however, especially as these were aggravated in the first hour when they lost two wickets for 48 runs. Parks was cleverly taken by short-leg at that total, the catch being the first of four by Birtwell during the day, and next ball Cox was bowled off his pads.

The fruitful nature of the wicket was none the less apparent when Cook joined John Langridge. The batsmen, indeed, showed every sign of settling into a safe stride on their long uphill journey, for when the first bowling changes were made in the late 70's, Langridge hooked Birtwell's first delivery for 4 – a very fine gesture indeed.

But misfortune befell them, as so often happens when a side are holding their position in time of peril, and the longer they hold it regardless of actual run-getting, the better.

Cook was the sufferer, through his own fault, being run out, most foolishly, at 89, miscalculating a flash of misfielding near point and being unable to get back. Disaster, moreover, seldom comes singly to a side in the position of Sussex, and at 98 another wicket fell, John Langridge being easily caught by square leg.

Fortunately Harry Parks and James Langridge were steadfast, and not only did they carry their partnership over the lunch interval, but they went on for an hour in the afternoon and hit an extremely welcome and heartening 155 before the stand was broken.

Parks batted with a freedom that would not have been ill-fitting if his side were on top, his driving and cutting being sound and powerful. He completed his 50 with a single when the fifth wicket had added exactly 100, and James Langridge followed suit a quarter of an hour later with a rousing straight drive off Sibbles.

Sandwiched between these two features had been the signalling of 200 in 3¼ hours – by no means a negligible speed in such circumstances.

On and on went the two batsmen, higher and higher rose the Sussex spirit; but unfortunately at 253 James Langridge paid the penalty of too much confidence and was stumped. He had batted about two hours.

Parks was still there, but the back of the innings was obviously broken. Two further wickets went down before tea, when Sussex were 267 for seven. Oakes was lbw in Birtwell's first over afterwards, and Parks followed him out 5 runs later, at 277, when he was only 2 short of his century.

The ill-luck of this dismissal was the greater because Birtwell's caught and bowled was a thrilling one, the bowler leaping to his left and taking the ball knee-high with both hands. Parks had batted masterfully for two hours and 50 minutes.

A grotesque little partnership for the last wicket by Tuppin and Cornford delayed the end of the innings for 40 minutes, 63 amusing runs being added, mainly off the edge of Cornford's bat, before Birtwell made his third catch.

Sussex were batting again at 5.35, and in the hour and 10 minutes left for play they lost John Langridge at 28, and yet reached 100 in an hour, through a stand by Parks and Cox, who survived in spite of poor light. Parks passed into the 50's after an hour with a leg glance at 103 off Birtwell, but just before the close he unexpectedly gave a simple return catch to the same bowler – and the crowd went home crestfallen.

Friday

The doom of Sussex fell upon them as the clocks struck three this afternoon, but not before they had merited as much praise as may properly be given even to the gamest losers.

Lancashire's triumph was by an innings and five runs – and it has sent them back to the North uncommonly eager for to-morrow's Battle of the Roses. Handsome though it was, however, and richly deserved, what really mattered most was the way Sussex lost.

Throughout the match 1,275 runs were made in 15 hours; eight new balls were called for; three batsmen reached three figures, and two reached the 90's. A memorable game, therefore, and not only because of Paynter's record-breaking.

To-day Cox became a century-maker, and so thoroughly did he master the Lancashire attack that there was always a chance of the reverse being averted as long as he remained at the crease, especially as Holmes played a captain's part with his bat later on, and carried it out for 48 at the bitter end.

Sussex were 112 for two wickets at the day's beginning, and they needed 188 if Lancashire were to bat again. Cook was bowled by Sibbles at 131, but James Langridge stayed until 210, with Cox, who had started with an overnight 47 unfinished.

Before Langridge left, leg-before at the end of an hour and 35 minutes, Cox had survived a perilous two balls from Sibbles, being nearly run out off the first and nearly bowled and stumped off the second; and a few minutes later he reached his fourth hundred of the season with a lovely boundary cut – off Iddon's bowling – and he drove the same bowler's next delivery through the covers for another 4. Gloriously typical, this, of Cox's aggression; it had lasted two hours and a quarter.

Two more batsmen followed Langridge out quickly. Harry Parks failed at 218, and ten runs later, Sibbles defeated Cox, sixth out, with a ball that moved deceptively in the air. Cox had batted for two hours 50 minutes all told, and the strength and courage of his innings were illustrated in his boundary hits, which totalled 15.

Sussex refused to say die even though the seventh and eighth wickets tumbled immediately after lunch – those of Hammond and Oakes – for the addition of two runs. Holmes and Tuppin put on 41 in half an hour, and we were estimating the amount of time that remained for play when Birtwell took the ball and bowled Tuppin with his first ball.

Another 10 minutes of smiles followed the arrival of Cornford, last man in, and another 24 runs were added, so that Holmes came within two of his half-century. But before he could complete it Cornford was bowled by Phillipson 'all over the shop' as the saying goes.

Holmes, who has become one of the most popular captains in the contemporary game, had resisted magnificently for an hour. It was not his fault, but his lack of authentic bowlers, that caused the second Sussex defeat of the season.

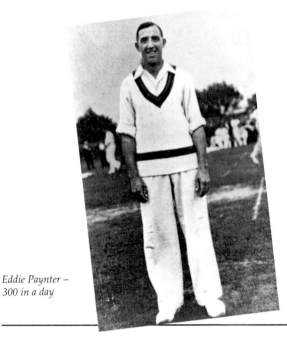

Eddie Paynter – 300 in a day

LANCASHIRE

Washbrook, c Parks (H.), b Parks (J.) 108	W.H.L. Lister, b Tuppin 7
Paynter, lbw, b Parkes (J.) 322	Pollard, c Parks (H.), b Parks (J.) 8
Iddon, run out 4	Duckworth, c Cornford, b Hammond 21
Oldfield, c Cornford, b Parks (J.) ... 92	B 14, l-b 13 27
Hopwood, not out 49	
Phillipson, c Holmes, b Parks (J.) ... 2	Total (8 wkts. dec.) 640
A.J. Birtwell and Sibbles did not bat.	

SUSSEX

Langridge (John), c Sibbles, b Pollard 39	lbw (n), b Phillipson 8
Parks (J.), c Birtwell, b Sibbles 31	c & b Birtwell 55
Cox, b Sibbles 0	b Sibbles 115
Cook, run out 16	B Sibbles 3
Langridge (Jas.), st Duckworth, b Sibbles 64	lbw, b Phillipson 24
	lbw (n), b Phillipson 7
Parks (H.), c & b Birtwell 98	not out 48
Flt-Lt. A.J. Holmes, b Pollard 10	c Washbrook, b Phillipson 0
Hammond, lbw, b Pollard 0	lbw, b Sibbles 0
Oakes (C.), lbw (n), b Birtwell 1	b Birtwell 12
Tuppin, not out 23	b Phillipson 11
Cornford (W.), c Birtwell, b Phillipson 40	B 2, l-b 10 12
B 9, l-0b 5, w 1, n-b 3 18	
	Total 295
Total 340	

LANCASHIRE – First Innings

	O	M	R	W		O	M	R	W
Hammond	26.2	1	118	1	Oakes	11	0	75	0
Tuppin	30	0	136	1	Cook	8	0	41	0
Parks (J.)	38	5	144	5	Langridge (John) ..	3	0	15	0
Langridge (Jas.) ...	20	2	84	0					

SUSSEX – First Innings

	O	M	R	W		O	M	R	W
Phillipson	25.1	5	89	1	Birtwell	27	5	79	2
Sibbles	25	5	70	3	Iddon	2	0	5	0
Pollard	24	3	79	3					

Second Innings

	O	M	R	W		O	M	R	W
Phillipson	29.4	4	91	5	Birtwell	10	2	37	2
Sibbles	23	5	80	3	Iddon	2	0	10	0
Pollard	18	0	65	0					

57: *Middlesex v Surrey*
LORD'S, 28–31 AUGUST 1937

Middlesex went into this match desperate for victory, as they attempted to wrest the County Championship from Yorkshire; as it turned out, Yorkshire secured the fifth of their seven titles of the 1930s, with Middlesex the runners-up – a position they occupied for five successive seasons, from 1936 to 1946, before winning the title in 1947. The other, and no less great, significance of this match was that it was 'Patsy' Hendren's last. Those who seek proof that cricket is more than a game should note Thomas Moult's account of the reception given to Hendren 'the well-beloved' when he went to the wicket, and the acclaim he received on scoring his hundred. He made 170 centuries in all, more than any other batsman except Hobbs.

Hendren (1889–1962) was the greatest middle-order batsman in England in the years immediately after the Great War. In his career, which began in 1907, he scored 57,611 runs, which only Hobbs and Woolley have surpassed. His average of 50.80 is better than either of them. He played 51 times for England, scoring 3,525 runs at an average of 48. He three times hit over 3,000 runs in a season, over 2,000 on another 12 and over 1,000 on another six, and four times scored 1,000 runs in a season abroad. He also played for Queen's Park Rangers and Manchester City at soccer. Errol Holmes (1905–1960), whose dubious tactic of bowling wides to push the score past 200 in order to claim a new ball caused chaos at the end of the game, captained Surrey from 1934 until 1938 and again in 1947 and 1948. He turned out for them sporadically from 1924 to 1955, scoring 13,598 runs at an average of 33 and taking 283 wickets at 34 each. He played five times for England.

Lord's, Saturday
By Thomas Moult

The spirit of Middlesex at Lord's was as willing as ever, but they were a team of physically tired cricketers afer their disheartening experience against Notts, which involved two consecutive days in the field. Their encounter with Surrey that promised such vitality, is consequently moving already to anti-climax.

Indeed, there are perils ahead for the would-be champions: Surrey have scored 448 for eight wickets.

Fishlock, Barling and Holmes are chiefly responsible for the thwarting of Middlesex. Fishlock and Barling scored centuries and Holmes came near to another. The left-hander's achievement was his third of three figures in successive innings.

He batted so masterfully that, opening the innings with Sandham, he made 101 out of 205 in two hours 50 minutes, his second 50 going up after 70 minutes. He drove with a power and judgement delightful to watch, and when Barling joined him the Middlesex bowlers, reinforced though they had been by G. O. Allen, were hit so unmercifully that the fourth wicket put on 142 in 105 minutes.

Fishlock eventually gave a catch behind the wicket, where Price had done his work heroically. He suffered acutely from a damaged right thumb, caused by a knock during the Trent Bridge match. His colleagues told me he could hardly bear to touch the ball.

Sandham hit Allen several times to the boundary before his off-stump was knocked down at 26, and

Gregory was caught in the gully off a mis-hook at 54. Fishlock and Squires stayed together until Fishlock entered the fifties, but Robins' policy of frequent bowling changes caused the partnership to be broken just before lunch, when Middlesex were feeling cheerless for more reasons than one – they had received news from Bournemouth that Yorkshire were already on the way to victory.

Robins and Allen made a pleasant gesture after the interval. The match was Hendren's last at Lord's and his farewell to Middlesex. They joined the great veteran at the professionals' gate and accompanied him on to the field, the other players following together.

Robins, I learn, has arranged a farewell dinner to Hendren this evening, and the whole team will be present.

Nearly 50 runs were added by Fishlock and Barling in the first half-hour of the afternoon. Fishlock hit Owen-Smith for 6, and then, in the next two overs, brought up Surrey's 200 and his own century. On the stroke of four o'clock his innings ended with Price's catch behind the stumps. Altogether he batted three and three-quarter hours, scoring 12 boundaries, principally through on-drives, in addition to his mighty 6.

Holmes continued, with Barling, where Fishlock left off so far as run-getting was concerned. He cut, drove and hooked without waiting to settle down, and by tea-time the score was 307. Barling was 30, and he went on to complete a chanceless 100 in two hours and three-quarters, and then gave a catch to mid-off at 361. He and Holmes put on 93 for the fifth wicket.

The Surrey skipper passed 50, saw Whitfield caught by short-leg 27 runs later, and then paid the penalty of not treating Jim Smith seriously as a fieldsman. He had to dive for his crease to save himself from being run out, and yet before long he again tried for a short run. This time Smith scattered his stumps while he was yards out, and a dashing knock, two hours long and including eleven 4's, was rudely ended. Watts followed his captain home first ball.

Monday

It hardly matters now, the result that to-day will bring, in the last match of the season for Middlesex at Lord's.

They saved the follow-on and scored 377 for six against Surrey's huge total of 509, but their flickering hope of winning the County Championship fluttered out like a candle's end.

But when their gallant, vain endeavour has receded so far into history that all the disappointment will have gone out of it as they look back, there is one of yesterday's memories that must remain bright and moreover, wonderful.

Wonderful, indeed, is the word the Middlesex president, Sir Pelham Warner, used to me at the close of the incident which moved nearly 13,000 onlookers in a way that has no parallel in English sport.

Hendren, the well-beloved, made a century in the last match he will ever play at his beloved Lord's. The scene that occurred when, with a single past Whitfield, the bowler, he made sure of a three-figure score was spontaneous, unanimous and, although deeply moving, most happy.

Earlier in the day Hendren had been given an intimation of the affection in which he is held by cricketers themselves, for, as he walked out, bat in hand, to open his innings amid a storm of clapping that lasted all thh way to the crease, the Surrey fieldsmen, who were apparently standing casually near the wickets, suddenly sprang to attention and, waving their caps, gave their veteran opponent three cheers.

But this was merely the prologue to the drama of the afternoon. For the next two hours, Hendren repaid Surrey by cracking the bowling about in a fashion that, more than once, recalled his heyday: and, then, immediately the crowd saw that the 170th hundred of his long career was an actuality, they clapped and cheered with such fervour that the game was suspended for several minutes.

Patsy stood raising his cap again and again. Reeves, the umpire, pulled out his watch and ticked off the moments to hide his emotion, and then, half in jest, took Hendren's arm and, as he told me afterwards, tried to make him retire there and then.

The applause faded, but the episode was not yet over, for a spectator under the Father Time stood and took off his straw hat and used it as a baton while he led the singing of 'For He's a Jolly Good Fellow.' The whole assembly joined in, and that of itself was unprecedented – choral music at Lord's!

'I can recall nothing like it,' Sir 'Plum' Warner told me afterwards. 'Hendren has deserved it. I am most happy about it.' The ex-president of the club, Mr. A.J. Webbe, who played for Middlesex in the 'eighties, went across to the professionals' room and gave Hendren his farewell congratulations.

His innings had thwarted Surrey, and, in a partnership with Edrich that put on 182 in two-and-a-half hours, saved Middlesex from a threatened collapse and possibly the humiliation of following-on.

Surrey increased their Saturday total of 443 for eight to 509. Parker and Brooks adding 77 altogether for the ninth wicket, the share of the amusing Brooks being 52; and then, when Middlesex began their reply at half-past 12, two batsmen were out for four runs.

Hart was bowled at 2 and Price, who, with a badly hurt thumb, is still hardly able to use his right hand, was lbw two runs later, Gover and Watts being the bowlers. This two-fold disaster brought Edrich and Hendren together, and it was four o'clock before Surrey had another success.

By that time the threat of Gover had so diminished that the wicketkeeper was able to stand up to him, and the Surrey attack became as tired and disheartened as the Middlesex bowling had been.

Hendren was soon the complete master; he hit five of his eight boundaries in forty minutes before lunch, contenting himself afterwards with placing the ball between the fieldsmen in a fashion that brought him apparently easy 2's and 3's.

He set the pace, all the same, and reached 51 out of 94 in 65 minutes. Not until he was 84 did Edrich complete his half-century – in 110 minutes – although the younger player had batted ten minutes longer.

Edrich offered a hot return catch to Whitfield at 153, which was not accepted; but Hendren was faultless. When he was 95 he received an unpleasant knock that held up the game; when he was 96 Fishlock ignored the appeal of the ring to 'let it go,' and saved an apparent 4 on the edge of the boundary, thus halting Hendren at 99. Only for an over, though; and when Hendren was caught at 103 his end was worthy of him. He was caught while trying to hit a six into the pavilion.

Edrich followed him out at 219, when tea was taken. He had missed his 100 by four, and in an excellent stay of two and three-quarter hours he hit 12 boundaries. Compton was well caught in the gulley at 281, and then Allen cracked a brisk 50 in 90 minutes that helped Middlesex so much that they only needed 45 to save the follow-on when left at 315. Owen-Smith, after sweeping Squires into the Tavern for 6, made sure of this by on-driving Watts to the boundary five minutes before the close of a memorable day.

Tuesday

To the very end the season at Lord's was full of life and surprise, nor could it have closed down on a more wideawake afternoon. The match between Middlesex and Surrey, indeed, continued after the ordinary stump-drawing time and the extra half-hour had been nearly used up, when the first innings points were awarded to Surrey.

During the day Surrey, who at one time looked like winning, were not consistently on top; Hendren, the hero of the Middlesex first innings, who helped to save his side with a splendid century, now got out for a duck; and the final moment seethed with controversy, stirred up by the action of the Surrey captain, who bowled wides into the sky so that Middlesex, with a gift of 22 extras, might be helped against their will into the second hundred, thus enabling his fast bowlers to claim the new ball.

This wholly legitimate policy, distasteful though it may be to some people, was followed by a scene of confusion which brought the game to a premature end, Middlesex being 92 runs behind with three wickets in hand.

In reply to the Surrey first total of 509 Middlesex made 419, the last four batsmen adding 83 at the outset. Then Surrey, with a lead of 90, hit up 204 for six and declared, leaving Middlesex to score 295 in 160 minutes – that is, at a speed of 108 an hour.

Middlesex did not succeed in their rather inconsistent endeavour; they scored 202 for seven.

Middlesex are naturally regretful that their great struggle for the championship has culminated in failure, but they have the consolation of never giving up.

They began the day with such eagerness that their not out batsmen, Owen-Smith and Robins, were act ally at the crease before the Surrey fieldsmen appeared: and then they set off at a pace which suggested that their ambition was to get as near as possible to that huge total of 509, put Surrey in and out as quickly as might be in the second innings and then hit off the victory runs!

An excellent crowd saw Robins pay the penalty of hitting out. He cracked Gover twice to the on-boundary in one over, and then, at 398, when he wanted 4 for his half-century, he was bowled leg-stump.

Owen-Smith was rather more fortunate than his captain, for he ran into the fifties before he was caught in the covers.

Middlesex were then 405 for eight, and taking the new ball that is nowadays a trouble-maker as well as a much-coveted fetish, Watts and Gover polished off Sims and Smith with ease. The innings ended soon after 12 o'clock, and Surrey had an hour and a quarter's batting before lunch.

Gover's figures for the innings were excellent, seeing how foot-weary he is after this arduous season – five for 130 in 25 overs.

Whitfield had been absent from the field; he fractured the little finger of his left hand while trying to catch Edrich off his own bowling the previous day, and it was announced that he would take no further part in the match.

This meant that Surrey were really three wickets down, not two, when Fishlock and Sandham left at 11 and 16. The left-hander was bowled middle-stump and Sandham was lbw, Smith being the destroyer of both.

The match became vital and full of possibilities when Squires turned Gray into short-leg's hands at 45, and Gregory was bowled middle stump by Gray at 54.

Lunch was taken with Surrey no more than 76 for 4. Middlesex thus finding themselves with a chance of victory for the first time. It receded, however, after lunch. Holmes and Barling hitting so vigorously that 102 were added for the fifth wicket in 55 minutes.

Holmes called his players in just before half past three, and now it was the turn of Middlesex to lose wickets. Thirty-two had been put on so quickly that a finish looked likely, but before long the interest faded again.

Then came Holmes's resolve to get the new ball; and the astonishing sequel, the players going in immediately he achieved his object by sending down all those wides and byes in an over.

From the news pages: Two England captains and a Test selector were the principal figures in an amazing incident at Lord's yesterday.

The match between Middlesex and Surrey was drifting to its close when E. R. T. Holmes, the Surrey captain and a Test selector, placed a fieldsman just in front of the pavilion, and then took the ball himself at the Nursery end.

To the surprise of the crowd he hurled three deliveries in succession high over the head of R. W. V. Robins, the batsman.

As the ball flew beyond the wicket-keeper towards the boundary MacMurray, the fieldsman, plainly acting under orders, watched it pass him on each occasion for four wides.

Holmes's purpose was to give runs to Middlesex so that his fast bowlers could use the new ball.

Altogether 22 were needed and after a fourth delivery, bowled straight, had been hit to a fieldsman hear the wicket, the fifth passed for four byes, the fieldsman again making no attempt to save the boundary.

The sixth and seventh deliveries were stopped by Robins's bat, and then Holmes bowled another ball high through the air, four wides again being signalled. The ninth ball was allowed to go for further extras.

The Middlesex total had now reached 202, and the crowd, having perceived Holmes's object, were booing and shouting 'Play the game!'

Meanwhile Robins and Allen, the batsman at the other crease, had responded to Holmes's action by

Patsy Hendren

Erroll Holmes

patting the pitch between the deliveries. Robins's feelings were indicated by the agitated manner in which he paced up and down near the wicket.

Everybody now expected that Holmes, with 10 minutes left for play of the extra half-hour that he had previously claimed, would call for the new ball in an attempt to dismiss the three outstanding Middlesex batsmen and force a last-moment victory.

Instead, to the general astonishment, the umpires pulled up the stumps and the players walked off the field.

It transpired that the match was abandoned in consequence of an appeal against the light by G. O. Allen.

The incident, however, had occurred in bright sunshine. It was apparent that this was only an excuse to bring to an end a situation which was becoming unhappy.

Robins and Holmes returned to the pavilion together. The Surrey captain was gesticulating in his attempt at an explanation. He was obviously within his right, as Robins admitted later, when he said:

'Holmes was perfectly fair and acting within the rules of cricket, but something ought to be done to alter the rules to prevent such bowling.'

In discussing the incident Holmes quoted precedents for runs being given away by the fielding side in an attempt to gain a victory. At the Oval, in June, Sussex bowled eight wides in order to get the new ball. In July, 1936, at Leeds, A. B. Sellers, the Yorkshire captain, gave away four byes and nine wides against Surrey.

The general impression at Lord's last night was that the unfortunate incident may have a sequel in an official inquiry.

SURREY

Sandham, b Allen	20	lbw, b Smith (J.)		4
Fishlock, c Price, b Smith (J.)	127	b Smith (J.)		8
Gregory, c Owen-Smith, b Smith (J.)	10	b Gray		19
Squires, st Price, b Robins	31	c Allen, b Gray		17
Barling, c Smith (J.), b Sims	114	not out		71
E.R.T. Holmes, run out	82	b Smith (J.)		58
Whitfield, c Gray, b Owen-Smith	10			
Parker, c Compton, b Robins	41	b Smith (J.)		1
Watts, b Sims	0	not out		26
Brooks, b Robins	52			
Gover, not out	0			
B14, l-b 7, n-b 1	22			
Total	509	Total (6 w., dec.)		204

MIDDLESEX

Price, lbw, b Watts	2	b Gover		23
Hart, b Gover	1	c Gregory, b Watts		10
Edrich, c Fishlock, b Gover	96	c Fishlock, b Watts		25
Hendren, c Gregory, b Squires	103	lbw, b Watts		0
Compton (D.), c Gregory, b Parker	28	b Watts		64
G.O. Allen, c Brooks, b Gregory	53	not out		35
H.G. Owen-Smith, c Gregory, b Gover	55	b Watts		1
R.W.V. Robins, b Gover	46	not out		9
Sims, b Watts	12			
Smith (J.), c sub, b Gover	6			
Gray, not out	0	c & b Gregory		1
L-b10, n-b 7	17	B 9, l-b 3, w 20, n-b 2		34
Total	419	Total (7 wkts.)		202

SURREY – First Innings

	O	M	R	W		O	M	R	W
Allen	21	0	84	1	Owen-Smith	23	0	100	1
Smith (J.)	24	7	42	2	Robins	20.1	1	90	3
Gray	20	1	89	0	Sims	23	1	82	0

Second Innings

	O	M	R	W		O	M	R	W
Smith (J)	12	2	44	4	Gray	15	0	76	2
Owen-Smith	5	0	21	0	Robins	3	0	21	0
Sims	8	1	45	0	Hart	1	0	5	0

MIDDLESEX – First Innings

	O	M	R	W		O	M	R	W
Gover	25.4	3	130	5	Gregory	8	2	19	1
Watts	20	1	87	2	Whitfield	5	0	20	0
Parker	15	2	39	1	Holmes	6	1	26	0
Squires	19	0	81	1					

Second Innings

	O	M	R	W		O	M	R	W
Gover	8	2	27	1	Gregory	14	5	34	1
Watts	14	0	62	5	Squires	5	1	25	0
Parker	8	0	20	0	Holmes	0.4	0		

Umpires – Reeves and Cooke

58: *Essex v Kent*
COLCHESTER, 13–15 JULY 1938

Arthur Fagg's feat of scoring two double centuries in a match remains unique. No batsman who has made a century and a double century in a match has ever come closer to the second double-hundred than scoring 157. Fagg (1915–1977) was only 23 at the time, so it seemed that a career of considerable promise lay ahead of him. He had already made his England debut at the age of 21, having first played for Kent in 1932. As Sutcliffe neared the end of his career Fagg was considered as an England opener, but was invalided home from MCC's tour of Australia in 1936–37 with rheumatic fever, missing all the 1937 season. His test career, which included just five games, ended with the war, sabotaged by ill health. On medical grounds he declined MCC's invitation to tour South Africa at the end of the 1938 season, and when war broke out in 1939 he was found medically unfit for the services. He spent the war as coach at Cheltenham and at first decided not to return to Kent after hostilities ceased; however, he was tempted back for a full season in 1947, scored over 2,000 runs, and stayed in the side until 1957. Altogether he scored 27,291 run at an average of 36, including 58 centuries. His best season was 1938: he scored 2,456 runs at an average of 52. From 1959 until his sudden death he was an umpire, eventually becoming one of the leading test umpires. In 1973 he threatened to withdraw from a test when members of the West Indies sides questioned his umpiring decisions, and a substitute umpire had to be found while Fagg was placated.

Tom Pearce (b. 1905), the Essex centurion, captained his county before and after the war, scoring over 12,061 runs at an average of 34, including 22 hundreds.

Colchester, Wednesday

A great innings of 244 by Fagg was the feature of the opening of the Colchester Festival yesterday, and thanks to him Kent scored 429, twelve of which Essex knocked off in the last quarter of an hour without losing a wicket.

A soft pitch did not play too easily at first, and Sunnucks and Levett were early and easily disposed of, but Fagg was full of confidence from the start and scored at a good pace while the other Kent men laboured after runs.

Todd and the captain, Chalk, helped Fagg in useful stands, but their part was merely to keep up one end while Fagg collared an attack badly weakened by the absence of Nichols and Peter Smith, who were playing for the Players at Lord's.

Fagg's best scoring shots were vigorous on-drives and powerful leg hits, and his timing was perfect. He scored 50 out of the first 55 in about 40 minutes and reached his century out of 125 in 94 minutes.

After lunch his methods were not quite so forceful, but his 200 was scored out of 305 and included twenty-six 4's. Todd helped him to put on 133 for the third stand in an hour and 40 minutes.

Fagg defied the attack for nearly five hours before mistiming a straight ball from Taylor. It was his first mistake. He hit thirty-one 4's.

Thursday

Arthur Fagg, the Kent opening batsman, who played no cricket at all last year after his unlucky illness while with the M.C.C. team in Australia, dominated the play at Colchester yesterday.

When Kent went in for a second time with a lead of 79 over Essex, Fagg forced the pace so brilliantly that before the close he had reached his second three-figure score of the match. Kent finished up 221 ahead with all their wickets in hand.

Fagg actually reached his century out of 134 in 69 minutes – the second fastest hundred of the season. Altogether in this match he has so far obtained 348 runs for once out. His 104 yesterday included 17 4's.

That Essex made as many as 350 was mainly due to a most courageous not-out innings of 137 by the captain, T. N. Pearce, and a fighting ninth-wicket stand of 131 between Pearce and Ray Smith.

Essex began the day by losing their first two wickets for 57, and in spite of a fine effort by O'Connor, who incidentally became the first Essex player to complete his thousand runs for the season, eight men were out for 207, and 73 runs were still needed to avert the follow-on.

Wright, the England leg-break bowler, was the chief cause of destruction, and in one spell of four overs he sent back four batsmen for six runs.

Friday

By scoring a double century in each innings of the match against Essex at Colchester, Arthur Fagg, the Kent opening batsman, set up a new world record, which even Bradman may find it difficult to surpass.

His figures for the match were: 244 out of 386 in five hours and 202 out of 313 in two hours and fifty

Fagg (left) is congratulated by T.N. Pearce, the Essex captain

minutes. He hit 31 fours in the first innings and 27 in the second. Fagg, who is only 23, had never before scored two centuries in a match.

Fagg's performance is all the more remarkable when it is remembered that less than eighteen months ago he was carried off the liner on a stretcher at Tilbury Docks on his enforced return from Australia through illness. He contracted rheumatic fever while on tour with the M.C.C. team, and was unable to play any cricket at all last season.

Essex and Kent players, as well as the spectators, joined in applauding Fagg on his return to the pavilion when Kent declared at 313 for the loss of Sunnucks, who was run out after scoring 82 and helping to add 283 in two hours 35 minutes for the first wicket.

Fagg scored almost twice as quickly as he did in the first innings. The drive, cut, hook, glide and solid hit to leg were all executed with the same certainty, and he did not make a false stroke all the time he was at the crease.

Essex, wanting 393 to win, made a deplorable start, losing Eastman and D. R. Wilcox for eight runs before lunch, but a downpour during the interval and another about three o'clock prevented any further cricket, and the match was left drawn.

Wade, the Essex wicket-keeper, accomplished a remarkable performance in not conceding a bye till 626 runs were on the board.

KENT

Fagg, lbw, b Taylor	244	not out 202
Sunnucks, c Wades, b Smith (R.)	3	run out 82
W.H. Levett, c Wilcox, b Daer (H.)	0	
Todd, b Smith (R.)	39	
Spencer, c Taylor, b Vigar	14	
F.G.H. Chalk, c Lavers, b Eastman	61	
Foy, c & b Taylor	25	
Harding, st Wade, b Vigar	9	
Wright, c Wade, b Taylor	2	
Watt, not out	24	not out 24
Lewis, c Vigar, b Taylor	5	
Lb 3	3	B 2, l-b 2, n-b 1 5
Total	429	Total (1 wkt dec) 313

ESSEX

D.R. Wilcox, c Harding, b Todd	5	b Watt 1
Eastman, lbw, b Todd	44	c Wright, b Todd 0
Taylor, b Lewis	37	not out 7
O'Connor, c Lewis, b Wright	63	not out 0
Avery, b Wright	1	
T.N. Pearce, not out	137	
A.B. Lavers, lbw, b Wright	1	
Wade, b Wright	4	
Vigar, lbw, b Wright	0	
Smith (R.), c Fagg, b Wright	37	
Daer, lbw, b Wright	4	
B 5, l-b 6, n-b 6	17	
Total	350	Total (2 wkts.) 8

KENTS – First Innings

	O	M	R	W		O	M	R	W
Smith (R.)	22	4	96	2	Vigar	19	3	91	2
Daer	10	3	51	1	O'Connor	2	0	6	0
Eastman	40	15	68	1	Pearce	10	0	43	0
Lavers	9	1	30	0	Taylor	10.1	1	41	4

Second Innings

	O	M	R	W		O	M	R	W
Smith (R.)	10	3	46	0	O'Connor	5	0	23	0
Daer	9	0	46	0	Vigar	13	0	75	0
Eastman	17	2	52	0	Wilcox	4	0	20	0
Taylor	10	0	46	0					

ESSEX – First Innings

	O	M	R	W		O	M	R	W
Todd	19	6	46	2	Wright	31.3	7	107	7
Watt	22	3	63	0	Lewis	26	7	83	1
Harding	5	1	34	0					

Wright bowled three no-balls, Harding two, Todd one.

Second Innings

	O	M	R	W		O	M	R	W
Todd	2	0	6	1	Watt	1.3	0	2	1

Umpires – Newman, Parker

59: *Glamorgan v Gloucestershire*
NEWPORT, 31 MAY–2 JUNE 1939

Glamorgan's remarkable recovery against Gloucestershire showed the quality of a side that would, shortly after the war, win the Championship for the first time. Since Glamorgan joined the Championship in 1921 they had finished only twice in the top ten, at eighth in 1926 and seventh in 1937. Although in this summer they would again perform poorly (coming 13th), the early post-war years would be fruitful. Gloucestershire had had a poor season in 1938, finishing 10th, but would finish third this year. Glamorgan's total was their highest in first-class cricket (though they were to overhaul it against Derbyshire in 1951, scoring 587) and

Emrys Davies' unbeaten 287 remains the highest score ever for the county: he also produced the best bowling in the match for Glamorgan. Hammond's 302 in Gloucestershire's innings was far less remarkable: it was his fourth treble century, though it was his 150th century in first-class cricket, accomplished at the age of 36.

Despite cricket being abandoned for six seasons because of the war, seven of the Glamorgan side returned to play in 1946 (and an eighth, Brierley, played for Lancashire). Most of them were still in the Championship-winning side of 1948, to be captained by Wooller, who spent much of the war in a Japanese prisoner-of-war camp. As has already been noted, Turnbull, the captain in 1939, was killed in action; Dai Davies became a first-class umpire and Mercer, already 44 when war broke out, played once for Northamptonshire (with whom he became county coach) in 1947. With the exception of Sinfield, who retired, the entire Gloucestershire side survived the war and turned out again for the county afterwards.

Newport, Wednesday

Gloucestershire had the better of the day's cricket at Newport, winding up within 56 of Glamorgan's total of 196 with seven batsmen still to be dismissed.

Dyson, for the sixth time, carried his bat through the innings, and but for his 99 not out the Welsh county would have failed completely. His was a painstaking innings lasting three hours 50 minutes.

Gloucester scored freely, especially during a third-wicket partnership between Hammond and Sinfield, 65 being added in 50 minutes. Hammond, with flashing cover drives and square cuts, went on to complete 50 out of 83 in 70 minutes, and was unbeaten at the close.

Thursday

Glamorgan set about the huge task set them by Hammond's brilliant innings of 302 at Newport yesterday with rare spirit, and at the close of play Dyson and Emrys Davies had knocked off 131 of the 309 needed to avoid an innings defeat without being separated.

Hammond's batting, of course, overshadowed everything on a day when the mastery of bat over ball was so great that only two wickets fell while 496 runs were scored. Hammond's innings equalled the biggest ever made against the Glamorgan bowling – his own 302 not out at Bristol in 1934 – and took him to within 73 of his 1,000 runs for the season.

Besides being his 150th century in first-class cricket, his score was his fourth of 300 or more. He overshadowed everybody else during the five hours and 40 minutes he was in, using a wide variety of stylish yet powerful strokes, and he hit two 6's –

one out of the ground – and 35 fours.

Taking 70 minutes to complete 50, he accelerated his pace, passing 100 in a further three-quarters of an hour, exceeding 200 in four hours, and adding his last 102 in a hundred minutes. He made his 302 out of 447. Emmett, who at one point obtained only three runs while Hammond got 50, served his side well for over two hours, during which 168 were added for the fourth wicket, and Crapp stayed the same length of time during a fifth partnership that realised 214.

Shortly after Hammond left to a skied catch behind the wicket Gloucestershire's innings was declared. The task presented no terros to Dyson and Emrys Davies, the Glamorgan opening pair, who scored at a brisk rate. In 35 minutes they sent up 50, and in 80 minutes had 100 on the board. Davies completed his 50 out of 74 in 50 minutes, and Dyson reached a similar figure just before the close, when Glamorgan had reduced the deficit to 178 without loss. .

Friday

On a pitch described as 'the best ever to be prepared in Wales' Glamorgan had little difficulty in saving their game against Gloucestershire at Newport, their score of 577 for four beating their previous highest in first-class cricket – 550 for five against Surrey at the Oval in 1936. E. Davies' 287 not out – his first double century – beat the previous highest individual score by a Glamorgan player – 280 not out by Duckfield, also at the Oval in 1936.

In Gloucestershire's first innings and Glamorgan's second innings 1,082 runs were scored for only nine wickets. The match aggregate was 1,278 for 19 wickets. The first-wicket stand of Davies and Dyson – who narrowly failed to make 100 in each innings – realised 255 in four hours. Bowlers had a heart-breaking task, and Glamorgan never looked in trouble.

Davies and Dyson overnight scored 136 and both reached their centuries almost simultaneously in three and a half hours. After Dyson left Davies dominated the cricket. Turnbull helped him to put on 138 in 80

The Glamorgan team of 1939

minutes, and D. Davies and Smart took part in further useful stands before the game was given up at six o'clock.

E. Davies defied Gloucestershire for seven and a half hours. He used every stroke, with the drive and hit to leg bringing him most of his 25 4's.

GLOUCESTERSHIRE

Barnett, c Davies (E.), b Mercer 15	Emmett, st Davies (H.),
Sinfield, b Davies (E.) 41	b Jones (E.C.) 53
Hopkins, c Turnbull, b Judge 13	J. P. Crapp, not out 60
W.R. Hammond, c Davies (H.),	W. L. Neale, not out 5
b Davies (E.) 302	B12, l-b 4 16
	Total (5 wkts., dec.) 505

Wilson, Scott, Lambert and Goddard did not bat.

GLAMORGAN

Dyson, not out 99		c Wilson, b Lambert 120	
Davies (E.), lbw, b Goddard 34		not out 287	
Brierley, b Scott 9		c Hammond, b Goddard 5	
M.J. Turnbull, c Wilson,		st Wilson, b Emmett 77	
b Lambert 18		c Lambert, b Sinfield 48	
Davies (D.), c Wilson, b Scott 1		not out 23	
Smart, b Scott 10			
W. Wooller, b Goddard 18			
Jones (E.C.), c Wilson, b Sinfield 0			
Davies (H.), c Wilson, b Sinfield 0			
Judge, c Neale, b Goddard 3			
Mercer, b Goddard 0			
B 1, l-b 2, n-b 1 4		L-b 17	
Total 196		Total (4 wkts.) 577	

GLAMORGAN – First Innings

	O	M	R	W		O	M	R	W
Scott	13	0	52	3	Sinfield	10	3	16	0
Barnett	4	0	18	0	Emmett	2	0	6	0
Lambert	14	2	50	1	Neale	1	0	5	0
Goddard	22.6	7	45	4					

Second Innings

	O	M	R	W		O	M	R	W
Scott	24	1	95	0	Neale	1	0	11	0
Lambert	16	0	128	1	Barnett	5	0	32	0
Goddard	38	7	123	1	Emmett	7	0	51	1
Sinfield	36	5	116	1	Hammond	1	0	4	0

GLOUCESTERSHIRE – First Innings

	O	M	R	W		O	M	R	W
Mercer	21	0	105	1	Davies (E.)	21	2	91	2
Judge	18	1	83	1	Davies (D.)	2	0	9	0
Wooller	23	1	124	0	Smart	6	1	36	0
Jones (E.C.)	9	0	41	1					

Umpires – Newman, Cruce

60: *Warwickshire v Nottinghamshire*
BIRMINGHAM, 24–25 JULY 1946

The first cricket season after the war received much less coverage in the press than its predecessors had. This was thanks to newsprint rationing, which meant that even reports of important matches sometimes found themselves reduced to little more than a scorecard. For taking all ten wickets in an innings Hollies was described as 'the first player to accomplish such a feat this season'. These days the feat is so rare – it has not been accomplished in first-class cricket in England since 1964 – that the expectation that it might happen more often in 1946 seems curious. Yet in the 11 seasons before the war it had happened 14 times, twice in 1939, and as late as 1956 was performed four times in a season (twice by Laker). Covered wickets, and the reduced help they give to bowlers, are the main causes of the rarity of the feat now.

Hollies' feat remains especially curious for two reasons. All his victims were bowled or leg-before, so he took all ten without help from a fieldsman. This remains unique in the Championship and only John Wisden, playing in 1850, has ever been recorded as having taken all ten in this way. Second, and less unusually, Warwickshire lost. Hollies (1912–1981) played for Warwickshire from 1932 until 1957, and took 2,323 wickets at 21 each bowling leg-breaks and

googlies. He played in 13 tests and was the man who bowled Bradman for a duck in his last test innings at the Oval in 1948. Hollies took 100 wickets in a season 14 times, and 1946 was his most successful year, when he took 184 wickets at under 16 each. In his long career Hollies scored only 1,600 runs at an average of five, his wickets easily exceeding his runs.

Eric Hollies

Birmingham, Wednesday

W. E. Hollies, the Warwickshire slow bowler, took all 10 Nottinghamshire wickets for 49 runs at Birmingham yesterday. He is the first player to accomplish such a feat this season. Perhaps the most remarkable feature of the performance is the fact that no other member of the Warwick side contributed directly to the fall of any of the wickets. Seven men were clean bowled by Hollies, the other three falling leg before wicket.

Warwick, who had scored 170, led on the first innings by 35 runs, Notts being able to total only 135 against the one-man assault of Hollies.

The last time a Warwickshire bowler took all 10 wickets was also on the Edgbaston ground, when H. Howell took the Yorkshire wickets for 51 runs.

And it was on the same ground, in 1939, that a bowler last dismissed a whole county side – but that time it was the Warwick wickets which fell to E. A. Watts of Surrey.

Thursday

The defeat by seven wickets of Warwickshire by Nottinghamshire at Edgbaston yesterday must have tended to make Eric Hollies feel that his remarkable feat of Wednesday, when he took all ten Notts wickets for 49 runs, had been in vain.

There was some consolation for him, however, in the fact that a collection taken on the ground in appreciation of his bowling realised over £100.

WARWICKSHIRE

P. Cranmer, c Heane, b Woodhead 1	R. Sale, lbw, b Jepson 7
R. Sale, c Heane, b Woodhead 30	J.M. Mills, c Meads, b Heane 16
R.H. Maudsley, b Jepson 0	R.H. Maudsley, c Meads, b Heane 22
H.E. Dollery, c Simpson, b Butler 2	H.E. Dollery, b Heane 25
J.M. Mills, c Jepson, b Butler 16	P. Cranmer, b Jepson 1
K.A. Taylor, b Butler 37	K.A. Taylor, b Jepson 18
J.S. Ord, c Heane, b Butler 0	J.S. Ord, b Butler 12
W.E. Fantham, lbw, b Heane 51	W.E. Fantham, b Butler 1
F. Mitchell, lbw, b Jepson 13	F. Mitchell, b Butler 0
C.C. Goodway, not out 9	C.C. Goodway, run out 5
W.E. Hollies, c Jepson, b Heane 2	W.E. Hollies, B Jepson 4
Extras (B 6, l-b 3) 9	Extras (B 1, l-b 1) 2
Total 170	Total 113

NOTTINGHAMSHIRE

W.W. Keeton, b Hollies 40	W.W. Keeton, not out 4
C.B. Harris, b Hollies 10	C.B. Harris, not out 80
R.T. Simpson, lbw, b Hollies 14	R.T. Simpson, b Maudsley 6
J. Hardstaff, lbw, b Hollies 0	J. Hardstaff, c Goodway, b Hollies 41
T.B. Reddick, b Hollies 1	T.B. Reddick, not out 19
G.F. Heane, lbw, b Hollies 4	
F. W. Stocks, not out 37	
A. Jepson, b Hollies 7	
H.J. Butler, b Hollies 8	
E.A. Meads, b Hollies 0	
F.G. Woodhead, b Hollies 8	
Extras (B 4, l-b 2) 6	
Total 135	Total (3 wkts.) 150

WARWICKSHIRE – First Innings

	O	M	R	W		O	M	R	W
Butler	25	9	49	4	Jepson	20	7	40	2
Woodhead	13	3	24	2	Harris	1	1	0	0
Heane	23.4	10	48	2					

Second Innings

	O	M	R	W		O	M	R	W
Butler	13	4	19	3	Jepson	20.3	6	43	4
Woodhead	12	6	17	0	Heane	19	8	32	3

NOTTINGHAMSHIRE – First Innings

	O	M	R	W		O	M	R	W
Mitchell	6	2	19	0	Maudsley	7	3	19	0
Hollies	20.4	4	49	10	Fantham	20	3	42	0

Second Innings

	O	M	R	W		O	M	R	W
Mitchell	5	2	10	0	Maudsley	7	1	22	1
Hollies	31	20	29	1	Fantham	10	1	36	0
Mills	18	4	46	0	Dollery	2	1	7	0

61: Middlesex v Sussex

LORD'S, 24–26 MAY 1947

There has never been such a summer in English cricket as 1947. English batsmen made thousands of runs on placid wickets. The two particular names that stand out from that summer – and are synonymous with it – are those of Denis Compton and Bill Edrich. Each broke the record for the highest number of runs scored in a season, established in 1906 by Tom Hayward, who scored 3,518 from 61 innings at an average of 66. Compton scored 3,816 runs from 50 innings at an average of 91; Edrich 3,539 from 52 innings at an average of 80. Of all the batsmen who have scored more than 3,000 runs in a season, only Herbert Sutcliffe bettered Compton's average, having scored 3,006 from 41 innings in 1931 at an average of 97. Compton and Edrich remain the two highest scorers in an English season, and unless the county programme is once more expanded, no-one is likely to beat them. Compton scored 18 centuries in the season, the most ever, surpassing Hobbs' 16 in 1925. Edrich made 12 centuries. Middlesex, having been runners-up in the five previous seasons, unsurprisingly won the Championship, the talent of the team running deeper than just Compton and Edrich.

Compton (b. 1918) played for the county from 1936 to 1958. In his career he scored 38,942 runs at an average of 52, including 123 centuries (among which was the fastest treble century in history, made in three hours in South Africa). He was also a useful slow left-arm bowler, taking 622 wickets at 32 each. He played 78 times for England, scoring 5,807 runs at an average of 50.

Lord's, Monday
By E. W. Swanton

Middlesex beat Sussex in two days at Lord's yesterday by 10 wickets, within five minutes of the end of the extra half-hour. After the stranglehold of the match which Middlesex had taken on Saturday the Bank Holiday performance, watched by more than 20,000, inevitably took on the character of a protracted and strenuous rearguard action by Sussex.

There was a time about half-past five when to the friends of Middlesex the prospect looked a little dreary. Cox and James Langridge were installed in great comfort for the third wicket on the easiest pitch possible, and the bowlers, after a long outing on one of the first real summer days, might well have been considered just about cooked. But with the second new ball Cox ended an innings of good Sussex vintage and a stand of 132 by being lbw to one that kept a little low – the sort of ball that cricketers have had to look out for at Lord's since time immemorial.

And soon afterwards Mann removed the other and more obdurate half of the partnership by catching Langridge beautifully full length to his left 20 yards from the bat on the leg side off a true hit.

Thereafter defence degenerated into flight, and by 7.25 p.m. Middlesex had another 12 points safely in the locker. The point is, though, that only a side alert, confident and admirably handled would have been capable of re-taking a complete grip of the match in the evening.

I cannot remember seeing Griffith bat with such a combination of soundness and discretion as he showed in a partnership with Bartlett that gave signs of rescuing the first innings. Unhappily the tail did little, and Robins, with a lead of 241, was obliged to make Sussex bat again.

MIDDLESEX

First Innings		Second Innings	
Robertson, c Parks b Cornford	10		
Brown, c Griffith, b Nye	3	Not out	2
W.J. Edrich, b Cornford	106		
Compton (D.C.S.) ... b C. Oakes	110		
R.W.V. Robins, c Griffith, b C. Oakes	23		
F.G. Mann, c Duffield, b Langridge (Jas.)	69		
Thompson, st Griffith, b Langridge (Jas.)	12		
Compton (L.), c Langridge (John), b Langridge (Jas.)	6	Not out	19
Sims, not out	20		
Young, c C. Oakes, b Langridge (Jas.)	0		
Gray, st Griffith, b C. Oakes	2		
Extras	19		
Total	380	Total	21

Bowling – 1st Inns: Nye 11–2–48–1, Cornford 30–5–98–2, Duffield 28–3–88–0, Jas. Langridge 13–3–38–4, Cox 4–0–17–0, C. Oakes 24–5–70–3, John Langridge 1–0–2–0.

2nd Inns: Cornford 2–0–13–0, Duffield 2–0–4–0, Bartlett 1–0–4–0.

SUSSEX

First Innings		Second Innings	
Langridge (John), c and b Gray	4	b Edrich	6
Oakes (C.), b Edrich	1	c sub, b Gray	32
Langridge (Jas.), c Edrich, b Sims	6	c Mann, b Young	85
Cox, lbw, b Edrich	22	lbw, b Gray	65
Parks, lbw, b Edrich	8	b Gray	17
S.C. Griffith, c Edrich, b Sims	45	b Sims	16
H.T. Bartlett, c Sims, b Gray	19	c Compton (L.), b Sims	9
Oakes (J.), not out	25	not out	16
Duffield, lbw, b Gray	1	c Compton (D.), b Sims	0
Nye, c Edrich, b Gray	0	st Compton (L.), b Compton (D.)	7
Cornford, c Compton (L.), b Compton (D.)	7	c Edrich, b Sims	0
Extras	1	Extras	6
Total	139	Total	259

Bowling – 1st Inns: Gray 12–1–28–4, Edrich 15–3–34–3, Sims 17–2–56–2, Robins 1–0–2–0, Young 4–1–12–0, Compton (D.) 3–0–6–1.

2nd Inns: Edrich 15–1–55–1, Gray 20–6–42–3, Young 17–4–40–1, Compton (D.) 13–4–42–1, Sims 20.3–2–46–4, Robins 8–1–28–0.

Edrich and Compton

62: Middlesex v Kent

LORD'S, 13–15 AUGUST 1947

Middlesex's progress towards the Championship in 1947 was not without its difficulties. This thrilling victory by Kent, whose fourth place this year was to be their last good Championship showing for almost 20 years, shows that the batting side was not impregnable. It was usual during this season for either Compton or Edrich (and, often, both) to perform spectacularly in each match in which they played. In this one it would have needed Edrich to provide more enduring support for Compton's 168 for his side to have had a chance. Edrich (1916–86) came from one of cricket's most famous families. A professional before the war, he served with great distinction as a RAF officer, winning the DFC, and became an amateur at the start of this season. He played for Middlesex from 1937 to 1958, captaining them from 1951 to 1957, and appeared 39 times for England. He made 36,965 runs in his career at an average of 42, and was also a useful fast bowler, taking 479 wickets at 33 each. In 1938, still only 22, he scored 1,000 runs before the end of May.

Kent's captain, Bryan Valentine (1908–83) played from 1927 to 1948, making 18,306 runs at an average of 30. Considering his test batting average of 65, it was odd that he played just seven times for England. Badly wounded during the war, he won the Military Cross. Doug Wright (b. 1914), whose 11 wickets were the main bowling contribution to the Kent victory, was unique, bowling medium-pace leg breaks. In a career that lasted from 1932 to 1957 he took 2,056 wickets at 24 each. This was his best season, in which he took 177 wickets at 21 each. Despite the expense of his test wickets – 108 at 39 each – he played 34 tests. Wright took seven hat-tricks in first-class cricket – a world record.

Lord's, Wednesday
By E. W. Swanton

The struggle at Lord's yesterday was as gripping as the one we saw at Canterbury, with the difference that this time Kent, being 168 runs on with three of Middlesex out, are not quite so comfortably placed as they were a week ago.

Even so, in getting out both Compton and Edrich for less than 50 between them they have done more than any side for a long time.

The pitch, though it took some spin from those who really turned their wrists was plumb and good, so that in bowling out Kent for 301, Middlesex had, as it were, struck off 100 or more from the total reason suggested when their opponents won the toss.

With Edrich looking on from slip, and Gray showing the strain of much hard labour the opening attack was made to seem very placid by two such craftsmen as Fagg and Todd. Ninety-three for 0 at lunch was horribly ominous, but Robins's departure afterwards to some secret pavilion conclave was the signal for a sharp rise in the fortunes of Middlesex.

First Todd, who had batted in the most refreshing way, was bowled by Sims, who caused Ames to die several deaths before he was caught by the keeper – 113 for two. This was fine bowling, and Valentine countered it aggressively in the true Kent way.

The crisis of the innings was at 179, when Young had the reward of some very steady overs by slipping one past Fagg. Davies, somewhat out of form, gave Leslie Compton another catch, and when Mann brought on Gray an off-break at once ended Valentine's admirable innings, and half Kent were out for 221.

Anson in the partnership with his captain had showed what a promising batsman was lost to Cambridge this summer. The comment that Kent's tail must be long and thin if Wright can get in at No. 9 was effectively answered with an innings full of such good strokes as we saw no glimpse of between Perth and Brisbane, whither he arrived, if my memory serves, without having bothered the scorers.

Kent had some early encouragement, for after Brown had guided one into the gully Robertson played as indifferently as even a really good batsman sometimes does when he is full of runs. But the deadly Wright came on and off, and 77 were up when Edrich, in on-driving, suddenly lifted his distinguished head like a very ordinary mortal.

Crisis deepened into tragedy when Compton, after a perfect beginning, was bowled round his legs with a huge leg-break to which he offered a strangely primitive blow.

Thursday

There was a fateful air about this grim day's cricket between Middlesex and Kent in the sunshine at Lord's. One had the strong impression that the championship was being lost and won, and one could sense the fearful thought that perhaps it was not being won

147

by Middlesex.

But once the great Valentine–Ames stand of 157 for Kent's third wicket was broken in the evening Middlesex were able to prevent their opponents pressing a good position home; at the end Kent led by 298 with 5 wickets left, and if ever a third day held the certainty of dramatic play to-morrow surely must be it.

Wright once again bowled beautifully for Kent, having entire charge of the Pavilion end to-day.

When the morning began a vast deal rested on the partnership of Robertson and Robins, who had withstood Wright so skilfully overnight. For the best part of an hour all went well. Wright, bowling again to his O'Reilly field of three short legs, diluting a dose of severe leg-breaks and googlies with occasional no-balls, faithfully struck by Robertson.

CAUGHT HIGH UP

Robertson's century came, his 12th this season, and an excellent innings in its latter part; then Robins sweeping at Wright hit the ball off the edge to long leg. A quick leg break and an admirable catch high up at slip sent back Mann, whereupon Robertson began to bat with a sense of desperation that hardly seemed warranted and quickly departed.

Young fought hard, and by painful ones and twos Middlesex crawled up to 229.

The sending back of both of Kent's openers put the spectators in wonderful heart but for their next wicket – and there was little hint of the traditional impartiality of Lord's about this crowd – they had to wait 2½ hours and to endure some batsmanship of wonderfully high quality from Valentine and Ames.

It was an especial joy to see Valentine playing so well again.

Compton, new style, bowled too many bad ones, and at last Robins began to tone up the game with Young one end and Compton, old style, (that is round the wicket in the classic left arm manner), at the other. Accuracy then tended to return to the attack and close on six Ames, having been bogged down, pushed Young into silly mid off's hands.

Soon after Valentine drove Compton inches only above the ground, Gray making a thrilling catch as he fell. Three-quarters of an hour then remained during which Robins continued to trust to the same pair. Davies' wicket fell, but Anson hardly ever looked like getting out.

Friday

The Kent and Middlesex match, than which few better have been seen of late at Lord's or anywhere else, ended in Kent's victory by 75 runs with just five minutes to spare, writes E. W. Swanton.

Kent declared at 10 minutes to 1 yesterday, leaving Middlesex to score 397 at 95 an hour. It was a tall order, but the three Middlesex Musketeers are no ordinary antagonists, and the fact of a strongly defensive field

being set soon after Compton and Edrich came together, though both openers had been got out for 28, was the measure of Kent's apprehension. Compton and Edrich, who was plastered plentifully with strapping, added 60, whereat Wright took a very nasty low catch and bowl to send back Edrich. With so long a Middlesex tail, Mann had now to be kept for a while from Wright, and the hour before tea suggested Middlesex's chief preoccupation was saving the day.

102 IN 40 MINUTES

At tea, taken in five minutes on the field, Compton was given orders to go to it, and for 40 minutes he did so with a brilliance that astonished even his admirers.

From there being 208 needed in 85 minutes the sum and ratio was actually decreased by the scoring of 102 in 40 minutes, 71 of them by Compton. Three-quarters of an hour and 101 runs divided Middlesex from victory, when Compton, turning himself inside out to force a ball wide of the leg stump over cover-point, failed to clear the fieldsman's head.

He had showed us strokes outside the imagination of any but a Hobbs or a Macartney, and Mann had backed him bravely and with skill. When Mann, too, was out just afterwards Middlesex had not quite the batting talent to withstand some inspired overs of off-breaks from Davies, and so the victory was snatched.

Doug Wright

KENT

First Innings		Second Innings	
Todd, b Sims	62	b Hever	7
Fagg, b Young	66	c Compton (L.), b Gray	6
Ames, c Compton (L.), b Sims	8	c Compton (L.), b Young	69
B.H. Valentine, b Gray	61	c Gray, b Compton (D.)	92
J.G.W. Davies, c Compton (L.), b Sims	4	lbw, b Young	11
G.F. Anson, lbw, b Sims	25	c Mann, b Young	51
Evans, lbw, b Compton (D.)	18	c Robertson, b Compton (D.)	56
Dovey, run out	7	not out	10
Wright, b Hever	36	c Edrich, b Young	11
Ridgway, b Compton (D.)	0		
Harding, not out	5		
Extras	9	Extras	11
Total	301	Total (8 wkts. dec.)	324

Bowling: Gray 17–3–44–1, Hever 10.1–2–32–1, Robertson 3–1–12–0, Young 16–8–24–1, Compton (D.) 24–2–87–2, Robins 2–0–6–0, Sims 19–0–87–4.

Bowling: Gray 19–3–70–1, Hever 15–3–37–1, Young 38.2–12–65–4, Compton (D.) 31–10–86–2, Sims 12–1–37–0, Robins 3–0–18–0.

MIDDLESEX

First Innings		Second Innings	
Brown, c Valentine, b Harding	0	b Harding	5
Robertson, c Evans, b Wright	110	lbw, b Harding	12
W.J. Edrich, b Dovey	28	c and b Wright	31
Compton (D.), b Wright	16	c Davies, b Wright	168
R.W.V. Robins, c Harding, b Wright	24	b Davies	21
F.G. Mann, c Fagg, b Wright	1	b Wright	57
Compton (L.), c Harding, b Wright	6	st Evans, b Wright	7
Sims, b Dovey	7	b Davies	7
Gray, c Todd, b Wright	7	not out	4
Young, c Fagg, b Wright	17	c Evans, b Davies	0
Hever, not out	8	b Davies	2
Extras	5	Extras	7
Total	229	Total	321

Bowling: Harding 5–1–22–1, Ridgway 13–1–46–0, Wright 33.2–5–92–7, Dovey 28–5–59–2, Davies 2–0–5–0.

Bowling: Harding 13–0–56–2, Ridgway 5–0–29–0, Wright 24–3–102–4, Dovey 20–2–69–0, Davies 19–3–58–4.

63: *Hampshire v Glamorgan*
BOURNEMOUTH, 21–24 AUGUST 1948

At last Glamorgan won their first title, convincingly, after 22 seasons of being near the bottom of the table. Glamorgan rose from ninth in 1947 to pip Surrey, whose insuperable side of the 1950s was almost complete, and Middlesex, the reigning champions, who could only finish third. On the first day there was just ten minutes play due to rain; a fact that made Glamorgan's victory over Hampshire (in Wisden's phrase) 'especially creditable'. By batting swiftly on the second day, and reducing Hampshire to 50 for 6 at the close, they made sure of the title.

As E.W. Swanton wrote in his report, there was much thought of Maurice Turnbull, killed in 1944, who had (as captain and secretary) turned Glamorgan round in the 1930s. Yet Wilfred Wooller (b. 1912), a former Cambridge blue who had become captain in 1947 and was to serve until 1960 in that post, led the side to victory. Between 1935 and 1962 he made 13,598 runs at an average of 22 and took 958 wickets at 27 each, performing the 'double' in 1954. He was later secretary of the county. Two other members of the side should be noted. Clay (1898–1973), another former captain, was a survivor from the first season in 1921. A highly effective slow bowler, as he showed in this fixture, he took 1,317 wickets in his career at under 20 each: his name became synonymous with Glamorgan cricket. The other main wicket-taker, Muncer (1913–1982), had spent much of the war in a Japanese prisoner-of-war camp with E.W. Swanton. He played for Middlesex from 1933 to 1946, and for Glamorgan from 1947 to 1954, after which he became senior coach at Lord's. Originally a batsman, he became an off-spinner, and this was his best season: he took 159 wickets at 17 each, decisive to Glamorgan's triumph.

Bournemouth, Wednesday
By E. W. Swanton

It is Glamorgan's championship. By winning the most conclusive of victories at Bournemouth against Hampshire yesterday they climbed beyond the reach of both Surrey and Yorkshire, neither of whom have greatly distinguished themselves in the matches just ended.

Thus the youngest of the 17 first-class counties becomes only the third outside those who used to be termed the big six to finish at the top since the competition was extended to more or less its present dimensions in 1895.

Glamorgan in 1948 will be remembered, with Warwickshire in 1911 and Derbyshire in 1936. Each of those two sides surprised the cricket world as Glamorgan have done this time. The present result is indeed a happy surprise for there could not have been a more popular success.

It is not necessary to flatter Glamorgan in order to praise them. They are deficient in several directions, especially batting. But they have shining virtues, and it is particularly appropriate that these include several of which our first-class cricket stands in need: quickness and 'drill' in the field, slow bowling which couples real spin with control, and that aggressive team spirit which has its mainspring in a strong captain who is himself an outstanding fielder.

Many on either side of the Welsh border will be thinking now of the late M. J. Turnbull, who fell in action with the Welsh Guards in Normandy on Aug. 5, 1944. Maurice Turnbull, from the moment of his taking over captaincy and secretaryship in 1930, was the maker of Glamorgan cricket.

As J. C. Clay wrote in the Wisden following his death: 'He converted a stumbling and shamefaced bankrupt into a worthy and respected member of society.' Turnbull was a great captain and a hero to every Welshman.

Now Clay and Wilfred Wooller carry on his work, one as the honorary secretary, the other as captain, and theirs is the chief credit for what has been achieved this summer.

Wooller's own fielding at short leg has been as brilliant as Turnbull's used to be, while Clay, at the age of 50, has come into the picture in the most dramatic way in the last two matches. Against Surrey he had 10 for 61, now against Hampshire nine for 79, so taking some of the burden from Muncer, whose seven wickets at Bournemouth brings his total for the summer to 150.

Muncer's off-breaks, often helped by Hever with the new ball, the all-round ability of Wooller, Watkins and the veteran Emrys Davies, and several spectacular innings by W. E. Jones have been the principal technical ingredients of their victories.

Wilfrid Wooller

GLAMORGAN – First Innings

Davies (E.), c Dawson (G.), b Shackleton	74
Dyson, hit wkt., b Bailey	51
Parkhouse, c Shackleton, b Bailey	2
Jones (W.E.), not out	78
W. Wooller, c & B Knott	29
Eaglestone, st Harrison, b Bailey	2
Muncer, lbw, b Bailey	40
J. Pleass, b Knott	0
Davies (H.), b Knott	0
Hever, c & b Bailey	18
J.C. Clay, c Herman, b Bailey	2
Extras	19
Total	315

Bowling: Herman 14–4–33–0; Shackleton 17–5–45–1; Knott 42–9–133–3; Bailey 41–8–85–6.

HAMPSHIRE

First Innings		Second Innings	
Arnold, lbw, b Clay	2	c Dyson, b Clay	16
Rogers, c Parkhouse, b Wooller	2	b Hever	11
Rev. J.R. Bridger, c Parkhouse, b Hever	0	b Clay	18
McCorkell, c Davies (H.) b Muncer	34	lbw, b Muncer	12
E.D.R. Eagar, c Wooller, b Muncer	0	b Muncer	39
Bailey, c Davies (E.), b Clay	3	run out	3
Dawson, c Wooller, b Clay	0	lbw, b Clay	4
Harrison, st Davies (H.), b Muncer	10	c Muncer, b Clay	5
Herman, b Muncer	21	b Clay	1
Shackleton, c Pleass, b Muncer	0	not out	0
C.J. Knott, not out	2	lbw, b Clay	4
Extras	10	Extras	3
Total	84	Total	116

Bowling: Wooller 6–4–8–1; Hever 6–3–10–1; Muncer 11.5–4–25–5; Clay 11–0–31–3.

Bowling: Wooller 6–1–19–0; Hever 4–1–9–1; Clay 20–5–48–6; Muncer 19–9–19–2; Jones (W.E.) 6–2–18–0.

64: *Middlesex v Nottinghamshire*
LORD'S, 7–10 MAY 1949

After slipping to third place in 1948, Middlesex returned to the top of the Championship in 1949. Nottinghamshire, in a period of relative decline, nonetheless very nearly beat them in Middlesex's first match of the

season at Lord's, holding them to what E.W. Swanton termed 'the most exciting of draws', thanks only to the injured Leslie Compton coming out to bat at the end of the last day. Middlesex's third great batsman – one sometimes undeservedly forgotten in the shadow of Denis Compton and Bill Edrich – was Jack Robertson, their regular opener. His century – one of seven he scored that season – in Middlesex's first innings allowed them to take a first innings lead. Robertson (b. 1917) played for the county from 1937 to 1959. He made 31,914 runs at an average of 37 in his career, including 67 centuries. He was picked only 11 times for England, despite having a test average of 46. His most remarkable performance in 1949 was scoring 331 not out in a day against Worcestershire at Worcester, in a total of 623 in a day. Sadly, because of newsprint rationing, that performance was hardly reported in *The Daily Telegraph*.

Leslie Compton (1912–84) was Denis's elder brother, a much less gifted cricketer but a better footballer, for many years centre-half for Arsenal and a record-breaker by gaining his first England cap at the age of 38. He played occasionally for Middlesex in the two seasons before the war and regularly for them afterwards until 1956. He averaged only 17 with the bat, but kept his place in the side as a wicketkeeper, making almost 600 dismissals. William Sime (1909–83), who almost bowled Notts to victory, played very occasionally for the county from 1935 to 1950. A prominent barrister, he became Recorder of Grantham and a circuit judge.

Lord's, Monday
From E. W. Swanton

Middlesex have struggled into a position of some small advantage in their first match of the season here against Nottinghamshire by taking two wickets late in the day, after declaring with three wickets in hand as soon as they had gained a lead on the first innings. Two old campaigners, Keeton and Hardstaff, now stand in the breach for Notts, who are only 18 runs ahead.

One needed to be a double-dyed enthusiast to enjoy the cricket in a bitter north-east wind and this was a pity for there was a great deal of a sound, unspectacular sort to appreciate.

PERSISTENT ATTACK

By a quarter past 12 Middlesex were 59 for 4, and Butler, Jepson and Woodhead were keeping up a persistently lively attack on a good wicket, but one with some pace to it. None of them gave anything away, and runs came slowly.

Gradually, with Sharp holding firm and Robertson's eye now thoroughly in, the scanty variety

at Sime's command became apparent. Indeed, what contrast there was, was provided by these three, all of something over medium pace.

Woodhead had a good slower ball and neither Butler nor Jepson belongs to the school that sends down six alike, so that the batsmen can, as it were, play their action. One was reminded of the subtleties of pace normally practised by the West Indies' bowlers.

At length we saw one real contrast, Harvey's leg-breaks. Again, this young cricketer, whom I saw bowling pretty well to the Australians last year, believes in length first, so much so that he can afford to dispense with deep square leg.

His spin perhaps is comparatively gentle, and he tends to cause most trouble by the overspun ball that comes on in to the bat, but these were characteristics of no less a bowler than Richard Tyldesley.

After lunch the play slowly became a little less pawky. Sharp went and as soon as the shine began to leave the new ball, Thompson brought more freedom to the scene with some handsome off-drives and several full-blooded hooks.

Thompson is never afraid to put his bat to the ball, and it was a pleasure to see him make such a good beginning to the season. He and Robertson carried the score from 110 for five to 212 for six, and then Compton (L.), after a tentative opening, during which he all but played on, took on the mantle of Thompson.

There were some fine, powerful off-drives, and some more rustic hits to mid-wicket, Robertson pursuing his virtuous way apparently unruffled by the fact of being at 99 for 40 minutes, including the interval for tea. The goal was all but reached before he was out, having played the slowest of all his valuable innings for Middlesex.

Harris hit the ball into his wicket when Notts went in again, and Stocks hung out the bat once too often against Edrich, who was working up a good pace down-wind from the nursery end.

Tuesday

The match between Middlesex and Notts ended this evening in the most exciting of draws, with the Middlesex last pair together 25 runs short of victory.

It had been a fight of shifting fortunes from first to last, and if Middlesex seemed to be most of the way to victory, both at lunch and again at tea, great credit was due to Notts, and especially to Sime, Woodhead and Jepson, in the closing stages for turning the game round.

From the Middlesex angle there was tragedy in a run-out of Compton which in all probability prevented their winning.

While the Notts third wicket lasted this morning and play was very good indeed, Sims and Compton inspired, perhaps by the steadiness of Notts yesterday kept the batsmen playing with the utmost concentration. It was from one of the very few bad ones that Hardstaff was missed by Sharp at deep mid-wicket off Compton.

Keeton, having been missed from an easy c. and b., was bowled in the same over, but it was Hardstaff's dismissal that caused the slump. He cut a leg-break hard to slip, where Edrich made a very nasty catch look simple. Sime could not resist a cow shot. Simpson pushed rather limply at another leg-spinner, and that was three out for two runs.

The Notts tail is rather disparaged, but Jepson and Meads, with some luck, batted lustily and well, while Harvey played promisingly, the last four wickets adding an unexpected 90 after lunch in 1¼ hours.

Early in the Middlesex second innings Notts had the worst possible luck, for Butler went off with a strain. Sime was thus left with two stock bowlers. After tea he stepped into the breach himself, bowling slow medium left arm extremely steadily, and soon taking a very hot c. and b. at the second attempt.

Robertson had left early, playing a highly speculative stroke in the effort to force. Edrich was soon showing plenty of strokes, and Brown nearly kept up, mostly by means of some crisp late cutting.

The hour before tea produced 73. Afterwards the proposition was to make 149 in 95 minutes. Compton had a lucky escape or two at the start and was batting under the handicap of a badly bruised right hand.

But he was beginning to improvise in his own ingenious way when he called Edrich for a push just wide of a very short third man which was refused, Edrich being the striker and the call therefore being properly Compton's. In the circumstances of the game it looked a fair run. One was left lamenting both in a general way, the tendency of several of the foremost present-day players to decline their partner's call, which is responsible for most run-outs, and in particular the failure of these two famous partners to evolve a sound and workable system of calling and running.

With an hour to go, 94 needed, and the great pair going well, the odds were on Middlesex. Compton left five minutes later, and Edrich's admirable effort was ended by a catch to mid-wicket at a quarter to six. Now the order was 71 in 45 minutes, with Compton (L.) injured and available to bat only with a runner.

Mann hit the bat straight and hard down deep extra cover's throat – 155 for five, and the chances had sunk sharply yet again. Sharp and Thompson continued to look for runs from anything, but at six o'clock Sharp was bowled, 168 for six and 44 needed. When Thompson was promptly stumped the game had turned right round and Middlesex were facing defeat.

Sime bowled Sims, but now Young and Gray stayed put. Jepson came back and at 6.25 knocked out Gray's off-stump. Mann ran for Compton who has injured an ankle. Notts now were all round the bat, for Jepson to Compton, no one more than six yards off. But his last over was safely played and that was that.

NOTTINGHAMSHIRE

First Innings			Second Innings	
Keeton, lbw, b Sims		39	b Young	50
Harris, c Compton (L.), b Edrich		77	b Gray	0
Stocks, b Compton (D.)		45	c Compton (L.), b Edrich	1
Hardstaff, lbw, b Young		46	C Edrich, b Sims	69
R.T. Simpson, b Sims		45	c Compton (L.), b Sims	10
W.A. Sime, lbw, b Sims		8	c Sharp, b Sims	36
Harvey, st Compton (L.), b Compton (D.)		1	c Thompson, b Compton (D.)	22
Jepson, not out		28	b Gray	36
Butler, b Compton (D.)		0	b Gray	0
Meads, st Compton (L.), b Compton (D.)		9	c Brown, b Compton (D.)	25
Woodhead, c Sharp, b Compton (D.)		1	not out	3
Extras		5	Extras	8
Total		304	Total	226

Bowling: Edrich 1–1–39–1, Gray 19–4–48–0, Young 21–8–40–1, Sims 36–5–92–3, Compton (D.) 21.5–1–73–5, Sharp 3–0–7–0.

Bowling: Edrich 12–3–30–1, Gray 6–1–21–3, Compton 26.2–4–76–2, Sims 25–2–56–3, Young 21–8–35–1.

MIDDLESEX

First Innings			Second Innings	
Robertson, c Meads, b Woodhead		120	lbw, b Jepson	12
Brown, b Butler		1	c & b Sims	39
W.J. Edrich, b Jepson		18	c Jepson, b Woodhead	68
Compton (D.), b Harvey, b Jepson		4	run out	23
F.G. Mann, c Harvey, b Woodhead		8	c Jepson, b Sime	9
Sharp, b Butler		24	b Sime	6
Thompson, lbw, b Jepson		53	st Meads, b Woodhead	14
Compton (L.), not out		60	not out	1
Sims, not out		8	b Sime	2
			Young, not out	16
			Gray, b Jepson	5
Extras		13	Extras	2
Total (7 wkts. dec.)		309	Total (9 wkts.)	197

Bowling: Butler 34–7–79–2; Jepson 41–12–105–3; Woodhead 30–13–52–2; Harvey 27–5–60–0.

Bowling: Butler 4–0–15–0; Jepson 15–2–56–2; Woodhead 15–0–61–0; Harris 2–0–12–0; Sime 19–2–51–4.

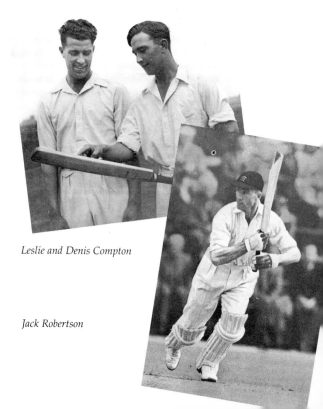

Leslie and Denis Compton

Jack Robertson

65: Yorkshire v Lancashire
SHEFFIELD, 27–30 MAY 1950

What started, as E.W. Swanton's report suggests, as a dour and grinding match typical of the series between Yorkshire and Lancashire, turned out to provide perhaps the most exciting cricket of the 1950 season, and the first finish in a Roses' Match since the war. Both sides were still at their pre-war eminence. Although Lancashire had finished 11th in 1949, they would share the championship this year with Surrey. Yorkshire were the reigning champions, and would finish third this year. Although, as Swanton also records, this match was watched by huge crowds, it was at about this time that cricket's post-war boom ended, and the sort of poor cricket that Swanton also describes on the first day began to drive people to other forms of recreation.

Much of Yorkshire's post-war success was built around Len Hutton (b. 1916), the England opener and one of the world's finest batsmen. Hutton is still best remembered for his 364 against Australia in 1938, but had, in 1949, enjoyed his best ever season, scoring 3,249 runs at an average of 68: that despite his left arm having been badly injured and shortened by an accident during the war. He was the first professional to captain England and was knighted on his retirement in 1956. He made 40,140 runs at an average of 55 in his career, and scored 6,971 for England in 79 tests. Norman Yardley (1915–1989), who so nearly secured a Yorkshire victory, captained his county and his country and was Yorkshire's leading all-rounder in the decade after the war. Johnny Wardle (b. 1923) was England's premier slow left-arm bowler. He took 1,846 wickets at 19 each in a career cut short, at the age of 35, by his criticism in print of the Yorkshire committee. He was sacked, and the tone was set for the internecine warfare of the 1960s, 70s and 80s.

Sheffield, Saturday
From E. W. Swanton

I assume that readers will have formed a fairly clear picture of Saturday's proceedings at Bramall-lane. Yardley, very properly, put in Lancashire on a pitch that started sluggish and later developed spasms of ill temper. It was one on which all but the most talented batsman could have been pinned down by a good length and driven into considerable straits if spin were added.

Fortunately for Lancashire they were not put under the constraint of having to fight hard for their runs. After three not-very-good strokes had cost three wickets for 54 and Yorkshire should theoretically have had their teeth into the enemy, Edrich and Wharton, under the sad gaze of the shrewdest of all cricket crowds, took competent toll of what they received.

Monday

Yorkshire stand 72 runs behind Lancashire with four first-innings wickets in hand here to-night. That, mathematically, is the position, and the remaining significant figure is the 5½ hours maximum that are left for play.

The two Lancashire spin bowlers – Berry, slow left-arm, and Tattersall, right-arm off-breaks – were able to peg down the Yorkshiremen to a scoring rate of 42 an hour by dropping the ball regularly and consistently on the good length, and they were assisted by first-class close fielding, especially by Grieves and Ikin.

The latter happily shows no ill-effects from his recent injury at Cambridge, and is prepared to stand on either side of the wicket extremely adjacent to the bat. As for Grieves, frankly I had not known he was so brilliant a catcher and stopper at short range.

If the summer is as wet as it promises to be, Lancashire should be much nearer their traditional and rightful position at the end of it. Wharton's batting gave the Lancashire innings its backbone this morning. Edrich was straightway well caught low wide right-handed, by Coxon at second slip from a fast-travelling snick.

Trueman, with the new ball, was unpredictable, but now and again fired in a good one that left the bat, and such a one was this. Just occasionally, too, the ball lifted, and Howard was unlucky enough to nick one of these as he attempted to withdraw the bat: but first he had shown one or two extremely powerful strokes on the off-side.

Lomax represented the last authentic line in the batting strength, and with an odd lapse or two he played decent, sensible cricket as second-string to Wharton. Once the latter gave a nasty wide catch to slip from a ball by Close that turned sharply, but mostly he manipulated the situation without undue difficulty and despatched the long hops safely.

His unfortunate dismissal seven short of his century was illustrative, sad to say, of the course of the cricket. He hit a long hop firm and flat out to long leg, where he was caught by Lester, who had just moved farther round, presumably either on a gesture from Yardley or a lucky hunch of his own.

Wharton had needed a little less than three hours' batting time, which on balance was good going, since if Yorkshire's length was kind, the wicket, especially on Saturday, was emphatically not.

Lancashire allowed their innings to jerk to its close even to the point of batting on after lunch with No. 11 at the wicket. This seemed to a southern mind the height of timidity, after so much time had been lost on Saturday. But I was informed by one of the past heroes of Lancashire that the extra runs would come in useful when it came to the follow-on, and felt suitably rebuked.

Of a follow-on there was never the slightest question once Hutton and Lowson had become established, but Lancashire did at least reflect the aggressive disposition shown by their old cricketer when they went into the field.

There was little in the wicket for Stone and Lomax, but as soon as Berry and Tattersall appeared there began the grimmest possible struggle for runs, with all Bramall-lane tense, alert, and, as ever, spontaneously appreciative.

When Hutton was batting to Berry the game at once was lifted to an altogether higher plane, and one was only sorry to have missed the treat of such a duel on Saturday, when the ball was biting more sharply then to-day. Hardly an over went by without Hutton making an obvious effort to seize the initiative, usually by making ground quickly with the object of hitting Berry on the full or otherwise jostling the rhythmical accuracy of his young adversary.

In his twenties Hutton must have got the benefit of the doubt in a stumping decision, Berry being the bowler. Then, when the partnership had climbed to 70, Grieves made a magnificent catch at short leg as he fell, clutching the ball inches from the ground.

Lowson had never been other than watchfully defensive, and with Hutton gone his progress was the subject of desultory derision. He is not quite in the runs to last year's extent. Perhaps that was a factor in his method. At all events, he had been batting three hours 20 minutes before he apparently mistook Grieves's googly, and was bowled.

Halliday already had given Grieves his second chance to show his exceptional reach and speed of eye, this time at slip, and after Lester had given an unaccepted chance at deep square-leg when nought he was ultimately nicely taken there by Place.

An off-break bowled Wilson, and Yorkshire were half out for 133. But now Close made a much more laudable mark on the game than hitherto with a fine straight six into Sheffield United's main stand and a generally punitory approach that made Lancashire's bowlers seem less formidable straight away. Yardley, too, batted rationally and confidently, and on his back rests the initial burden to-morrow morning.

Tuesday

Lancashire beat Yorkshire here this afternoon by 14 runs after a day of agonising excitement which, many a year from now, will set tingling the blood of all those – and there were some 16,000 of us – who were lucky enough to have been present at Bramall-lane.

After the Yorkshire innings this afternoon had gone through many palpitating changes of fortune, Wardle, at number nine, came in to join his captain, Yardley, with only 125 on the board of the 182 needed, and, with respect to Brennan, no substantial batting to follow.

The wicket was spasmodically spiteful still though scarcely the venomous treacherous thing on which Lancashire had been bowled out for 117 in the morning.

The odds seemed long, but Yardley was playing most admirably, and whatever impious critics may say of certain technical limitations on faster wickets, he is, as he has always been, an excellent batsman when the turf is taking the spin. No one who saw his partnership with Hammond on that evil day at Brisbane in the first Test of 1946 could doubt that.

The mood of the whole day's cricket had been to 'get at him before he gets at you.' Only Hutton with his superb method, had been above and beyond the necessity of chancing his arm. Wardle was the last man to close up at such a moment, and in hardly more than a quarter of an hour 27 more came for the eighth wicket, mostly runs truly made against bowling that remained steady and fielding that took inspiration from the occasion.

This was a moment, almost the only one in the match, when Yorkshire seemed really on top. And then, when another four or two would have counted beyond price, Wardle drove Berry hard off the meat of the bat straight back.

Berry clung safely to the ball, and in that there was poetic justice since the game from its beginning had developed largely into a duel between these two left-arm bowlers and the Lancastrian had proved a clear and worthy winner.

With 30 needed Brennan took Wardle's place and began with a fine snick for four past the wicket-keeper to a roar that must have been heard far away in the heart of the city.

Yardley now monopolised the situation, drawing everything off his stumps with an easy dexterity that made it all look almost safe. His 50 arrived to a crescendo of cheering and then Brennan swung at an off-break and Wharton held a good, hard hit chest-high at short mid-wicket.

Now it was simply Yardley or no one. He declined single runs from each of the first three balls of Berry's next over, tried for the last time to back the fourth off his wicket round the corner and so get the next over, and the ball, lifting, lobbed gently in the air to within reach of any of three men round the bat.

Thus it ended and Lancashire had beaten their ancient enemies for the first time since on this same ground Iddon's fine bowling had won the day 13 years before.

This has not been a happy match for young Close, but he had his brief moments of glory, pulling his first ball, from outside the off stump, for a thrilling six to square-leg, sending Berry whistling over extra cover to the boundary, and giving his captain cause to hope that the improbable might after all be brought to pass.

The manner of his end was a tragedy for Yorkshire. Yardley declined a youthfully optimistic call for a second run. Close turned, and could no doubt have made his ground, but slipped up badly (was he properly studded?) and a quick pick up by Berry, followed by the slickest of returns ran him out.

On Saturday Yardley gave Lancashire a more vicious wicket to bat on than Yorkshire themselves found yesterday; and when he declared afer three overs this morning 64 behind with two wickets left including his own, he obliged them to bat on the unpleasantest one of all.

I wrote last evening that a further judicious fall of

rain might make for a battle, and so indeed it proved. Lancashire had a desperately sticky time of it this morning, and how few they might have been skittled for but for Grieves no one can say.

The first three wickets had gone for 35 when he came to the crease, and he made 52 out of the next 76 in well under the hour. As with Yardley, it was a case of a fine eye and quickness of judgement overcoming the attack against all the odds. As ever, when an Australian is assaulted, he hits back good and hard.

Wardle at any rate, though still inclined to drop short on the leg stump, bowled a fuller length than in the first innings, yet Grieves found a variety of strokes with which to belabour him and to put heart into a succession of young partners at the other end.

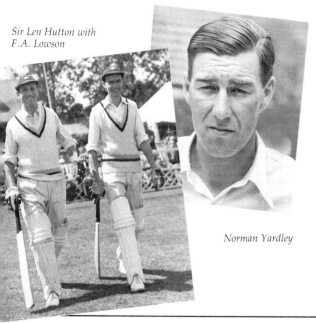

Sir Len Hutton with F.A. Lowson

Norman Yardley

LANCASHIRE

First Innings		Second Innings	
Place, c Coxon, b Wardle	15	b Close	18
Ikin, c Halliday, b Close	19	c Brennan, b Wardle	3
Edrich (G.A.), c Coxon, b Trueman	70	c Coxon, b Close	2
Grieves, c Hutton, b Wardle	1	b Wardle	52
Wharton, c Lester, b Wardle	93	c Hutton, b Wardle	11
H.D. Howard, c Brennan, b Trueman	11	b Wardle	5
Lomax, c Trueman, b Coxon	27	c Wilson, b Close	6
Stone, not out	9	b Wardle	0
Tattersall, c Hutton, b Close	2	c Lester, b Close	14
Barlow, lbw, b Coxon	1	c Brennan, b Wardle	5
Berry, c Yardley, b Close	3	not out	0
Extras	6	Extras	1
Total	257	Total	117

Bowling: Trueman 15–4–39–2; Coxon 20–8–38–2; Wardle 41–17–77–3; Close 30.2–10–66–3; Halliday 7–2–15–0; Yardley 4–0–16–0.

Bowling: Trueman 4–1–4–0; Coxon 2–1–2–0; Wardle 21.2–9–44–6; Close 20–4–66–4.

YORKSHIRE

First Innings		Second Innings	
Hutton, c Grieves, b Tattersall	39	c Ikin, b Tattersall	45
Lowson, b Grieves	49	b Berry	3
Halliday, c Grieves, b Berry	10	c Howard, b Tattersall	9
Lester, c Place, b Grieves	16	c Grieves, b Tattersall	2
Wilson, b Grieves	14	b Berry	9
N.W.D. Yardley, not out	27	c Ikin, b Berry	51
Close, b Berry	22	run out	17
Coxon, c Ikin, b Tattersall	6	b Tattersall	1
Wardle, b Berry	0	c and b Berry	13
D.V. Brennan did not bat		c Wharton, b Tattersall	5
Trueman did not bat		not out	0
Extras	10	Extras	12
Total (8 wkts. dec.)	193	Total	167

Bowling – First Innings: Lomax 7–3–11–0; Stone 4–0–5–0; Berry 36.3–17–50–3; Grieves 18–2–51–3; Tattersall 43–15–66–2. Second Innings: Stone 1–0–4–0; Tattersall 30–11–60–5; Berry 22.4–8–67–4; Grieves 9–2–24–0.

66: *Somerset v Gloucestershire*
TAUNTON, 12–15 MAY 1951

Both Gloucestershire and Somerset suffered a decline in 1951. On paper this was an evenly-placed match, as both sides had shared 7th place in the previous season's Championship. In 1951 Gloucestershire would

fall to 12th, Somerset to 14th. This match, though, had all the excitement of a top-of-the-table contest, with Gloucestershire eventually scoring their 108 runs to win in 49 minutes. There were some glittering names among the teams.

Harold Gimblett (1914–1978) was Somerset's leading batsman during his career from 1935 to 1954; Wisden called him 'the most exciting English batsman of his day'. Called into the Somerset team in 1935 to make up the numbers, he made the fastest century of the season on his debut. In 1948 he took 310 off Sussex, the highest score ever made for Somerset at the time. In his career he made 23,007 runs at an average of 36, and was most unlucky to play in only three tests.

Arthur Milton, the Gloucestershire centurion, played for the county from 1948 to 1974 and was a far more valuable player than his brief international career – just six tests – might suggest. He made 32,150 runs in his career at an average of 34, including 56 centuries, and 16 times made 1,000 in a season. An Arsenal and Bristol City footballer, he also played soccer for England in this season. Maurice Tremlett (1923–84), who bowled so well in Gloucestershire's first innings, had been considered one of the leading fast bowlers of the post-war period. However, after two disastrous overseas tours his international career ended, and he concentrated instead on his batting; 1951 was the only season in which he made 2,000 runs. He made 16,038 runs at an average of 25 in his career from 1947 to 1960, and took 351 wickets at 31 each.

Taunton, Monday
From E. W. Swanton

The ancient battle between Somerset and Gloucestershire turned strongly towards Gloucester here on this most charming ground in a day which held much interesting and inspiring cricket.

Praise be, several young players earned good marks and helped vitally to shape the course of the game, notably T. W. Graveney, Milton, Tremlett and Stephenson.

At the end Gloucestershire had taken their lead to 113 with four wickets in hand and it is a matter of whether Somerset can hold out over a full day's play to-morrow.

The critical partnership of the Gloucestershire innings was one of 113 between Crapp and Graveney. Young and the Graveney brother who is principally a bowler, J. K., had given their side a useful opening partnership of 48, Graveney, a left-hander having been sent in out of turn overnight.

Then Somerset took three wickets inside a quarter of an hour and for quite a spell after that were clearly on top. Not without a little luck when facing Tremlett, Crapp and T. W. Graveney gradually assumed the

initiative and by the time the stand was broken Somerset were patently missing the services of a bowler. Hazell had badly strained a leg when batting on Saturday and will be out of cricket for a fortnight.

When Graveney was beaten by the pace of a quicker ball by Tremlett, Milton took more than a half share in another century partnership with Gloucestershire's acting captain. Crapp, when three short of his hundred, was surprised by a ball that turned sharply and lifted, after which Milton saw to it that his side should continue to capitalise on their advantage.

The bowling was tamed before Milton's arrival and so he had an easier passage. How tight his defence is could not therefore be judged. But what we could see was almost wholly admirable.

He made many runs by forcing the ball on the off-side off his back foot, he sorted out the one to hit with good judgement and for a comparatively inexperienced player he placed his scoring strokes with the coolest skill.

The three quick wickets before lunch were due to two brilliant stumpings by Stephenson and a fine diving catch at leg-slip by Lawrence, who then demonstrated his utility by bowling his leg-breaks almost unrelieved from the pavilion end.

There is something of Evans about Stephenson's keeping. It is all so keen and eager and one can imagine days when he makes mistakes that a quieter keeper might avoid. At all events his best is good indeed and these two pieces of work, first a very wide stumping on the off-side, and then one at lightning speed when Emmett barely lifted his back leg as the ball passed behind him, were worthy of anyone past or present.

Lastly Tremlett's bowling. He had a shattering experience in the corresponding game a year ago, losing all control of the ball and bowling an embarrassing series of wides. Afterwards, though he made plenty of runs, he took only 12 wickets all the summer. Thus there was an important psychological background to his performance to-day and the crowd sensing this gave him all the encouragement possible.

With a short run and swing of the shoulders after the Tate-Bedser manner he made the ball hustle off even this sleepy wicket and he kept at it like a Trojan. He might easily become a fine bowler yet.

Tuesday

The most stirring of finishes here this evening ended in a Gloucester victory over Somerset by seven wickets six minutes from time.

After an excessively stodgy first day this has been an excellent match with the right side winning and the losers up to the very end making brave amends for their miserable batting on Saturday.

Gloucester's last four wickets added 40 more runs this morning, which gave them a lead of 153. Somerset, suffering many violent shifts of fortune, responded with 257.

Gloucester had only 55 minutes to score their 105, but they have been experts at forcing against the clock ever since they were encouraged in the technique by B. H. Lyon, and the hitting of Emmett, Crapp and J. K. Graveney in the final phase drew generous cheers from the ranks of Tuscany.

The game swayed to and fro in the liveliest manner from the moment Somerset began their second innings. After several risky spars at Lambert, Gimblett began to put his bat to the ball in a succession of strokes that beat the field from the moment of impact.

No-one's bat has a truer ring than Gimblett's when he is in the vein and this innings, combined with the fact that he seems to have lost the best part of two stone in weight as a result of his tour in India, tends to indicate a good season for Somerset's No. 1 batsman.

Gimblett's first 50 came inside the hour and although he decelerated after lunch the first-wicket partnership of 142, of which his share was 87, took only a little over two hours.

When Gimblett got out Somerset with eight more effective wickets, were 11 behind and there was a bare three hours' playing time left. The game was more than half saved.

Three-quarters of an hour later they had lost four more wickets and were only six runs ahead. Angell's patient innings was ended by the first of three remarkable catches by J. K. Graveney, fielding a point only a yard off the popping crease to Cook's bowling.

No one, surely has stood so close since Hammond fielded at the very point of the bat for the great Charlie Parker.

Now Tremlett, by the boldest counter-attack in the 25 minutes before tea went a long way towards repairing the damage. In this time 59 were made, 44 by him, including three towering sixes into and around the pavilion from Cranfield's off-spinners.

When Crapp took the new ball directly afterwards Tremlett sensibly changed his game and with Lawrence showing every sign of holding firm Somerset's resistance continued until Cook made a fine catch at short leg, throwing himself full length forward.

The tail-enders each stayed for useful periods while Lawrence grew quite ferocious, especially at the expense of Lambert whom he hooked time and again. Perhaps the decisive item was a magnificent wide leg-side stumping of Stephenson by Wilson off J. K. Graveney, to which there was an added savour for those who saw the plot being quietly hatched before the over began.

The last Somerset wicket went down at 5.25 and Graveney had a part in every dismissal except one.

The features of the finale were many strokes of a power altogether belying his size by Emmett, a very good deep-field catch by Hill that could have saved the game and the scrupulous briskness with which Tremlett and Buse bowled and the Somerset fielders crossed over for the left-handed batsmen.

SOMERSET

First Innings		Second innings	
Gimblett, run out	29	c Wilson, b Graveney (J.)	87
Angell, c Wilson, b Lambert	1	c. Graveney (J.), b Cook	52
Hill, b Lambert	10	c Scott, b Graveney (J.)	0
Smith, c Graveney (J.), b Cook	17	c Graveney (J.), b Cook	3
Buse, b Cook	51	c Graveney (J.), b Cook	2
Tremlett, b Graveney (J.)	3	c Cook, b Graveney (J.)	47
Lawrence, b Lambert	89	not out	43
S.S. Rogers, c Lambert, b Cook	8	b Lambert	4
Stephenson, b Milton	0	st Wilson, b Graveney (J.)	1
Robinson, c Milton, b Cook	11	c Cook, b Graveney (J.)	2
Hazell, not out	5	absent hurt	0
B 3, l-b 5	8	B 8, l-b 4, w 4	16
Total	232	Total	257

GLOUCESTERSHIRE

First Innings		Second Innings	
Young, c Lawrence, b Tremlett	22		
Graveney (J.), st Stephenson, b Lawrence	22	not out	25
Emmett, st Stephenson, b Tremlett	2	c Gimblett, b Buse	38
Graveney (T.), b Tremlett	50	c Stephenson, b Tremlett	2
Crapp, c Tremlett, b Robinson	97	c Hill, b Buse	20
Milton, c Robinson, b Tremlett	125		
Wilson, b Lawrence	22		
Lambert, c and b Tremlett	16		
Scott, c Stephenson, b Buse	0	not out	16
Cranfield, c Angell, b Tremlett	9		
Cook, not out	2		
B 7, l-b 5, w 5, n-b 1	18	B 1, l-b 5, w 1	7
Total	385	Total (for 3 wkts)	108

SOMERSET – First Innings

	O	M	R	W		O	M	R	W
Buse	26	6	66	1	Robinson	42	13	91	1
Tremlett	37.2	14	67	6	Smith	3	0	17	0
Lawrence	57	14	126	2					

Second Innings

	O	M	R	W		O	M	R	W
Buse	7.5	0	60	2	Tremlett	8	0	41	1

GLOUCESTERSHIRE – First Innings

	O	M	R	W		O	M	R	W
Lambert	24.1	4	50	3	Milton	17	2	39	1
Graveney (J.)	24	6	44	1	Cranfield	13	5	25	0
Cook	35	17	51	4	Scott	6	0	15	0

Second Innings

	O	M	R	W		O	M	R	W
Lambert	20	4	72	1	Cranfield	10	1	65	0
Graveney (J.)	21.1	5	50	5	Scott	11	1	22	0
Cook	21	9	32	3					

Umpires – E. Boulton-Carter and E. Pothecary

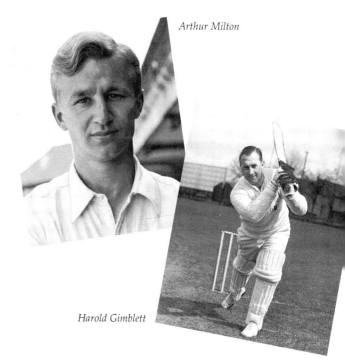

Arthur Milton

Harold Gimblett

67: Surrey v Warwickshire
THE OVAL, 16 MAY 1953

For the first time since 1897 – when they had scored 164 and beaten Leicestershire (35 and 35) at Leicester, Surrey won in a day. It was the third instance since the war and there was to be another that season, three weeks later, when 'Bertie' Buse, the Somerset professional, was to find his benefit match at Bath ending in a day. Surrey were champions, and would be again this year: and for five years after that, the longest run of supremacy in the competition's history. Surrey had world-class batsmen and bowlers and, although they relied on some good luck to sustain their run, were a very hard side to beat. This victory was all the more remarkable in that play began late, because of heavy overnight rain. Moreover, Warwickshire were being dined at the House of Commons on the Monday evening by Sir Anthony Eden, one of the county's MPs, so had to spend two days idly in London waiting to fulfil this engagement.

Alec Bedser (b. 1918) was a top-rank medium-pace bowler. This year he was to help England win the Ashes, taking 39 wickets at 17 each in the series. This was his best season: he took 162 wickets at 16 each. In his career, from 1939 to 1960, he took 1,924 wickets at 20 each. After his retirement he was a test selector for 20 years, and chairman of the selectors for 12. Jim Laker (1922–1986), who took the third of his four hat-tricks in this match, was one of the most successful bowlers in the game's history. His record 19 wickets for 90 runs against Australia in 1956 is unlikely ever to be beaten. In partnership with Lock he helped bowl Surrey to their seven titles. Between 1946 and 1964 he took 1,944 wickets at 18 each. He played occasionally for Essex after leaving Surrey, and later became a leading television cricket commentator.

The Oval, Saturday

Surrey dismissed Warwickshire twice in two hours and 25 minutes at the Oval on Saturday, winning by an innings and 49 runs.

The first Warwick innings, when the wicket was least obnoxious, lasted an hour and a quarter. Their second venture, when it was at its worst, survived for only an hour and 10 minutes.

Between whiles Surrey offered much firmer resist-ance, but their score of 146 came largely from enter-prising batting by Constable and desperate hitting by Surridge (three sixes), Laker (one six) and Lock.

Although Surrey dismissed their opponents twice and there were, in the two innings, 12 failures to score, not once did the Surrey bowlers hit the stumps. Nine men were caught in the first innings, seven in the second.

This remarkable victory was engineered by Alec Bedser and Laker. Bedser, using a crosswind to attack the leg stumps, first took eight wickets for 18 – equalling a similar performance against Notts at the Oval last year – and followed with four for 17, for match figures of 12 for 35.

Laker, for the second time in his career did the hat-trick. His previous success was at Gloucester in 1951.

The Surrey innings ended with an accident to Lock, who was hit over the eye by a ball from Grove and taken to hospital. There was no serious injury, however, and he is expected to be fit for the match with Gloucestershire at the Oval on Wednesday.

Alec Bedser

WARWICKSHIRE

First Innings		Second Innings	
Gardner, c Laker, b Bedser (A.)	7	c Laker, b Bedser (A.)	7
Cartwright, lbw, b Bedser (A.)	0	lbw, Laker	9
Taylor (Don), c Fletcher, b Bedser (A.)	0	lbw, Bedser (A.)	20
Spooner, c Whittaker, b Bedser (A.)	16	c & b Laker	0
Dollery (H.E.), c Lock, b Bedser (A.)	8	c Surridge, b Laker	0
Hitchcock, c Whittaker, b Lock	3	c Bedser (A.), b Laker	0
Townsend, c McIntyre, b Lock	7	run out	0
Weeks, not out	0	c Surridge, b Bedser (A.)	0
Grove, c Fletcher, b Bedser (A.)	3	c Constable, b Laker	10
Dollery (K.), c Brazier, b Bedser (A.)	0	not out	0
Hollies, c Laker, b Bedser (A.)	0	c sub, b Bedser (A.)	0
Extras	1	Extras	6
Total	45	Total	52

Bowling – 1st Inns.: Bedser (A.V.) 13.5–4–18–8; Surridge 6–1–17–0; Lock 7–3–9–2. 2nd Inns.: Bedser (A.V.) 13.4–7–17–4; Laker 13–6–29–5.

SURREY

Bedser (E.A.), b Dollery (K.)	5
Fletcher, c Townsend, b Weeks	13
Constable, c Grove, b Dollery (K.)	37
Clark, c Dollery (K.), b Hollies	2
Brazier, c Townsend, b Hollies	6
Whittaker, b Dollery (K.)	0
McIntyre, c & b Dollery (K.)	9
Laker, c Dollery (H.), b Hollies	18
W.S. Surridge, b Grove	19
Bedser (A.V.), not out	5
Lock, retired hurt	27
Extras	5
Total	146

Bowling: Grove 10.1–3–29–1; Dollery (K.) 11–4–40–4; Weeks 8–1–24–1; Hollies 10–4–48–3.

68: Surrey v Worcestershire
THE OVAL, 25–26 AUGUST 1954

Some of Surrey's success in the 1950s must be attributed to their captains, first Stuart Surridge and then Peter May. Surridge's determination to secure the Championship for the third successive year led to his astonishing declaration at only 92 for three on the first day, Worcestershire having been bowled out for 25, in order to get the visitors in again before the close on a drying wicket; not a tactic that could be used today, with the covering of pitches denying such opportunities and the spin-bowler's art declining accordingly. Worcestershire's total was just one better than the lowest in their history, made against Yorkshire at Huddersfield in 1903. The aggregate for the game was, as Michael Melford says in his report, the lowest ever in the Championship and the lowest this century anywhere in the world; both those records still hold.

Surridge (b. 1917) captained Surrey from 1952 to 1956, winning the Championship each year. A medium-pace bowler, he played for Surrey from 1947 to 1959, taking 506 wickets at 29 each. Tony Lock (b. 1929), who with Laker defeated Worcestershire, played for Surrey from 1946 to 1963, Leicestershire from 1965 to 1967 (captain in the last two seasons), and for Western Australia in the winters from 1962–63 to 1970–71. He took 2,844 wickets in his career at 19 each, 14 times taking 100 in a season, including two seasons when he took more than 200. He is the last bowler ever to take 200 wickets in a season, with 212 in 1957. He did the hat-trick four times (including, for Leicestershire, the first ever taken in first-class cricket in England on a Sunday), and once took all ten wickets in an innings, against Kent at Blackheath in 1956 (see game 71).

The Oval, Wednesday
By Michael Melford

Surrey's advance along the last leg of their journey to the championship reached a more precipitous pace here today than even they have achieved before.

They put Worcestershire in, bowled them out for 25, declared at 92 for three themselves and took two second-innings wickets for 13, all between two o'clock and half-past six. A half share in the championship has thus already been won. The other half must surely follow early tomorrow.

Worcestershire's total of 25 is only one run more than the lowest in their history, and is the lowest, in first-class cricket, since Somerset were bowled out by Gloucestershire for the same figure in 1947. The last eight wickets fell for only five runs.

The feats of Lock and Laker have been eulogised often enough recently. It need only be said here that it is hard to imagine any other bowlers in the world making more out of this wicket than they did and that today Lock with his pace through the air and bite off the wicket was the senior partner. His five wickets for two runs were taken in only 32 balls.

The Worcestershire batsmen doubtless found the

amiable tracts of Worcester poor practice ground for a wicket like this. Their confidence, moreover, was undermined from the first over of the day in which Richardson was caught low down at first slip off a ball that lifted sharply to find his glove.

For 45 minutes afterwards, however, Kenyon and Outschoorn went warily and not too perilously against Bedser and Loader until Kenyon was caught at second slip.

Laker then came on, followed three overs later by Lock and they swept through the later batsmen, taking seven of the last eight wickets in 35 minutes. The other wicket was a run-out for which the honours were divided between Barrington, the thrower, and Laker, the bowler. The innings lasted 105 minutes.

Surrey's innings of 92 for three occupied only 75 minutes of brisk purposeful batting. The wicket seemed much as before, but only Perks bowled on it with any distinction and the lead was taken in half an hour with only one wicket down.

Clark and Stewart began the assault and May and Constable later added 46 in only 25 minutes, Constable hooking and pulling with great zest.

Not the least pleasant part of the day was the sight of May playing again with grandeur and sureness of touch.

At half-past five the wicket showed no signs of losing its spirit and Surridge decalred. The main question then was whether the match could be won and the Championship clinched this evening.

When Kenyon in the first over and Outschoorn a few minutes later had gone to balls that turned and lifted impossibly, a finish with the help of the extra half-hour seemed a possibility. But throughout the last half-hour Richardson showed a most laudable skill against the turning ball. Broadbent supported him stoutly and further disaster was averted.

Thursday

Surrey brought the County Championship to the Oval yesterday for the third year in succession with a historic win over Worcestershire. The match occupied only 4 hours 50 minutes of actual playing time and Surrey's score of 92 for three declared was enough to give them victory by an innings and 27 runs.

Worcestershire's second innings total of 40 made their tally for the match 65 for 19 wickets (one batsman retired hurt) and meant that only 157 runs were scored in the whole match.

This is the lowest aggregate for a completed match ever recorded in the County Championship.

It is the lowest in England since 1878 when M.C.C. (33 and 19) lost to the Australians (41 and 12 for one).

It is the lowest this century anywhere in the world.

Thus Surrey reached the climax of a wonderful run of devastating cricket and as they will be the first to admit, good fortune. The run began on July 28 when

Surridge – a great captain

Tony Lock

they stood eighth in the table, 46 points behind Yorkshire with two matches in hand.

On the wet wickets that have persisted since, they have won eight out of nine matches. They have won the toss when it most mattered, suffered less than their rivals from the floods, yielded only the most junior of their four illustrious bowlers to the Test match and enjoyed a remarkably easy fixture list.

The hour which Surrey needed to finish off Worcestershire yesterday was an eventful one. It began with Richardson being caught at the wicket off Laker's second ball which turned and leapt up as he tried to withdraw his bat.

This was followed by a curious incident in which Umpire Cooke refused an appeal thinking it was for a catch at the wicket, called over and walked away. His colleague, Lee, at square-leg had seen Hughes hit his wicket and after a pause informed Cooke who at once changed his decision.

For the rest the story was as on Wednesday, of fine bowling this time by Bedser and Laker (Lock was not needed), of an unpleasant but not impossible wicket and of thoroughly bad batting. There was also a difficult slip catch which Laker made look easy.

Devereux, one of the few batsmen to cope adequately had to retire with a suspected fractured finger, and the last pair came together at 26. At this point Loader was given a chance to become the fourth Surrey bowler to take 100 wickets this season.

After Yarnold had hit the only two fours of the innings and earned glory by becoming the only Worcestershire batsman in either innings to reach double figures, the chance was taken. Just after half-past 12 Bedser at first slip held an awkward catch with majestic calm and the Championship was won.

There followed much cheering, a speech to a crowd of 3,000 by Surridge, whose leadership has been as effective and ebullient as ever – and then the Oval was left deserted, ironically in glorious late summer sunshine.

WORCESTERSHIRE

Kenyon, c Surridge, b Bedser (A.V.)	8	c Stewart, b Lock	0
P.E. Richardson, c May, b Bedser (A.V.)	0	c McIntyre, b Laker	9
Outschoorn, b Laker	9	c Lock, b Laker	3
Broadbent, c Laker, b Lock	3	c McIntyre, b Laker	1
Hughes, run out	0	hit wkt, b Bedser (A.V.)	2
Devereux, not out	2	retired hurt	
Jenkins, c Stewart, b Lock	1	c Laker, b Bedser (A.V.)	1
Yarnold, c Barrington, b Lock	1	not out	14
Perks, c Barrington, b Laker	0	b Bedser (A.V.)	2
Flavell, c Constable, b Lock	0	c Clark, b Laker	3
Ashman, c and b Lock	0	c Bedser (A.V.), b Loader	2
Extras	1	Extras	2
Total	25	Total	40

SURREY

Clark, c Richardson, b Parks	10
Stewart, c Flavell, b Perks	11
P.B.H. May, not out	31
Constable, c and b Ashman	29
Barrington, not out	10
Extras	1
Total (for 3 wkts dec)	92

McIntyre, Laker, W.S. Surridge, Bedser (A.V.), Lock and Loader did not bat.

SURREY – First Innings

	O	M	R	W		O	M	R	W
Bedser (A.V.)	9	4	12	2	Loader	6	3	5	0
Laker	8	3	5	2	Lock	5.3	4	2	5

Second Innings

	O	M	R	W		O	M	R	W
Lock	10	7	3	1	Laker	17	9	25	4
Bedser	6	3	7	3	Loader	2.4	1	3	1

WORCESTERSHIRE – First Innings

	O	M	R	W		O	M	R	W
Perks	12	1	43	2	Flavell	3	1	17	0
Ashman	8	3	29	1	Devereux	1	0	2	0

69: *Somerset v Hampshire*
WESTON, 17–18 AUGUST 1955

Derek Shackleton (b. 1924) was the most consistent bowler of the post-war period. He played for Hampshire from 1948 to 1969, and in 20 consecutive seasons from 1949 to 1968 took over 100 wickets in a season with his right-arm medium pace; a record. He took 2,857 wickets in his career at an average of 19 each, but for a bowler of his high abilities enjoyed relatively little success in tests, playing in only seven and taking 18 wickets at a cost of 43 each. His remarkable return in this match, 8 for 4 in Somerset's first innings, was the second cheapest eight-wicket return in cricket history. Only Laker, who took 8 for 2 for England against the Rest at Bradford in 1950 has surpassed it. Shackleton's match return of 14 for 29 equalled the cheapest ever 14 wickets in a game, W. C. Smith having taken 14 for 29 for Surrey against Northamptonshire at the Oval in 1910. Shackleton was central to Hampshire's success in 1955. Their third position in the Championship was their highest ever, coming after years of

dismal performances, and the side would eventually win the title in 1961. Somerset, by contrast, were going through perhaps the roughest patch in their history. This was the fourth of four consecutive seasons in which they came bottom.

James Hilton (b. 1930), the off-spinner whose hat-trick briefly gave Somerset the advantage on the first day, was to enjoy little more success in county cricket. Having spent two fruitless seasons with Lancashire in the early 1950s he played for Somerset from 1954 to 1957, taking just 135 wickets at 27 each. Rayment (b. 1928), the Hampshire centurion, played for the county from 1949 to 1958, making 6,338 runs at an average of just 20.

Weston, Wednesday

Hilton performed the first hat-trick of his career when he dismissed Harrison, Shackleton and Burden with successive balls at Weston-super-Mare, but Somerset fared disastrously when they went in, and finished 129 behind Hampshire, with half their side out.

161

Thursday

Better all-round cricket enabled Hampshire to race to victory over Somerset at Weston-super-Mare yesterday. They won by 264 runs in extra time.

The main credit must go to Shackleton, who followed up his performance of eight for four in the first innings by taking six for 25 in the second. Somerset could find no answer to him on the awkward pitch.

Only Laker, the Surrey and England off-spinner, has taken eight wickets for fewer runs in first-class cricket. He secured eight for two for England against the Rest in a Test trial at Bradford in 1950.

C. H. Palmer, of Leicestershire, had an analysis of eight for seven against Surrey at Leicester in May this year.

Hampshire, 117 ahead on the first innings after Somerset had mustered only 37 in an innings lasting 74 minutes, had to thank Rayment and Horton for their ability to declare when 362 ahead with seven wickets down.

Rayment's first championship hundred of the season included 12 fours and took 160 minutes. He shared in partnerships of 89 with Horton and 103 with Harrison.

Stephenson, who hit nine fours in scoring 52 in 50 minutes, alone offered serious resistance for Somerset in their second innings. The side were all out for 98 in 110 minutes.

HAMPSHIRE

First Innings

Gray, c Lawrence, b Hilton 43
Marshall, c Stephenson, b Saeed 5
Horton, c Lawrence, b Hilton 43
Rayment, c Lawrence,
  b McMahon 12
Rogers, c Williams, b Hilton 2
Barnard, c McMahon 19
Harrison, c Williams, b Hilton 9
Sainsbury, not out 13
Shackleton, st Stephenson,
  b Hilton 0
Burden, b Hilton 0
Cannings, c Hilton, b McMahon 0
  Extras 8
                                      ——
  Total 154
Bowling: Lobb 11–4–23–0; Saeed 7–2–16–1; Hilton 24–7–49–6; McMahon 27.3–10–58–3.

Second Innings

lbw, b McMahon 4
c Lobb, b Saeed 12
b Tordoff 59
c Tordoff, b McMahon 104
c Williams, b Tordoff 10
b McMahon 5
not out 35

b Hilton 4
  Extras 12
                                      ——
  Total (7 wkts dec) 245
Bowling: Saeed 5–0–14–1; Lomax 2–1–2–0; McMahon 32–2–122–3; Lobb 6–1–12–0; Hilton 12.2–0–50–1; Tordoff 11–1–33–2.

SOMERSET

First Innings

G.G. Tordoff, b Shackleton 0
G.L. Williams, c Rogers,
  b Shackleton 2
Lawrence, lbw, b Shackleton 8
Tremlett, c Gray, b Shackleton 8
Wight, c Marshall, b Shackleton 2
Lomax, c Rogers, b Sainsbury 0
Stephenson, not out 18
Y. Saeed, c Barnard, b Shackleton .. 0
Hilton, b Shackleton 0
McMahon, run out 1
Lobb, c Rayment, b Shackleton 0
  Extras 6
                                      ——
  Total 37

Second Innings

c Marshall, b Shackleton 0
c Burden, b Shackleton 2
c Gray, b Sainsbury 4
b Shackleton 0
c & b Burden 10
c Rayment, b Shackleton 20
c Horton, b Sainsbury 52
c Barnard, b Shackleton 0
b Shackleton 0
not out 9
c Burden, b Sainsbury 0
  Extra 1
                                      ——
  Total 98

Bowling: First Innings: Shackleton 11.1–7–4–8; Cannings 4–2–5–0; Sainsbury 7–2–22–1. Second Innings: Shackleton 16–7–25–6; Cannings 4–2–3–0; Sainsbury 13.4–0–63–3; Burden 2–0–6–1.

James Hilton

Derek Shackleton

70: *Essex v Gloucestershire*
ROMFORD, 23–24 MAY 1956

During the early 1950s Essex's success in the Championship had been far less than this rout of Gloucestershire (who were to finish third this year, compared with Essex's eleventh) might suggest. Essex were about to begin a reasonable run in the Championship that would last until the early 1960s, thanks largely to their two regular amateurs, Insole and Bailey. Doug Insole (b. 1926), who dominated the Essex innings, captained the county from 1950 to 1960 and played for them from 1947 to 1963, scoring 25,241 runs at an average of 38. He played in nine tests. Trevor Bailey (b. 1923) was England's leading all-rounder. He played for the county from 1946 to 1967, succeeding Insole as captain. He scored 28,641 runs at an average of 33 and took 2,082 wickets at 23; in his 61 tests he won a reputation for slow scoring (he was known as Barnacle Bailey), and a test was never lost while he was at the wicket. He later became a famous radio commentator and cricket writer.

Tom Graveney (b. 1927) played for Gloucestershire from 1948 to 1960, leaving them after a disagreement over his captaincy of the county, and then for Worcestershire from 1961 to 1970. He was one of the greatest batsmen of the 1950s and 1960s, and among the best of all time. His aggregate of 47,793 runs at an average of 45 has been bettered by only eight other batsmen, and he made 122 centuries. He was a consistent test batsman, scoring 4,882 runs in 79 tests at an average of 44, and commanding a place in the England side until 1969, when he received a short ban from tests for playing in the Sunday league on a rest day. He made 1,000 runs in a season 20 times, including 2,000 seven times, and after his retirement became a well-known television commentator.

Romford, Wednesday
From R. A. Roberts

August conditions prevailed here to-day, run-making was a pleasant occupation, and under the industrious influence of their captain, Insole, Essex prospered after a sluggish start.

Two hours' play before lunch produced only 70 runs, but Gloucestershire could not staunch an ever-accelerating flow afterwards, and four hours later Essex closed at 356 for nine wickets.

Insole, in such busy fettle that three times he left the middle to run to the sightscreen helping to save time as well as aiding in shifting operations, scored 159 out of 240 in three-and-a-quarter hours. His third 60 came in half-an-hour.

Dodds, obviously struggling to regain his normal free and easy touch, and Barker made heavy weather of the first hour before, at 34, Dodds touched a ball from Milton, Gloucestershire's tidiest bowler at medium-pace, to slip.

The second hour was no brighter. Both Barker, a compact batsman, patently full of cricket, and the left-handed Taylor looked the part without transferring this appearance into tangible results on an excellent batting wicket.

They had more purposeful designs afterwards and added another 30 in 15 minutes, whereupon Milton took a sharp gully chance offered by Taylor with typical deceptive nonchalance.

Barker's 50 came in two and half hours after his first hour had yielded only 10, and then Insole took the stage and commanded it until 20 minutes from the end of a sun-drenched day.

Insole is among the most difficult batsmen to quieten when he is in the mood, and clearly he was seeing the ball early and timing it sweetly from the moment he took guard.

He proceeded by a series of short-armed clips to all points of the compass, including some very good straight blows, to 59 in 75 minutes and to 100 in two and three-quarter hours. Bailey helped him add 66 in even time before retiring with a dislocated finger, which was quickly repaired.

After a century partnership with the promising young left-hander, Bear, Insole really cut loose upon reaching his century and the on-side fielders especially had a trying time. Altogether he hit one six and 20 fours.

All credit to Gloucestershire for some excellent catching, including efforts by Rochford, a neat wicket-keeper, and by Milton and Crapp in the deep, towards the end of a tiring day. This resulted in five wickets falling while 15 runs were added in the final 20 minutes.

Thursday

Tom Graveney dominated the scene here to-day even more markedly than Insole had done yesterday, but with nothing like comparable support, and so Essex ran out victors by an innings and 96 runs with a day and a bit to spare.

Some good seam bowling by Ralph, the Ilford amateur, and Bailey, allied to some frankly bad batting – always excepting Graveney – and careless running between the wickets, contributed to this pronounced success by Essex in a strange, sometimes exciting, day's cricket.

Gloucestershire were unfortunately deprived of Young's services through a fractured finger, but on a good, fast batting wicket failed miserably in being dismissed twice inside four and a half hours.

True 260 runs were made in that period, but Graveney contributed no fewer than 167 of them in two delightful innings. He is obviously in his best form and spirits and if he can play anything like as well throughout the second month of the season as he has done in the first the cause of England cricket could be well served.

Graveney began his first innings after the first 25 minutes has been used up in scoring seven runs. He was into his stride immediately, driving surely with that full and fluent swing of the bat off either foot, and in a generous arc between mid-wicket and square cover. Cuts and deflections and firm leg hits were also part of an entrancing pattern.

But for the loss of several partners, of the strike at a vital period, and through the wanderings of a large black dog of varied antecedents, he must have reached his hundred in the fastest time of the season. As it was this fourth hundred of the month occupied only two hours, and contained 17 fours.

Only during his second-wicket partnership in the first innings with Milton, when 84 were added in an hour, did Gloucestershire's batting show at both ends the class of which it is capable. A good throw by Preston then beat Milton home on the third run, and from that point wickets fell with ever-increasing frequency throughout the day.

Gloucester followed on 203 behind and their second innings was all over in under two hours. Milton was immediately lbw padding off, the tried and trusted campaigners Emmett and Crapp failed for the second time inside a day, a rare enough occurrence, and Mortimore achieved a pair.

It all seemed so illogical with Graveney breezing along unconcernedly at the other end. He made 67 out of 102 in 95 minutes, and then was very well caught, off a mistimed hit, by Insole running backwards from slip.

Ralph thereupon gobbled up Gloucester's notorious tail, finished with his best-ever return of seven for 42, and added a one-handed catch at long leg for good measure.

Essex – First Innings

Dodds, c Graveney, b Milton	19
Barker, c Graveney, b Lambert	56
Taylor, c Milton, b McHugh	30
D.J. Insole, c Rochford, b Cook	159
T.E. Bailey, c and b Mortimore	24
Bear, b Mortimore	43
Smith (R.), c Rochford, b Cook	1
Smith (G.), c Milton, b Cook	1
Greensmith, not out	6
R. Ralph, c Crapp, b Mortimore	2
Preston, not out	5
Extras	10
Total (9 wkts dec)	356

Bowling: Lambert 28–3–100–1; McHugh 25–6–78–1; Milton 14–4–53–1; Wells 11–6–22–0; Cook 16–2–49–3; Mortimore 11–0–44–3.

Gloucestershire

	First Innings		Second Innings	
Emmett, c Taylor, b Ralph		5	c Taylor, b Ralph	15
Milton, run out		32	lbw, b Bailey	0
Graveney, c Taylor, b Ralph		100	c Preston, b Ralph	67
Crapp, c Preston, b Insole		0	b Ralph	6
Mortimore, b Bailey		0	c Taylor, b Ralph	0
Lambert, b Bailey		9	c Insole, b Ralph	2
Rochford, not out		1	b Ralph	7
Cook, run out		0	b Ralph	0
Wells, run out		4	c Ralph, b Preston	5
McHugh, b Ralph		0	not out	0
Young, absent, hurt		0	absent, hurt	0
Extras		2	Extras	5
Total		153	Total	107

Bowling – First Innings: Preston 7–2–9–0; Ralph 13.2–3–34–3; Smith (R.) 6–0–35–0; Insole 11–2–42–1; Bailey 12–4–31–2. Second Innings: Bailey 13–4–49–1; Preston 4.5–1–11–1; Ralph 11–1–42–7.

Tom Graveney

71: Kent v Surrey
BLACKHEATH, 7–10 JULY 1956

This was Lock's match. He took all ten wickets in an innings for the only time in his career, and his 16 for 83 in the match was his best match return ever, and remains the best ever for Surrey. This season was to bring the fifth of their seven successive Championships, by 20 points from Lancashire, nowhere near as heavy as their victory had been in 1955. However, 1956 was one of the wettest seasons on record. For Kent it was a disastrous season; they finished 16th, with only four victories from their 28 matches.

Although so often Surrey relied on exemplary bowling by Lock, Laker, Loader and Bedser to secure victory, they also had a formidable batting side. Peter May (b. 1929) was one of the greatest of post-war batsmen. He made his debut, for the Combined Services, in 1948, and for Surrey in 1950 after his first summer at Cambridge. He was a blue in all of his three years and, while still an undergraduate, scored a century on his England debut. His career was all too short; indifferent health and a prospering business career ended his regular appearances in 1961. He made 27,592 runs in his career at an average of 51, including 85 centuries. He was one of England's most successful captains ever, leading them in 44 of his 66 tests. For England he made 4,537 runs at an average of 47. He made 1,000 runs in a season 11 times, five of those over 2,000 runs. He succeeded Alec Bedser as chairman of the selectors in 1982, and his six years in charge coincided with some of the poorest performances in English cricket. His fellow centurion in this game, Clark (1924–1981), here made the highest score of his career, in which he made 11,490 runs at an average of 29.

Blackheath, Monday
From Michael Melford

Lock bowled his way magnificently through Kent to-day. By tea their first innings had ended for 101, a quarter of Surrey's 404 for four declared. By this evening they had lost six second-innings wickets for 128.

From the first innings Lock emerged with six wickets for 29. In the second he has so far taken all six for 54, making an extraordinary tally of 22 against Kent in the last two week-ends.

To-day the wonderful batting wicket and fast outfield which Surrey enjoyed on Saturday were altogether more difficult to come by though for much of the day the sodden pitch was not much more than awkward.

It was, one felt, very much the sort of pitch on which Surrey, with their strength in spin and close catching, prosper where others achieve little. Laker is resting a slightly damaged finger, but Lock did the job supremely well.

The ball turned a little for him, but, until this evening, not at any speed. He attacked all the time with great control and many of the runs he yielded this evening were give away with a purpose.

The catch with which Stewart, fantastically close in the gully, removed Fagg in the first innings was a fair sample of the support Lock gets.

The stroke was respectable enough, the ball barely 2in off the ground, and if Stewart had been fielding at normal range it would scarcely have occurred to anyone that a chance had been given.

Having given credit to Lock, and, indeed, Alec Bedser, and acknowledged Kent's ill-fortune in not having Saturday's conditions, one must say that, Cowdrey and Phebey excepted, Kent batted dismally in the first innings.

Cowdrey and Phebey made 55 for the first wicket and the score was 81 for four before Cowdrey left. Of the other nine batsmen Dixon reached double figures with the help of four overthrows. None of the other eight scored more than two.

The Rectory Field's powers of recovery, summer and winter, are ever a source of wonder. This morning, after the thunderstorm, play started no more than 40 minutes late, though, a grim, grey light and intermittent drizzle made it a cheerless business.

If the batsmen could not see very well, the bowlers had trouble in holding the ball and keeping their feet. Cowdrey and Phebey played fairly comfortably for over an hour.

Before long Cowdrey was brightening the scene with a series of glorious, effortless strokes. One remembers a cover drive and an on drive in the same over off Bedser and a shot off the back foot off Lock, all for four. Once he pulled a no-ball from Loader equally easily to a great height behind square leg for six.

Just before drizzle sent them off for lunch ten minutes early Phebey hit over and across a ball from Lock and was bowled.

Tuesday

In just under 25 minutes this morning Lock added the last four Kent wickets to the six he had taken yesterday and joined the 60 other bowlers who have taken all 10 wickets in an innings in a first class match.

Ten for 54 were the figures, making his total contribution to Kent's defeat by an innings and 173 runs 16 wickets for 83.

During most of this very fine piece of bowling the wicket was by no means impossibly difficult. This morning, however, the ball did turn and lift much quicker and Lock, fresher now, swept through the tail, taking the four wickets in 19 balls without yielding a run.

Nearly everything that can be said about the quality of Lock's bowling in this match was said after his 47 overs yesterday. It need only be added now that coming at a time when a doubt existed about his fitness the performance is all the more remarkable and all the more welcome.

Some 150 people came to the Rectory Field this morning, many perhaps drawn there by a small hope of seeing an historic event. They were not kept waiting long.

The first ball of Lock's second over turned and lifted sharply and had Ridgway caught off his hand by Stewart, head high and very close in the gully. The fourth ball of the same over stopped and was lobbed gently to cover-point by Halfyard.

On these occasions much, of course, depends on what is going on at the other end. As it happened the wicket held little for anyone else and Ufton was able to contain Loader comfortably. He was safely kept at that end and Lock began his third over to Page. The fifth ball of it was a quicker one which knocked the off-stump out of the ground.

Needing one for game, as it were, Lock had one ball at Wright which was played uppishly but safely on the offside. Loader then bowled an over to Ufton which was not perhaps the most hostile ever bowled and Lock had another chance.

The first ball of his next over was of good length pitching around middle and leg and knocked back Wright's off stump as he pushed forward.

The little crowd raised a creditable cheer and gathered in front of the pavilion to welcome the hero back.

SURREY

Clark, b Ridgway	191
Stewart, c Fagg, b Wright	13
Barrington, c Ridgway, b Wright	32
P.B.H. May, not out	128
Pratt, c Phebey, b Page	21
Bedser, E.A., not out	11
Extras	8
Total (4 wkts dec)	**404**

Swetman, W.S. Surridge, Lock, Bedser (A.V.) and Loader did not bat.
Bowling: Ridgway 15-3-53-1; Halfyard 28-4-104-0; Wright 25-3-85-2; Page 25-2-107-1; Dixon 9-0-44-0; Cowdrey 1-0-3-0.

KENT

	1st	2nd
Phebey, b Lock	22	b Lock	12
M.C. Cowdrey, c. Swetman, b Bedser, A.V.	49	lbw, b Lock	8
Wilson, c Barrington, b Lock	2	b Lock	32
Evans, b Loader	1	c & b Lock	19
Fagg, c Stewart, b Lock	2	c Bedser, A.V., b Lock	21
Dixon, c May, b Lock	13	b Lock	2
Ufton, b Lock	0	not out	17
Ridgway, c Surridge, b Lock	6	c Stewart, b Lock	7
Halfyard, c Pratt, b Bedser, A.V.	1	c Barrington, b Lock	0
Page, not out	1	b Lock	0
Wright, c Loader, b Bedser, A.V.	2	b Lock	0
Extras	2	Extras	12
Total	**101**	**Total**	**130**

Bowling: Loader 16-6-38-1; Bedser, A.V. 11-0-28-3; Lock 21-12-29-6; Bedser, E.A. 3-2-4-0.

Bowling: Loader 8-3-7-0; Bedser, A.V. 16-5-41-0; Lock 29.1-18-54-10; Bedser, E. 18-10-16-0.

Trevor Bailey

72: *Northamptonshire v Surrey*
NORTHAMPTON, 5–7 JUNE 1957

Surrey's perpetual dominance of the championship was coming towards its close. Champions in the previous five years, they would win again this season and the next, but that was to be the end of their run. Northamptonshire had revived spectacularly in the 1950s, and as our correspondent points out, the county were particularly good at defeating Surrey. In 1957 Northamptonshire finished second in the table, their highest since 1912, so this was a most important fixture. It took on historic significance through Mickey Stewart's then unique achievement of being the only non-wicketkeeper to catch seven batsmen in an innings. Stewart (b. 1932) was Surrey's main middle-order batsman from 1954 to 1972, scoring over 26,492 runs at an average of 33. He captained Surrey from 1963 to 1972, became the side's manager in 1979, and later became the first full-time England manager. He took 77 catches in 1957, the second highest number ever in a season to Hammond's 78 in 1928.

Surrey's side was laden with test players. By contrast, Northamptonshire had two irregular test bowlers upon whom the county greatly relied. George Tribe (b. 1920) was an Australian all-rounder. He had played just three tests for his country immediately after the war. He joined Northamptonshire in 1951 and played nine seasons with them, performing the 'double' in seven. In his career he took 1,378 wickets at 20 each, bowling slow left-arm, and scored over 10,177 runs at an average of 27. Frank Tyson (b. 1930) was said to be the fastest bowler in England, with only Trueman to rival him. In a short career from 1952 to 1960 he took 767 wickets at 21 each, before emigrating to Australia to coach Victoria and become a leading cricket commentator.

Northampton, Wednesday

Northants, seeking their fifth consecutive victory over Surrey and second successive double over the champions, made a steady recovery after early shocks here to-day.

After losing their opening pair and left-hander Livingston for only nine they fought back grimly to reach 213 in five and a half hours.

Barrick rescued Northants from what might have been a disastrous collapse by hitting a resolute 86 out of 138, including a six and eight fours, in a stay of 200 minutes. He was caught behind the wicket, attempting to cut a ball from Lock, when he seemed set to score a chanceless century.

Barrick put on 77 in 105 minutes with the help of the left-hand Lightfoot – a 21-year-old playing in his first match of the season for Northants. He had the support of another left-hander, Tribe, in a fighting fifth wicket stand of 59 in 75 minutes, raising the Northants total to 145.

Eric Bedser ended the resistance of the middle order batsmen by taking two wickets in two balls with his off-spinners, thus emulating the feat of his twin brother, Alec, who had also taken wickets with successive balls earlier in the day.

Both Bedsers took their wickets with the last ball of one over and the first of the next.

Tribe did not make his second scoring stroke until he had been at the wicket for almost 40 minutes. He carved out a promising 22, but was bowled by Eric Bedser with a ball which scurried beneath his bat to take the off-stump.

Manning was bowled middle stump between bat and pad by Bedser's next ball. Andrew, who saved the hat-trick, made some neat shots to justify his promotion in the batting order, but was run out before his partnership with Tyson could develop into something useful.

Thursday

In a long struggle for first innings lead between Northamptonshire and Surrey here to-day, only the batting of May relieved the cold and gloom which restricted the crowd to a mere 1,000.

It was May's effort which carried Surrey to their target, and at the end, after the later batsmen had pushed the score on in easier circumstances. Surrey led by 98 runs on the first innings and had also secured the bonus points.

Fletcher and Stewart opened the Surrey innings with considerable caution, and there were those present who regretted the absence of Clark, whose customary aggressive approach to new ball bowlers is one of the most heartening qualities of Surrey's batting.

With 58 runs on the board Manning's left-arm spin found the edge of Stewart's bat on the forward defensive stroke with the only ball of the day which turned sharply.

Soon afterwards Fletcher swung a long-hop from Tribe accurately to square-leg and May, 10 minutes before the luncheon interval, went to the wicket with the obvious task of reviving a match showing distinct signs of ennui. In this he was successful and, aided by Constable, instilled some purpose into the batting.

Their stand of 79 in as many minutes was broken by the first ball of the day from Allen – the youngest of Northants' trio of left-arm spinners – who found Constable woefully late in cutting. Barrington, normally of attacking mentality, took an hour to score eight runs – and it was left to May to carry Surrey past the Northants total.

May weathered the new ball assault of Tyson and Kelleher until Surrey achieved their hard-fought lead, whereupon he edged Tyson to first slip, denying himself a century which had seemed a near-certainty.

Tribe, a third left-arm spinner, disposed of the Surrey tail, though Eric Bedser showed some spirit with an innings of 46 which ended – as did play for the day – with a catch at mid-wicket.

Friday

Cricket history was made here to-day when, in Surrey's defeat of Northamptonshire by 10 wickets, Michael Stewart held seven catches during Northants' second innings.

No fielder, other than a wicket-keeper, has taken so many catches in a single innings and only two wicketkeepers have achieved the feat.

Stewart took six of the seven at short leg and the other in the gully of the left-hander Livingston. He said afterwards: 'Everything stuck that came to hand and after not holding a catch in Northants first innings, I never dreamt I should collect seven in the second.'

Thus Surrey avenged last week's defeat by 72 runs from Northants at the Oval, and ended a sequence of four consecutive defeats against this county.

After being restricted by rain to 45 minutes' play before lunch they dismissed Northants for 111 in 115 minutes and then Stewart and Fletcher hit off the 14 runs required for victory.

Alec Bedser lifting the ball uncomfortably took four wickets for 31 in 47 balls and Lock, aided even more by Stewart's eager hands, took four for 20.

Apart from a third wicket stand of 41 between Reynolds and Barrick, Northants struggled all the time. Livingston, Stewart's first victim, failed to score for the second time in the match and hits for six by Tribe off Lock were merely token resistance in the later stages of the innings.

NORTHAMPTONSHIRE

Brookes, c Lock, b Bedser, A.V. 7	c Lock, b Bedser, A.V. 6
Reynolds, b Loader 2	c Stewart, b Bedser, A.V. 26
Livingston, b Bedser, A.V. 0	c Stewart, b Bedser, A.V. 0
Barrick, c McIntyre, b Lock 86	c Barrington, b Bedser, A.V. 33
Lightfoot, lbw, b Laker 29	c Stewart, b Lock 5
Tribe, b Bedser, E.A. 22	c Stewart, b Lock 11
Manning, b Bedser, E.A. 0	c Stewart, b Laker 10
Andrew, run out 6	not out 12
Tyson, not out 34	c Stewart, b Laker 4
Allen, b Bedser, A.V. 5	c McIntyre, b Lock 0
Kelleher, b Laker 13	c Stewart, b Lock 0
Extras 9	Extras 4
Total 213	Total 111

Runs per over: 2.02
Bowling: Loader 26-9-54-1; Bedser, A.V. 26-6-56-3; Laker 13-3-10-2; Lock 2-3-10-45-1; Bedser, E.A. 16-2-33-2

Bowling: Loader 9-2-26-0; Bedser, A.V. 16-6-43-4; Laker 12-6-14-2; Lock 9-2-4-20-4; Bedser, E.A. 1-0-4-0.

SURREY

Fletcher, c Manning, b Tribe 37	not out 8
Stewart, c Andrew, b Manning 24	not out 6
Constable, b Allen 42	
P.B.H. May, c Kelleher, b Tyson ... 96	
Barrington, b Kelleher 10	
Bedser, E.A., c Livingston,	
b Tyson 46	
McIntyre, b Tribe 27	
Lock, st Andrew, b Tribe 0	
Laker, c Manning, b Tribe 11	
Loader, c Brookes, b Tribe 4	
Bedser, A.V., not out 0	
Extras 14	
Total 311	Total (no wkt.) 14

Runs per over: 2.58 (bonus points)
Bowling: Tyson 25.4-8-47-2; Kelleher 22-7-39-1; Manning 26-10-81-1; Tribe 26-3-73-5; Allen 20-8-57-1.

Bowling: Manning 1.5-1-8-0; Allen 1-0-6-0.

Micky Stewart

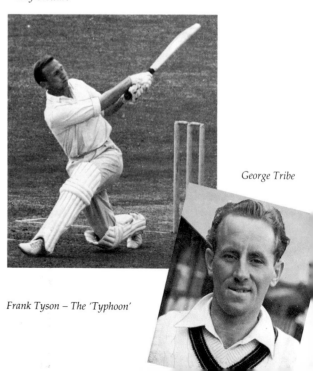

George Tribe

Frank Tyson – The 'Typhoon'

73: *Derbyshire v Hampshire*
BURTON, 13–14 AUGUST 1958

Hampshire, in 1958, had never won the Championship; and in this year, which brought Surrey's seventh successive title, they were doomed to come second. Being caught on a drying wicket at Burton at this crucial moment in their campaign finished off their chances, though they were to be successful, at last, in 1961. With the exception of 1956, when they had a poor season and finished 12th, Derbyshire were one of the most consistently good sides of the 1950s; and, as Michael Melford points out in his report, were superior to Hampshire in terms of experience and suitability for these conditions. That 39 wickets could go down in a day, though, was down to some especially fine bowling on both sides.

Malcolm Heath (b. 1934), who took 13 wickets for Hampshire, had his best season in 1958, taking 126 wickets at 16 each. He never again took a hundred in a season, and left the game relatively young in 1962, having taken 527 wickets at 25 each. For Derbyshire, Harold Rhodes (b. 1936) was one of the most controversial bowlers of the age. He was no-balled three times for throwing between 1960 and 1965, but ultimately the MCC judged his action to be fair, after he had had his arm painted black and white and been specially filmed as evidence. Despite being 'cleared', he remained under suspicion until his career ended. In his career, between 1953 and 1975, he took 1,073 wickets at under 20 each, and played twice for England in 1959. His fast bowling partner, Les Jackson (b. 1921) took 1,733 wickets at 17 each in a career that lasted from 1947 to 1963, and 1958 was his finest season. He headed the averages with 143 wickets at 10.99 each, the lowest average of the century for a bowler taking 100 wickets.

Malcolm Heath

Burton-on-Trent, Wednesday
From Michael Melford

The forecast to-day was mainly dry, but that did not stop rain ending play here this morning when Hampshire, after putting Derbyshire in had taken one wicket for eight runs.

I imagine that Ingleby-Mackenzie's decision to field, taken after much weighty consideration, was based partly on the prowess of the Derbyshire seam bowlers.

If there was something in the wicket they would certainly find it – and Derbyshire have not been beaten on this ground for a long time.

In the 20 minutes' play which took place, before the advance guard of what must have been a large crowd, the ball moved about just a little. When the roller's effects had worn off, the pitch might have held rather more for Shackleton and Heath. No-one could say for certain.

As it was, they bowled for part of the time with a wet ball, and all that Hampshire gained was the wicket of Lee.

After starting very promisingly he touched a ball from Shackleton off the inside edge on to his pad, whence it rebounded to be well caught by Horton rolling over at forward short leg. Green, next year's Cambridge captain, had no sooner come in than they had to go off.

Thursday

Thirty-nine wickets fell here in a remarkable day's cricket which ended with Derbyshire beating Hampshire in the extra half-hour by 103 runs. In the process they bowled out the championship leaders for 23 and 55.

Various melancholy records were set up by Hampshire's 23 in the first innings. It was the lowest since 1939, and the lowest ever against Derbyshire, two runs fewer than the previous lowest made by Kent and Lancashire in the 1870s.

No less extraordinary was the fact that there was not a single bowling change in the match until 6.40 this evening, when Morgan replaced Rhodes. During the previous 6hr 40min of play to-day Jackson and Rhodes bowled for Derbyshire, Shackleton and Heath for Hampshire.

The pitch had had no rain for 20 hours, and a breeze and a hot sun dried it out more quickly than anyone expected.

Derbyshire won, not because they had the best of the wicket, but because they were much better equipped for these unusual conditions.

Well as Shackleton bowled without reaching his best, he was not as fast as Jackson. Heath, though he took 13 wickets, was not as accurate in length and direction as Rhodes, and nothing like as fast.

The watcher could, with a stretch of imagination, have pictured himself standing up to Shackleton and Heath this morning. Nobody without a suit of armour could have been other than appalled by the thought of facing Jackson and Rhodes.

The best of the four was the tall young Rhodes, who dug the ball in from his considerable height, moved it off the pitch either way, and took four of the first six wickets in the first innings.

Jackson was a little short at first this morning, but went through the tail quickly enough. He must soon have realised that batsmen fearing all sorts of horrors from the lifting ball were peculiarly vulnerable to the half-volley and yorker, and the ball which did not lift.

This brings me to the second of Derbyshire's advantages – their batting which had more experience than Hampshire's, particularly in the middle.

Fortitude was one requisite for batting to-day, but the technique of thumping the half-volley and fending off or avoiding everything else, is only learnt by experience.

Thus Carr and Dawkes in the first innings, and Carr and Morgan in the second (with a stand of 54) made invaluable contributions.

Derbyshire's third advantage was that in Morgan, Carr had a third bowler of pace in reserve. Ingleby-Mackenzie had to work Shackleton and Heath long after they had reached normal weariness.

The Derbyshire first innings, resumed at eight for one, lasted another 95 minutes this morning.

The ball moved in the air besides kicking off the pitch, and Heath had some difficulty in controlling the outswinger. But in time the ball began to lift more often from a length and a series of catches close to the wicket, including a very fine one by Horton flinging

himself forward, reduced Derbyshire to 35 for six.

So far they had tried to play normally. Now they threw the bat at anything, obviously anxious, among other things, to get Hampshire in.

Johnson and Dawkes both hit Heath back over his head, Carr laid about him as well, and the last four wickets added 39 in half an hour.

Carr and Dawkes both holed out to deep square-leg, and other catches went to hand fairly accommodatingly. All but two were held, and the misses were not costly.

The pitch was obviously not dry enough yet to roll out plumb, but Hampshire must have hoped that Marshall might perhaps get them a quick 30 before the roller's effect wore off. The first of several magnificent catches killed that hope. In Rhodes' second over Dawkes hurled himself far to his right and scooped the ball up close to the ground.

Gray, having been dropped at third slip – Derbyshire's only miss – was promptly bowled, and a fine throw by Johnson, after Carr had back-heeled the ball close to the third-man boundary, surprised Pitman at the end of a third run. The score was seven for three and the worst of the pitch was yet to come.

At lunch Hampshire were 17 for five and Ingleby-Mackenzie, hit several times on the hand, had had to retire for five minutes for repairs. Immediately after lunch he cut Rhodes with immense power from the middle of the bat and Lee miraculously hung on to it.

Hampshire's last chance of getting near Derbyshire's score had gone. A few minutes later the last man, Burden, came in, had his head grazed by the first ball which reared from a length, and was bowled by the second, which kept fairly low.

So the innings ended a painful, often frightening, life after 70 minutes.

Heath still tended to bowl short in the second innings, and Lee and Brailsford achieved a prodigious opening stand of 21 before Brailsford was caught off a

Harold Rhodes

skier at mid-on.

Green was caught at first slip trying to play a ball from Shackleton, and Heath, temporarily on a better length now disposed of Lee and Hamer. This was 40 for four at four o'clock.

The stand by Morgan and Carr which followed came at a time admittedly when Heath seemed very tired, and was bowling shorter than ever, but both batsmen played very sensibly.

It seemed now that Ingleby-Mackenzie must rest Heath soon. He and Shackleton had bowled two long spells each of 95 minutes – but he kept him on after tea, and saw him at last find a good full length.

At 94 Morgan hit too soon at Shackleton, whereupon Heath took four wickets in a row, and the last six fell for 13 runs.

Hampshire needed 159 to win with 90 minutes left this evening, but it might just as well have been 1,000 once Marshall had been lbw first ball. Jackson brought one back off the pitch at a normal height when Marshall had been expecting it to lift.

Gray was caught at the wicket in Rhodes's first over trying not to play, and the only question soon became whether Hampshire could keep enough wickets in hand to-night to be able to continue, perhaps on a better wicket to-morrow.

At seven o'clock six wickets were down, and Carr claimed the extra half-hour. Only 15 minutes of it was needed.

DERBYSHIRE

	First innings		Second innings	
Lee	c Horton, b Shackleton	8	c Horton, b Heath	6
Brailsford	c Barnard, b Heath	4	c Horton, b Heath	14
D.J. Green	c Sainsbury, b Heath	6	c Barnard, b Shackleton	4
Hamer	c Pitman, b Heath	5	c & b Heath	7
Morgan	c Horton, b Shackleton	3	c Marshall, b Shackleton	46
D.B. Carr	c Burden, b Heath	12	lbw b Heath	19
Johnson	c Harrison, b Heath	4	c & b Shackleton	6
Dawkes	c Burden, b Heath	19	b Heath	0
Rhodes	b Shackleton	0	c Sainsbury, b Heath	2
Smith	not out	6	b Heath	0
Jackson	b Shackleton	4	not out	0
Extras		3		3
Total		74		107

Scoring rate: 2-26 (bonus points).
Fall of wickets: 1-8, 2-13, 3-24, 4-27, 5-27, 6-35, 7-52, 8-56, 9-68.
Bowling: Shackleton 16.4-8-36-4; Heath 16-5-35-6.

Fall of wickets: 1-21, 2-25, 3-25, 4-40, 5-94, 6-100, 7-100, 8-106, 9-107.
Bowling: Shackleton 18.2-4-52-3; Heath 18-4-52-7

HAMPSHIRE

	First innings		Second innings	
Marshall	c Dawkes, b Rhodes	4	lbw, b Jackson	0
Gray	b Rhodes	0	c Dawkes, b Rhodes	1
Horton	b Jackson	5	b Jackson	8
Pitman	run out	0	c Carr, b Rhodes	11
Barnard	c Morgan, b Rhodes	5	c Carr, b Jackson	16
A.C.D. Ingleby-Mackenzie	c Lee, b Rhodes	2	c Rhodes	4
Sainsbury	b Jackson	4	c Dawkes, b Jackson	4
Harrison	not out	2	c Jackson, b Morgan	0
Shackleton	c Lee, b Jackson	0	c Jackson, b Morgan	1
Heath	b Jackson	0	b Morgan	4
Burden	b Jackson	0	not out	0
Extras		1		6
Total		23		55

Scoring rate: 1-38
Fall of wickets: 1-4, 2-5, 3-7, 4-12, 5-17, 6-17, 7-23, 8-23, 9-23.
Bowling: Jackson 8.4-5-10-5; Rhodes 8-3, 12-4.

Fall of wickets: 1-1, 2-1, 3-13, 4-23, 5-32, 6-46, 7-47, 8-47, 9-55.
Bowling: Jackson 15-8-16-4; Rhodes 9-1-29-3, Morgan 5-3-3-4-3.

Umpires – J.S Buller and H.G. Baldwin.

74: *Middlesex v Sussex*
LORD'S, 17–20 MAY 1959

By the end of the 1950s both Middlesex and Sussex were looking like teams from which the glory had departed. Only Robertson was left of the formidable Middlesex batting line-up of the immediate post-war years, and although Sussex had colourful names like Dexter and Marlar among their number the side was, at the best, erratic. Middlesex's victory here, by one run, rates among the more astonishing in the game's history. Sussex's own triumph seemed unstoppable, after they had reduced Middlesex to 138 all out in the second innings, and when with the goal in sight the visitors had needed just 29 with five wickets standing.

D.V. Smith (b. 1923), who had set up the supposed Sussex victory, played for the county from 1946 to 1962, making 16,960 runs at an average of 30; he was also a useful left-arm medium-pace bowler, taking 340 wickets at 28

each, and had a short and unsuccessful test career, playing three times for England. Ted Dexter (b. 1935), who supported him in the second innings, is better known today as England's cricket supremo, a talented amateur golfer and public relations man. One of the most attractive attacking batsmen of his day, he played for Sussex from 1957 to 1968 after a glittering career at Cambridge. He made 21,150 runs (including 51 centuries) in his career at an average of 41 and took 419 wickets at 30. He captained both Sussex and England, playing 62 tests. Alan Moss (b. 1930) whose bowling undid Sussex in the second innings, was one of the leading quick bowlers of the time, though he never commanded a regular England place, playing just 9 tests. In his career he took 1,301 wickets at an average of 21, five times taking 100 in a season.

Lord's, Monday
From E. W. Swanton

It was a bright day but a cool one, with a sharpish wind blowing from the nursery which made the free seats a much more comfortable watching-place than the pavilion or the Warner Stand.

There were 13,000 spectators, including members, and for most of them the frequent fall of wickets and the general incident went a fair way, perhaps, to make up for the indifferent quality of the batting.

I wish I could give a convincing excuse for the failure of the Sussex first innings and the Middlesex second, but frankly it is impossible to find one. What can be said in extenuation is that the pitch showed the old Lord's tendency for the ball to keep low, and that a certain mistrust of it confined the batsmen's strokes.

It was not that they got out to balls that did unusual things. The only man who seemed to do so was, ironically, Robertson, who, judging by the applause that lasted all the way of his walk to the wicket, was being willed to succeed by everyone.

Batsmen and sides get complexes about pitches, and both these sides played as if their runs were desperately hard to get. The pace of this one was, it seemed, thoroughly easy, and if the bat had ever got on top either side might have made anything up to 400.

However, there was a regular distaste for playing right-forward – which when in doubt is always the classic recipe at Lord's – and, of course, with certain exceptions the spinners were allowed to wheel up their wares to a cluster of short-fielders with acres of space stretching to the boundary boards untenanted.

If one examines, for instance, Titmus's first innings analysis of seven for 54, the sorry truth emerges that two of the most distinguished Sussex batsmen were bowled literally playing back to half-volleys, the hopeful forward push accounted for two more, to catches near the wicket, while a fifth was offering a stroke which charity forbids my beginning to describe.

Titmus, indeed, bowling apparently more slowly than last year, varied his pace nicely and flighted his off-breaks skilfully into the breeze. But as a sophisticated cricketer he will know what his analysis was really worth.

He could have bowled just as well and taken two for 80 (perhaps having said which I might add that Titmus's first innings of 43 has been distinctly the most stylish and trouble-free innings of the game so far).

Sussex played woefully badly, while as to the Middlesex batting it is true to say that character is missing somewhat from it: or, at least, that the young men who occupy all but one of the first eight places in the order are still struggling to put their personality across.

Two or three, one might add, seem to have the ability to come to the front. At the moment there is a fair degree of promise running neck and neck.

The prospect of Sussex reaching the Middlesex score on first innings disappeared very early in the morning with the departure of Parks first ball and Dexter for four.

Parks, stretching forward outside the off-stump, touched a comfortable catch to slip. Such a large proportion of Sussex's runs so far – and for that matter so many of the catches taken – have been credited to Parks that this was a grievous blow.

Dexter, not yet in practice, probed outside the off-stump, the head, it seemed some way from the line of the ball. Cooper played in a workman-like way until he took a justifiable dip at the end, while Thomson either presented a cautious defensive bat or offered a good old-fashioned swing.

Ninety runs ahead, Middlesex began again with 29 for the first wicket, mostly scored by Russell, before Gale was caught from too fine a glance by Parks standing back.

Russell continued a succession of useful scores, and batted very pleasantly despite a slight crouch in the stance which somewhat reduces his reach.

Robertson is taking a second benefit this year against Yorkshire, not having been very lucky with his first, and his cause was appropriately recommended to the spectators over the loudspeaker system by the Middlesex captain, who reminded his hearers that Robertson began his career with Middlesex at Whitsuntide 21 years ago with an innings of 80.

Alas! this afternoon the hero made 80 fewer, being lbw to a near shooter, but this did not prevent the crowd from subscribing the handsome sum of £288.

The only two Middlesex players to do anything once Russell went were Parfitt and Tilly. Parfitt, left-handed, short but strongly built with a shock of fair hair, he hit the ball crisply, especially to leg.

He is a good glancer and hooker, and there is no nonsense with him of letting the leg-side ball go by for fear of being snapped up by one of the sharks around the corner. This valuable and enterprising innings should have sharpened his confidence.

Tilly batted a while in the manner of a latter-end bowler, with several whole-hearted smacks to leg and one or two more ambitious hits through and over extra-cover. It was in chasing one of these that Lenham failed to avoid the boundary board and was assisted off with a sprained ankle.

The ligaments are torn, and Lenham is thought to be out of cricket for two weeks. At all events he is not expected to bat to-morrow.

Marlar for the most part stuck to his quicker bowling, and Bates rewarded him with a particularly steady performance.

When Sussex went in just before half-past five in search of 229 to win, their batting was much more presentable than hitherto. Oakman and Smith, neither so far this year in prime form, played with confidence and at times freedom.

Oakman was yorked just on half-past six, but

Smith remains with Bell, the slow left-arm bowler who recently distinguished himself with the bat against Essex. All in all the last day has an intriguing prospect.

Tuesday

Middlesex had their second split-hair finish in successive matches here this afternoon. A week ago they beat Kent by two runs in a game wherein by all accounts the ranks of Tuscany were at least divided as to which side deserved the heartier cheer.

To-day the margin was one run, and although Sussex were much to be sympathised with in the absence of Lenham, who tore the ligaments of an ankle yesterday and had returned to Brighton, as the play went no impartial person could either withhold full credit from Middlesex for snatching the game from the fire nor, for that matter, could they refrain from the thought that Sussex had seemed somewhat chicken-hearted in the crisis.

It was all, needless to say, palpitatingly exciting from the moment when Middlesex took the new ball at 200 for four. Sussex then were only 29 runs from victory and Parks and Suttle, having been in half an hour or more, had had time to become set.

The score was 209 when Parks flipped an out-swinger to Murray standing back to Warr.

This left five effective wickets to make a further 20, and the very next ball Cooper repeated Parks's stroke and Murray, going for a rather wider catch which would probably have carried comfortably to first slip, put it on the floor.

In the next over Cooper obliged again, and Murray made no mistake, and now, of course, Middlesex were really scenting blood. This sixth wicket fell at 210, and in Moss's next Thomson fended off a short fast one, but the ball reached second slip low down and Sussex were 212 for seven.

Suttle had been in earnest consultation with his partners between overs for some time and henceforward the conferences were continuous, Middlesex perhaps rather abetting them as Moss and Warr grew tired.

The trouble for Sussex was that Suttle was not batting well enough to take charge, and the tail were patently fallible against these two fast bowlers with their tails up and the ball still red.

With Bates in, Suttle was constrained to risk a couple of cow-shots against Warr which aimed straight good-length balls to square leg. One trickled up the hill for four, but it was from a more orthodox push round the corner that the penultimate misfortune for Sussex occurred.

Suttle placed the ball in a vacant plot around the square-leg umpire, and Warr, the bowler, was the first man to reach it. By this time Suttle and Bates had turned and were both well on their way for the second. Suddenly, however, Suttle stopped and shouted Bates

back to the batting end. His wretched partner, in full stride, had no hope whatever of stopping, turning, and getting back – and that was 219 for eight.

Enter now the Sussex captain, with 10 runs wanted, and for 25 more minutes the agony lasted, and the small boys squawked away as an occasional single accrued or either Moss or Warr were unavailingly played at outside the off-stump.

Apart from a fair proportion of these dabbles, Marlar looked at least as safe as Suttle, and it was he who suddenly opened his shoulders and hit Warr truly and well straight over his head to the pavilion.

One to tie, and Suttle's turn to face Moss. Warr had everyone in now to save the single. Five straight good-length balls yielded no run, and before the sixth Warr ostentatiously dropped two men back on the leg-side.

TRAP BAITED
'Try a Bouncer'

The trap was elaborately baited. Lip-readers with field glasses no doubt may well have seen Warr at mid-off mutter to his tiring partner: 'Try a bouncer.'

Was it bluff or double bluff? As one cogitated the thought, Moss steamed up for the last time, dug in a fast short one, little Suttle aimed to swat as the ball flew over his head, and a shout from Middlesex united proclaimed that he had snicked and Murray had safely grasped the catch.

So after the best part of an hour the drama ended and Middlesex came in happy at the knowledge of 40 points, precious if precariously gained, from their three matches. Moss, with five for 42 from 23 overs, had the place of honour at their head.

For most of the morning it had looked that Sussex were gathering the game comfortably into their keeping. Bell, the promoted tail-ender, stayed in while 40 for one overnight grew to 61, then fell to a stroke a good deal below his heightened station.

Thereupon Dexter joined Smith in a stand which in just over 1½ hours added 102 and seemingly had taken Sussex into the realms of safety.

Smith had not found his best touch hitherto this season, while Dexter had had no practice since New Zealand until the middle of last week. There were signs of uncertainty about both which, in the circumstances, was understandable. Smith waved a good deal at the faster bowling, while Dexter's timing took a while to develop.

When he had made only three, with Smith in the late thirties, Dexter drove Moss extremely hard to mid-off and Tilly could not hold a nasty catch around his boots.

Gradually, however, the stand prospered, and Smith especially played some fine strokes, off-drives, a straight hit or two, and a pull off the front foot to mid-wicket which is almost the left-hander's signature tune, and which Warr was slow to guard against with a man on the boundary boards.

Dexter came to terms with himself with a straight-

Dexter hits to leg

hit six off Hurst, later repeated at the other end. When he connects the ball travels extremely fast from the bat, and during this stand one reflected not for the first time, how small the 75-yard boundary makes a field when, as now, the turf is well-rolled and hard.

Gradually, I believe, county captains will come to realise that in such circumstances the confounded inner-ring principle is far too expensive, as well as encouragement to bowlers to pitch short, and they will man the boundaries more strongly.

The Middlesex attack stood up reasonably well during this partnership, the key man being Titmus, who had several moral successes, especially against Smith. Will he, I wonder, make the big step forward this year which seemed only a matter of time several summers ago?

Before lunch Warr gave Gale an over of leg-breaks – which apparently is a regular item. It seems a scant chance to offer if Gale can really drop the ball and spin it.

In this case it cost two straight fours from Dexter, their being no fieldsman in front of the pavilion, but Gale would have had a slightly fortuitous scalp if Parfitt had held a hard-hit hook at short mid-wicket.

Smith left in the following over, bowled by Moss when he missed an attempted hook, and Dexter did not stay long afterwards, being caught in the covers trying to force off the back foot.

Parks, bothered by the sore finger that had been dislocated on Saturday, never looked himself, and it was his comparative failure that first gave Middlesex a gleam of hope.

For Sussex the result must have come as a sad disappointment. But the match at least had its compensations for them in Smith's return to form, and in the first real example of his ability, so far as his county are concerned, by Dexter. He was given a Sussex cap during the day, having earned an England one some 10 months before.

MIDDLESEX

Gale, c Parks, b Thomson	6	c Parks, B Bates	5
Russell, lbw b Bates	52	b Thomson	32
Parfitt, c Parks, b Bell	20	c Dexter, b Bates	60
Robertson, c Parks, b Smith	1	lbw, b Bates	0
White, c Smith, b Bell	35	b Dexter	6
Titmus, c Oakman, b Marlar	43	b Smith	2
Murray, b Marlar	3	c Suttle, b Dexter	1
Tilly, c Parks, b Marlar	5	c Bell, b Bates	23
J.J. Warr, b Bell	14	c Parks, b Thomson	0
Hurst, c Suttle, b Bates	16	b Bates	0
Moss, not out	19	not out	0
Extras (lb 6)	6	Extras	9
Total	220	Total	138

Fall of wickets: 1-12, 2-65, 3-66, 4-82, 5-153, 6-165, 7-166, 8-171, 9-191.

Scoring rate: 2.64.

Bowling: Thomson 17-7-33-1; Bates 10.2-2-37-2; Dexter 5-0-16-0; Smith 9-2-18-1; Bell 26-5-60-3; Oakman 8-3-21-0; Marlar 8-1-29-3.

Fall of wickets: 1-29, 2-31, 3-43, 4-70, 5-73, 6-74, 7-134, 8-138, 9-138.

Bowling: Thomson 18.1-5-29-2; Bates 16-1-32-5; Dexter 9-3-23-2; Smith 6-0-13-1; Bell 4-0-17-0; Marlar 3-1-15-0.

SUSSEX

Oakman, c Murray, b Tilly	28	b Moss	19
Lenham, b Titmus	25	absent hurt	0
Smith, b Titmus	17	(D.V.), b Moss	90
Suttle, b Titmus	8	c Murray, b Moss	28
Bell, c Watt, b Titmus	?	b Titmus	7
Parks, c Russell, b Titmus	0	c Murray, B Warr	15
E.R. Dexter, c Russell, b Moss	4	c Russell, b Titmus	58
Cooper, b Titmus	19	c Murray, b Moss	0
Thomson, lbw, b Warr	14	c Russell, b Moss	0
B.G. Marlar, lbw, b Titmus	3	not out	5
Bates, not out	4	run out	0
Extras (lb 5)	5	Extras (lb 2, lb 3)	5
Total	130	Total	227

Scoring rate: 1.98.

Fall of wickets: 1-28, 2-70, 3-71, 4-80, 5-80, 6-85, 7-85, 8-118, 9-121.

Bowling: Moss 14-3-28-1; Tilly 7-2-20-1; Warr 10-3-10-1; Titmus 25.2-5-54-7; Hurst 5-2-6-0; Parfitt 3-1-6-0; Gale 1-0-1-0.

Fall of wickets: 1-38, 2-61, 3-163, 4-179, 5-209, 6-210, 7-212, 8-219, 9-227.

Bowling: Moss 23-8-42-5; Warr 16-3-47-1; Titmus 25-11-58-2; Hurst 18-6-47-0; Tilly 4-0-9-0; Parfitt 3-1-10-0; Gale 1-0-9-0.

75: *Leicestershire v Glamorgan*
LEICESTER, 30 MAY–2 JUNE 1959

Leicestershire in the late 1950s had inherited the role of their neighbours, Northamptonshire, in propping up the championship table. Between 1954 and 1964 the county was bottom four times, one from bottom four times, and only once finished higher than ninth. This season was one where they came 16th, despite occasional fine batting performances by Maurice Hallam. Hallam (b. 1931) played for the county from 1950 to 1970, and in his career made 24,488 runs at an average of 29. He exceeded 1,000 runs in a season 13 times, and three times made more than 2,000, including 1959, when he made 2,070 at an average of 34. He became only the fifth batsman to score a double century and a century in the same championship match, a feat he would repeat two years later against Sussex. His 210 not out was the best score of his career and one of two double centuries he scored in this season.

Willie Watson (b. 1920), the Leicestershire captain who helped Hallam win the match with a fast half-century, was the side's leading player. He enjoyed his best season in 1959, scoring 2,212 runs at an average of 55. He played for Yorkshire from 1939 until 1957, going to Leicestershire as a professional captain in 1958, staying there until 1964. In his career he made 25,670 runs at an average of just under 40. He played in 23 tests but never matched his form at county level, managing under 900 runs at an average of 26. Allan Watkins (b. 1922), the Glamorgan centurion, was an all-rounder for the county from 1939 until 1962. In his career he made 20,361 runs at an average of 30 and took 833 wickets at 25, achieving the 'double' twice. He played 15 times for England.

Leicester, Monday
From T. H. Evans Baillie

A chanceless innings of 210 not out by Hallam, his second double hundred of the season, carried Leicestershire almost single-handed to first-innings points but not to bonus points.

As Hallam, followed by the Glamorgan side, walked off at the declaration which followed, Wooller, the selector, was subjected to some friendly banter by the crowd.

Glamorgan were left with an hour and three-quarters batting and made 106 for the loss of Hedges, brilliantly caught by Phillips low down at half deep square-leg. Parkhouse in particular had been driving with great power and style.

On a pitch kind to batsmen and against bowling that was short of any sustained pace runs came for the most part casually and with a preponderance of deflection.

Once Hallam took three 4's off an over from Wooller, but Van Geloven, trying to drive, edged the ball shoulder high to gully.

This discouraged any levity and though Hallam proceeded soberly to his fifth 50 of the season, having taken 110 minutes, Phillips just defended dourly.

At 102 Phillips missed a ball from Walker. Revill, who succeeded him, set about the bowling at once, sweeping boundaries off Shepherd and also having a lucky snick that went for four. This stirred Hallam to emulation and he took 14 off an over from McConnon.

The 150 was reached in three hours, helped by some untidy ground fielding, which was stressed by the contrast of Ward and Hedges, both agile and skilful.

Hallam's 100, reached in 191 minutes, preceded a lunch score of 172 for two, but the new ball was taken on the resumption and Revill, jumping out to sweep, missed and was leg before.

Watson, after a few of his classic cover and off-drives, had his middle stump hit attempting a stroke rather unworthy of him. But he had injected needed speed into the scoring and at 214 for four the bowling was on its way to being collared.

Wooller himself toiled heroically ringing the changes between medium-fast and slow-medium with a very occasional fizzer, and was never easy to play.

But generally Watkins, Pressdee, McConnon and Shepherd posed few problems, though keeping a fair length, and Walker gave him the best support.

It took the seventh and eight bowlers tried, both off-spinners, to tie down the batsmen. These two were Ward and Devereux.

Ward met with immediate success, getting Burch caught at cover, and runs came mainly one at a time, though a succession of 12 singles by Hallam was broken by an overthrow for two.

Hallam, however, went steadily along, his placing to leg, late-cuttings and cover-driving serving him well. When he carried his bat he had been there 328 minutes and hit 27 boundaries.

His is the highest score in post-war cricket by a Leicestershire player.

Tuesday

Maurice Hallam, Leicestershire's opening batsman, who is challenging for an England place, followed up his 210 not out in the first innings with 157, including the season's fastest hundred (71 minutes), against Glamorgan here to-day. He is now only 17 away from being the first player to reach 1,000 runs.

Leicester eventually won by eight wickets with nearly half an hour to spare.

Three individual scores of 50 or over had enabled Wooller to make the third declaration of the match, leaving Leicester to make 269 in three hours at 90 an hour.

Parkhouse, Watkins and Devereux were Glamorgan's second-innings run-makers, with the dynamism coming from Watkins, who in 49 minutes drove and pulled 59 runs. In one 17-minute spell he and Devereux put on 50.

Van Geloven, Leicester's first-change bowler, did better than most by taking another four wickets at reasonable cost, which made eight altogether in this batsman's revel, 1,189 runs scored for 23 wickets. His accurate medium-paced deliveries move a little either way.

Leicester scored four runs in two overs before lunch, and there might have been no shine on the ball to judge by the play when it was resumed.

Hallam was soon showing all the strokes, though he did not late cut with quite the delicacy Watkins had achieved. Runs raced by almost twice as fast as minutes. The 50 was reached in 27 minutes, the 100 in 57.

When he was 79 Hallam broke this enjoyable monotony by giving his first chance, a sharp one to slip. He was becalmed, perhaps as a result, in the 80s, but his 100 came soon enough.

The 150 total came in 87 minutes and though Van

Geloven, who had played his part tactfully, left at 158 Watson at once attacked and soon it was a matter of only 60-odd needed in an hour.

At 247 Hallam (18 fours and a six) was snapped up at the wicket, but Watson, who hit two sixes in his 47-minute 50, and Revill completed the job.

GLAMORGAN

Parkhouse, c Smith, b Van Geloven	17	c Julain, b Boshler	50
Hedges, c Hallam, b Van Geloven	53	c Phillips, b Savage	33
Pressdee, c Spencer, b Van Geloven	0	b Van Geloven	38
Devereux, lbw, b Van Geloven	38	c Burch, b Van Geloven	56
Watkins, c Revill, b Spencer	132	b Van Geloven	59
Walker, c Smith, b Spencer	12	b Van Geloven	0
W. Wooller, c Savage, b Smith	14	not out	9
Ward, c Watson, b Boshler	12	c Hallam, b Boshler	11
McConnon, b Boshler	5	not out	4
Evans, not out	12		
Extras (b 11, lb 16)	27	Extras (lb 4)	4
Total (for 9 dec)	322	Total (7 wkts. dec)	271

Fall of wickets: 1-44, 2-44, 3-95, 4-133, 5-166, 6-190, 7-247, 8-253, 9-322.

Scoring rate: 3.59 per over.

Did not bat: Shepherd.

Bowling: Spencer 24.4-1-97-2; Boshler 21-3-53-2; Van Geloven 24-3-82-4; Savage 13-2-45-0; Smith 7-2-18-1.

Fall of wickets: 1-56, 2-112, 3-129, 4-215, 5-215, 6-244, 7-254.

Bowling: Spencer 17-3-53-0; Boshler 12-1-32-2; Van Geloven 14-2-47-4; Savage 13-2-67-1; Smith 18-4-68-0.

LEICESTERSHIRE

Hallam, not out	210	c Evans, b Walker	157
Van Geloven, c Pressdee, b Watkins	19	c Shepherd, b Walker	37
Phillips, lbw, b Walker	13		
Revill, lbw, b Wooller	30	not out	15
Watson, b Walker	19	not out	59
Burch, c Hedges, b Ward	11		
Julian, not out	19		
Extras (lb 2, w 2)	4	Extras (b 1, lb 2)	3
Total (5 wkts. dec.)	325	Total (2 wkts.)	271

Scoring rate: 2.75.

Fall of wickets: 1-51, 2-102, 3-184, 4-215, 5-257.

Did not bat: Smith, Spencer, Savage, Boshier.

Bowling: Walker 30-11-61-2; Wooller 32-7-80-1; Watkins 14-2-36-1; Shepherd 12-1-36-0; McConnon 8-3-33-0; Pressdee 2-0-7-0; Ward 10-0-40-1; Devereux 10-2-28-0.

Fall of wickets: 1-158, 2-247.

Bowling: Wooller 16-1-92-0; Watkins 7-0-40-0; Shepherd 14-1-53-0; Walker 12-0-78-2; Ward 1.3-0-5-0.

Umpires – C.S. Elliott and W.F. Price

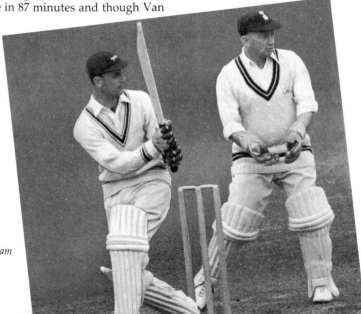

Maurice Hallam

76: Kent v Worcestershire
TUNBRIDGE WELLS, 15 JUNE 1960

This match is the last in first-class cricket to be finished in a day. Unless there is a revolution in the preparation of wickets, and unless the modern unacceptably slow over rates are improved, this feat may never happen again. Another factor against it is the new regulation whereby counties are docked championship points for producing bad wickets. This 'brute of a wicket', as our correspondent termed it, at Tunbridge Wells would surely have qualified for this censure. Nor would it be likely now that the victorious home captain would be as sporting as Colin Cowdrey was, and describe the wicket prepared by his groundsman as 'disgraceful'.

That part of Kent's victory that cannot be attributed to the lethal wicket was down to their opening bowlers, Brown and Halfyard. David Halfyard (b. 1931) played for Kent from 1956 to 1964, retiring prematurely because of injury problems. He went on to the first-class umpires' list from which, probably uniquely, he returned to play three seasons for Nottinghamshire between 1968 and 1970. He took over 100 wickets in a season five times, with 1958 being his best season, and took 963 altogether in his career, at an average of nearly 26. When he retired for the second and last time he once more became a first-class umpire. Alan Brown (b. 1935) played for Kent between 1957 and 1970, taking 743 wickets at just under 25 each. Only once did he take 100 wickets in a season, with 116 in 1965 at an average of 19. He played twice for England, on MCC's tour of India and Pakistan in 1961–62, but without any success.

Tunbridge Wells, Saturday

On a brute of a wicket at Tunbridge Wells yesterday Kent bowled out Worcestershire twice in two hours 50 minutes for 25 and 61 to win in a day by an innings and 101 runs.

The pitch, brown and grassless, never gave the batsmen a chance and Kent captain, M. C. Cowdrey, afterwards described it as 'disgraceful.' It is the first County Championship to finish in a day since Lancashire beat Somerset on June 6, 1953, at Bath.

Worcester's first innings total of 25, scored in 75 minutes, is the lowest of the season and only two more than Hampshire's 23 against Derbyshire at Barton

David Halfyard

in 1958.

It was the Kent seam bowlers, Brown and Halfyard, who caused these two collapses yesterday after Worcester had already dismissed their opponents for 187.

Brown took six for 12 in the first innings and Halfyard four for seven. They did most of the damage when Worcester batted again, Brown taking three for 22 and Halfyard five for 20.

Worcester would have fared as badly on their second time out as they did on their first but for a fighting 22 by Broadbent. He apart, Worcester's batsmen had no answer, for so long as the bowlers kept the ball on the stumps, the wicket did the rest.

Commendably aggressive batting by the left-hander Jones helped Kent reach 187. Going in with four wickets down for 68, he stayed one hour 35 minutes for 73 before being ninth out at 179.

Worcester's first innings began at 10 minutes to four. It was over at 5.25. Even a misdirected delivery spelled danger.

Eight of the ten batsmen dismissed were bowled and seven failed to score.

The target to avoid the follow-on, 38, was almost forgotten, and inevitably Worcester did go in again. With three wickets down for seven runs a repeat performance looked likely.

But Brown and Halfyard lost some of their length and direction. Broadbent fought for 70 minutes before he was eighth out at 51. Shortly after Cowdrey conferred with Dews and agreed to the extra half-hour being played.

Worcester were out at 10 minutes past seven, their second innings lasting one hour, 35 minutes. Halfyard bowled throughout the two innings, taking nine for 27.

Alan Brown

KENT

Phebey, b Gifford	16
Richardson, b Flavell	23
M.C. Cowdrey, c Broadbent, b Pearson	17
Wilson, c Headley, b Flavell	0
Leary, st Booth, b Slade	23
Jones, c Broadbent, b Slade	73
Dixon, c Dews, b Pearson	17
Catt, st Booth, b Gifford	0
Halfyard, st Booth, b Gifford	0
Brown, b Gifford	1
Shenton, not out	7
Extras	10
Total	187

Scoring rate: 2.71 (bonus points).
Fall of wickets: 1-41, 2-43, 3-43, 4-68, 5-104, 6-151, 7-154, 8-161, 9-179.
Bowling: Flavell 18-8-25-2; Pearson 16-7-35-2; Slade 18-5-54-2; Gifford 17-5-63-4.

WORCESTERSHIRE

Sedgley, c Leary, b Brown	7	c Richardson, b Brown	2
Headley, b Halfyard	0	c Wilson, b Halfyard	0
Spencer, b Brown	0	c Leary, b Brown	4
Richardson, b Brown	0	b Halfyard	2
Broadbent, b Halfyard	0	c Catt, b Halfyard	22
Dews, lbw, b Brown	0	b Brown	0
Booth, b Brown	2	c Shenton, b Halfyard	7
Slade, b Halfyard	9	c Leary, b Shenton	11
Gifford, not out	0	c Brown, b Shenton	4
Pearson, b Halfyard	0	c Cowdrey, b Halfyard	2
Flavell, b Brown	1	not out	0
Extras	6	Extras	7
Total	25	Total	61

Scoring rate: 1.45.
Fall of wickets: 1-6, 2-7, 3-8, 4-9, 5-9, 6-9, 7-24, 8-24, 9-24.
Bowling: Halfyard 9-4-7-4; Brown 8.1-5-12-6.

Fall of wickets: 1-0, 2-6, 3-7, 4-17, 5-18, 6-40, 7-51, 8-51, 9-61.
Bowling: Halfyard 13-4-20-5; Brown 8-2-22-3; Shenton 4.5-0-12-2.

Umpires – T.J. Bartley & J.S. Buller

77: *Sussex v Nottinghamshire*
EASTBOURNE, 6–7 JUNE 1962

It is something of an achievement to declare before the close on the first day, having made 406, but to lose before the end of the second, 'It stretched credulity to the limits' wrote our correspondent. Probably not for the reasons he intended, Dexter's gamble of putting the visitors in after he had won the toss paid off, though at the end of the first day it looked very much like recklessness. Dexter did, though, do more than any other player to win the match; and Nottinghamshire's batting in the second innings was a largely inexplicable disaster. This was, incidentally, the last season in which the distinction between amateurs and professionals pertained. On the scorecard hereafter all cricketers would have the distinction of their initials preceding their surname.

Alan Oakman (b. 1930) was a cornerstone of the Sussex side from 1947 to 1968. He made 21,800 runs at an average of 26 but was also a useful off-spinner, taking 736 wickets at 28 each in his career, and one of the best slip fielders of his age. He played twice for England. Ken Suttle (b. 1928) was another indispensable feature of the Sussex side. He record of 423 consecutive Championship matches between 1954 and 1969 is unsurpassed by any other county player. In his career between 1949 and 1971 he made 30,225 runs at an average of 31, scoring 1,000 runs in a season 17 times; this was his best season, in which he made 2,326 runs at an average of 39. Norman Hill (b. 1935), whose batting on the first day had given Nottinghamshire such an advantage, played for the county from 1953 to 1968, eventually captaining them. He made 14,303 runs in his career at an average of 29.

Eastbourne, Wednesday
From E. A. Roberts

Notts achieved the season's fastest first-day scoring in the County Championship, when they made 406 for eight declared in 310 minutes against Sussex to-day, the rate being 3.49 an over.

Hill, the left-handed opening batsman, batted for all but 15 minutes of that time for 193, which is the highest innings in the championship so far. It was eight short of his best, also taken off Sussex at Worksop a year ago.

Dexter is not one for strict conventions and his decision to field on a Saffrons pitch glistening with promise of abundant runs no doubt caused a few Sussex eyebrows to shoot upwards in questioning gestures.

However, Dexter's choice obviously stemmed from an honest appraisal of his own bowling resources, and his hunch that it is better to be chasing runs on the last afternoon here instead of stopping them, might yet prove right.

But Notts lost little time expressing their gratitude for first innings. Norman Hill and Winfield, casting off Portsmouth cares, reached 50 together in 40 minutes. In the next hour Maurice Hill struck three sixes with disarming ease and made 44 out of 75.

Although young Rhodes began rather too decorously, Norman Hill, always a close watcher of the ball, busily pulled, cut and deflected at a rate that kept his side on proper terms with the clock.

And even if the early play of the afternoon lacked inspiration, the day and setting were sublime, the elms in their full cloaks of greenery screening the new block of flats arising behind the pavilion, while the croquet on the adjoining lawns went on oblivious of Hill, Dexter, transistors and Epsom.

Hill, helped by Rhodes in a third wicket stand of 112, none the less reached 101 out of 211 in three hours and 10 minutes and then fairly skipped along adding a third 50 in 35 minutes.

With Poole at the other end the floodgates were open and an endless permutation of limited bowling resources did nothing to staunch the flow. By the time the new ball was due, Notts were on the brink of 300, a salutary reminder of what a fast scoring ground this is.

Hill, in fact, had 28 fours and also contributed one of his team's half a dozen sixes, a vast pull on to the pavilion roof, before he was caught at slip off Lenham, one of eight bowlers tried.

Despite their pummelling, Sussex always fielded keenly and bowled their overs well above 20 to the hour. Lenham, landing his back-of-the-hand spinners presentably, doubled his previous career wicket aggregate, and Cooper worked tirelessly for the wicket he eventually earned for himself with a brilliant return catch.

It was inevitably a day for batsmen, however, and although they started unconvincingly this evening, Sussex should find it another one to-morrow.

Thursday

All things are credible in cricket but events here, as

Ken Suttle

Sussex sensationally gained an eight-wicket victory half-way through the extra half-hour of the second day stretched credulity to the limits.

At tea Sussex declared, having just gained first-innings lead and bonus points with vigorously sustained batting, which carried them from 20 for one to 423 for four in under 4½ hours.

Forecasts naturally centred upon a further scoring spree and the likely target Sussex would face to-morrow in their second innings.

One hundred minutes later, Notts had been bowled out for 57 – on a good, fast wicket on which 829 runs had been made at a rate of 70 a wicket and 80 an hour. Sussex required 41, and with the extra period had 45 minutes at their disposal to finish off the game.

The abrupt change in events is explicable only in the unpredictability that is part and parcel of the game, but it was certainly a personal triumph for Dexter and a vindication of his gamble in fielding first.

He shared in one of the two big partnerships that had Oakman as the cornerstone, reached his 100 in 97 minutes and took four for 14 when Notts dramatically collapsed.

This morning Sussex in two and a half hours added 209.

Oakman, with his reach turning the good length ball into a half-volley, was soon sending his cover-drives swerving wide of the fieldsmen and Suttle bristled with activity, once finding the enthusiasm to dash over to gully in pursuit of a ball from Davison that

179

had slipped only to find the wicket-keeper had beaten him to it.

For much of the second-wicket partnership, the left-hander with his partiality for the leg side conspicuously evident, scored the faster but as both men drew within range of the century Oakman gained more of the strike.

Although Pratt bowled six maiden overs to him Oakman reached his century in 176 minutes and at the same time put up a double-century stand in 160 minutes. Suttle, five runs needed for his own hundred, was out in the next over, trying to run a widish one down to third man. N. Hill, the sole slip, took the chance very well on his left hand.

Oakman, in an eventful last over before lunch, hit Corran to long off for six, slashed a short one fiercely to point where Pratt made a brave attempt to make a catch, and then swayed away from a bumper which Millman took standing up at the wicket.

Parks provided a second wicket in a good spell by Corran, but it was a mixed blessing for the fielding side because Dexter now arrived, having had a lengthy 'net' beforehand, and was soon blasting the ball through the field with a controlled ferocity that tended to make one overlook Oakman's own brisk progress.

Oakman did survive a chance to long-leg made awkward as it came directly out of the strong sunlight during a century partnership in only an hour. Dexter's share was 60 including a hook for six off Corran that carried the mid-wicket boundary by almost 100 yards.

Notts have some ponderous movers in the field, but the spirit obviously is willing. M. Hill and Rhodes retrieved splendidly in the covers where Winfield also picked up an excellent catch to end Oakman's innings.

Oakman hit 28 fours and two sixes and curiously, like N. Hill yesterday was within range of emulating the double century each achieved when these two teams met at Worksop last year.

The new ball only went faster off the bat than the old one and Dexter, taking three successive fours off Davison, brought himself into calculations for the fastest century of the season.

Although he reached his first championship century for Sussex in two seasons by driving Wells (who sportingly kept the ball right up) for six in an over

costing 17, his time of 97 minutes was just outside the quickest. He lost fully five minutes, however, while a car was being covered to prevent reflection from the sun.

Dexter thereupon declared and by tea on the second day 829 runs had been scored with almost eight hours to go. Suddenly and surprisingly, however, the bowlers came into the game and Notts lost their first four wickets for 30.

Thomson, experimentally bowling round the wicket, started it, Bates took three in 19 balls, Cooper smartly ran out Millman, and then Dexter ran through the remainder, while N. Hill, the hero of Notts' first innings, was a helpless bystander at the other end and carried out his bat – all in vain.

NOTTINGHAMSHIRE

Hill, N., c Oakman, b Lenham	193	not out 23
Winfield, c Oakman, b Dexter	18	c Parker, b Thomson 0
Hill, M., c & b Bell	44	b Bates 0
Rhodes, W.E., c Langridge, b Bell	35	c Suttle, b Bates 9
Poole, b Thomson	30	b Bates 12
Millman, b Lenham	41	run out 0
Wells, run out	8	b Thomson 5
A.J. Corran, not out	11	c Parks, b Dexter 0
Davison, c & b Cooper	6	c Bates, b Dexter 2
Extras (b 12, lb 6, w 1, nb 1)	20	Cotton, b Dexter 0
		Pratt, b Dexter 0
		Extras (b 4, lb 2) 6

Total (8 wkts., dec.) 406   Total 57

Did not bat: Cotton, Pratt.
Scoring rate: 3.49.
Fall of wickets: 1-51, 2-126, 3-238, 4-304, 5-376, 6-388, 7-391, 8-406.
        Fall of wickets: 1-1, 2-2, 3-16, 4-30, 5-38, 6-38, 7-44, 8-48, 9-52.
Bowling: Thomson 11-1-32-1; Dexter 15-1-44-1; Bates 17-0-57-0; Cooper 36-1-9-89-1; Bell 18-2-78-2; Lenham 6-1-24-2; Suttle 7-1-43-0; Ledden 6-0-19-0.
        Bowling: Thomson 8.2-2-14-2; Bates 11-2-23-3; Dexter 8-2-14-4.

SUSSEX

Oakman, c Winfield, b Davison	177	not out 13
Langridge, c Millman, b Davison	0	c Millman, b Davison 7
Suttle, c Hill, N., b Corran	95	c Hill, N., b Corran 13
Parks, lbw, b Corran	9	not out 8
E.R. Dexter, not out	114	
Lenham, not out	12	
Extras (b 15, w 1)	16	

Total (4 wkts dec) 423   Total (2 wkts.) 41

Scoring rate: 4.02.
Fall of wickets: 1-6, 2-212, 3-244, 4-380.
        Fall of wickets: 1-11, 2-28.
Did not bat: Cooper, Ledden, Thomson, Bell, Bates.
        Bowling: Davison 4-1-15-1; Corran 3-0-25-1; Rhodes 1-1-0-0; Winfield 0-3-1-0.
Bowling: Cotton 10-2-42-0; Davison 23-2-99-2; Corran 28-0-114-2; Pratt 32-10-79-0; Wells 9-0-73-0; Poole 1-1-0-0.

Sussex – 14 points
Umpires – F.A. Gibbs & J.F. Crapp.

Alan Oakman

78: Sussex v Warwickshire
WORTHING, 6–9 JUNE 1964

By the mid-1960s county cricket was in serious decline. While financial salvation had been found, from 1963 onwards, in sponsored limited-over competitions, these flourished only at the expense of three-day cricket, whose programme was ultimately reduced in size to accommodate the one-day matches, and to which it became ever harder to attract crowds. The introduction of so much prize money into the game, and the abolition of amateur status after the 1962 season, also changed the character of the game. With so much at stake for the professionals, cricket became increasingly defensive and unattractive, attitudes verging on the unsportsmanlike crept in, and the acquisition of skills needed in the one-day game began to cause decay in the skills needed for successful three-day matches.

Exceptional achievements still occurred, though more rarely. Ian Thomson's 10 for 49 in Warwickshire's first innings is the most recent occasion in England that a bowler has taken all ten in an innings. Thomson (b. 1929) played for Sussex from 1952 to 1965, though came out of retirement to play for them during 1972. He took 100 wickets in a season 12 times, and in his career took 1,597 wickets at 20 each. He played five times for England on MCC's tour of South Africa in 1964–65, without any success. Thanks to Sussex's disastrous second innings, the lowest county score for 40 years, he joined the ranks of bowlers who have taken all ten for a losing side. Jack Bannister (b. 1930), who was the chief cause of Sussex's defeat, was a Warwickshire medium-pace bowler from 1950 to 1968. He took 1,198 wickets in his career at an average of 22, and later became a well-known television commentator.

Worthing, Monday
By Tony Goodridge

No one plays better on the uncertainty of the batsmen than that doughty warrior Ian Thomson, 35, who has so often come to the rescue of Sussex. Here to-day he crowned all previous achievements by taking the 10 Warwickshire first-innings wickets for 49 and collecting two more in the second.

Warwickshire, the joint leaders in the champion-

Ian Thomson – the last man to take all ten in England

ship, having led on the first innings, by 76 runs, had scored 54 for four wickets in their second innings to lead by 130.

All told 22 wickets fell during the day on a pitch which was always suspect although rather grudging in the pace with which it lent its help to the bowlers.

Still the batsmen obviously did not trust it and so far as the bowlers were concerned that was half the battle.

Warwickshire, with 103 runs in the bag after Saturday's play, and with eight wickets still in hand were moved to score as quickly as possible.

They had to live dangerously for the wicket, although in general very slow, did take a certain amount of spin and the occasional ball was apt to do something eccentric.

Some of the batsmen's strokes were enthusiastic rather than realistic and no one is more calculated to exploit a situation such as this than the Sussex seam bowler, Thomson, who took all 10 wickets for 49.

It was fitting that it should have happened here for it was at Worthing in 1953 that he was awarded his county cap while playing against Hampshire.

Thomson started his work of destruction by having Barber, who had made a good half-century on Saturday, caught at second slip in the third over of the day.

Thereafter only M. J. K. Smith and Cartwright gave promise of staying for long. The latter reached a good 50 in 84 minutes with a six and five fours to help.

In the course of the morning Thomson, who started with six consecutive maidens, took eight for 30 and all told 10 for 49 in 34 overs.

The Sussex batting subsequently did little to enhance this splendid effort of Thomson. The Warwickshire seam bowlers, Brown, Bannister and Cartwright, bowled accurately and economically and they were supported by some good close catching.

The batsmen were all at sea in their estimation of the pace of the wicket and Suttle, Lenham, Oakman and Cooper were all out playing far too soon.

Bell and Snow provided the most rewarding stand of the evening by putting on 39 for the ninth wicket. But the side could muster only 120 and Warwickshire were left with 95 minutes in which to increase a first-innings lead of 76.

On the whole they thrived and finished the day 130 runs ahead with six wickets still in hand. Again good catches were held by Sussex, notably an excellent one by Gunn behind the wicket, which dismissed Barber and one by Pountain close in on the off side which sent back Horner.

Tuesday

Warwickshire imposed their authority on Sussex here to-day in the manner of would-be champions. Having set Sussex to get 206 runs in the last innings the Warwickshire seam bowlers in 55 minutes had Sussex all out for 23, the lowest total by a county since 1924, when Lancashire scattered Glamorgan for 22 at Liverpool.

Bannister, bowling from the same end from which Thomson had caused such havoc during the Warwickshire batting, was the chief agent of destruction.

Making full use of an awkward spot on a length from which the ball was liable to do all manner of unexpected things, he took six for 16 in six overs.

He was ably assisted by Brown from the pavilion end and when he was succeeded by Cartwright the latter polished off the innings by taking the last two wickets with his first two deliveries.

But it was Thomson who once again spread the initial confusion of the day. When Warwickshire began this morning 130 runs ahead with six wickets in hand two of Thomson's first three deliveries lifted ominously and the fourth one crept perilously close to Jameson's off-stump about an inch above the ground.

Warwickshire did well under the circumstances to set Sussex the target which they did. Thomson once again proved what a formidable adversary he can be and his five wickets for 26 brought his match total to 15 for 75.

Jack Bannister

In the last 60 years only R. G. Marlar has taken 15 wickets in a match for Sussex. He did it twice, first in 1952 against Glamorgan at Swansea (15 for 133) and in 1955 against Lancashire at Hove (15 for 119).

Sussex's final agony began at once. In Bannister's first over Langridge, just as he had done in the first innings, turned him into the leg trap. At 15 Lenham was lbw to a ball that kept very low. Oakman returned a catch to the bowler and Suttle sent one to mid-wicket.

Two runs later Cooper was caught at point off a ball that rose very sharply and Pountain, all poised for a drive at Brown, merely deflected the ball on to his off stump.

At 21 Thomson was caught at wide mid-on and Buss shuffled vaguely towards the off and hung out his bat but not apparently in the line of flight because he was bowled.

Cartwright then appeared at the pavilion end and Snow advanced to hit his first ball but checked on the shot and Barber at mid-on took the catch. Gunn knew little or nothing about the next ball and that, so far as Sussex were concerned, was very much the end.

WARWICKSHIRE

Batsman	1st innings		2nd innings	
N.F. Horner	c & b Thomson	0	c Pountain, b Thomson	11
R.W. Barber	c Suttle, b Thomson	57	c Gunn, b Buss	15
K. Ibadulla	c Buss, b Thomson	17	lbw, b Thomson	0
M.J.K. Smith	lbw, b Thomson	42	c Gunn, b Buss	19
J.A. Jameson	b Thomson	7	c Buss, b Thomson	16
T.W. Cartwright	st Gunn, b Thomson	54	c Cooper, b Snow	24
R.E. Hitchcock	lbw, b Thomson	2	c Bell, b Buss	0
A.C. Smith	b Thomson	2	c & b Snow	7
J.D. Bannister	c Gunn, b Thomson	1	b Thomson	0
R. Miller	b Thomson	7	c Buss, b Thomson	0
D.J. Brown	not out	0	not out	25
Extras	(b 2, lb 3, nb 2)	7	(b 4, lb 4, nb 4)	12
Total		**196**		**129**

Fall of wickets: 1-10, 2-48, 3-107, 4-122, 5-133, 6-151, 7-155, 8-163, 9-181.
Bowling: Thomson 34-2-19-49-10; Buss 12-1-42-0; Snow 16-2-52-0; Bell 11-3-35-0; Oakman 5-2-11-0.

Fall of wickets: 1-18, 2-26, 3-26, 4-31, 5-64, 6-74, 7-93, 8-100, 9-100.
Bowling: Thomson 25-2-15-26-5; Buss 12-6-58-3; Snow 7-1-33-2.

SUSSEX

Batsman	1st innings		2nd innings	
K.G. Suttle	c M.J.K. Smith, b Brown	33	c Hitchcock, b Brown	8
R.J. Langridge	c M.J.K. Smith, b Bannister	0	c M.J.K. Smith, b Bannister	1
L.J. Lenham	c Ibadulla, b Bannister	2	lbw, b Bannister	6
A.S.M. Oakman	c Brown, b Cartwright	10	c & b Bannister	0
G.C. Cooper	c Hitchcock, b Brown	7	c Ibadulla, b Bannister	2
F.R. Pountain	b Cartwright	3	b Brown	0
N.I. Thomson	c M.J.K. Smith, b Cartwright	8	c Brown, b Bannister	4
A. Buss	c & b Brown	3	b Bannister	0
J. Snow	not out	21	c Barber, b Cartwright	2
R.V. Bell	not out	25	not out	0
T. Gunn	lbw, b Brown	0	b Cartwright	0
Extras	(b 8)	8		
Total		**120**		**23**

Fall of wickets: 1-1, 2-25, 3-50, 4-50, 5-60, 6-62, 7-68, 8-80, 9-119.
Bowling: Brown 16-5-4-50-4; Bannister 15-7-26-2; Cartwright 26-11-36-3.

Fall of wickets: 1-1, 2-15, 3-15, 4-15, 5-17, 6-17, 7-21, 8-21, 9-23.
Bowling: Brown 6-3-7-2; Bannister 6-2-16-6; Cartwright 0.2-0-0-2.

Warwickshire 10 pts
Umpires – J. Arnold & A.E. Fass.

79: *Yorkshire v Hampshire*
MIDDLESBROUGH, 19–20 MAY 1965

When Yorkshire cricket went into decline after the 1960s – their Championship success of 1968 was their most recent – the decline was sudden. They came fourth in 1965, and would win the title for the three following seasons, but in their humiliation by Hampshire (who would finish 12th) there was, perhaps, a sign of the weaknesses to come. Yorkshire's 23 was the lowest score in their history, though to be fair it should be noted that 1965 was one of the grimmest seasons for batsmen for many years, with only four averaging over 45 and a player of the calibre of Boycott not managing to score a century all summer. Wisden said of the debacle at Middlesbrough that 'their [Yorkshire's] policy of under-preparing pitches for county games' was directly responsible. Referring to the predominant malaise in the game, it continued: 'Is it any wonder batting in county cricket has become so unattractive when such conditions exist?' Gates were falling continuously, and seldom has confidence in the quality and appeal of first-class cricket been as low as it was at this time.

White (b. 1935), who led the rout of Yorkshire, played for Hampshire from 1957 to 1971, and played twice for England. In his career he took 1,143 wickets at 24 each, four times taking 100 in a season. Although on this occasion he contributed most with the bat, Freddie Trueman (b. 1931) was Yorkshire's and England's most famous fast bowler. It was in this summer that he played the last of his 67 tests for England, in which he became the first man to take 300 test wickets. He finished with 307 at a cost of 22 each. Known as 'Fiery Fred', he took 2,304 wickets at 18 each in his career. He later became a renowned radio commentator.

Middlesborough, Wednesday
By A Special Correspondent

Twenty-two wickets fell during the day here, which was notable for some lusty batting by Trueman and fine bowling by Shackleton, the Hampshire opening bowler.

Yorkshire, all out for 121, were four runs behind on first innings but went three runs ahead only to lose Hampshire and Boycott, without adding to the score before the close.

When Yorkshire batted they had no idea what they had undertaken. Shackleton made the new ball move alarmingly from the seam after pitching. Several good length deliveries hit the batsmen on the knuckles or passed waist-height to the wicket-keeper. Only occasionally the ball kept low.

For 36 minutes without scoring a run Boycott defended with all the skill he possessed and was then tempted to try to hit a slower ball from Shackleton, and was bowled by him.

The Yorkshire batsmen came and went. Hampshire was caught in the leg trap, Close played on, Padgett was lbw, Sharpe was caught and Illingworth bowled.

The seventh wicket fell with only 47 runs on the board. But then came Trueman, and the situation changed. With four mighty wallops he hit Shackleton for four successive boundaries. In another over from Shackleton after lunch he collected 26 runs.

He scored 55, Hutton, by far the best looking of the Yorkshire batsmen scored 22 and the total reached a respectable 121. Shackleton, with yet another fine performance, finished with six wickets for 64 runs – and 47 of them had been taken by Trueman.

Rolling between the innings seemed to change the character of the pitch. Marshall and Barnard scored 27 runs before Trueman caught and bowled Barnard.

Yorkshire hopes soared when Horton and Livingstone were dismissed cheaply but Marshall found no difficulty and scored 51 before being bowled by Hutton.

Against a steady and perservering Yorkshire seam attack, the Hampshire batsmen now began to fall. That is, apart from Keith. In the light of recent performances, this player will have to be promoted in the batting order. He scored 17 not out and saw Hampshire to a first innings lead of four runs.

In the closing half-hour Hampshire again struck into the Yorkshire batting and claimed the wickets of Boycott and Hampshire while conceding only seven runs.

Thursday

Yorkshire were bowled out for 23 runs in their second innings here to-day, the lowest total recorded in the history of the club, and suffered a completely humiliating 10 wickets defeat in less than two days at the hands of Hampshire.

After the match, A. C. D. Ingleby-Mackenzie, the Hampshire captain, said: 'It is a sporting pitch and we have the bowlers for the job.' They certainly had.

D. W. White took six wickets for 10 runs, and at one time had five without conceding a run.

It was, of course, the best performance by this fast right-arm bowler – he bats left-handed – who has played in two Tests against Pakistan. There were seven maidens in his 10 overs.

The Yorkshire-born D. Shackleton took two for seven, to add to his six wickets in Yorkshire's first

David White

Fred Trueman

innings, and Cottam, a native of the neighbouring Lincolnshire, also had two wickets which cost him two runs.

The pitch was extremely helpful to the fast bowlers, and White in particular seemed to produce extra pace from it.

He made the ball kick from a good length, and the Yorkshiremen could do nothing with it, except edge it to the slips or into their stumps.

Binks, Close, Illingworth and Hutton were among his victims in this way, and Sharpe, who had defended better than most for 20 minutes, pushed a catch to short leg.

As usual Shackleton bowled immaculately. He had Padgett caught with a gem of an outswinger at the start of the day.

At one time when six wickets were down for eight runs it seemed that Yorkshire might be dismissed for the lowest total of all time.

Four byes gave them double figures, but the position was already hopeless. They had been four behind on the first innings.

When they had lost eight for 13, Ingleby-Mackenzie replaced Shackleton with the faster Cottam.

Trueman's fighting spirit enabled him with Wilson to produce the only stand, 10 runs between them, but Cottam brought this remarkable innings to a dramatic end with the last two wickets.

Neither Trueman not Nicholson could find such life in the pitch as White had, and the scoring of 20 runs which Hampshire needed by Marshall and Barnard was almost an anti-climax. Yorkshire were completely beaten.

YORKSHIRE

G. Boycott, b Shackleton	0	lbw, b White	5
J.H. Hampshire, c Horton, b Shackleton	10	c Keith, b Shackleton	2
D.E.V. Padgett, lbw, b Cottam	12	c Keith, b Shackleton	0
*D.B. Close, b Shackleton	2	c Barnard, b White	1
P.J. Sharpe, c Horton, b Cottam	9	c Sainsbury, b White	1
R. Illingworth, b Cottam	3	b White	0
R.A. Hutton, c Timms, b Shackleton	22	c Barnard, b White	0
†J.G. Binks, c Sainsbury, b Shackleton	3	c Keith, b White	0
F.S. Trueman, c Marshall, b Shackleton	55	lbw, b Cottam	3
D. Wilson, b Cottam	0	not out	7
A.G. Nicholson, not out	2	c Livingstone, b Cottam	0
Extras	3	Extras (b 4)	4
Total	121	Total	23

Fall of wickets: 1-9, 2-14, 3-16, 4-34, 5-37, 6-40, 7-47, 8-113, 9-115.
Bowling: Shackleton 22.5-10-64-6; White 7-4-9-0; Cottam 15-3-45-4.

Fall of wickets: 1-7, 2-7, 3-7, 4-7, 5-8, 6-8, 7-12, 8-13, 9-23.
Bowling: Shackleton 9-5-7-2; White 10-7-10-6; Cottam 1.4-0-2-2.

HAMPSHIRE

R.E. Marshal, b Hutton	51	not out	10
H.M. Barnard, c & b Trueman	19	not out	6
H. Horton, c Binks, b Nicholson	1		
D.A. Livingstone, run out	2		
P.J. Sainsbury, c Padgett, b Hutton	11		
*A.C.D. Ingleby-Mackenzie, c Sharpe, b Hutton	6		
G.L. Keith, not out	17		
†B.S.V. Timms, c Hampshire, b Close	3		
D. Shackleton, b Close	0		
D.W. White, b Nicholson	6		
R.M. Cottam, b Trueman	0		
Extras	9	Extras (lb. 4)	4
Total	125	Total	20

Fall of wickets: 1-27, 2-29, 3-31, 4-86, 5-91, 6-100, 7-118, 8-118, 9-124.
Bowling: Trueman 9-2-2-15-2; Nicholson 18-3-59-2; Hutton 16-5-33-3; Boycott 5-2-5-0; Close 1-0-4-2.

Bowling: Trueman 4-2-3-0; Nicholson 4-0-13-0.

Hampshire 10 pts.
Umpires – F.C. Gardner & A.E.D. Smith.

80: *Middlesex v Glamorgan*
LORD'S, 18–20 AUGUST 1965

Although their insipid attitude to batting in this game would not suggest it, Glamorgan were one of the more attractive sides of the 1960s. Their second Championship title would come in 1969 and this season they would finish third. This match was remarkable as it included the last occasion in a first-class match in England that a batsman was given out 'handled ball'. It had happened only once before since the Championship had been officially constituted in 1890, when the Nottinghamshire batsman C.W. Wright was given out in a game against Gloucestershire at Bristol in 1893. As John Thicknesse writes, it had not happened in any first-class match in England

for 58 years. After Rees's dismissal it did not occur again in a first-class match until 1971–72, in Pakistan, after which it occurred 18 times in 15 years, mostly on the Indian sub-continent.

Rees (b. 1938) was a Welsh rugger international who subsequently became a professional rugby league player. He played for Glamorgan from 1955 to 1968, making just 7,681 runs at an average of 24. Titmus (b. 1932), one of England's leading all-rounders, was in the first of four difficult seasons as his county's captain. He played for the county from 1949 to 1982, with the exception of two seasons spent at the Oval as Surrey's coach in the late 1970s. In his career he scored 21,588 runs at an average of 23, and with his off-spin took 2,830 wickets at 22 each. He played 53 times for England and was most successful as a bowler, taking 153 wickets at 32 each. He achieved the 'double' eight times, taking 100 wickets in a season 16 times. Halfway through his career he lost four toes when he was hit by a boat when swimming.

Lord's, Wednesday
By John Thicknesse

Middlesex did Northamptonshire a great service here by smiting Glamorgan all round the ground for 380 for seven declared. Russell and Brearley put on 151 for the first wicket, Murray made 57 in 70 minutes, and finally Parfitt scored a century in 2¼ hours, the second 50 occupying 43 minutes.

In the final quarter-hour Glamorgan scored eight without loss, but their chances of winning seem slight. Even the prospects of a slogging match on the third day have receded in the light of Middlesex's commanding score.

There was only one sticky phase in the Middlesex innings when, in poor light after lunch, they went from 151 for no wicket to 167 for three in 40 minutes. Otherwise it was a story of bat lustily put to ball, a matter greatly facilitated by an over rate of 20 an hour.

By lunch Russell and Brearley had made 123 off 41 overs both clearly sighting the ball early in the brightest sunshine of the day. Brearley played some uppish strokes into the covers off Pressdee, but the one real alarm came when Russell, having reached 50 in 90 minutes, mis-hit Slade gently to mid-off.

There Lewis, of all people, who used to make swirling touch kicks in front of 60,000 at Twickenham look as easy as shelling peas, dropped it with something to spare. At lunch Russell was 70, Brearley 49.

But 25 minutes afterwards Russell mis-timed a drive and was caught at cover, whereupon Jones, in his second spell from the pavilion end, disposed of Brearley and Clark, the latter to a catch joggled on by Pressdee to Walker at first slip.

Wheatley at that moment must dearly have wished Shepherd was fit enough to prise the door farther open. But with the appearance of Murray, Middlesex at once got a second wind and the next two hours produced 170.

Murray, having given Parfitt 40 minutes to start, caught him at 21 and went ahead with three fours in an over from Wheatley. He reached 50 in 55 minutes with his seventh boundary, and was out when a cut made minimal contact and Evans caught him at the wicket.

With Radley as his partner, Parfitt took over where Murray had left off, and aided by swift running between wickets, they put on 75 in less than an hour.

Parfitt hit the ball harder through the covers than

Fred Titmus

I have seen him, and cut with a fine cleaving smash. At 93 he was lucky to lob Jones over the slips to the boundary, and at 99 ran out Radley, but he completed his 100 with another good boundary through extra cover.

Contrary to expectations, Titmus delayed the declaration 20 minutes. Middlesex added another 37 runs, losing Parfitt to a stumping and the captain to a ludicrous run-out.

Thursday

Glamorgan made batting look hard work today. Setting their sights unashamedly on the 231 needed to save the follow-on, they just scraped home with Rees and the last man, Wheatley, together. At this point the innings had occupied 139 overs, or six hours' batting time.

It would be mincing words to say that the spectacle provided was anything but excruciating, particularly when contrasted with Middlesex's fine batting that brought 380 for seven yesterday.

At the same time, one could appreciate, if not sympathise with, Glamorgan's tactics. Needing to win this match to retain any real chance of catching Northants, they had only two reasonable courses.

The first was to score 500 and try to win on merit, which was probably discarded without much trouble. The other was to limit Middlesex's lead to something below 150 and hope that Titmus would set them a target against time on the third day.

They pursued the second course, but with a degree of strokelessness that would have caused Mackay to shed tears of envy. Glamorgan achieved their object, certainly – but whether they will find Titmus in magnanimous mood tomorrow is open to question. Nobody at Lord's today would blame him if he was not.

Hedges was out, having added 17 to his overnight

Eastbourne, Monday
By Rex Alston

The players did their best to make up the loss of Saturday's play at Eastbourne and Surrey had the better of the day's play by making 300 for four declared off 82.5 overs, to which Sussex replied with 110 for three off 41 overs.

The basis of Surrey's big score was a forceful first-wicket partnership of 130 between Edwards, restored to the side in Storey's place, and Lewis. Both were out to Michael Buss mis-timing attacking strokes chasing bonus points.

The rest of Surrey's batsmen carried on the good work, with Owen-Thomas and Younis flashing at the faster bowlers and giving catches to Parks. Each played some fine strokes and the ball raced to the boundary over the fast out field.

The Sussex reply was sustained by Graves and Prideaux and the latter was still there, 50 not out, with Spencer as night watchman. Spinners Pocock and Intikhab were a teasing proposition and Sussex struggled against them in the last hour.

Tuesday

Pat Pocock, the Surrey off-spinner, took seven wickets, including the hat-trick for four runs in his final two overs to deny Sussex victory at Eastbourne yesterday. His efforts, plus a run-out off the last ball of the match left Sussex three runs short with a wicket to fall.

Incredible is the only word that can be applied to Sussex's failure to win the match and to their losing five wickets in the last over.

Set 205 to win in about 130 minutes, Sussex lost their first wicket for 27, then Greenidge and Prideaux added 160 in 80 minutes and victory seemed sure for 18 were needed off the final three overs with only one man out.

Greenidge went for 68 off the first ball of the 18th over. Pocock took two more wickets in the over and conceded two runs as Sussex continued to charge after victory.

Eleven runs came from the other end and the final over began with Sussex needing five runs with six wickets standing.

Panic set in as their batsmen rushed to the destruction Pocock coolly offered them. Even Prideaux, who in the morning had scored 50 in the first hour to complete an admirable century, joined the hara-kiri with his score at 97.

Prideaux was caught on the boundary off the first ball of Pocock's remarkable over, the hat-trick was duly completed and only Spencer's single off the fourth ball prevented Surrey from accomplishing the impossible.

The scoreboard records the over as WWW1W1 (run out).

SURREY

First Innings		Second Innings	
M.J. Edwards, c Joshi, b M.A. Buss	81	c Phillipson, b Spencer	6
R.M. Lewis, c Greenidge, b M.A. Buss	72	st Parks, b Spencer	28
D.R. Owen-Thomas, c Parks, b Spencer	31	c Griffith, b M.A. Buss	32
Younis Ahmed, c Parks, b Phillipson	26	c A. Buss, b Joshi	26
G.R.J. Roope, not out	43	not out	21
*M.J. Stewart, not out	34	not out	1
Intikhab Alam		c Spencer, b Joshi	6
Extras (b 6, lb 7)	13	Extras (b 4, lb 6)	10
82.5 overs Total (4 wkts. dec.)	300	Total (5 wkts. dec.)	130

Did not bat: A.R. Butcher, A. Long, P.I. Pocock, R.D. Jackman.
Fall of wickets: 1–130, 2–167, 3–212, 4–232.
Bowling: Spencer 22.5–4–56–1; A. Buss 17–3–74–0; Phillipson 13–1–37–1; M.A. Buss 15–3–58–2; Joshi 15–5–62–0.

Fall of wickets: 1–8, 2–61, 3–95, 4–101, 5–117
Bowling: Spencer 11–0–29–2; A. Buss 12–1–35–0; Joshi 6–0–27–2; M.A. Buss 5–1–29–1.

SUSSEX

First innings		Second Innings	
G.A. Greenidge, c Long, b Butcher	6	b Pocock	68
P.J. Graves, b Pocock	35	c Roope, b Jackman	14
R.M. Prideaux, not out	106	c Jackman, b Pocock	97
M.A. Buss, c Long, b Pocock	8	b Pocock	0
J. Spencer, lbw, b Intikab	0	not out	1
†J.M. Parks, c Roope, b Intikhab	29	c & b Pocock	2
*M.G. Griffith, not out	29	c Lewis, b Pocock	6
J.D. Morley		st Long, b Pocock	0
A. Buss		b Pocock	0
U.C. Joshi		run out	1
Extras (b 6, lb 7)	13	Extras (b 4, lb 8, w 1)	13
72.1 overs. Total (5 wkts. dec.)	226	Total (9 wkts.)	202

Did not bat: C.P. Phillipson.
Fall of wickets: 1–12, 2–80, 3–104, 4–117, 5–190.
Bowling: Jackman 7–1–29–0; Butcher 15–4–33–1; Pocock 24–8–69–2; Intikhab 26.1–6–82–2

Fall wickets: 1–27, 2–187, 3–187, 4–189, 5–200, 6–200, 7–200, 8–201, 9–202.
Bowling: Jackman 13–1–62–1; Butcher 3–0–13–0; Pocock 16–1–67–7; Intikhab 12–2–47–0

Sussex 5pts, Surrey 8
Umpires – D.J. Constant and A.G.T. Whitehead

84: Kent v Surrey
MAIDSTONE, 4–6 JULY 1973

In this match Colin Cowdrey (b. 1932) scored the 100th of his 107 first-class centuries. He was only the 16th player to reach this landmark, only the fifth since the war, and only the third Kent player to do it, after Woolley and

Ames. Cowdrey was also the first man to play in over 100 test matches, having established this record in an age when fewer tests were played than today by being a regular member of the England side for 15 years, and playing his first and last tests 20 years apart after winning a famous recall, in 1974–75, to help save England on Denness's disastrous tour of Australia. He first played for Kent as an amateur in 1950, having become one of the finest public school batsmen. He was the youngest player ever to appear in a major match at Lord's, making his debut there for Tonbridge in 1946 aged 13. He captained Kent from 1959 until 1971, and led England 27 times in his 114 tests, finally retiring in 1976. He made 42,719 runs at an average of 43, with a top score (for MCC against South Australia on the 1962–63 tour) of 307.

Playing against Cowdrey in this match was another batsman who would make a hundred hundreds, John Edrich. Edrich (b. 1937) came from the renowned Norfolk cricketing family, and was a cousin of W.J. For twenty seasons Edrich went in first for Surrey, from 1959 until he retired in 1978, and 19 times made 1,000 runs in a season (including six seasons when he made more than 2,000). He made 103 centuries in all and scored 39,790 runs at an average of 45, playing 77 times for England. He was one of the most courageous batsmen of his age, unflinching in the face of the most hostile bowling, with an unshakeable nerve. He captained Surrey successfully from 1973 until 1977.

Maidstone, Wednesday
By John Mason

Geoff Howarth, Surrey's New Zealander, spent an adventurous four hours mauling Kent's bowlers on a splendidly true batting pitch at Maidstone yesterday. Only John Shepherd successfully withstood the attack.

Surrey, also usefully served by Owen-Thomas, declared at 367 for six, Howarth's 159 being his second century this summer and his highest career score so far. He struck 21 boundaries.

Kent, left with 20 minutes batting to complete another day of high summer, reached eight wickets without loss. Surrey's bowlers may have had troubled dreams last night, and it will be hard labour today unless the weather changes.

Edwards must have watched the subsequent events of the day with a heavy heart. He has been in no sort of form for some time, but yesterday he had an opportunity in perfect conditions to play a long innings again.

He failed, and in marched Howarth in the sixth over to start a partnership of 131 in 45 overs with Edrich. The extent of that stand will have gratified Surrey for there were moments of doubt.

Edrich, angular, poker-faced, turned not a hair when playing and missing at Shepherd and Elms. Howarth shuffled about unhappily once Johnson's off spin was employed. Nor was the running everything it might have been.

Howarth, though, was wonderfully quick to attack anything short and Surrey prospered until Edrich flicked one on the leg-side for Nicholls to swoop upon. Younis drove ambitiously on the up and Topley made ground to deep mid-off for the catch.

Owen-Thomas settled in due course and, like several colleagues, was anxious not to let slip a marvellous chance to get runs. Meantime, Howarth – his driving becoming even more fiercely forthright – was looking better and better.

Topley's left-arm spin slowed him only briefly; the initiative was always his. When, in the 85th over, 10 runs were wanted for a sixth batting point, Howarth got 12 and passed his previous best of 156. Then came Shepherd with the new ball.

Thursday

Shortly before 4.45 p.m. yesterday Colin Cowdrey, a fraction misty-eyed but smiling broadly, left the field at Maidstone, his 100th hundred safely and sweetly gathered in. His Kent colleagues formed a guard of honour at the pavilion steps. Even as the crowds converged, the applause a continuous happy shout, the spitting rain grew more heavy and wet-weather drill after days of unrelenting sunshine was with us again.

Kent declared 41 behind Surrey at 326 for five the moment Cowdrey, placing the ball gently square on the off-side, sped through for a single off Jackman to reach 100 not out – his second century at Maidstone this week.

Nor was yesterday's innings – 'the last milestone of my career' was how he put it – a poor imitation of the Cowdrey of summers ago. This was brisk (140 minutes, 14 fours), hugely entertaining and of considerable importance to Kent.

Cowdrey, batting at No. 7, a position in itself worthy of comment, was fortunate to be associated on this notable day with Asif Iqbal. In pure cricketing terms Asif's 119 not out was the better innings.

That, though, is a relative comment only. Not a person on Maidstone's green and pleasant ground would deny that this was Cowdrey's day – the day he became the 16th player to score 100 hundreds – the first since Tom Graveney in 1964, and the third in Kent's history.

Cowdrey began his innings 10 minutes before lunch when Kent were 124 for five in the 48th over. Surrey, especially Intikhab's wrist spin, had had a profitable morning. Kent had been surprisingly fragile for all that.

There were no further alarms before lunch: Kent 129 for five (50 overs); Asif 23, Cowdrey 1. One way of describing the afternoon, spoilt only by the disappearance of the sun and the return of rain, is to indicate the tea score: Kent 310 for five (90 overs); Asif 114, Cowdrey 89.

In 125 minutes and 40 overs, Asif and Cowdrey put on 181. Driving, pulling, cutting (late and square), hooking – yes Cowdrey hooked at least once – these two completely altered the course of the match in which Surrey had been doing rather well for themselves.

The excitements – and Cowdrey's former cricket master at Tonbridge, C.H. Knott, and his uncle, John Taylor, were among those present – were not confined to Cowdrey's runs and the undefeated stand of 202. The chase for batting points was controversial and thrilling.

The scoreboard got into a muddle in the 77th over. It caught up in the 84th, having been an over behind, but by then the batsmen were thoroughly confused for they had one over, not two, to score six runs for a fifth point.

They got four runs and, off the last ball, Cowdrey could scramble a single only, by which stage the square-leg umpire, Cec Pepper, was signalling energetically 'no ball' under Law 44. Surrey had more than two onside fieldsmen behind the popping crease at the instant of delivery.

Asif took the single off the extra delivery and Surrey, at one point controlling affairs, must have felt hard done by. Smith was off with a groin strain. Owen-Thomas was limping, Intikhab had hurt an arm and Storey was not at all happy about something.

The events of the morning seemed a long way off: deft foot-work by Jackman to run out Luckhurst, a fine caught and bowled by Smith and Intikhab's persistence and craft. He bowled Johnson (51) round his legs and had Ealham playing no recognisable stroke.

There was a break of 45 minutes after Kent's declaration and time for four overs only before the rains came again when Surrey were three for no wicket, 44 ahead. We were soon reflecting about Cowdrey again – and his intention to play two more seasons, probably.

Friday

Rain at the end of the fifth over of the 20 that must be bowled in the last hour spoilt what promised to be a tight finish between Kent and Surrey at Maidstone yesterday. No further play was possible and the match was drawn.

Surrey declared at 147 for eight having batted for 78.4 overs and all but four of those on a rain-affected but drying, turning pitch. They required Kent to score 189 in 47 minutes and, in the last hour, 20 overs.

The challenge was keenly accepted. In those 47 minutes, Kent scored 81 in 12 overs, the debit side being that Luckhurst, Johnson, Shepherd (four, six and out in six balls) and Asif had been dismissed. Fieldsmen had stiff necks, so often was the ball in the air.

Nicholls was still present with Ealham. Both men, at a period in the game when instant cricket has little room for some traditional batting skills, know how to belt a ball. They could bring Surrey down.

But not yesterday. Ealham aimed a huge blow at Intikhab in the first over of the last 20, at which stage 108 were wanted, and was caught by Jackman. Nicholls continued to punch away.

Pocock, having bowled a wider one to Asif and got him stumped, ended that threat as Nicholls, stretching, skied to mid-off. That was 94 for six, 17 overs to go. Cowdrey and Denness played two more overs in increasing rain and that was that.

The storms of Thursday evening and early yesterday morning meant a busy period for the ground staff. Greatly to the credit of all concerned, the start was

Colin Cowdrey

John Edrich

delayed only 20 minutes, making the aggregate time lost then an hour and 40 minutes.

Edrich and Edwards, resuming at three for no wicket, belaboured the pitch with the backs of their bats urgently and energetically in between picking off the occasional loose ball from Elms. The start, if noisy, was without alarms.

Woolmer came on at the Elms end, and, three overs later, Johnson replaced Shepherd, who had barely wasted a delivery (8–5–6–0). That was a few minutes after midday, and Johnson's off-spin was to be used for 31 overs until the declaration two hours 45 minutes later.

Johnson's first ball turned and lifted. Edwards could not control it and backward short leg took the catch. A drying pitch, plenty of humidity and occasional flashes of hot sun was a combination that could destroy batting that demonstrated anything less than cool judgment, precise care.

Edrich, bat close to the body, jaw jutting, is purpose-built for such situations and in Howarth he had an associate who has grown up this summer. For an hour, they firmly resisted temptation and, for the most part, error.

It was an important hour for Surrey because when Edrich bottom-batted a ball to short mid-wicket 20 minutes before lunch, two more wickets fell, both to Johnson before the break. Surrey, 78 for four, then led by 119 with a maximum of 200 minutes remaining, less the gap between innings.

Bearing in mind Kent's limited over skills, Edrich's declaration was bound to be later than sooner. By the time it came Luckhurst's rarely used left-arm spin had claimed three wickets, but not that of the obdurate Howarth – two hours 45 minutes for 42 and another innings of consequence.

SURREY

First Innings		Second Innings	
J.H. Edrich, c Nicholls,			
b Shepherd	59	c Asif, b Topley	40
M.J. Edwards, c Nicholls,			
b Shepherd	6	c Luckhurst, b Johnson	15
G.P. Howarth, c Asif,			
b Shepherd	159	not out	42
Younis Ahmed, c Topley,			
b Woolmer	12	st Nicholls, b Johnson	0
D.R. Owen-Thomas, not out	89		
S.J. Storey, c Nicholls,		c Nicholls, b Johnson	3
b Shepherd	7	c Denness, b Johnson	7
Intikhab Alam, c Asif,			
b Woolmer	19	c Asif, b Luckhurst	20
†A. Long		c Denness, b Luckhurst	0
R.D. Jackman		lbw, b Luckhurst	11
Extras (b 4, lb 9, w 2, nb 1)	16	Extras (b 3, lb 6)	9
	—		—
Total (6 wkts. dec.)	367	Total (8 wkts. dec.)	147

Fall of wickets: 1–9, 2–141, 3–177, 4–305, 5–322, 6–367.

Bowling: Elms 21–1–67–0; Shepherd 30–8–85–4; Woolmer 16.2–3–63–2; Johnson 26–1–93–0; Topley 8–2–26–0; Cowdrey 1–0–17–0.

Did not bat: P.I. Pocock, D. Smith.

Fall of wickets: 1–27, 2–71, 3–72, 4–76, 5–96, 6–121, 7–121, 8–147.

Bowling: Elms 5–1–15–0; Shepherd 8–5–6–0; Woolmer 7–2–13–0; Johnson 31–8–57–4; Topley 15–5–24–1; Luckhurst 12.4–4–23–3.

KENT

First Innings		Second Innings	
B.W. Luckhurst, run out	20	c Long, b Jackman	4
G.W. Johnson, b Intikhab	51	c Owen-Thomas, b Jackman	16
†D Nicholls, c Pocock, b Intikhab	14	c Smith, b Pocock	35
*M.H. Denness, c & b Smith	15	not out	4
Asif Iqbal, not out	119	st Long, b Pocock	10
A.G.E. Ealham, c Howarth,		c Jackman, b Intikhab	11
b Intikhab	4		
M.C. Cowdrey, not out	3	not out	9
		J.N. Shepherd, c Edwards,	
		b Smith	10
Extras (lb 2, w 1)	3	Extras (lb 3)	3
	—		—
Total (5 wkts. dec.)	326	Total (6 wkts.)	102

Fall of wickets: 1–47, 2–77, 3–94, 4–105, 5–124.

Bowling: Jackman 24.2–3–81–0; Smith 15–4–37–1; Intikhab 25–4–88–3; Storey 15–1–45–0; Pocock 13–1–72–0.

Fall of wickets: 1–4, 2–25, 3–35, 4–61, 5–84, 6–94.

Bowling: Jackman 6–0–34–2; Smith 4–0–31–1; Pocock 4–1–16–2; Intikhab 3–0–18–1.

Kent 6pts, Surrey 3

Umpires – J.F. Crapp and C.G. Pepper

85: *Warwickshire v Gloucestershire*
BIRMINGHAM, 27–29 JULY 1974

In various attempts to stimulate better cricket in the Championship, the regulations have, in recent years, been altered several times. One of the most pernicious and damaging decisions, which applied from the 1974 season, was to limit the first innings for each county to 100 overs, though a county bowling out its opponents in under 100 overs could bat on using the 'spare' overs from the other side's allocation. This rule denied lower-order batsmen many chances of an innings, robbed captains of tactical flexibility in prolonging innings into a second day, and was abandoned after eight seasons. But for it, who knows how many Jameson and

Kanhai might have made for the second Warwickshire wicket? Their 465 unbroken partnership remains a world record for the second wicket, and for any Warwickshire wicket. It was the highest partnership for any wicket in the Championship since Bowley and Langridge's 490 for Sussex in 1933 (see game 51). It was also the first time two Warwickshire batsmen had scored double centuries in the same innings.

John Jameson (b. 1941) was one of the most attractive strikers of the ball then playing. In his career from 1960 to 1976 he scored 18,941 runs at an average of 33. His 240 in this match was his highest score. He later became a first-class

*Kanhai and Jameson
– a record stand*

umpire, and then a cricket administrator. Rohan Kanhai (b. 1935) played for Warwickshire from 1968 until 1977. In his career from 1954 to 1977 he became one of the greatest West Indian batsmen of all time, scoring 28,774 runs at an average of 49, including 6,227 at an average of 47 in 79 tests, ultimately captaining his country.

Birmingham, Saturday
By John Mason

John Jameson's 240 not out for Warwickshire against Gloucestershire at Edgbaston on Saturday was his highest in first-class cricket. That achievement, in itself, barely merits attention.

This was only one of six records Jameson and Rohan Kanhai set as they took Warwickshire to 465 for one in 100 overs, having begun after Abberley's dismissal in the first over without a run scored.

Their partnership beat the world record for the second wicket by 10 runs and was a Warwickshire record for any wicket. They also established national and Warwickshire records for the second wicket, besides being the first Warwickshire players to score double hundreds in the same innings.

Even those of us who dislike and disapprove of the slavish devotion of some to the statistics of sport,

have to confess to being slightly impressed by the rich haul of Jameson and Kanhai, who was 213 not out.

Jameson, in for 310 minutes, hit 34 fours and a six; Kanhai 30 fours and a six. It seems gratuitous to add that earlier in the week against Lancashire on the same ground they put on 231 – small fry!

Gloucestershire's five bowlers, three of whom have little first-class experience, had a fearful day, though such was the state of numb disbelief in the field that at 447 and 448 both men were missed, two outstanding catchers putting down simple chances.

Gloucestershire answered with 75 in an hour and 10 minutes for the loss of Knight.

Monday
By Mike Stevenson

Warwickshire ground Gloucestershire's inexperienced side (seven of them are under 22) into the Edgbaston turf yesterday, winning an embarrassingly one-sided contest by an innings and 61 runs.

The pitch was certainly not the culprit, as Jameson and Kanhai had proved on Saturday, though Hemmings, who is taking wickets at a furious rate these days, managed to turn the ball appreciably though slowly.

He took six for 87 off 25.5 overs in Gloucester's first innings.

197

Stovold batted fairly well for Gloucester, and Dunstan registered his maiden half-century in championship cricket, but there was little else to cheer the visitors, who followed on 222 behind.

Again their innings started disastrously, Willis and Blenkiron bowling them to 61 for four at tea.

Procter showed glimpses of his class until he was caught behind cutting against Hemmings's spin, but thereafter apart from a competent knock by Brown and another promising effort from Dunstan, it was something of a procession, the match ending in the extra half-hour.

WARWICKSHIRE

First Innings	
R.N. Abberley, c Brown, b Dixon ...	0
J.A. Jameson, not out	240
R.B. Kanhai, not out	213
Extras (b 7, lb 5)	12
	—
100 overs, Total (1 wkt.)	465

Fall of wicket: 1–0.

*M.J.K. Smith, A.I. Kallicharran, †D.L. Murray, E.E. Hemmings, W.A. Bourne, W. Blenkiron, R.G.D. Willis and D.J. Brown did not bat.

Bowling: Dixon 17–2–91–1; Shackleton 20–2–88–0; Knight 20–2–103–0; Mortimore 31–5–87–0; Thorn 12–1–84–0.

GLOUCESTERSHIRE

First Innings		Second Innings	
†A.W. Stowold, c Murray, b Willis	49	b Willis	9
R.D.V. Knight, c Jameson, b Hemmings	27	c Hemmings, b Blenkiron	5
A.J. Hignell, c Willis, b Hemmings	11	c Abberley, b Willis	0
M.J. Procter, c Murray, b Hemmings	20	c Murray, b Hemmings	46
J.C. Foat, c Murray, b Bourne	34	b Blenkiron	7
M.S.T. Dunstan, b Bourne	52	c Bourne, b Hemmings	32
A.S. Brown, c & b Hemmings	4	b Blenkiron	40
P. Thorn, not out	14	c Murray, b Willis	0
J.B. Mortimore, c Kanhai, b Hemmings	13	b Willis	0
J.H. Shackleton, b Blenkiron	2	b Blenkiron	11
J.H. Dixon, c Kallicharran, b Hemmings	7	not out	0
Extras (b 5, lb 3, nb 2)	10	Extras (lb 4, w 4, nb 3)	11
	—		—
69.5 overs Total	243	Total	161

Fall of wickets: 1–69, 2–89, 3–100, 4–110, 5–187, 6–198, 7–202, 8–229, 9–236.

Fall of wickets: 1–14, 2–18, 3–18, 4–36, 5–100, 6–114, 7–115, 8–115, 9–150.

Bowling: Willis 13–3–40–1; Brown 11–1–44–0; Hemmings 25–5.5–87–6; Bourne 11–2–32–2; Jameson 4–0–16–0; Blenkiron 5–1–14–0.

Bowling: Willis 15–6–31–4; Blenkiron 9.3–4–18–4; Brown 11–4–31–0; Hemmings 19–5–45–2; Bourne 3–0–25–0.

Warwick 18pts, Glos 2

86: *Hampshire v Sussex*
SOUTHAMPTON, 30 AUGUST–2 SEPTEMBER 1975

The importation of overseas players made Hampshire one of the most powerful sides of the mid-1970s. They won the Championship in 1973, though after that a gradual decline set in – they came second in 1974 and third in this season. As John Mason points out in his report, Hampshire's failure to bowl out Sussex twice on this plumb wicket, a task made harder by Roberts' injury, hindered them in the pursuit of the Championship. Hampshire's overseas trio of Barry Richards and Gordon Greenidge – the most exciting opening partnership in the land – and West Indian fast bowler Andy Roberts – made them a hard side to beat. Greenidge (b. 1951), whose 259 included more sixes (13) than had ever been hit in an innings in first-class cricket, was not really an overseas player at all. His family had settled in Berkshire when he was a child and he had had the option of playing for England, but he chose his native West Indies,and became one of the world's leading batsmen.

Barry Richards (b. 1945) would have been one of the great test batsmen in the world, had it not been for the international ban on South Africa. In the four tests he played for them before the ban was imposed he had an average of 72. He played for Hampshire from 1968 to 1978, as well as for Natal, Transvaal and one match for Gloucestershire in 1965. He also had a season with South Australia in 1970–71, during which he became only the third batsman in Australia to score 300 in a day during an innings of 356. In his career he made 28,358 runs at an average of 55. Mark Faber (b. 1950), whose dour innings prevented a Hampshire victory, had the best season of his short career in 1975, making 1,060 runs at an average of 30.

Andy Roberts

Southampton, Saturday

Hampshire, by adding Saturday's four batting points, lead the County Championship at the moment. Pleasurable as that is to them, Hampshire people are not exactly grinning from ear to ear, writes John Mason.

No matter the heroic proportions of Gordon Greenidge's 259 against Sussex at Southampton, or the 501 for five declared scored from 99.5 overs. Hampshire are slightly bothered; Andy Roberts has sore shins, and has been ordered to rest for a week.

He limped off, dejected and upset, without bowling a ball, having broken down during his practice run-up before the Sussex innings started. Roberts – 57 wickets at 15.80 – may have bowled less this summer, but he has a major part in Hampshire's efforts to win the title.

Having watched Greenidge 273 not out last season at Eastbourne, I can visualise easily events at Southampton – 13 sixes, 24 fours, 308 minutes, the sixes beating Charlie Barnett's championship record of 11 in an innings. Greenidge's back injury has mended, it seems.

Barry Richards

Monday

Until the last hour, Hampshire claimed Sussex wickets reasonably regularly at Southampton yesterday. They enforced the follow-on, having restricted Sussex to 259 for eight, but progress was less assured after that.

At the close, Sussex were 151 for three in the second innings, needing another 91 to make Hampshire, who took seven bonus points, bat again. In the odd way the bonus system operates, Sussex have five points.

Sussex's relative prosperity second time round followed an unfinished fourth-wicket stand of 65 between Groome and Faber. Hampshire's pressure was not all it might have been, perhaps, but it had been a long day and Roberts was absent.

Sussex, having lost their first wicket to the last ball of Saturday's proceedings, resumed 451 behind. The figure was so daunting that much could be excused, even Hampshire's leniency in the field. They did not catch well for a time.

Barclay stayed for 10 overs and four more runs before being caught bat and pad. But if he was uneasily circumspect and unable to get the ball off the square, Parsons and Graves were not. They shared a pleasant partnership of 56.

Gilliat rotated his bowlers, giving them attacking fields. Taylor was the least fortunate, Southern the busiest. Justice was done when Taylor had Graves caught behind at 126 as he forced off the back foot. Parsons pressed on.

Sainsbury presented a turning, lifting delivery for Faber that Greenidge did well to reach from shortish gully. Then the gallant Parsons skied Southern to extra cover immediately after lunch, having batted 150 minutes for 65.

After Hoadley had played on to Southern, Buss threatened for a while until seeking a run to Sainsbury at short mid-wicket that did not exist. Spencer swung happily, but in the 10 overs remaining the only doubt was the size of the follow-on figure.

The 100 overs' total of 259 for eight, Mansell having been marvellously caught left-handed at second slip by Greenidge, left Sussex 242 behind. Though not all out, the follow-on did apply in these rare circumstances if Hampshire wished.

They did and at 3.40 p.m. Barclay and Groome began Sussex's second innings. Jesty and Rice, who was awarded his county cap at lunchtime, used the new ball and though there were runs to be taken, there were wickets to fall, too.

Barclay offered a firm square drive or so before Jesty bowled him as he came forward, and at the same total, 36, Parsons who had been so determined previously, was lbw to his third ball from Jesty. Groome, amid these mishaps, played carefully.

He and Graves added 50 for the third wicket and Hampshire were beginning to wonder when they would next strike when Graves top-edged his sweep. Groome, though, had a valuable ally in Faber to see out the last hour.

Tuesday

Sussex, the last-placed side in the county championship table, seriously interfered with Hampshire's attempts to win the title by batting through the day on a slow pitch at Southampton. Hampshire took seven points from the drawn game, Sussex five.

For five hours, including an hour on Monday, Mark Faber resolutely resisted Hampshire's efforts to remove him. His reward was a career best 176 – and a less than gracious reception for an innings of undeniable value.

The avoidance of defeat does not demand swashbuckling enterprise and Faber, irrespective of the 32 boundaries he hit – some of which he could hardly avoid – knew that. His colleagues initially followed suit.

Hampshire hindered themselves; Groome was missed off the fourth ball of the morning without having added to his overnight 58; Faber was missed when 84 and 128; Hoadley, when two.

So Sussex, having resumed 91 behind at 151 for three, plodded on to 524 all out. After tea Stephenson, having passed wicket-keeping gloves and pads to Jesty, bowled amiable rubbish and time was played out.

Groome and Faber carried the fourth-wicket partnership to 129 in 2½ hours, mostly against Sainsbury and Southern, the spinners. Rice, Taylor and Jesty intervened at times. Richards aired his off-spin and Greenidge joined in, too – numbering the weary Faber's among his three wickets.

Groome departed for 70, smartly held after some sleight of hand at wide second slip. After lunch Sainsbury dived to his right round the corner to catch Buss, by which time Sussex led by 14.

That, for Hampshire was the last moment of much consequence. They thought they had dismissed Faber when 133, an appeal for a catch at short extra off Sainsbury being rejected. The rest barely mattered.

Spencer (79) whacked six sixes and seven fours in 25 minutes and looked to be en route to an absurdly fast century. I select 'absurdly' deliberately, for Gilliat was providing the fodder. Heigh-ho!

HAMPSHIRE

First Innings

B.A. Richards, c Spencer, b Buss	49
C.G. Greenidge, c Groome, b Barclay	259
D.R. Turner, c Mansell, b Phillipson	62
T.E. Jesty, lbw Spencer	34
R.M.C. Gilliat, lbw Barclay	61
M.N.S. Taylor, not out	10
Extras (b 12, lb 11, w 1, nb 2)	26
Total (5 wkts. dec.)	501

Overs 99.5

Did not bat: P.J. Sainsbury, J.M. Rice, G.R. Stephenson, A.M.E. Roberts, J. Southern.

Fall of wickets: 1–88, 2–253, 3–344, 4–465, 5–501

Bowling: Spencer 19–1–85–1; Phillipson 29–5–126–1; Buss 19–3–93–1; Waller 19–1–84–0; Barclay 12.5–0–65–2; Hoadley 1–0–22–0.

SUSSEX

First Innings		Second Innings	
J.R.T. Barclay, c Jesty, b Rice	12	b Jesty	21
J.J. Groome, c Greenidge, b Richards	38	c Greenidge, b Sainsbury	70
A.E.W. Parsons, c Turner, b Southern	65	lbw, b Jesty	0
*P.J. Graves, c Stephenson, b Taylor	35	c Richards, b Sainsbury	26
M.J.J. Faber, c Greenidge, b Sainsbury	9	st Stephenson, b Greenidge	176
M.A. Buss, run out	36	c Sainsbury, b Richards	7
S.J. Hoadley, b Southern	6	c Sainsbury, b Greenidge	58
†A.W. Mansell, c Greenidge, b Sainsbury	23	not out	51
J. Spencer, not out	21	c Turner, b Greenidge	79
C.E. Waller, not out	4	run out	0
		C.P. Phillipson, st Jesty, b Gilliat	16
Extras (lb 3, w 1, nb 6)	10	Extras (b 5, lb 3, w 8, nb 4)	20
100 overs, Total (8 wkts.)	259	Total	524

Did not bat: C.P. Phillipson.

Fall of wickets: 1–50, 2–70, 3–126, 4–153, 5–180, 6–207, 7–215, 8–248.

Bowling: Jesty 10–2–18–0; Rice 21–4–45–1; Southern 32–13–78–2; Taylor 12–3–41–1; Richards 7–1–42–1; Sainsbury 16–6–25–2.

Fall of wickets: 1–36, 2–36, 3–86, 4–215, 5–256, 6–345, 7–410, 8–502, 9–504.

Bowling: Jesty 15–2–44–2; Rice 19–5–55–0; Taylor 12–5–18–0; Southern 56–27–114–0; Sainsbury 40–22–49–2; Richards 19–8–49–1; Greenidge 16–3–84–3; Turner 3–0–12–0; Stephenson 5–1–28–0; Gilliat 4.3–0–51–1.

Hants 7 pts, Sussex 5
Umpires – K.E. Palmer & D.G.L. Evans

87: *Somerset v Gloucestershire*
TAUNTON, 29 MAY–1 JUNE 1976

Victories after following on are rare, and while this was not the most spectacular of the genre – that honour must belong to Hampshire, in their match against Warwickshire in 1922 (see game 36) it does display a rare example of attacking cricket in an age when negativity threatened to force the terminal decline of the first-class game. This remarkable achievement by Gloucestershire was the first such victory in the Championship since Glamorgan had overwhelmed Nottinghamshire, bowled out for 75 when chasing 103, in 1957. Gloucestershire, who would eventually come third in the Championship, were given an early indication of the abilities of Botham, then in just his third season with Somerset. The visitors were

unlucky to meet, in Botham, a bowler who could capitalise upon difficult atmospheric conditions, in one of the rare breaks in the weather during the heatwave summer of 1976.

Whether or not Somerset would have declared and put their opponents in before the close on the first day, had the 100-over rule not ended their innings anyway, we cannot tell. It was certainly what gave Somerset the initial advantage, as Gloucestershire were reeling by the close of play, and ultimately followed on 254 behind. Zaheer was having a vintage season. He made 2,554 runs at an average of 75, at this point the highest total made since the reduction of the Championship, and his century was one of 11 he made during the season. Yet it was Procter

(b. 1946), a South African whose career record of 21,748 runs at an average of 36 and 1,395 wickets at 19 each made him one of the greatest all-rounders, whose devastating bowling secured victory for Gloucestershire.

Taunton, Monday
By Gerald Pawle at Taunton

Celebration turned into frustration for Brian Close at Taunton yesterday as Somerset, having gained a first-innings lead of 254 over Gloucestershire, had to operate with two of their bowlers – Burgess and Clapp – out of action.

Gloucestershire were dismissed by an already depleted attack for 79 in the morning – the last six wickets falling for 27 runs – but it was a different story when they followed on, thanks to a century by Zaheer.

At the close, Gloucestershire led by 71 runs with four wickets standing.

Botham, who took six for 25, bowled splendidly before lunch, removing Stovold and Brown with successive balls.

Zaheer made amends in the second innings, scoring his 141 which included 23 boundaries in 2¾ hours.

Tuesday

Though they had followed on 254 runs behind the previous day, Gloucestershire snatched an astonishing victory over Somerset by eight runs at Taunton yesterday.

When Gloucestershire's last four wickets fell for 47 runs in the morning, Somerset were left with all the time in the world to make 119 to win on a wicket still playing easily.

But a brilliant and unconventional spell by Procter, alternating – often in the same over – fierce speed with slow off-breaks, saw them collapse.

When play began, Botham again bowled well and Gloucestershire had Shackleton and Brassington to thank for stiffening the tail. They added 44 in an hour before the innings ended at 372, Botham finishing with five for 125 after 37 overs.

Zaheer Abbas

Rose and Slocombe began confidently enough and had put on 36 by lunch. But, after the interval, Brown, moving the ball enough to compel close concentration, got rid of Slocombe and Denning in the same over.

Even when Close was brilliantly caught low down at cover by Shackleton off a humming square drive, however, there was little reason to anticipate a Somerset defeat, because Rose was still there, driving fluently and playing well off his legs.

Crisis came upon them at 97 when Shackleton took another catch to remove Kitchen. Then next ball, Procter suddenly whipped in a thunderbolt that Taylor edged to Sadiq.

Three runs later came the crucial wicket of Rose, caught high above his head by Shepherd at deep mid-off after making an excellent 48.

Gloucestershire were fielding like demons and, after Procter had bowled Botham, Brinkwell swung at a long hop from Graveney and was magnificently caught by Shepherd.

When Procter had Jennings caught at the wicket seven runs later, it was left to the 'walking wounded' – Burgess, with seven stitches in a gashed brow and Clapp, with a badly strained side – to get the last eight runs.

Gloucestershire were not to be denied, however, and Procter settled the issue when he had Clapp

Mike Procter

snapped up by Sadiq at short leg. In his last seven overs, Procter had taken six for 13, his final figures being six for 35. Brown claimed three for 27.

SOMERSET

First Innings		Second Innings	
B.C. Rose, c Brassington,		c Shepherd, b Procter	48
b Graveney	104		
P.A Slocombe, lbw, b Brown	36	lbw, b Brown	17
P.W. Denning, b Brown	41	c Sadiq, b Brown	4
D.B. Close, b Brown	0	c Shackleton, b Brown	10
M.J. Kitchen, b D Graveney	69	c Shackleton, b Procter	10
D.J.S. Taylor, not out	41	c Sadiq, b Procter	0
G.I. Burgess, retd hurt	10	not out	1
I.T. Botham, b Graveney	13	b Procter	3
D. Breakwell, b Davey	0	c Shepherd, b Graveney	0
K.F. Jennings, not out	3	c Stovold, b Procter	6
		R.J. Clapp, c Sadiq, b Procter	1
Extras (b 5, lb 9, nb 2)	16	Extras (b 4, lb 5, nb 1)	10
Total (7 wkts.)	333	Total	110

Innings closed
Did not bat: R.J. Clapp
Fall of wickets: 1–58, 2–138, 3–138, 4–237, 5–290, 6–326, 7–327.
Bowling: Davey 20–2–82–1; Shackleton 10–1–34–0; Procter 16–5–32–0; Brown 28–8–64–3; Graveney 24–4–94–3; Sadiq 2–0–11–0.

Fall of wickets: 1–43, 2–47, 3–73, 4–97, 5–97, 6–100, 7–101, 8–108, 9–108.
Bowling: Procter 14.3–4–35–6; Davey 5–0–20–0; Brown 9–2–27–3; Graveney 4–9–18–1.

GLOUCESTERSHIRE

First Innings		Second Innings	
Sadiq Mohammad, c Breakwell,		c & b Jennings	8
b, Botham	2		
N.H.C. Cooper, b Botham	1	b Botham	38
Zaheer Abbas, b Clapp	5	b Close	141
M.J. Procter, c Taylor, b Botham	7	c Breakwell, b Close	32
†A.W. Stovold, c Close, b Botham	18	b Botham	58
D.R. Shepherd, b Clapp	27	lbw, b Jennings	30
*A.S. Brown, lbw, b Jennings	0	b Botham	4
D.A. Graveney, lbw, b Jennings	2	b Botham	0
J.H. Shackleton, c Close, b Clapp	0	st Taylor, b Breakwell	30
A.J. Brassington, not out	4	not out	15
J. Davey, b Botham	1	b Botham	0
Extras (b 4, lb 2, nb 1, w 5)	12	Extras (b 8, lb 7, nb 1)	16
39.1 overs. Total	79	Total	372

Fall of wickets: 1–3, 2–9, 3–9, 4–29, 5–52, 6–52, 7–61, 8–68, 9–74.
Bowling: Clapp 13–6–18–3; Botham 16.1–6–25–6; Jennings 8–1–24–1;Close 1–1–0–0; Kitchen 1–1–0–0.

Fall of wickets: 1–11, 2–126, 3–209, 4–236, 5–319, 6–325, 7–325, 8–327, 9–371.
Bowling: Botham 37.1–6–125–5; Jennings 25–6–71–2; Close 27–9–90–2; Kitchen 3–0–21–0; Rose 4–0–9–0; Breakwell 24–12–40–1.

Somerset 8pts, Glos 13
Umpires – H. Horton & A.E. Fagg

88: *Glamorgan v Worcestershire*
SWANSEA, 29 JUNE – 1 JULY 1977

Glenn Turner (b. 1947), the New Zealand test batsman, was the mainstay of the Worcestershire batting for over a decade. In 1982, his last season, he scored 311 not out in a day for his county against Warwickshire, the highest score ever made (until the coming of Hick) for Worcestershire. In 1973, when a member of the New Zealand touring party, he had become the first cricketer since 1938 to score 1,000 runs by the end of May. By the time he retired he had scored 34,346 runs at an average of almost 50, and in scoring 103 centuries had become the first New Zealander to score a century of centuries. It was often said that Turner dominated his side, though that discounted the considerable talents of his colleagues, not least Basil d'Oliveira. No batsman, though, has ever dominated a side quite to the extent that Turner did in this fixture.

His 141 scored out of 169 was, at 83.4 per cent of the total for the completed innings, the highest percentage one batsman has ever made of his team's all-out total; and it was equally astonishing that Turner's 141 was 134 higher than Gifford, the second-highest scorer, could manage, and no batsman reached double figures. Both sides in this match had a poor season –

Glamorgan finished 14th, one place lower than Worcestershire – and this could have been an opportunity for Glamorgan to earn a badly-needed victory had the weather not intervened, and the last day's play not been lost to the rain. Nor could the 100-over rule, which forced Glamorgan's first innings to close with only four wickets down, have helped them to impose the maximum advantage over their rivals.

Swansea, Wednesday

Mike Llewellyn and Gwyn Richards, two of the younger Glamorgan batsmen, inspired a brilliant revival against Worcestershire at Swansea yesterday.

Glamorgan had opened so slowly that in two and a half hours before lunch their scoring rate was just over two runs per over.

When Llewellyn, 23, and Richards, 25, came together Glamorgan had lost four wickets for 148 off 62 overs and were in danger of losing valuable bonus points.

But in a punishing unbeaten fifth wicket partnership Llewellyn and Richards not only raised the tempo, but changed the whole character of the cricket. They added 161 off 38 overs before the Glamorgan innings closed at 309 for four.

Llewellyn hit two sixes and seven fours in his 91, his championship best, while Richards' 74 included

Basil d'Oliveira

Glenn Turner – the highest percentage

eight boundaries. It was his best score of the season.

Norman Gifford took three for 91 for Worcester hire on an unresponsive pitch.

Worcestershire had an hour's batting before the close and lost opener Barry Jones and Phil Neale to finish at 44 for two off 19 overs. Glenn Turner was 39 not out.

Thursday

Glenn Turner, New Zealand's captain, gave a marvellous one-man show for Worcestershire against Glamorgan at Swansea yesterday, carrying his bat for 141 out of 169 – a world record for the percentage of runs scored by a batsman in a completed innings.

He batted for 220 minutes, starting on Wednesday evening, and hit a six and 18 fours.

Turner's century was scored out of 128 in 173 minutes, and the only blemish came when he was 92, Ontong missing a second-slip catch off Nash.

No other Worcester batsman reached double figures. The next highest score was seven by Gifford, who figured in a ninth-wicket partnership of 57 in 50 minutes. This late stand not only enabled Turner to complete his second century of the season, but also saved Worcester from following on.

While wickets were crashing around him, Turner played all the bowling with ease, driving powerfully. He said later there was nothing wrong with the pitch.

Glamorgan had a lead of 140, and when they batted a second time scored 142 for seven before bad light and rain ended play 45 minutes early.

GLAMORGAN

First Innings		Second Innings	
*A. Jones, lbw, b Gifford	48	b Holder	7
J.A. Hopkins, lbw, b Pridgeon	28	c Neale, b D'Oliveira	45
R.C. Ontong, st Humphries, b Gifford	21	b Cumbes	56
C.L. King, c D'Oliveira, b Gifford	25	c D'Oliveira, b Holder	2
M.J. Llewellyn, not out	91	b Holder	12
G. Richards, not out	74	lbw, b Cumbes	0
		†E.W. Jones, b Cumbes	4
		M.A. Nash, not out	5
		A.E. Cordle, not out	4
Extras (b 4, lb 6, nb 12)	22	Extras (lb 5, nb 2)	7
100 overs. Total (4 wkts.)	309	Total (7 wkts.)	142

Did not bat: E.W. Jones, M.A. Nash, A.E. Cordle, B.J. Lloyd, A.H. Wilkins.
Fall of wickets: 1–57, 2–98, 3–117, 4–148.
Bowling: Holder 19–1–54–0; Cumbes 19–3–54–0; Pridgeon 14–1–45–1; Gifford 30–8–91–3; D'Oliveira 18–8–43–0.

Fall of wickets: 1–17, 2–23, 3–82, 4–119, 5–124, 6–132, 7–137.
Bowling: Holder 9.3–6–48–3; Cumbes 14–4–30–3; D'Oliveira 17–4–32–1; Gifford 12–6–25–0

WORCESTERSHIRE

First Innings	
G.M. Turner, not out	141
B.J.R. Jones, lbw, b Nash	1
P.A. Neale, c E.W. Jones, b Wilkins	3
E.J.O. Hemsley, b Cordle	3
B.L. D'Oliveira, c E.W. Jones, b Cordle	0
D.N. Patel, c E.W. Jones, b Nash	4
†D.J. Humphries, c Llewellyn, b Cordle	0
V.A. Holder, lbw, b Cordle	4
*N. Gifford, c Llewellyn, b Lloyd	7
J. Cumbes, lbw, b Nash	5
A.P. Pridgeon, lbw, b Cordle	0
Extras (lb 1)	1
68 overs. Total	169

Fall of wickets: 1–18, 2–35, 3–68, 4–71, 5–71, 6–82, 7–87, 8–93, 9–150.
Bowling: Nash 31–14–51–3; Cordle 24–9–53–5; Wilkins 7–0–33–1; Ontong 3–0–20–0; Lloyd 3–1–11–1.

89: Northamptonshire v Essex

NORTHAMPTON, 18–21 AUGUST 1979

In 1978 Essex had come second in the Championship. The following summer they not only won it, for the first time in 85 years in the competition, but they did so by such a margin that victory was confirmed by this defeat of Northamptonshire, with four matches in their programme left to complete. They finished 77 points ahead of the runners-up, Worcestershire, and they won the Benson and Hedges Cup too. For half the season they were without their star player, Gooch, on test duty, as in this match. Yet so deep were the county's reserves that the absence of such talent could be endured, and in this match it was left to Turner, for 20 years a hard-working all-rounder who never represented his country, to take 10 wickets, allowing Essex to come from behind on first innings and win the match, and the Championship title.

In a season when Essex made a habit of winning by an innings whenever they could, this victory was one of their hardest, and yet they made it with half-an-hour to spare on the Tuesday evening. Willey, who held together the Northants first innings, was one of the leading all-rounders of the time and in and out of the England side for years. Hardie, whose reputation as an unattractive batsman was unfairly based on a slow-scoring record he had established five years earlier (when he had taken 142 minutes to score four runs), carried out his bat for five hours to ensure that his side won. Essex would have been far astray in the first innings had it not been for McEwan, their South African batsman, who was one of the most exciting and prolific players in England at that time.

Northampton, Saturday

The two questions one might ask of champions elect Essex are: were they lucky with the weather, and is success going to spoil them? I am delighted to tell you that skipper Keith Fletcher answered exactly as expected here at Northampton yesterday, writes Bob Farmer.

To the first question he diplomatically replied: 'We have been fortunate with the weather, but we won those matches and that is what counts.' To the second he said: 'We couldn't change the character of this county.'

That is immensely satisfying for Essex are a joy and a credit to the English sense of sportsmanship. We should all enthuse over their success this season. Before yesterday they needed only 20 points for the title. By close of play that target had been reduced to 16.

Peter Willey stopped uninhibited Essex joy with an excellent 131 in 210 minutes, with 20 fours, as Northamptonshire totalled 224 after an awful start of nine for three.

Why England will not give him a second chance is down to our dreadfully biased selectors. Were he with Middlesex, Surrey, Kent or Yorkshire, he would walk into the England team.

Monday
By John Mason

Essex relying upon disjointed bursts of excellence, inched closer towards their first Schweppes Championship at Northampton yesterday. Having been dismissed for 199, a deficit of 25, they took eight Northamptonshire wickets for 174. The light was so poor late in the day that play ended five minutes early – but not before Stuart Turner nipped in with two lbws from successive deliveries, which should lighten Essex's task today.

Though, depending on events in the Derby-Worcester match, Essex could win the title today, they will need to bat far more convincingly. The most positive innings was from Alan Lamb (66), who was one of eight lbw dismissals.

With four bowling points safely tucked away and a Saturday total of 82 for one from 33 overs in reply to Northants' 224, Essex were well on course for maximum bowlers points when play resumed. The morning was grey but humid; the pitch damp.

McEwan, his bat ringing true after some discordant days, moved easily into his strokes and Denness, tidy in appearance and cricketing style, was equally at ease first thing. In 14 more overs they extended their stand to 96.

From that point on the control exerted by Essex, the Schweppes champions elect, was less than sure. Not a bad case of timiditis, championshipitis, perhaps, but the symptoms were a shade worrying to their many friends as Sarfraz beckoned the batsmen to the tumbrils.

The catching of Yardley at first slip did much to pull Essex down. At 118 his first swoop accounted for Denness and later there were better catches still to despatch Pont and East as nine wickets fell for 81.

The threatening McEwan received a beast of a delivery that kept low at 121, having batted well for 70. The heady reaches of No. 5 looked appealing to Pont until the first ball of a new spell by Griffiths. Suddenly, Essex's prosperity depended importantly upon Fletcher.

The gnome-like captain applied himself as Sarfraz and Griffiths worked efficiently and quickly through the order. That Fletcher was missed before he had scored is not a fact upon which Willey – or Tim Lamb, the bowler – will care to dwell.

Fletcher's prime aim was a second batting point. But not all the right decisions were made.

After Lever, going for a second, had been run out by Larkins, Fletcher, though stroking three fours in an over, lost the strike and Acfield departed at 199, one run short of that second point.

Sarfraz finished with six for 60, his best championship return this summer, and Larkins and Cook, both on sundry short lists for Australia, extended

Northamptonshire's lead of 25 to 60 before Larkins, who had been enjoying the contest, was beaten by Lever's late movement.

Williams made a similar discovery six runs later when on the front foot and in marched Alan Lamb, second in the national batting averages. A further quick dismissal here and Essex were in business. Cook and Lamb were not cooperative.

A stand of 63 followed involving the most positive batting of the day. Lamb was untroubled by the variable bounce and, though losing the competent Cook at 104 and Willey third ball two runs later, he made the Essex bowlers struggle.

Turner, all menace and bristle, could not disturb Lamb though at any moment Yardley looked to be on the list. This amused the batsmen rather more than Turner who had the last laugh when in worsening light Sharp and Sarfraz were lbw to successive deliveries.

Tuesday

On the dot of six o'clock yesterday evening Essex became the 1979 Schweppes County Champions for the first time. Half-an-hour previously victory by seven wickets over Northamptonshire at the County Ground had brought them 17 points – enough to put them out of reach of all challengers.

But were they the champions? The remarkable events at Derby meant a nerve-racking wait of half an hour plus for the Essex players before they knew that Worcestershire had only drawn.

Victory yesterday was the 11th in Essex's most successful season in their 103-year history. It was gained more easily than had seemed likely for much of Monday, when 17 wickets fell in the day, and fittingly Keith Fletcher, the captain, played a major role.

Amid the jubilation and celebration – Essex secretary Peter Edwards had thoughtfully packed champagne in the boot of his car before leaving home – there were many congratulations for Brian Hardie, who was 103 not out at the end.

The victory operation was a perfect example of the county's team skills that also brought them the Benson and Hedges Cup this season, the first major competition Essex have ever won. Someone, somewhere in the camp, has invariably contributed importantly.

Yesterday, the mechanics of wrapping up the championship began with Northants 174 for eight in their second innings, a lead of 199. It had rained overnight but the Northampton pitch which had assisted the seam bowlers on Monday, was docile – slow and low in the vernacular of the cricketers.

Jim Watts did delay Essex for 50 minutes, the time it took to dismiss Tim Lamb, bowled by Turner as he pushed indeterminately forwards, and Griffiths, who was lbw to Lever at 203. That dismissal was the 14th lbw of the match, 11 of them against Northants.

Essex had five hours to secure 229 and make certain of the most prized crown in the domestic game. Those calm, correct cricketing Scotsmen, Denness and Hardie, moved surely along what has been an eventful path since May. There was no need to hurry.

The opening partnership was worth 113 before Denness, having immediately before been roundly applauded for his 50, cut against the spin of Williams and

Brian Hardie

Peter Willey

played the ball into his wicket. Hardie nodded dourly and pushed on. The flourishes he left to McEwan.

There was an enormous six to the wall beyond the mid-wicket boundary and then, facing Willey, McEwan selected the wrong line and umpire Wight agreed with the lbw appeal. Not for the first time in this match a batsman looked less than pleased.

Hardie's next partner was Fletcher, now in his 20th season with the county, the last six of which have been as captain. He does not believe in wasted effort or undue risk. Steadily Essex advanced towards their goal.

Fletcher and Hardie shared a stand of 78, mostly against Willey and Williams with willing assistance from Griffiths, the seamer.

Sarfraz was absent, nursing back trouble, having been off the field before lunch. But he expects to play for Northants today in the Gillette Cup semi-final against Sussex.

At 210 that expert slip catcher, Yardley, pounced as the determined Fletcher edged.

Pont offered a couple of handsome strokes and, with overs and time in hand, stepped back to permit the sturdy Hardie to complete a valiant century (270 minutes, 12 fours) and stroke the winning runs that secured the championship for Essex, who still have four games to play.

NORTHAMPTONSHIRE

First Innings		Second Innings	
G. Cook, lbw Turner	32	b Turner	38
W. Larkins, lbw Lever	0	lbw, b Lever	17
R.G. Williams, b Phillip	1	lbw, b Lever	1
A.J. Lamb, c Hardie, b Phillip	2	lbw, b Phillip	66
P. Willey, lbw Turner,	131	lbw, b Turner	2
T.J. Yardley, b Turner	1	c Denness, b Phillip	24
G. Sharp, lbw Lever	9	lbw, b Turner	2
P.J. Watts, c Fletcher, b Turner	12	not out	25
Sarfraz Nawaz, b Turner	5	lbw, b Turner	0
T.M. Lamb, not out	3	b Turner	2
B.J. Griffiths, c Smith, b Phillip	3	lbw, b Lever	2
Extras (b 4, lb 12, w 2, nb 7)	25	Extras (b 2, lb 13, w 1, nb 8)	24
Total	224	Total	203

Overs: 69.4

Fall of wickets: 1–1, 2–7, 3–9, 4–71, 5–83, 6–149, 7–205, 8–212, 9–219.

Bowling: Lever 22–4–77–2; Phillip 17.4–6–35–3; Turner 17–2–70–5; Acfield 13–4–17–0.

Fall of wickets: 1–35, 2–41, 3–104, 4–106, 5–161, 6–166, 7–174, 8–174, 9–195.

Bowling: Lever 22.3–4–71–3; Phillip 15–2–52–2; Turner 25–2–56–5; East 2–2–0–0.

ESSEX

First Innings		Second Innings	
B.R. Hardie, lbw, b Sarfraz	11	not out	103
M.H. Denness, c Yardley, b Sarfraz	31	b Williams	51
K.S. McEwan, lbw, b Sarfraz	70	lbw, b Willey	11
K.W.R. Fletcher, not out	52	c Yardley b Larkins	39
K.R. Pont, c Yardley, b Griffith	6	not out	8
S. Turner, lbw, b Griffiths	6		
N. Phillip, b Sarfraz	2		
†N. Smith, b Sarfraz	0		
R.E. East, c Yardley, b Sarfraz	3		
J.K. Lever, run out	1		
D.L. Acfield, c Sharp, b Griffiths	0		
Extras (b 1, lb 6, w 2, nb 8)	17	Extras (b 1, lb 16)	17
79.4 overs. Total	199	Total (3 wkts.)	229

Fall of wickets: 1–22, 2–118, 3–121, 4–143, 5–157, 6–165, 7–169, 8–183, 9–187.

Bowling: Sarfraz 27–7–60–6; Griffiths 23.4–6–65–3; T.M. Lamb 19–6–35–0; Willey 10–4–22–0.

Fall of wickets: 1–113, 2–132, 3–210.

Bowling: Sarfraz 7–2–23–0; Griffiths 21–5–55–0; T.M. Lamb 12–4–23–0; Willey 28–7–42–1; Williams 15–5–29–1; Larkins 7–3–15–1; Watts 5–1–22–0; Yardley 0.3–0–3–0.

Northants 6pts, Essex 17

Umpires – K.E. Palmer & P.B. Wight

90: *Somerset v Gloucestershire*
TAUNTON, 24–27 MAY 1980

Ian Botham (b. 1955) was the most famous – and, thanks to the attention he received from the popular press on and off the field, infamous – cricketer of his time. Though his reputation was finally sealed by his Ashes-winning performance of the following summer, he was already established as England's premier all-rounder by 1980, and was captaining England against the West Indian tourists. In losing only one test and drawing four, his record was most successful compared with what was to follow in the 1980s. 1980 itself was a better year for Botham with the bat than with the ball, his 1,149 runs coming at an average of 42, but his 40 wickets costing 34 each.

With batting sides still hampered by the 100-over limitation on the first innings, Somerset did well to pile up 534 for 6 before the innings was closed. This was largely thanks to Botham. His 228, the highest score of his career, took just over three hours, and the 310 he put on with Denning for the fourth wicket was a Somerset record. With Vivian Richards playing for the touring West Indians Somerset had secured the Indian master batsman, Gavaskar, as their overseas player for the season, but by his standards he played poorly, averaging just 34. On the Gloucestershire side, and also enjoying a comparatively lean season, was Zaheer Abbas (b. 1947), one of the most prolific batsmen in county cricket at this time and the first Pakistani to score more than 100 centuries. In his career he made 34,843 runs at an average of 52, and played in 78 tests. His 173, which saved the match for his side, was his highest of the season. As the game subsided to a draw Botham kept wicket to allow Taylor, like his ten team-mates, to have a bowl.

Taunton, Saturday

Ian Botham, blossoming from controlled aggression into brazen belligerence, hit the first double century of his young and distinguished career on Saturday to England's delight and the special pleasure of one selector, Brian Close, writes Michael Austin.

When Botham reached 200 against Gloucestershire at Taunton, he achieved a distinction which eluded Close, his mentor, throughout a 30-year reign in first-class cricket.

Close's highest score was 198, but his pupil, with a subtle sense of timing, in view of Wednesday's Prudential Cup match against the West Indies, swept to a peerless 228 which included 10 sixes and 27 fours.

Botham's first century occupied 107 minutes, his second spanned only 58 minutes and the fourth-wicket stand of 310 with Peter Denning (98) broke the county record and hurried Somerset to the prosperous regions of 534–6.

Monday

Despite a sparkling 62 from Zaheer and a fighting 80 by Hignell, Gloucestershire followed on 295 behind at Taunton yesterday, concluding a harrowing day against the Somerset seam attack, 258 in arrears with nine wickets remaining.

Gloucester's second innings had proceeded reasonably until, in lowering light, Dredge had Stovold senior caught at second slip. Zaheer, sent in to face the final 20 minutes, was not required to take strike, bad light intervening.

In cool, overcast weather, the pitch was not completely dry when the quest for Somerset's vast total began.

Sadiq hooked the first short ball of the day straight to fine leg, but despite the slight seam movement and bounce variations, Stovold and Zaheer convincingly added a brisk 70 before Stovold flashed to slip.

Zaheer, clearly in prime form against an attack still lacking Botham, moved delightfully to 62 in 26 overs before driving firmly to mid-wicket and calling for a run. Obviously he had not heard of Slocombe's recent run-out successes against Boycott, Hampshire and, less meritoriously, Gavaskar, and so paid the penalty.

Now while the medium-paced Jennings steadily reduced the rest, Hignell, on his return after severe injury, bravely and productively held the fort.

Often in severe trouble, and escaping a couple of technical close chances, he worked doggedly forward, cover-driving, hooking, and square-cutting as opport-

unity arose. Procter, not in form, dropped a return catch, then it was nearly all Hignell, just keeping things afloat.

His partners battled stoutly for survival, Graveney and Brassington lasting for some 40 minutes apiece.

Tuesday

Highly accomplished batting by Zaheer, who scored 173, and Hignell, with a steady 100 not out, comfortably saved Gloucestershire at Taunton yesterday when, having followed on 295 behind Somerset, they ended the match with 394 for five.

Zaheer and Hignell put on 254 in 3½ hours for the third wicket. Botham bowled for the first time since May 11 and ended the match as wicket-keeper: with Somerset's chance of victory long since gone, all 11 players had a bowl.

Gloucestershire resumed at 37 for one and over-night rain, followed by morning sun, gave the spinners appreciable turn, usually at a slowish pace. Sadiq was just opening out when he unluckily played on to

Botham on the attack

Breakwell at 92 with the pitch perhaps at its worst.

Previously, in Marks's first over Zaheer had been missed at short leg when eight, the diving fielder just losing the ball as he fell. This was Somerset's last glimpse of victory.

Hignell worked his way carefully through the most difficult task, and gradually, with Zaheer leading brilliantly, the bat gained complete ascendancy as the pitch dried and became amiable.

Botham produced four lively overs at the start, later purveyed some variably interesting off-breaks, then had three experimental overs with the second ball before taking his place behind the stumps.

Zaheer and Hignell were largely helping themselves, but at last Zaheer was out for 173 in 4¾ hours,

Sunil Gavaskar

having hit two sixes and 24 fours.

Hignell eventually reached a worthy hundred in a minute under four hours, with 13 fours, as the final proceedings became amusingly irrelevant.

SOMERSET

First Innings

*B.C. Rose, c Sadiq, b Brain	32
S.M. Gavaskar, c Sadiq, b Wilkins	75
P.A. Slocombe, lbw, b Brain	0
P.W. Denning, c and b Graveney	98
I.T. Botham, c Sadiq, b Procter	228
V.J. Marks, lbw, b Procter	0
†D.J.S. Taylor, not out	57
D. Breakwell, not out	22
Extras (lb 18, nb 4)	22
Total (100 overs) (6 wkts.)	534

Did not bat: H.R. Moseley, C.H. Dredge, K.F. Jennings.
Fall of wickets: 1–78, 2–78, 3–119, 4–429, 5–429, 6–486.
Bowling: Procter 24–5–81–2; Brain 21–0–134–2; Wilkins 18–4–112–1; Partridge 21–2–104–0; Graveney 16–4–81–1.

GLOUCESTERSHIRE

	First Innings		Second Innings	
A.W. Stovold, c Marks, b Dredge	32	c Botham, b Dredge	14
Sadiq Mohammad, c Dredge, b Moseley	4	b Breakwell	55
Zaheer Abbas, run out	62	c & b Jennings	173
A.J. Hignell, c Taylor, b Dredge	80	not out	100
*M.J. Procter, c & b Jennings	23	c Marks, b Slocombe	32
M.W. Stovold, c Botham, b Jennings	2	lbw, b Jennings	1
M.D. Partridge, b Jennings	15	not out	3
D.A. Graveney, c Taylor, b Jennings	1		
†A.J. Brassington, c Rose, b Moseley	3		
A.H. Wilkins, c Taylor, b Moseley	7		
B.M. Brain, not out	0		
Extras (lb 6, w 1, nb 3)	10	Extras (b 3, lb 10, nb 3)	16
81 overs. Total	239	Total (5 wkts.)	394

Fall of wickets: 1–12, 2–82, 3–112, 4–142, 5–159, 6–184, 7–204, 8–231, 9–237.
Bowling: Moseley 21–3–66–3; Dredge 21–5–51–2; Jennings 25–9–87–4; Marks 14–5–25–0.

Fall of wickets: 1–33, 2–92, 3–346, 4–356, 5–390
Bowling: Moseley 10–1–35–0; Dredge 17–4–58–1; Marks 31–3–66–0; Botham 15–4–57–0; Breakwell 16–6–39–1; Jennings 15–4–59–2; Gavaskar 7–2–29–0; Rose 5–0–25–0; Slocombe 1–0–7–1; Denning 1–0–2–0; Taylor 2–1–1–0.

Somerset 8pts, Glos 4
Umpires – D Shackleton & P.G.S. Stevens

91: *Leicestershire v Northamptonshire*
LEICESTER, 29 AUGUST–1 SEPTEMBER 1981

L eicestershire, having won their first Championship six years earlier, were one of the stronger sides of the early 1980s. Their neighbours and close rivals, Northamptonshire, finished 15th in the table in 1981 despite having a consistently good batting side built around the South African all-rounder Allan Lamb, who would play his first test for England the following year. Cook, who like

many Northants players had been recruited from the North-East, made his England debut the following winter against Sri Lanka, but was never able to reproduce his consistent county form at test level.

It was this solid batting that kept Northants ahead for almost the whole match, but a misjudgement by Cook let Leicestershire snatch an unlikely victory. Leicestershire's success was due principally to Gower, then at the peak of his form, and a player who always seemed to perform much better for his country than for his county, though he averaged 56 for them this summer. Cook's invitation to Leicestershire to make 261 in three hours seemed to favour the home side. When Leicester were still more than 200 behind with seven wickets left at tea, Cook tried to buy wickets to force a Northants victory. However, Gower played to the limits of his excellence and the home side made their runs with time to spare, Gower's century including 16 fours. It was sad that, in subsequent years, the combined pressures of the captaincy of both his county and his country seemed to inhibit Gower, depriving Leicestershire of the best of his talent, and allowing positive cricket such as this to give way to carelessness.

Leicester, Monday

David Gower's failure to make a big score was a disappointment at Grace Road yesterday on a frustrating day for Leicestershire, which ended with Northamptonshire leading by 77 runs with 10 wickets standing.

Gower, who has not scored a hundred since June, looked equal to the task when he reached 50 in 98 minutes, but was soon out to begin a down-curve of the Leicestershire batting, totalling 251–9 declared in reply to 300 by Northants on the easy-paced wicket.

Leicestershire's innings revolved around Cobb, Gower and Davison, who each made 50 in individual fashion. Cobb, in his third championship match, took twice as long in reaching his first class best, but his defensive play provided a good foil.

Gower, in sparkling form, was unfortunate to be out on the stroke of lunch for 53 (seven fours), the ball dislodging a bail as he attempted to hook Griffiths. Davison started slowly but increased the tempo to reach his 50 in 88 minutes, with nine fours.

Northants, at the start of the day needed only six overs to advance the overnight score from 256–4 to 300 without loss.

Tuesday
By Stuart McLean

Persuasive captaincy by Northamptonshire's Geoff Cook helped to produce a decisive result at Grace Road yesterday, when David Gower responded to the challenge of quick runs with an unbeaten 117, giving Leicestershire victory by four wickets.

Set a target of 261 in 130 minutes plus 20 overs, after Northants had made a brisk 211 for three, Leicestershire appeared to have settled for a draw when 47 for three at tea.

But Cook encouraged them to make a game of it by bowling himself and keeping off-spinner Williams on for an expensive 26 overs.

Gower's century, scored in 163 minutes and including 16 fours, overshadowed Allan Lamb's feat of 2,000 runs for the season, and he received good support from Clift and Garnham. The fourth-wicket stand with Clift added 138 in 99 minutes.

Allan Lamb

David Gower

NORTHAMPTONSHIRE		
First Innings	**Second Innings**	
*G. Cook, c Gower, b Briers 117	c Taylor, b Clift 71	
J.P.C. Mills, c Garnham,	run out 16	
b Parsons 29		
R.G. Williams, c Garnham,	b Cook 22	
b Taylor 63		
A.J. Lamb, not out 36	not out 78	
R.J. Boyd-Moss, c and b Clift 5	not out 23	
T.J. Yardley, not out 25		
Extras (b 4, lb 11, nb 10) 25	Extras (lb 1) 1	

Total (4 wkts. dec.) .... 300 Total (3 wkts. dec.) 211

Fall of wickets: 1–62, 2–216, 3–236, 4–248.

Fall of wickets: 1–47, 2–94, 3–118,

Did not bat: Sarfaz Nawaz, B.J Griffiths, T.M. Lamb, R.M. Carter, †G. Sharp.

Bowling: Taylor 4–0–16–0; Parsons 5–2–3–0; Cook 25.3–9–71–11; Balderstone 18–2–58–0.

Bowling: Taylor 20–2–61–1; Parsons 18.1–2–66–1; Cook 13–2–55–0; Clift 15–7–29–1; Balderstone 11–3–42–0; Briers 12–4–22–11.

LEICESTERSHIRE		
First Innings	**Second Innings**	
*J.C. Balderstone, run out 11	run out 10	
R.A. Cobb, c Mills, b Carter 54		
D.I. Gower, b Griffiths 53	not out 117	
B.F. Davison, c Sarfraz,	b Sarfraz 2	
b Williams 55		
N.C. Briers, c Sarfraz, b Williams .. 22	c Sarfraz, b Griffiths 5	
T.I. Boon, c Cook, b Williams 0	b Griffiths 0	
P.B. Clift, lbw, b Williams 17	c T.M. Lamb, b Williams 73	
†M.A. Garnham, c Yardley,	b Griffiths 41	
b Williams 0		
N.G.B. Cook, c A.J. Lamb,		
b Sarfraz 5		
G.J. Parsons, not out 15	not out 4	
L.B. Taylor, not out 5		
Extras (b 6, lb 7, nb 1) 14	Extras (b 3, lb 6, nb 2) 11	

91 overs. Total (9 wkts. dec.) ...... 251 Total (6 wkts.) 263

Fall of wickets: 1–16, 2–102, 3–181, 4–184, 5–184, 6–223, 7–223, 8–230, 9–230.

Fall of wickets: 1–16, 2–17, 3–28, 4–166, 5–241, 6–243.

Bowling: Sarfraz 17–4–47–1; Griffiths 13–5–43–1; T.M. Lamb 18–10–30–0; Williams 34–11–101–5; Carter 9–4–16–1.

Bowling: Sarfraz 6–2–18–1; Griffiths 9–0–35–3; Williams 26.2–5–100–1; Cook 12–4–38–0; Carter 1–0–6–0; T.M. Lamb 8–0–55–0.

Leics 20 pts, Northants 8

Umpires – R. Aspinall & R.S. Herman

92: *Lancashire v Warwickshire*
SOUTHPORT, 28–30 JULY 1982

Wisden described this game as 'one of the most remarkable matches in the history of the County Championship', which if anything was an understatement. Humpage (b. 1954), the Warwickshire wicketkeeper, enjoyed a career with the bat that alternated between short periods of gloriously successful savagery and long periods of unexceptional competence. This match was representative of the former: his 254 was his highest first-class score, its 13 sixes were the most ever hit by an Englishman in an innings. The 470 he put on with Kallicharran (whose 230 was his third double century of the season) was the highest for any Warwickshire wicket, beating Jameson and Kanhai's 465 eight years earlier; the highest for the fourth wicket in English cricket, beating Hayward and Abel's record of 448 in 1899; and the fourth highest fourth-wicket stand in the world.

Yet Lancashire secured a mind-boggling victory. Fowler (b. 1957), who made his test debut a month later, not only scored a century in each innings, but did so both times with a runner, having injured himself on the first day in the field. MacFarlane's career-best bowling performance left Lancashire ample time to score their runs, which they did without losing a

wicket. Notwithstanding the personal feats that won Lancashire the match, Lloyd's shrewd captaincy in declaring more than 100 behind on first innings, on a wicket that promised nothing to the bowlers, was the crucial feature of the match; though Lancashire were greatly assisted by inept Warwickshire batting in the second innings, which demonstrated how well-deserved this apparently fine batting side's reputation for inconsistency was.

Southport, Wednesday
By Michael Austin

Geoff Humpage, with an astonishing career-best innings of 254, and Alvin Kallicharran, who made an unbeaten 230, overpowered Lancashire with an English first-class record for the fourth wicket of 470 as Warwickshire reached 523 for four declared at Southport yesterday.

Humpage hit 13 sixes, a total exceeded only once in cricket history, by John Reid, who struck 15 in a New Zealand provincial match in 1962–63, and the partnership, occupying 293 minutes, was the best for any Warwickshire wicket.

Kallicharran's double century was, remarkably, his third this season. He hit 34 fours and, like Humpage, offered only one chance, a return catch to

Graeme Fowler

Abrahams at 177. Humpage was later dropped at 185, by Scott.

With Croft and Allott injured, Lancashire were in an unexpected position of promise when Warwickshire wobbled at 6–2, but Kallicharran, hooking and driving disdainfully in a dictatorial innings, transferred the initiative as cloud cover heralded blissful sunshine.

McFarlane's initial success in encouraging Dyer to divert a sharp catch to second slip and then having Amiss caught off bat and pad owed much to his extraction of extra bounce but thereafter, McFarlane and Lancashire bowled lamentably at Kallicharran's strength around middle and leg.

A dry and placid pitch belied a green appearance, a fast and gently sloping outfield rewarded Humpage's pugnacity and Kallicharran's unhurried and deliberate shots so that Clive Lloyd could merely share the load of punishment around his seven bowlers.

Folley induced an edge from Andy Lloyd to usher in Humpage and runs came in a flood with Kallicharran's century including 20 fours and his double century taking him towards 1,500 runs in his best English season.

Humpage's flow of 24 fours was interrupted by a barrage of sixes and, with a rich sense of occasion, the wicket-keeper-batsman broke an 83-year-old record

when hooking a full toss from Abrahams on to the railway line.

The English record had previously belonged to R. Abel and T.W. Hayward, who scored 448 for Surrey against Yorkshire at the Oval.

Thursday

David Brown, the former England fast bowler, yesterday became the first substitute to take a wicket in county cricket as Warwickshire and Lancashire contributed to another highly eventful day at Southport.

Fowler, the Lancashire batsman with a thigh strain, scored 126 with the aid of a runner, and Cockbain missed a maiden century by two runs.

After Lancashire declared at 414 for six, Warwickshire lost Dyer and Lloyd in extending their lead to 123.

After the English fourth-wicket stand of 470 between Humpage and Kallicharran the previous day, Brown added a second piece of cricket history when his pace and movement defeated Scott, the nightwatchman.

Brown, 40, Warwickshire's team manager, was permitted to take a full part as fielder and bowler, and if required, as a batsman under a regulation catering for a player, in this case Small, being withdrawn during a match to join the Test squad.

The substitution was approved by Lord's and, after Brown bowled a 13-over spell before lunch, Small, finally not required by England rejoined the game, following a motorway dash, all of which prompted chunterings and confusion among Lancashire members.

Lancashire's batsmen were undismayed and made uncomplicated progress, though the wicket assisted Sutcliffe and Kallicharran, off-spinners whose accuracy commanded respect. Warwickshire's seam bowlers were treated with less ceremony.

Fowler, confirming his England potential as an opener, hinted at the season's fastest hundred, decelerated and then reached his eighth first-class century – and his third against Warwickshire – with a pulled six off Brown, in 109 minutes. In all, he hit 23 fours and two sixes.

Thereafter Clive Lloyd, below his best and later dismissed by a ball which turned and lifted, shared a century stand with Cockbain, a stylish strokeplayer who was becalmed in the nineties and then nervously edged a catch to backward short-leg.

Abrahams played vigorous strokes in Lancashire's confident advance beyond 374, the target to save the follow-on, and there was just time for McFarlane to dismiss Dyer, for a pair, and Lloyd before completing a bizarre day by delivering a wide with the hat-trick ball.

Friday

Warwickshire's astonishing collapse from a dictatorial position of 523 for four in their first innings, was poignantly completed yesterday when Graeme Fowler's second century helped Lancashire to a 10-wicket win in a remarkable match of multiple records.

Fowler followed his inspirational 126 with an unbeaten 128, both centuries being scored with the aid of a runner, a cricket rarity also achieved by Amiss, against Derbyshire last summer.

Ironically, Amiss dropped a straightforward slip catch off Hartley with Fowler on two and, thereafter, David Lloyd, unbeaten on 88, and Fowler were blissfully untroubled in making the required 221 for victory with seven overs to spare.

Warwickshire suffered assorted problems, batted abjectly in the morning and even had the symbolic experience of being dismissed for 111, the cricketers' bad luck number known as Nelson, which was curiously appropriate at the Trafalgar Road ground.

McFarlane, 30, the former Northants and Bedfordshire fast bowler in his first season with Lancashire, prompted the early extinction of Warwickshire's innings with a career-best six for 59, four wickets fell at 47 and five batsmen failed to score.

Kallicharran's second-ball dismissal to an excellent catch at backward short leg, highlighted the athleticism of Lancashire's fielding. Folley bowled economically and O'Shaughnessy took three prime wickets.

Warwickshire, 107 for 9 and sinking, wistfully viewed the lunch-time scoreboard which had been returned to their first innings total for a pictorial commemoration of Humpage's record stand with Kallicharran, but they found no escape.

Fowler hit 16 fours and two sixes, welcome labour-saving devices for his runner, Folley, and the fluent David Lloyd hit fourteen fours, turning Warwickshire's first day jubilation into weariness and frustration in broiling heat.

Humpage – a powerful wicketkeeper-batsman

WARWICKSHIRE

First Innings		Second Innings	
*D.L. Amiss, c Abrahams, b McFarlane	6	c Scott, b McFarlane	24
R.I.H.B. Dyer, c Simmons, b McFarlane	0	c Abrahams, b McFarlane	0
T.A. Lloyd, c Scott, b Folley	23	b McFarlane	0
A.I. Kallicharran, not out	230	c D. Lloyd, b O'Shaughnessy	0
†G.W. Humpage, b D. Lloyd	254	c Abrahams, b O'Shaughnessy	21
Asif Din		c Hughes, b O'Shaughnessy	21
S. H. Wootton		b McFarlane	0
C. Lethbridge		c Hughes, b Folley	18
G.C. Small		lbw, b McFarlane	0
P. Hartley		c Scott, b McFarlane	16
S.P. Sutcliffe		not out	7
Extras (b 1, lb 6, w 1, nb 2)	10	Extras (b 1, lb 2, w 1)	4
Total (4 wkts. dec.)	523	Total	111

100 overs: 441–3.
Fall of wickets: 1–5, 2–6, 3–53, 4–523.
Bowling: McFarlane 11–2–90–2; Folley 15–3–64–1; O'Shaughnessey 15–2–62–0; Simmons 20–2–97–0; Hughes 20–2–79–0; Abrahams 15–3–76–0; D. Lloyd 10–1.1–45–1.

Fall of wickets: 1–1, 2–1, 3–47, 4–47, 5–47, 6–47, 7–76, 8–81, 9–99.
Bowling: McFarlane 20–3–59–6; Folley 11–5–19–1; O'Shaughnessey 7.1–0–29–3; Simmons 1–1–0–0.

LANCASHIRE

First Innings		Second Innings	
G. Fowler, b Asif Din	126	not out	128
D. Lloyd, c Humpage. b Small	10	not out	88
*C.J. Scott, lbw, b Brown	9		
L Cockbain, c Amiss, b Kallicharran	98		
*C.H. Lloyd, c Humpage, b Kallicharran	45		
D.P. Hughes, c Small, b Kallicharran	14		
J. Abrahams, not out	51		
S.J. O'Shaughnessy, not out	26		
Extras (lb 13, w 3, nb 19)	35	Extras (lb 2, nb 8)	10
Total (6 wkts. dec.)	414	Total (no wkts.)	226

100 overs: 357–6.
Did not bat: J. Simmons, I. Folley, D.L. McFarlane.
Fall of wickets: 1–34, 2–109, 3–194, 4–305, 5–327, 6–333.
Bowling: Small 15–4–38–1; Hartley 14–0–66–0; Sutcliffe 38–9–103–0; Lethbridge 14–5–58–0; Brown 13–3–47–1; Asif Din 6–1–35–1; Kallicharran 13–3–32–3.

Bowling: Small 11–2–30–0; Hartley 9–1–38–0; Sutcliffe 19–5–60–0; Lethbridge 9–2–27–0; Asif Din 5–0–25–0; Kallicharran 6–0–35–0; Lloyd 1–0–1–0.

Lancs 21pts, Warwick 6
Umpires – H.D. Bird & J. van Geloven

93: Essex v Surrey
CHELMSFORD, 28–31 MAY 1983

Essex were the supreme team of the 1980s. Following their first Championship victory in 1979, they only finished outside the top 10 once in the next ten years, won three other championships (including in this year), and were three times in the top four: and they had limited-over success to match. When a side bowled out Essex reasonably cheaply – and anything under 300 could be considered in that category – its own batsmen could be reasonably sure they would fare even more miserably. No side, though, crashed quite as spectacularly as Surrey on this occasion.

Their 14, scored on the second afternoon of a rain-blighted match, with no play on the first day, was the lowest score in their history, undercutting the 16 they had made against Nottinghamshire at the Oval in 1880. Only four sides (two in the Championship) ever made lower scores, and Surrey missed by just three runs being the lowest scoring side of all time: at 8 for 8 before Clarke's late flourish, this seemed eminently possible. Only one other side, Hampshire in 1922, had made fewer than 20 runs in an innings since the Great War (see game 36). Philip (b. 1948), the main destroyer of the Surrey batsmen, was a fine West Indian all-rounder in the tradition begun at Essex by Keith Boyce. In an age when competition to play for the West Indies was stiff, Philip played just nine tests for his country in the late 1970s. Foster (b. 1962), his partner, was to enjoy a brief period as England's premier fast bowler during the difficult years in the late 1980s. His decision to join a rebel side to play in South Africa in 1990 effectively ended a test career that, while having moments of great success, had (like his county performances) been dogged by injury.

Chelmsford, Monday
By Rex Alston

Surrey were bowled out for 14 when they replied to Essex's total of 287 in the Schweppes County Championship match at Chelmsford yesterday. Keith Fletcher, the Essex captain, had made 110.

Surrey's total was only two runs better than the

Foster – a destroyer of Surrey

lowest in first class cricket – 12 by Northamptonshire at Gloucester in 1907, and by Oxford University, batting a man short, against MCC and Ground at Oxford in 1877.

Yesterday's innings lasted 14.3 overs. Norbert Phillip took six wickets for four in 7.3 overs and Neil Foster, 21, four for 10 in seven overs.

Foster had a serious back operation a year ago and made his first appearance in the senior side since then only because John Lever has a hairline fracture of his right foot.

The heavy roller had been on the pitch between innings, but this could not account for Surrey's disastrously feeble batting.

Butcher began the procession when he was well caught at the wicket and the next six batsmen to depart were out for nought. Most of them played back to Phillip, who kept the new ball well pitched up.

Foster disposed of Needham, and Phillip was surprised and delighted to have the dangerous Knight and Lynch lbw.

Clinton, top scorer with six, watched these disasters from the other end before swinging on the leg side and giving David East a good catch.

When Clarke joined Monkhouse at eight for eight it looked as though Surrey would set a new world record, but a wild slog by Clarke just reached the square leg boundary for the only four of the innings and Monkhouse edged a two before giving Phillip his third lbw.

Surrey started well when Thomas in his first over, hit Gooch's leg stump as the batsman aimed to long leg, and soon afterwards Hardie played forward to Clarke and was bowled.

Fletcher and McEwan set about restoring the situation and with a series of easy strokes hoisted the 100 before McEwan was caught at the slip. This was reward for a very tidy spell of accurate medium pace from Knight.

With the slow pitch inhibiting the pace of Clarke and Thomas, Surrey's slow and medium-paced bowlers, Pocock and Knight, made steady inroads into Essex's middle order whilst Fletcher held the other end firm.

Turner put up the 200 with a straight six and was then marvellously well caught by Knight throwing himself to his left.

Fletcher's fine innings ended with an attempted slashed cover drive after he had batted for nearly four hours for his second century of this abbreviated season.

Tuesday

A fine not-out century by Roger Knight restored Surrey's morale after Monday evening's debacle and ensured a draw with Essex at Chelmsford. He and Clinton had a third wicket partnership of 167 and the game ended peacefully on a lovely afternoon.

Knight batted for 210 minutes and hit only seven fours in his 101 not out and the faithful Clinton played through the innings, four hours for 61 out of a total of 185 for two.

So it was back to normal after Monday's freak performance. Play was delayed for 90 minutes when Surrey set out to try to save the game – 273 behind on first innings.

Heavy overnight rain had seemingly not affected the pitch and sun and warmth permeated the atmosphere as Butcher and Clinton began the innings. The perpetrators of Surrey's disasters naturally continued where they had left off but they met more resolute battling until Butcher touched a fast one from Foster and Gooch held the simple slip catch. Seven runs later Phillip had Needham lbw, so at 18 for two Surrey were up against it as Knight joined Clinton.

The pitch played true, though the occasional ball may have moved a little, and neither batsman looked assured. However, they saw off Monday's executioners, Phillip and Foster, and had no problem with Gooch's medium pace, around the wicket, and Acfield's off-spin.

The real crunch came after lunch, taken at 56. If Essex were to break through, this was their chance, but all the bowlers met two obdurate left-handed batsmen.

Knight should have been caught in the gully when 24 off Turner but there were no obvious other chances. The batsmen grew in stature and confidence as Fletcher went through his bowling repertoire.

As Pocock had bowled well on Monday, Fletcher might perhaps have made more use of spinners Acfield and East as Knight and Clinton played the fast men comfortably.

Knight, as usual, drove easily through the covers, at first defensively and later with more abandon, while Clinton was the ever-reliable sheet anchor.

After tea 90 minutes remained and Essex needed a quick break-through if they were to have a chance. But it was not to be and soon Fletcher was employing his occasional bowlers to fill in the time till 5.30.

ESSEX

First Innings

G.A. Gooch, b Thomas	1
B.R. Hardie, b Clarke	16
*K.W.R. Fletcher, c Lynch, b Monkhouse	110
K.S. McEwan, c Lynch, b Knight	45
K.R. Pont, b Pocock	12
N. Phillip, b Pocock	8
S. Turner, c & b Knight	20
R.E. East, c Lynch, b Clarke	19
†D.E. East, c Butcher, b Pocock	17
N.A. Foster, not out	19
D.L. Acfield, run out	0
Extras (b 4, lb 10, nb 6)	20

89.5 overs. Total 287

Fall of wickets: 1–1, 2–27, 3–113, 4–156, 5–179, 6–222, 7–238, 8–252, 9–276.

Bowling: Clarke 20–3–58–2; Thomas 20–2–78–1; Monkhouse 13–2–49–1; Knight 17–6–33–2; Pocock 19.5–6–49–3.

SURREY

	First Innings		Second Innings	
A.R. Butcher, c D.E. East, b Phillip	2	c Gooch, b Foster	5
G.S. Clinton, c D.E. East, b Foster	6	not out	61
A. Needham, b Foster	0	lbw, b Phillip	4
*R.D.V. Knight, lbw, b Phillip	0	not out	101
M.A. Lynch, lbw, b Phillip	0		
†C.J. Richards, c Turner, b Phillip	0		
D.J. Thomas, lbw, b Foster	0		
I.R. Payne, b Phillip	0		
G. Monkhouse, lbw, b Phillip	2		
S.T. Clarke, b Foster	4		
P.I. Pocock, not out	0		
Extras	0	Extras (b 1, lb 8, w 2, nb 3)	14

14.3 overs. Total 14   Total (2 wkts.) 185

Fall of wickets: 1–2, 2–5, 3–6, 4–8, 5–8, 6–8, 7–8, 8–8, 9–14.

Fall of wickets: 1–11, 2–18.

Bowling: Phillip 7.3–4–4–6; Foster 7–3–10–4.

Bowling: Phillip 13–2–39–1; Foster 13–2–33–1; Turner 7–3–16–0; Gooch 22–6–45–0; Acfield 17–7–23–0; R.E. East 1–0–5–0; Pont 1–1–0–0.

Essex 7pts, Surrey 4

Umpires – W.E. Alley and J.W. Holder

94: Nottingham v Warwickshire
TRENT BRIDGE, 25–28 AUGUST 1984

Although they managed only to come second in the Championship, 1984 was possibly Nottinghamshire's most successful season ever, as they were also runners-up in the Sunday league and semi-finalists in the Benson and Hedges Cup. Much of this success was attributable to their overseas players, their South African captain Clive Rice and New Zealand all-rounder Richard Hadlee. This match was remarkable for Hadlee (b. 1951): he became the first player to achieve the 'double' of 1,000 runs and 100 wickets in a season since Titmus in 1967, and the first therefore since the reduction of the Championship programme after 1968. He achieved the feat during his innings of 39, though it was his nine wickets in this match that really set up Nottinghamshire's victory. Hadlee's end-of-season figures were 1,179 runs at an average of 51, with a top score of 210 not out, and 117 wickets at 14 apiece; such excellence placed him in the highest rank of all-rounders in cricket history. Four years later Franklyn Stephenson, another Nottinghamshire all-rounder and overseas player, emulated Hadlee. How far the difficulty of performing the 'double' was due to less cricket being played, and how far due to the decline of genuine all-rounders, is a moot point.

The Nottinghamshire side of the mid-1980s was rich in talent. In addition to Rice and Hadlee, this side included players of past and future test calibre in Robinson, Randall, French and Hemmings. In the Warwickshire side, though, Dennis Amiss (b. 1943) – the mainstay of both innings – was enjoying an Indian summer in a career that was to last 28 seasons and bring him 43,423 runs, including 102 centuries, at an average of 43.

Nottingham, Saturday

Poised to become the first cricketer to achieve the cherished 'double' since F.J. Titmus in 1967, the remarkable Richard Hadlee yesterday took 6 for 55 in yet another fine display of fast bowling to keep Notts' title hopes simmering nicely, writes Julian Baskcombe.

Hadlee, with 100 wickets already safely secured, helped bowl Warwickshire out for 261 after Notts had won the toss.

Notts' problem was that Hadlee received scant support from his fellow bowlers and the experienced Amiss and Humpage accumulated 91 for the fourth wicket before Randall's dive at mid-off accounted for the solid Amiss on 70.

Saxelby and Cooper both suffered the full blade of Humpage's aggressive drives, but Hadlee's fourth spell saw Paul Smith snaffled at slip and Ferreira and Lethbridge palpably leg before to successive deliveries.

Pick, again, proved an astute change, trapping Humpage in front of his stumps for an invaluable 89, but although Notts achieved their objective of maximum bowling points, the visitors had undoubtedly fared rather better than most in similar circumstances.

Notts replied with a steady 68 for one, but were fortunate to see opener, Robinson, put down at third slip by Dyer off Small when only seven.

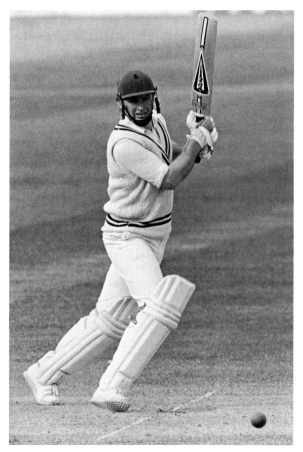

Dennis Amiss

Monday
By Doug Ibbotson

Nottinghamshire's championship aspirations were handsomely served at Trent Bridge yesterday, when Derek Randall and Tim Robinson, with a rousing second-wicket partnership of 178, enabled Clive Rice to declare at 350 for six – 89 runs ahead of Warwickshire.

By close of play Warwickshire had lost four wickets in reversing the advantage by only 10 runs and Nottinghamshire today confidently expect to claim 24 crucial points.

If Robinson, unluckily dismissed for 97, and Randall, whose 113 included 11 fours, claimed centre stage for much of the day then Richard Hadlee, who reached the elusive double of 1,000 runs and 100 wickets almost stole the show.

Nottinghamshire's two major innings were favoured by fielding errors. Robinson was dropped at seven on Saturday and when Randall had reached 40 yesterday Amiss, a first slip, parried but failed to hold a chance off Ferreira.

Warwickshire's ground fielding was also generally below par, though partially redeemed by Lethbridge, whose alertness in the covers helped contain the burgeoning second-wicket partnership.

Nevertheless, Robinson, in particular, looked especially fluent. Having reached his 10th half-century of the season, he seemed assured of his fifth century when, within three runs, he chopped a ball from Ferreira on to his leg stump.

Randall, having resumed at 22, made an uncertain start, fencing at Small and showing a shuffling respect for the accurate Old. But having reached his 50 with a superb square cut off Lethbridge, he joined Robinson in a blistering boundary assault on Paul Smith.

On 99, Randall suffered an excruciating maiden over from Old, but having completed his third century of the summer twice advanced down the pitch to drive the same bowler for four. However, an extravagant and fatal attempt to cut Small looked sacrificial – especially as the promoted Hadlee was next man in.

If the pleasantly rounded entertainment now assumed an element of tension then Hadlee, in typically crisp and nerveless pursuit of his 21st and 1,000th run of the season, quickly dispelled it.

His first dozen runs included a lofted cover-driven boundary off Old and another to long-on off Small. Then in Old's next over Hadlee hit a magnificent six over long-on and with a first bounce blow to the mid-wicket boundary reached his prime objective.

Immediately after another celebratory six off Lethbridge, Hadlee departed for 39 and it remained for French to relieve the inevitable air of anti-climax with an attractive and undefeated 37.

On reaching 21 runs at Trent Bridge yesterday Richard Hadlee became the first player since Fred Titmus in 1967 to achieve 1,000 runs and 100 wickets in a season.

The modest but determined New Zealander then confirmed that his successful attempt for the double was statistically planned and programmed at the start of the season. It began, he said, as a challenge and developed into an obsession.

Hadlee, who claimed the 100th wicket in his 20th championship match at Blackpool last week topped the 1,000 runs in his 21st – some way ahead of a schedule which did not include the two universities or the touring sides.

'I worked on the need to average 50 runs and 4½ wickets a match – 60 wickets at Trent Bridge and the rest, along with most of the runs, in away games. The double century against Middlesex at Lord's gave me a four-match bonus.

'A month ago I felt burned out, but the double was a tremendous incentive. Now it's done I'm going to relax and really enjoy my cricket.'

Tuesday

Nottinghamshire, with a grateful eye on the spin bowling skills of Eddie Hemmings and an anxious ear for intelligence from the Oval, duly beat Warwickshire by seven wickets at Trent Bridge yesterday to harvest 24 valuable Championship points.

In taking six wickets for 49, Hemmings achieved his best figures of the season – a performance that restricted his former county to a forlorn lead of 116 with 70 overs in prospect. Even so, Nottinghamshire moved somewhat ponderously in their victory quest.

To some extent, the day's events were protracted by Nottinghamshire's understandable determination that the end rather than the means was paramount. Added to which, Warwickshire, with little expectation of success, did rather better than anticipated.

They resumed their second innings at 99 for four with a slender lead of 10. In Gladstone Small they had a nightwatchman who subsequently saw little of the morning.

Having despatched the first ball from Pick to third man for three, he fell to Hadlee's second, smartly caught by Birch at slip, and Warwickshire were 104 for five.

Nevertheless the redoubtable Amiss was still there and soon demonstrating his wakefulness by clipping Hadlee to the mid-wicket boundary.

In company with the flaxen-haired Smith (24), and the swarthy Ferreira (30), Amiss then proceeded to a leisurely half-century of 176 minutes and six fours. By now however, Hemmings was extracting the maximum benefit from a helpful pitch and his rich fund of experience.

Smith contributed to his own downfall by nudging a simple catch to Robinson at silly point, while Ferreira sportingly walked on looping a silent bat-and-pad chance to wicket-keeper French.

Old, who might better have chanced his arm, was bowled for one offering, an impassive prod, and

Lethbridge, seemingly uncertain whether survival was most likely against Hemmings or Hadlee, fell for 11, rashly attempting to drive the latter.

Amiss, meanwhile, plodded on until, when joined by the veteran Gifford, he lunged down the wicket to meet Hemmings and slogged a steepling catch to Birch at wide mid-on.

Warwickshire's lead was modest and the overs in the can plentiful, yet, when Nottinghamshire set out, Small proved lively, Old accurate and Ferreira splendidly consistent in both respects.

There were tremors then before all was safely gathered in. Newell, splendidly caught by Humpage on the leg side, Randall, capriciously departing for one and the admirable Robinson, the victim of another fine catch by Kallicharran at second slip, all left before skipper Rice steered his side home with an unbeaten 41.

Richard Hadlee – a famous double

WARWICKSHIRE

First Innings

R.I.H.B. Dyer, c French, b Hadlee		24
K.D. Smith, c Randall, b Hadlee		4
A.I. Kallicharran, c Rice, b Pick		22
D.I. Amiss, c Randall, b Cooper		70
†G.W. Humpage, lbw Pick		89
P.A. Smith, c Rice, b Hadlee		1
A.M. Ferreira, lbw Hadlee		12
C. Lethbridge, lbw Hadlee		0
C.M. Old, not out		21
G.C. Small, lbw Saxelby		4
*N. Gifford, b Hadlee		3
Extras (b 2, lb 3, w 3, nb 3)		11
Total		261

Overs: 87.2

Fall of wickets: 1–7, 2–33, 3–76, 4–167, 5–190, 6–210, 7–210, 8–241, 9–258.

Bowling: Hadlee 26.2–9–55–6; Saxelby 23–2–68–1; Cooper 23–7–63–1; Pick 13–1–52–2; Hemmings 2–0–12–0.

Second Innings

b Pick		26
c Rice, b Hemmings		11
lbw, b Hadlee		25
c Birch, b Hemmings		62
b Hemmings		3
c Robinson, b Hemmings		24
c French, b Hemmings		30
c French, b Hadlee		11
b Hemmings		1
c Birch, b Hadlee		3
not out		0
Extras (lb 4, w 1, nb 4)		9
Total		205

Fall of wickets: 1–29, 2–58, 3–76, 4–99, 5–104, 6–140, 7–180, 8–182 9–205.

Bowling: Hadlee 24–7–48–3; Saxelby 11–2–41–0; Hemmings 27.1–11–49–6; Cooper 8–2–14–0; Pick 14–2–44–1.

NOTTINGHAMSHIRE

First Innings

M. Newell, b Old		10
R.T. Robinson, b Ferreira		97
D.W. Randall, c Humpage, b Small		113
*C.E.B. Rice, c Humpage, b Ferreira		20
R.J. Hadlee, c Ferreira, b Lethbridge		39
J.D. Birch, c Kallicharran, b Ferreira		16
†B.N. French, not out		37
E.E. Hemmings, not out		2
Extras (lb 6, w 1, nb 9)		16

98 overs. Total (6 wkts. dec.) 350

Did not bat: R.A. Pick, K. Saxelby, K.F. Cooper.

Fall of wickets: 1–23, 2–201, 3–257, 4–292, 5–292, 6–337.

Bowling: Ferreira 26–5–65–3; Old 29–7–93–1; Small 23–3–67–1; Smith 7–1–35–0; Lethbridge 11–1–71–1; Gifford 2–0–3–0.

Second Innings

c Humpage, b Small		2
c Kallicharran, b Ferreira		33
c Humpage, b Old		4
not out		41
not out		28
Extras (b 6, lb 3)		9
Total (3 wkts.)		117

Fall of wickets: 1–16, 2–23, 3–61.

Bowling: Small 8–2–26–1; Old 8–3–20–1; Ferreira 12–3–41–1; Gifford 9–3–15–0; Lethbridge 2–0–6–0.

Notts 24pts, Warwick 5

Umpires – P.B. Wight & B. Dudleston

95: Somerset v Warwickshire
TAUNTON, 1–4 JUNE 1985

Since overseas players were introduced into County cricket in the late 1960s West Indians have made the biggest impression. Vivian Richards' contribution matched that of two of his predecessors as West Indies' captain, Sir Garfield Sobers and Clive Lloyd. Much of the success of the West Indies against England in recent years has been attributed – somewhat dubiously – to the intimate knowledge almost all their players have of English players and conditions throughout county cricket. It always seemed, though, that Richards (b. 1952) needed no such help. Although he did not know it at the

time, 1985 was his penultimate season for Somerset, since the county chose to dispense with his services (and those of Joel Garner) in 1986; and in doing so they lost, in protest, Ian Botham, absent from this match. Following the announcement of his sacking, Richards' supporters forced a vote of confidence in the Somerset committee, which the committee won. Richards played league cricket for a season, then led his country against England, and but for injury would have resumed his county career with Glamorgan in 1989.

Richards' treble century was only the fifth in

the Championship since the war. It was the highest score ever made for Somerset, beating Gimblett's 310 that had stood since 1948. He made his runs out of 479 from 258 balls in six minutes under five hours, making it one of the fastest treble centuries scored in the Championship. Nor was this Warwickshire side meagre opposition: in Small they had one of England's leading strike bowlers of the next five years, and in Gifford one of the most experienced slow bowlers in the game. Richards, though, was unconquerable.

Taunton, Saturday

An amazing innings of 322 by Vivian Richards sent the records tumbling at Taunton as Somerset, after a shaky start, reached a remarkable 566–5 declared against Warwickshire, who responded with 23 for no wicket in nine overs, writes Eric Hill.

Richards arrived after Bail had retired following a blow on the helmet from an extremely menacing Small, who immediately had Felton well taken at slip.

Richards began rather sketchily, edging Small several times, was beaten a time or two, and, after a flurry of crisp strokes struck firmly on the thumb by the aggressive Smith. This seemed to renew his thirst for runs as he peeled off a seemingly endless array of strokes – glorious, elegant, powerful, and outrageous, and running his runs rapidly to the very end.

Popplewell gamely overcame his early troubles for a valuable 55 as they added 122. Then Ollis smoothly helped in a stand of 174. Small was extremely unlucky not to remove both in an excellent afternoon spell as, on a slightly grassy pitch, there was often some help for the sweating, toiling bowlers.

Richards passed the highest Somerset innings and his own highest score as he went to 100 in 105 balls and 300 in 244 balls to a standing ovation and hand-shakes all round.

Having a slog, Richards finally played on for 322 in 258 balls, with eight sixes and 42 fours – an incredible effort. Marks reached a crisp half century in a partner-ship of 183.

Not without anxious moments – Dyer being caught off a Davis no-ball when eight – the Warwick-shire openers survived the final testing period.

Monday
By David Green

The Taunton run glut abated only slightly yesterday as Warwickshire replied to Somerset's daunting 566 for five with 442 for 9 declared. In the final 10 minutes Somerset lost Bail in extending their lead to 133.

Consistency was the key for Warwickshire. Andy

Lloyd made 61 while Dennis Amiss (81) and Paul Smith (93, a championship best) shared in a fourth-wicket stand of 161 in two hours and Anton Ferreira made a handsome unbeaten 101.

Tuesday

County cricket was seen at its most pointless yesterday at Taunton, where Warwickshire, not surprisingly, made no attempt to reach 351 for victory off 53 overs and finished 170 short with eight wickets standing.

Alvin Kallicharran took the opportunity of batting practice and made an increasingly fluent 89 while Robin Dyer scored 63 not out. Vic Marks made an unbeaten 66 in Somerset's second innings of 226 for 5 declared.

Several reasons may be advanced for the stiffness of Marks's declaration. Certainly runs had been scored freely throughout the match, and Warwickshire – even without the injured Humpage – are a powerful batting side.

Then too, Somerset had lost all three of their home matches this season. Marks could also say that, as Warwickshire had a maximum of 205 minutes to get the runs, more than 53 overs would probably be bowled.

When Somerset resumed their second innings in the morning 133 runs ahead, Gard and Popplewell had an uneasy time against Small, bowling with pace and hostility, and the lively Smith. Small soon had Poppl-ewell caught at mid-off.

Gard, however, interspersing nicks with powerful blows in front of the wicket, scored rapidly until run out by Smith's direct hit. Ollis was immediately lbw, at which point Gifford brought on Lloyd and Kallicharran to feed Somerset some quick runs.

When the declaration finally came, Warwick-shire's hopes of flying start were rapidly dispelled by Garner. Lloyd was caught behind, Dyer hit on the shoulder and then almost caught at third slip.

With Davis also bowling well in the steamy atmos-phere, runs came slowly. Kallicharran used his feet well to the spinners and looked set for one of the

Viv Richards

easier centuries when he was caught behind cutting at Marks. Thereafter Dyer and Amiss decorously observed the last rites.

SOMERSET

First Innings		Second Innings	
N.F.M Popplewell, c Tedstone, b Hoffman	55	c Hoffman, b Small	27
P. Bail, ret hurt	8	c Kallicharran, b Small	0
N.A. Felton, c Kallicharran, b Small	0	c Small, b Lloyd	45
I.V.A. Richards, b Ferreira	322		
R.L. Ollis, c Hoffman, b Ferreira	55	lbw, b Wall	0
*V.J. Marks, st Tedstone, b Gifford	65	not out	66
M.R. Davis, not out	25		
M.S. Turner, not out	17	not out	24
†T. Gard		run out	47
Extras (b 1, lb 9, w 1, nb 8)	19	Extras (lb 13, nb 4)	17
Total (5 wkts. dec.)	**566**	**Total (3 wkts. dec.)**	**226**

Overs: 100.
Did not bat: J. Garner, S.C. Booth.
Fall of wickets: 1–28, 2–150, 3–324, 4–507, 5–533.
Bowling: Small 16–3–70–1; Wall 18–3–72–0; Smith 11–0–73–0; Ferreira 23–0–121–2; Hoffman 14–0–85–1; Gifford 18–1–135–1.

Fall of wickets: 1–1, 2–62, 3–103, 4–105, 5–175.
Bowling: Small 8–0–31–2; Smith 9–1–43–0; Hoffman 2–0–12–0; Wall 5–2–7–1; Lloyd 16–0–64–1; Kallicharran 11.4–0–66–0.

WARWICKSHIRE

First Innings		Second Innings	
T.A. Lloyd, lbw, b Richards	61	c Gard, b Garner	7
R.I.H. Dyer, lbw, b Turner	33	not out	63
A.I. Kallicharran, c Garner, b Davis	36	c Gard, b Marks	89
D.L. Amiss, c Davis, b Marks	81	not out	14
P.A. Smith, c Turner, b Marks	93		
A.M. Ferreira, not out	101		
†G.A. Tedstone, b Turner	22		
G.C. Small, c Davis, b Turner	3		
S. Wall, lbw, b Turner	1		
D.S. Hoffman, run out	0		
*N. Gifford, not out	0		
Extras (b 1, lb 6, w 1, nb 3)	11	Extras (lb 5, w 1, nb 2)	8
Total (9 wkts. dec.)	**442**	**Total (2 wkts.)**	**181**

100 overs: 372–5
Fall of wickets: 1–84, 2–108, 3–151, 4–312, 5–312, 6–399, 7–419, 8–431, 9–431.
Bowling: Garner 20–3–59–0; Davies 23–4–1–115–1; Turner 22.4–2–74–4; Richards 12–4–31–1; Marks 25–3–97–2; Booth 13–3–59–0.

Fall of wickets: 1–18, 2–158.
Bowling: Garner 6–2–16–1; Davis 9–2–19–0; Marks 16–1–56–1; Turner 1–0–9–0; Booth 21–4–72–0; Bail 2–0–4–0.

Somerset 6pts, Warwicks 6
Umpires – A.A. Jones & P.B. Wight

96: Yorkshire v Northamptonshire
SCARBOROUGH, 10–12 SEPTEMBER 1986

This turned out to be Geoffrey Boycott's last match. For years Yorkshire cricket, once legendarily successful, had been in turmoil. This was not simply because of failure (the county that had won more Championships than any other had not enjoyed any success since 1968), for the problems stemmed from the days of success. In-fighting and dressing-room tensions had characterised Yorkshire cricket since the war; and the row over whether or not Boycott (b. 1940) remained first captain, and then a player was the most painful and enduring that the county had to bear.

Boycott's application and statistical achievements were of the first order; yet he had a reputation as a man playing for himself and not for his team, and that – fairly or unfairly – was to be his downfall. By the time he left the field in this game he had amassed 48,426 runs at an average of 57, including 151 centuries. Only Hobbs, Woolley, Hendren, Mead, W.G. Grace, W.R. Hammond and Sutcliffe have scored more hundreds; and it is a further sign of Boycott's greatness that his average was higher than any of theirs. Though stigmatised as an agonisingly slow and cautious player who would grind away at bowlers, he could be devastating in attack on his day. Towards the end of his career, though,

attrition – both on and off the field – predominated. He acquired an unfortunate reputation for running partners out. His mode of dismissal in his last innings in first-class cricket should be carefully noted: as should the complete loss of advantage that Yorkshire suffered after plodding to a reasonable position, a situation all too often repeated in their most difficult years.

Scarborough, Wednesday
By David Green

Yorkshire accelerated after a slow start at Scarborough yesterday and reached 352 for seven by the close, Jim Love making a handsome 109, his first championship century for two years, and Geoff Boycott a painstaking 61.

Yorkshire, who omitted their England opener Martyn Moxon, were 129 for four after 60 overs, tedious going on a placid pitch, but Love played with refreshing freedom for three and a half hours, hitting two sixes and 14 fours.

After Bairstow had been deftly caught at second slip by Harper, Carrick joined Love in a partnership of 108 in 23 overs which was notable for the powerful driving of both players.

Love was severe on Nick Cook, driving him for two sixes, one of them on to the press box roof.

Geoffrey Boycott

Carrick's useful innings ended when he played on to Capel and Love was caught at mid-wicket just before the close.

Yorkshire began quietly on a cool autumnal morning against Mallender, who had problems with length and direction and Capel who troubled Metcalfe on several occasions before having him lbw with one that nipped back a little.

Capel also had Boycott, on 15, dropped at first slip, a straightforward chance to Bailey, but it was Nick Cook who ended Blakey's uncomfortable innings via a simple catch at silly point off bat and pad.

Boycott meanwhile was looking more and more solid, impenetrable defence being occasionally relieved by crisp on and straight drives. Sharp batted more freely, but paid the penalty when he drove Harper into the hands of short extra cover.

Boycott had been batting for 200 minutes when Love edged Capel to third man. Boycott seeking a second run, advanced a few strides up the pitch. Love sent him back, but he could not beat Walker's excellent throw.

Love, despite using the middle of the bat, found it difficult to beat the field, but Bairstow, dropped by Wild at Cover off an awkward skier when four, played aggressively, taking four fours in an over from Capel.

Thursday

Yorkshire, assisted by some profligate first-innings batting by Northamptonshire, established a strong position yesterday at Scarborough, where the visitors, with six second-innings wickets still standing, lead by only three runs.

Northants collapsed after a promising start and followed-on 155 runs behind. Chris Shaw, Yorkshire's improving medium pacer, took a career-best five for 38 and Richard Blakey, keeping wicket in place of the injured Bairstow, held three catches.

Northants fared rather better at their second attempt, despite the absence of their captain, Geoff Cook, with a broken finger sustained in the morning. Duncan Wild made a most attractive 52 not out, which included 10 fours.

Northants' first innings started at a furious pace, the bat of Larkins in particular whirling like the blades of a helicopter as Dennis and Fletcher conceded runs at the rate of seven an over.

Larkins had hit seven fours and a six in 45 minutes when he attempted an on-drive and front-edged the ball to extra cover. Boyd-Moss never really settled and soon lost his middle stump to Fletcher.

Cook then walked in front of one from Shaw and Capel was caught at short mid-wicket off the debutant off-spinner Berry.

A complete transformation then ensued. Steady bowling from Shaw, particularly, and Dennis, combined with some inappropriate strokes, caused a dismal collapse, Northants' last six wickets falling for 27 runs in only 11 overs.

Friday

Yorkshire's final championship match ended in one of the more tedious draws at Scarborough yesterday, with Northants having followed on 155 runs behind Yorkshire, batting out the final day to finish at 422 for eight.

Northamptonshire's Yorkshire-born wicketkeeper, David Ripley, was the backbone of their rearguard action, making 134 not out, the first century of his career. Duncan Wild scored an attractive 74 and Nick Cook made 45.

The visitors thus redeemed their profligate first innings batting performance and Yorkshire rarely looked like dislodging them on a placid pitch, though had Ripley been caught at slip by Love off Fletcher when 47, the end might possibly have been different.

Carrick, acting captain in the absence of Bairstow who has a broken finger, was reluctant to use himself and the young off-spinner Berry during the morning,

when Northants were most vulnerable, preferring the seamers of Fletcher, Shaw and Dennis.

Northants, 158 for four overnight, lost Harper early on to Dennis and Wild had his off stump removed by Shaw but both Cooks held on doggedly with Ripley, who batted in all for 293 minutes and hit 19 fours.

YORKSHIRE

First Innings

G. Boycott, run out	61
A.A. Metcalf, lbw, b Capel	15
R.J. Blakey, c Bailey, b N. Cook	12
K. Sharp, c N. Cook, b Harper	33
J.D. Love, c Bailey, b Walker	109
†D.L. Bairstowe, c Harper, b Walker	37
P. Carrick, b Capel	46
S.J. Dennis, not out	18
P.J. Berry, not out	4
Extras (b 6, lb 8, nb 3)	17
Total (7 wkts. dec.)	352

100 overs 285–5
Did not bat: S.D. Fletcher, C. Shaw.
Fall of wickets: 1–25, 2–59, 3–117, 4–129, 5–193, 6–301, 7–348.
Bowling: Mallender 21–3–67–0; Capel 25–4–89–2; Walker 19–4–56–2; N. Cook 24–7–78–1; Harper 25–6–48–1.

NORTHAMPTONSHIRE

First Innings		Second Innings	
*G. Cook, lbw, b Shaw	47	b Sharp	26
W. Larkins, c Berry, b Dennis	40	c Metcalfe, b Carrick	40
R.J. Boyd-Moss, b Fletcher	10	c Carrick, b Fletcher	4
R.J. Bailey, c Blakey, b Shaw	47	c Berry, b Dennis	18
D.J. Capel, c Carrick, b Berry	14	lbw, b Fletcher	20
D.J. Wild, c Boycott, b Shaw	6	b Shaw	74
R.A. Harper, c Blakey, b Dennis	1	c Blakey, b Dennis	14
†D. Ripley, b Shaw	1	not out	134
N.G.B. Cook, c Sharp, b Shaw	5	c Carrick, b Shaw	45
N.A. Mallender, c Blakey, b Dennis	11	not out	11
A. Walker, not out	1		
Extras (b 3, lb 6, w 1, nb 4)	14	Extras (b 13, lb 13, w 3, nb 7)	36
50.2 overs. Total	197	Total (8 wkts. dec.)	422

Fall of wickets: 1–74, 2–98, 3–123, 4–153, 5–170, 6–173, 7–176, 8–182, 9–195.
Bowling: Dennis 162–3–71–3; Fletcher 12–2–45–1; Shaw 17–3–38–5; Carrick 7–0–24–0; Berry 4–1–10–1.

Fall of wickets: 1–18, 2–42, 3–79, 4–138, 5–186, 6–213, 7–309, 8–362.
Bowling: Fletcher 46–15–105–2; Shaw 30–5–77–2; Dennis 12–0–63–2; Berry 35–12–73–0; Carrick 33–16–58–1; Sharp 7–2–20–1.

Yorks 7pts, Northants 3
Umpires – B. Dodleston and J.A. Jameson

97: *Glamorgan v Derbyshire*
CARDIFF, 2–4 SEPTEMBER 1987

Neither Glamorgan nor Derbyshire enjoyed much success in the Championship during the 1980s. Glamorgan finished 1987 in 13th position: they had finished in the top 10 once since 1970, making them one of the most consistently poor performers of modern times. For Derbyshire, 1987 was their best season for 20 years, and

they finished sixth. This thrilling victory, achieved when Maher hit the last ball of the match (a short-pitched delivery from Holmes) for six over mid-wicket, was one of the finest finishes in the history of the Championship. The match was a perfect example of closely-contested county cricket between two well-matched sides, and proved the point that even unglamorous teams can produce fine cricket.

Maynard (b. 1966), whose commanding innings on the first day saved his county from humiliation, was the best batting prospect the Welshmen had produced for years. He made his test debut the following summer in England's disastrous series against the West Indies. Butcher (b. 1954), the centurion of the second innings, was one of the most consistent county batsmen of the time, though he never received the full recognition some felt his talent deserved. He began his career with Surrey, and while at the Oval played one test for England, against India in 1979. Derbyshire had a better share of talent. Kim Barnett (b. 1960), their captain, enjoyed a brief test career, but failed to establish himself in the England side. In Michael Holding, Derbyshire had one of the finest fast bowlers in cricket history, now reaching the end of his career; and their registration of Ole Mortensen, a Dane, enabled by Common Market regulations, set a precedent that other counties were slow to follow.

Cardiff, Wednesday
By Edward Bevan

Two outstanding individual performances held centre stage at Sophia Gardens yesterday as Matthew Maynard took on the Derbyshire battery of seam bowlers almost singlehanded, and played a majestic innings of 119, while Michael Holding, sensibly used in short spells, took five for 41 with a perfect demonstration of controlled swing bowling.

When bad light ended play nine overs early, Derbyshire were 106 for two, 133 behind, and grateful for an enterprising opening partnership of 75 between Barnett and Maher.

The heavy atmosphere and a wicket that had a tinge of green about it influenced Barnett's decision to put in the opposition. His action was quickly justified when Holding took two wickets in his third over.

Glamorgan's fortunes were restored thanks to a partnership of 84 for the third wicket between Morris and Maynard.

Holding was by far the most hostile of Derbyshire's bowlers, and, when he was rested after an opening spell of two for 19 off seven overs, the batsmen took advantage of the other bowlers who, by comparison, were not in the same league.

After Morris was out, cutting at Sharma's offspin, Glamorgan stuttered in mid-innings. Holding bowled quite beautifully to a cluster of seven men around the bat, and, with the batsmen tentatively probing, Maher picked up five catches behind the wicket.

Maynard's batting, however, was delightful and merciless. Although he offered a difficult chance behind the wicket when he had scored 71, he continued to strike the ball cleanly and reached his century off 131 deliveries, 18 fours and one six coming in his total of 119.

The remainder of the innings was notable chiefly for a rear-guard action from Glamorgan's tailenders who added 52 for the last two wickets.

Thursday

Glamorgan ended the second day's play at Sophia Gardens on 55 for no wicket, an overall lead of eight over Derbyshire, and the final day of the season in Wales could well prove eventful with two imaginative young captains in control

Consistency was the hallmark of Derbyshire's batting. No one reached 50 but nearly all the batsmen made reasonable contributions.

Twenty-eight overs were lost due to early morning rain and, in the nine overs possible before lunch, Derbyshire lost Roberts caught behind and O'Gorman, who was making his debut, was well held by Todd in the gully.

Morris, meanwhile, had looked in imposing form, punishing anything short of a length, and he looked set for a big innings before slicing Derrick to his namesake at slip.

All the Derbyshire batsmen were in attacking mood, and after Sharma was taken at second slip, Finney and Warner consolidated with a useful partnership of 44 before Todd took his fourth catch to remove Finney.

At 238 for seven honours were pretty even; but Warner, playing every ball on its merit, and Holding, with more unconventional means brought about a useful lead for Derbyshire.

Holding struck three fours and a six in his rapid 26, before he was beautifully caught by Maynard at deep mid-wicket. Reminiscent of a rugby fullback fielding an up-and-under with a rampaging pack of forwards in pursuit, Maynard kept his eye on the ball as he covered 25 yards and took the catch over his right shoulder.

Base removed the tail, and the medium pacer has recently experienced something of an Indian (or Welsh) summer. In the last five innings he has taken 22 wickets after previously taking just six all season.

Glamorgan's start to their second innings was positive. Butcher was soon into his stride with two fours but he was then hit on the shoulder by a short-pitched delivery from Holding, and had to retire hurt.

Friday

The ebb and flow of the first two days was maintained throughout the last at Sophia Gardens yesterday, as Bernie Maher hit a six off the last ball for a Derbyshire win.

They needed eight to win off the last over and only managed two off the first five deliveries, but Maher swung lustily at Holmes's last ball and hit it high over square leg.

Derby had looked home and dry earlier with Glamorgan 105 for seven, just 58 ahead. But Alan Butcher (113 not out) with assistance from the tail-enders, notably Ian Smith (45), added 157.

Barnett and Finney – combined championship wicket tally 22 before this – brought about the collapse as Glamorgan lost seven for 32.

Butcher played an innings of the highest stature. Authoritative and composed, he hit 12 fours, facing 207 balls.

Derbyshire needed 216 to win and Barnett and Morris gave them a flying start with 71 off 13 overs before Morris was caught at long off.

Barnett and Roberts kept up the momentum before Barnett was acrobatically stumped off Ontong, and Warner holed out to long on.

Roberts and Holding struck boldly and could have won it more comfortably, but both got themselves out at crucial moments.

GLAMORGAN

First Innings		Second Innings	
A.R. Butcher, c Maher, b Holding ..	6	not out	113
*H. Morris, c Maher, b Sharma	30	c O'Gorman, b Finney	25
G.C. Holmes, c Maher, b Holding ..	0	st Maher, b Barnett	36
M.P. Maynard, c Maher,		c Maher, b Finney	0
b Mortensen	119		
R.C. Ontong, c Sharma, b Holding .	6	c Morris, b Barnett	9
P.A. Todd, c Finney, b Holding	0	b Finney	5
J. Derrick, c Morris, b Holding	4	lbw, b Barnett	0
†C.P. Metson, not out	23	lbw, b Barnett	0
I. Smith, c Maher, b Mortensen	1	b Holding	45
S.J. Base, c Warner, b Malcolm	18	c Barnett, b Malcolm	9
S.R. Barwick, b Mortensen	5	b Holding	3
Extras (b 5, lb 16, w 1, nb 5)	27	Extras (lb 8, w 4, nb 5)	17
Total (69.3 overs)	239	Total	262

Fall: 1–10, 2–10, 3–94, 4–138,
5–138, 6–169, 7–181, 8–184,
9–213.

Fall: 1–73, 2–73, 3–98, 4–98, 5–104
6–105, 7–105, 8–183, 9–237.

Bowling: Holding 17–7–41–5;
Malcolm 15–2–43–1; Warner 13–2–53–0; Sharma 4–1–21–1;
Mortensen 203–4–60–3.

Bowling: Holding 21.4–3–72–2;
Warner 5–1–13–0; Mortensen 5–1–12–0; Malcolm 9–1–40–1;
Finney 28–11–47–3; Barnett 31–11–70–4.

DERBYSHIRE

First Innings		Second Innings	
*K.J. Barnett, c Todd, b Ontong	48	st Metson, b Ontong	45
†B.J.M. Maher, c Todd, b Smith	39	not out	12
B. Roberts, c Metson, b Smith	20	c Derrick, b Ontong	47
J.E. Morris, c Morris, b Derrick	38	c Butcher, b Smith	39
T.J.E. O'Gorman, c Todd, b Base ...	2	not out	11
R. Sharma, c Maynard, b Base	17	st Metson, b Ontong	4
R.J. Finney, c Todd, b Ontong	29	run out	13
A.E. Warner, c Metson, b Base	43	c sub, b Holmes	4
M.A. Holding, c Maynard,		b Ontong	32
b Ontong	26		
O.H. Mortensen, not out	5		
D.E. Malcolm, b Base	3		
Extras (b 1, lb 10, nb 5)	16	Extras (b 4, lb 5)	9
Total (83.3 overs)	286	Total 7 wkts.	216

Fall: 1–75, 2–103, 3–122, 4–139,
5–172, 6–194, 7–238, 8–270,
9, 282.

Fall: 1–71, 2–109, 3–116, 4–153,
5–166, 6–190, 7–192.

Bowling: Barwick 11–1–37–0; Base
18.3–2–67–4; Derrick 14–4–47–1; Ontong 20–8–46–3; Holmes 2–1–9–0; Smith 18–3–69–2.

Bowling: Base 5–0–33–0; Smith 6–0–34–1; Ontong 16–1–85–4;
Holmes 12–1–55–1.

Glamorgan 8pts, Derbyshire 7
Umpires – B. Dudleston & R.A. White

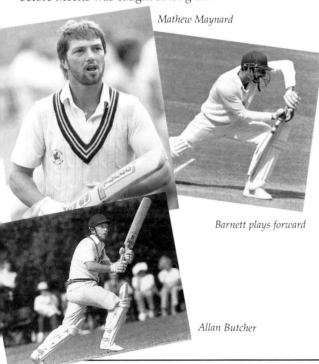

Mathew Maynard

Barnett plays forward

Allan Butcher

98: *Essex v Kent*
CHELMSFORD, 21–25 APRIL 1988

Four-day cricket was introduced into the Championship, on an experimental basis for three seasons, in 1988. This match, one of the first round of four-day games ever to be played, remains perhaps the most exceptional. The game was played throughout in bitterly cold weather; its aggregate of 1,570 runs was the highest recorded in the Championship (see game 35), a record made less remarkable by the extra day and since surpassed by Surrey and Lancashire at the Oval in 1990. Gooch (b. 1953) was one of the finest attacking batsmen of his generation: his score was the highest he had ever made, and he was within 25 runs of becoming only the second Essex batsman to score 300, 84 years after Perrin's feat (see game 19). Essex equalled their highest score this century, passing 600 for the first time since 1921. Fletcher (b. 1944), their captain, whose last season this was, did overhaul Perrin: during his innings he passed Perrin's aggregate of 29,172 in all matches for Essex, and became the highest scorer for the county. He finished his career with 37,665 runs in all cricket at an average of 38.

Kent's mistake, in retrospect, was to declare their first innings closed. Even another 25 runs might have put the match beyond Essex's reach. Fighting back, helped by maiden centuries from G. Cowdrey and Marsh, the wicketkeeper, they were able to set Essex a demanding target of 169 at nearly seven an over. The wicket remained blameless, the Kent bowling was unpenetrative, and Essex (thanks to a masterpiece of aggression by Gooch) won with 22 balls to spare. For much of the history of cricket Kent had dominated this traditionally hard-fought local contest: Essex's ascendancy, sadly for Kent, coincided exactly with a period of decline for their opponents.

Chelmsford, Thursday
By Trevor Bailey

A double century stand between openers Mark Benson and Neil Taylor ensured that Kent enjoyed the better of the first day in their Britannic Assurance Championship match at Chelmsford. Benson and Taylor put on 208 in a splendid partnership and after Kent had faltered, losing three quick wickets after tea, the elegant Hicks and Christopher Cowdrey enjoyed a lively partnership before the former was caught in the covers off a casual drive. Kent finished the day on 303 for four.

Essex gave the impression that they are likely to have problems bowling out the opposition this season, though on this occasion they did not help themselves by missing two comparatively easy chances, both off Childs. Cowdrey, having called correctly, elected to bat on a firm, benign pitch, which had to be watered last week. It was still not quite quick enough.

The Essex attack, without the injured Neil Foster, lacks real pace and Benson and Taylor were seldom troubled. By sound workmanlike batting they took the score to 80 at lunch by which time Benson had reached his half-century.

The afternoon belonged entirely to Kent. Benson a stocky left-hander, played especially well, though strangely for a small man he is not a good cutter.

He completed a chanceless century and his partner Taylor, with a technique not dissimilar to that of Tavaré, supported him well, though he should have

been caught by Gooch. At tea the pair were still together with 199 on the board, Fletcher having used seven bowlers.

Kent were hoping to accelerate in the final session but received two early setbacks. Topley, who until then had looked the least impressive of the seamers, removed both batsmen in the same over.

Hinks, a tall graceful left-hander, was able to maintain the pressure and when Tavaré became Topley's third victim he found an equally aggressive partner in his captain.

Friday

Essex survived the loss of two early wickets to make a spirited and sparkling reply of 279 for three against Kent's formidable total of 400 for seven declared on a bitterly cold day and a pitch lacking in pace.

Gooch scored another majestic undefeated century but the most satisfactory feature of the day for Essex supporters was the brilliant 88 not out by Pringle.

In the morning the Cowdrey brothers resumed with Kent strongly placed at 303 for four against the second new ball. The need was quick runs, but they were never really forthcoming with a long, very accurate spell by Lever the main obstacle.

Saturday

Graham Gooch, who managed a mere 131 runs in 10 innings at Chelmsford last season, joyously greeted the new season with a mammoth 275 yesterday.

And to the chagrin of his suffering Kent opponents, Gooch had the gall to say afterwards: 'I am a little disappointed not to have got to 300. Still, I played as well as I have ever done in the last 18 months.'

Essex amassed 616, which left Kent wondering why they had deigned to declare at a modest 400 for 7. Derek Pringle, his eyes on a Test comeback, also completed a career-best 128 along with Gooch in an awesome fourth-wicket stand of 259 and even Keith Fletcher, joined in the fun.

Kent's miserable day was complete as they ploughed to 76 for four in their second innings with the wicket taking spin and face a possible innings defeat!

Monday

Essex beat Kent by eight wickets at Chelmsford in a match which produced a remarkable 1,570 runs. Needing 169 to win in 25 overs they reached their target with four overs to spare.

Gooch and Hardie provided the ideal start, 45 runs coming in only five overs. But when the latter departed, Border, the Australian captain, took over and demonstrated exactly why he is so hard to bowl against in a run chase. Besides running quickly between the wickets and taking singles he has the ability to hit boundaries in unexpected areas, especially square on either side of the wicket.

Gooch was again in majestic form before being leg before for a spectacular 73 but Pritchard finished the game off with a flurry of fours.

In the morning session Kent moved from the danger of 74 for four to 200, losing two wickets in the process, both to Childs.

He was easily the most effective bowler, having the nightwatchman caught in the gully and the Kent captain off a miss-sweep. However, Graham Cowdrey and Marsh launched a controlled counterattack and despite a couple of difficult chances were still together at lunch on 54 and 38 respectively.

The two Kent batsmen dominated the afternoon's proceedings on a pitch which was still slow and easy, although it did take a certain amount of spin.

The Essex bowlers struggled and it was surprising that Miller did not try a few overs from around the wicket.

The new ball was eventually taken and this ended Marsh's innings and also accounted for Penn, who in this situation played a most injudicious stroke.

After tea Childs claimed his fifth victim and Topley bowled Graham Cowdrey for 145, which set the scene for an eventful climax.

KENT

First Innings		Second Innings	
M.R. Benson, c East, b Topley	110	c Gooch, b Topley	13
N.R. Taylor, b Topley	94	c Miller, b Childs	24
S.G. Hinks, c Prichard, b Gooch	35	st East, b Miller	10
C.J. Tavaré, c East, b Topley	13	c East, b Childs	0
*C.S. Cowdrey, c Border, b Pringle	48	c Gooch, b Childs	54
G.R. Cowdrey, c Gooch, b Lever	35	b Topley	145
†S. Marsh, lbw, b Lever	7	c Border, b Lever	120
C. Penn, not out	25	c Prichard, b Topley	1
R.P. Davis, not out	10	c Border, b Childs	1
A.P. Igglesden		c Fletcher, b Childs	3
H.L. Alleyne		not out	0
Extras (b 2, lb 15, w 1, nb 5)	23	Extras (b 3, lb 10)	13
Total (7 wkts. dec.)	400	Total	384

100 overs: 259–3

Fall of wickets: 1–208, 2–209, 3–254, 4–295, 5–327, 6– 7–363

Bowling: Lever 33–11–62–2; Topley 39–6–124–3; Pringle 37–7–77–1; Gooch 9–3–19–1; Childs 24–6–65–0; Miller 7–1–30–0; Border 3–1–6–0.

Fall of wickets: 1–27, 2–49, 3–49, 4–49, 5–89, 6–122, 7–344, 8–357, 9–372.

Bowling: Lever 19–4–85–1; Topley 21.2–5–57–3; Childs 45–16–113–5; Miller 28–6–95–1; Border 4–0–21–0.

ESSEX

First Innings		Second Innings	
G.A. Gooch, b Davis	275	lbw, b Davis	73
B.R. Hardie, c C.S. Cowdrey, b Penn	20	c Taylor, b C.S. Cowdrey	22
P.J. Prichard, c Benson, b Penn	0		
A.R. Border, c Marsh, b C.S. Cowdrey	31	not out	15
D.R. Pringle, c Marsh, b Alleyne	128	not out	55
*K.W.R. Fletcher, c sub, b Davis	58		
G. Miller, b Davis	16		
†D.E. East, c Tavaré, b Davis	29		
T.D. Topley, c Marsh, b Penn	1		
J.K. Lever, not out	13		
J.H. Childs, b Davis	7		
Extras (b 6, lb 24, w 1, nb 7)	38	Extras (b 1, lb 4)	5
Total	616	Total (2 wkts.)	170

100 overs: 361–3

Fall of wickets: 1–33, 2–33, 3–126, 4–335, 5–539, 6–543, 7–591, 8–594, 9–605.

Bowling: Igglesden 13–1–57–0; Alleyne 20–2–80–1; Penn 41–7–160–3; C.S. Cowdrey 31–3–93–1; Davis 39.5–8–132–5; G.R. Cowdrey 17–1–64–0.

Fall of wickets: 1–53, 2–150

Did not bat: D.R. Pringle, *K.W.R. Fletcher, G. Miller, † D. East, T.D. Topley, J.K. Lever, J.H. Childs.

Bowling: Cowdrey (CS) 7–0–59–1; Alleyne 6–0–40–0; Davis 4.2–0–34–1; Cowdrey (GR) 4–0–32–0.

Essex (21pts) beat Kent (4) by 8 wkts.

Umpires – R. Julian and K.J. Lyons

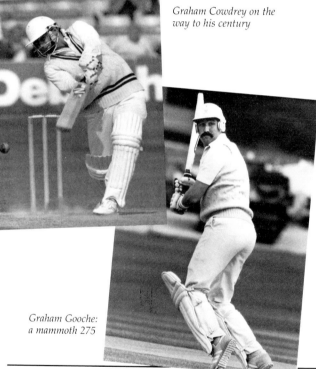

Graham Cowdrey on the way to his century

Graham Gooche: a mammoth 275

99: *Somerset v Worcestershire*
TAUNTON, 5–9 MAY 1988

Graeme Hick's form in his first few seasons of county cricket led to him being regarded, apparently universally, as the great hope of the future of English cricket. His ability to translate hope into performance was checked by his Rhodesian birth. Despite occasional attempts to review the residential qualifications (born largely out of despair at the dismal record of the English test team in the late 1980s), Hick remained barred from representing his adopted country until 1991. Performances such as this phenomenal feat of batsmanship, in a four-day match at the beginning of the season in which Worcestershire won their first championship for 14 years, did little to temper the excitement with which Hick's international debut was awaited.

In 1987 Hick (b. 1966) had had just an averagely brilliant season, scoring 1,879 runs at an average of 52. He had wintered successfully in New Zealand, where he averaged 63 for Northern Districts: but nothing presaged this carnage at Taunton. His was only the second quadruple-century scored on English soil in a first-class game. The other, A.C. MacLaren's 424 in 1895, was also made against Somerset at Taunton (see game 7). Without an eye on the record books Neale, Worcestershire's captain, declared his side's innings closed only five runs short of matching the county's highest ever score, and with Hick needing just 20 runs to overtake MacLaren. Nothing would have been lost by carrying on, as Somerset subsided only 90 minutes into the final day. Hick, who had made 410 runs in April, then had a lean patch, taking three weeks to make the 185 runs needed to score 1,000 runs by the end of May. In doing so, he became the first county cricketer to achieve this since 1938.

Taunton, Thursday
By David Green

An unbeaten 179 from the remarkable Graeme Hick, assisted by Steven Rhodes' dogged 44 not out in an unbroken sixth wicket stand of 180, carried Worcester-shire to a healthy 312 for five against Somerset at Taunton yesterday.

Hick scored his runs in just under five hours, hitting 22 fours and a six. Defensive field placings and a sluggish outfield slowed him at times but the power and variety of his strokeplay meant that he was never really contained.

Yesterday he came in at 78 for one in the 31st over, Curtis and Lord having dealt competently with some moderate seam bowling until Lord sliced Dredge to gully. Hick struck his first ball cleanly through mid-wicket for four.

He went into lunch having scored 31 off 25 balls with six fours but greatly improved bowling after the interval from Rose and Mallender caused the fall of four quick wickets and brought circumspection and even a hint of fallibility.

Curtis dragged a short ball from Rose on to his stumps and two balls later the same bowler had

Richard Illingworth congratulates Hick on his 400

405 – Hick's record score

D'Oliveira caught by Roebuck at slip. Shortly after-wards Neale was neatly taken at gully off Mallender.

Botham, with previous Championship scores of three and four behind him, played across a full-length ball from Rose and was bowled, which meant that Worcestershire had declined from 111 for one to 132 for five in 10 overs.

During this period it became evident that the pitch, whitish and of modest pace, permitted some movement off the seam and that the bounce, though generally on the low side, was not entirely consistent.

Hick continued to drive firmly but his but his half-century, reached after 81 minutes, came from an edged four over slip off Rose and when he was 67 he offered a very difficult slip chance to Crowe off Jones.

Thereafter, Hick appeared to play with caution but his second 50 took only another 72 minutes, his century having been scored out of 120 – a proportion which is a clear indication of his dominance.

After reaching his century Hick added only a single in half an hour but then asserted his mastery once more, the grooved orthodoxy of his attacking strokes giving little hope for Somerset's toiling bowlers.

On 141 Hick pulled Mallender fiercely to midwicket where the leaping Felton got half a hand to the ball. After this he plainly played for today when his career-best score of 230 will surely be threatened.

Friday

Graeme Hick, Worcestershire's 21-year-old Zimbabwean batting prodigy, made further claim to be included among the great names of cricket with a monumental innings of 405 not out against Somerset at Taunton yesterday.

Worcestershire, who shortly after lunch on Thursday had been tottering at 132 for five, declared at tea yesterday at a highly prosperous 628 for seven and by the close had Somerset struggling at 103 for four.

Hick's innings occupied nine-and-a-quarter hours and included 35 fours and 11 sixes. It is the second highest County Championship score, exceeded only by Archie MacLaren's 424 for Lancashire on the same ground in 1895.

Breakdown of Hick's 400

	Mins	Balls	4's	6's
1st 100	153	126	13	–
2nd 100	189	151	11	1
3rd 100	142	134	5	2
4th 100	71	58	6	8
Total:	555	469	35	11

Frank Wheeldon

Other records were established along the way, Hick's sixth-wicket stand of 265 with Rhodes, who made 56, and his unbroken eighth-wicket partnership of 177 with Richard Illingworth, 31 not out, both eclipsing the previous best for the county.

Hick's runs were scored out of 550 made while he was at the wicket, a startling proportion, particularly as Somerset captain Peter Roebuck frequently had five men on the fence when Hick was facing, while settling attacking fields for his partners.

Hick said: 'I started getting tired towards the end of each session but I enjoyed a bit of luck after getting 300 and I took it as it came.'

A feature of Hick's play, which throughout was masterful, powerful and strictly orthodox, was the almost metronomic rate of his scoring until a tremendous late surge of strokes brought him his last 105 runs in only 71 minutes.

When Hick, on 179, and Rhodes on 40, resumed their innings yesterday morning Worcestershire were well placed at 312 for five. The pitch, though placid, seemed likely to take spin increasingly so Worcester-

shire were naturally looking for a massive total.

The batsmen proceeded with care against steady medium fast-bowling from Jones, Mallender and Rose. Marks's tidy off-spin was also treated with respect and the dogged Rhodes took 100 minutes to advance to his half century.

After five-and-a-half hours' resistance Rhodes struck a long hop from Dredge straight to midwicket. Lunch came with Hick on 257 and one was slightly surprised that his measured play had produced as many as 78 runs during the morning.

Newport lent valuable assistance as Hick, now confronted entirely by fields designed to prevent boundaries, picked up ones and twos steadily. When Marks bowled Newport with one that turned considerably Somerset were certainly more concerned than their opponents.

Hick now began to cut loose, reaching his 300 with two sixes in three balls from Rose, one straight and one over mid-off. From that point Somerset's weary bowlers had no chance of stopping his gallop.

Hick's fourth hundred, which came off only 58 balls, contained eight sixes and six fours. He reached the target with his final six, over midwicket off the hapless Dredge, who was playing in his first championship game since 1986.

Neale's declaration at tea was designed to give Worcestershire sufficient time to dismiss their opponents twice. He was not, apparently, aware of the proximity of MacLaren's record score which certainly saved him much agonising.

Roebuck found that misfortunes seldom come singly as, bent with care, he fell leg before to Radford's second ball. Then Hick, whose energy throughout his innings had been astonishing, came on to bowl off-spin, with almost immediate success.

Felton, who had shaped confidently, soon drove him into short extra's hands. Radford had Hardy caught behind, Hick trapped Harden leg before and Somerset still need 376 to avoid following on.

Saturday

Somerset, bowled out for 222 in their first innings having started the day at 103 for four, followed on 406 runs behind Worcestershire and struggled to 143 for six of which Martin Crowe has made 47 not out, writes David Green.

The shadow of Graeme Hick's colossal unbeaten 405 loomed large over yesterday's play. His innings underpinned a total so vast that Somerset needed to reach 479 to avoid following on. Worcestershire, therefore, could set attacking fields with impunity.

Crowe and Marks started off confidently enough against Dilley and Radford but the fast-medium Newport's bursts of four wickets in 29 balls swiftly reduced them from 147 for four to 173 for eight.

Botham's marvellous one-handed diving catch at second slip accounted for Marks, a trimmer found the edge of Crowe's bat, Rose was well caught at fourth slip and Mallender was caught at the wicket, after which Radford mopped up the tail.

When Somerset batted again, resolute play by Roebuck and Felton demonstrated that the pitch was far from spiteful and they had scored 48 runs together when Roebuck ran into difficulties.

With his score on 17, he survived a shout for caught behind off Botham, was caught by Botham off a Newport no ball, dropped by Botham when he edged Radford and, finally, leg before to Radford.

Another four-wicket burst from Newport plunged Somerset into deeper trouble. He bowled Hardy, had Felton caught by Rhodes, trapped Harden leg before and had Marks caught at second slip.

Poor light caused the introduction of spin with Hick's offspin and Illingworth's slow left arm. Burns obliging swept at Hick, who can do nothing wrong at present, and lobbed a catch to square leg.

Monday
By David Green

Worcestershire needed only 90 minutes to take the last four Somerset wickets at Taunton yesterday, recording their third handsome victory in three championship matches, in this case by an overwhelming innings and 214 runs.

Phil Newport took the last two wickets to finish with six for 50, giving him match figures of 10 for 109. Martin Crowe made 53 and Graeme Rose 30, in a vain but conscientious rearguard action.

Somerset resumed their second innings at 143 for six still needing 263 to make Worcestershire bat again. Crowe had just reached his half century after 2¼ hours when he aimed to play Radford wide of mid-on. The ball stopped a little and a dolly catch to mid-off via the front edge resulted.

Mallender did not survive for long, Radford beating him for pace to have him leg before. By now, Newport had relieved Dilley and, as throughout this match, obtained movement both ways.

Rose had survived for almost two hours by

employing a straight bat and a long front leg, but Newport soon had him in difficulty around off stump, finally inducing a thin edge to the wicketkeeper.

Dredge offered some hearty blows but eventually he tried to run the ball through an offside catching cordon of six fielders and was caught at fourth slip.

WORCESTERSHIRE
First Innings
T.S. Curtis, b Rose	27
G.J. Lord, c Mallender b Dredge	49
G.A. Hick, not out	405
D.B. D'Oliveira, c Roebuck, b Rose	0
*P.A. Neale, c Marks, b Mallender	0
I.T. Botham, b Rose	7
†S.J. Rhodes, c Felton, b Dredge	56
P.J. Newport, b Marks	27
R.K. Illingworth, not out	31
Extras (b 6, lb 16, nb 4)	26
Total (7 wkts. dec.)	628

100 overs: 287–5
Fall of wickets: 1–78, 2–112, 3–112, 4–119, 5–132, 6–397, 7–451.
Did not bat: N.V. Radford, G.R. Dilley.
Bowling: Jones 32–4–97–0; Mallender 32–9–86–1; Marks 50–6–141–1; Rose 31–8–101–3; Dredge 34.5–8–133–2; Roebuck 10–0–48–0.

SOMERSET
First Innings		Second Innings	
N.A. Felton, c Radford, b Hick	24	c Rhodes, b Newport	36
*P.M. Roebuck, lbw, b Radford	0	lbw, b Radford	17
J.J.E. Hardy, c Rhodes, b Radford	39	b Newport	0
M.D. Crowe, c Rhodes, b Newport	28	c Lord, b Radford	53
R.J. Harden, lbw, b Hick	2	lbw, b Newport	3
V.J. Marks, c Botham, b Newport	42	c Hick, b Newport	7
†N.D. Burns, c Botham, b Radford	32	c Illingworth, b Hick	11
G.D. Rose, C Curtis, b Newport	12	c Rhodes, b Newport	30
N.A. Mallender, c Rhodes, b Newport	3	lbw, b Radford	1
C.H. Dredge, b Radford	16	c Curtis, b Newport	17
A.N. Jones, not out	8	not out	3
Extras (lb 6, nb 10)	16	Extras (b 2, lb 1, nb 11)	14
Total (70.5 overs)	222	Total	192

Fall of wickets: 1–1, 2–70, 3–70, 4–75, 5–147, 6–152, 7–166, 8–173, 9–203.
Bowling: Dilley 20–0–40–0; Radford 23.5–1–77–4; Newport 17–4–59–4; Hick 8–3–18–2; Illingworth 1–0–4–0; Botham 9–3–18–0.

Fall of wickets: 1–49, 2–59, 3–62, 4–74, 5–90, 6–111, 7–154, 8–167, 9–185.
Bowling: Dilley 14–2–40–0; Botham 6–2–25–0; Radford 17–6–39–3; Newport 15.3–3–50–6; Illingworth 11–4–20–0; Hick 11–4–15–1.

Worcestershire (23pts) beat Somerset (4) by an innings and 214 runs.
Umpires – R. Julian and R. Palmer

100: Essex v Yorkshire
SOUTHEND, 22–25 JULY 1989

Only one of the two significant features of this match was apparent when it was actually played; the other became manifest seven weeks later. Essex became the first county to be docked 25 points for preparing an unsatisfactory wicket, a rule brought in at the

beginning of the 1989 season. One other side, Nottinghamshire, would suffer this ignominy during the season. However, the 25 points that Nottinghamshire lost did not make the difference between them winning and losing the County Championship; but that is exactly what it meant for Essex, and for the second successive year Worcestershire won the title. That was not the end of the irony. Essex had no control over the preparation of the wicket at Southchurch Park, the exclusive fiefdom of the Southend Corporation groundsmen's department. Only a threat to take their cricket festival elsewhere by the understandably aggrieved county club led to any more fixtures being planned for Southend after this catastrophe.

Yorkshire had their second worst ever season in 1989, coming 16th, so would scarcely have been a match for Essex on a good wicket. As Robert Steen wrote in his first report, the sorry performance was brought about by 'paranoia and downright bad batting'. The difference between the two sides was manifest in the depth of young talent the home county was able to field in comparison with Yorkshire. The highest scorers for Essex, Stephenson (b. 1965) and Hussain (b. 1968) were both educated in the county and both were called up for England before the end of the season; Stephenson opening with Gooch for England at the Oval, and Hussain being picked for the 1989–90 West Indies tour. They remain two of England's brightest prospects for the 1990s.

Southend, Saturday

As Yorkshire, party to another pitch complaint at Headingley the previous day, disintegrated for 115 in 41.4 overs on a grassy Southend wicket, it was hard to avoid the suspicion that this was a severe embarrassment to Essex.

The Yorkshire batsmen did little to help their cause. Admittedly, Moxon and Carrick were helpless against vicious lift, but Robinson, Metcalfe and Jarvis all departed with wanton waves of the wand.

Even from a distant vantage point square of wicket 120 yards away, Jarvis seemed intent on donning his specialist hat as soon as possible. When he did he despatched Gooch and Prichard in his opening two overs.

Four overs later, however, Jarvis was smarting from figures of 2–41 as Stephenson put Yorkshire's tribulations into perspective, eventually passing a thousand runs in a season for the first time en route to an exuberant 85 studded with 18 boundaries.

Carrick persuaded the odd delivery to turn but Hussain's silken touch was again in evidence, after Waugh and Stephenson had rattled up 97 in 22 overs.

Jarvis returned to wreck the middle order with a burst of four for 30, but by the close Essex were usefully placed at 205 for eight.

Now to the controversial business of the day. This Southchurch Park creation is not obviously inferior to the undulating strip reported as poor during Essex's two-day victory over Kent.

The county are aware, however, that another adverse ruling from the same umpires, Plews and Palmer, will almost certainly result in a 25-point penalty.

At lunch, in fact, with Yorkshire 86 for eight following a spell of four for 30 from Topley that included the scalps of Robinson, Sharp and Carrick in one over, neither umpire seemed to believe that anything suspicious had occurred. At stumps Plews asserted, 'We haven't even discussed it yet.'

True, 18 wickets fell yesterday but there was no real indication of a sub-standard pitch. The main cause was paranoia and downright bad batting.

Monday
By Robert Steen

Predictably perhaps, the maligned Southchurch Park square was reported again yesterday. Indeed, the only consolation for Essex was that Yorkshire's batsmen conspired with resolution to prevent a two-day defeat.

Whether or not Essex are found guilty of producing a sub-standard pitch, Southend's future as a first-class venue seems very tenuous following the decision of umpires Nigel Plews and Ken Palmer to report a pitch there for the second time in four days.

Harry Brind, the Test and County Cricket Board pitch consultant, is expected to make a re-appearance at Southend today. Yorkshire, who insisted the wicket had deteriorated since their swift dismissal on Saturday, will thus feel vindicated.

Moxon, who spent 52 minutes rooted on 29, Robinson and Carrick, displayed the necessary resolution to delay Essex. But only one delivery was needed to justify the complaints.

Shortly after lunch, Foster pitched a good length ball into one of two holes outside the right-hander's off-stump at the pavilion end. Rearing viciously, it flew via Blakey's bat handle to the left side of his visor, then bounced off to smash the other side.

Foster immediately raced over to place a concerned hand on the shoulder of his dazed near-victim. After a seven-minute delay, Blakey fished nervously at the next ball and departed.

Presumably recognising that another such incident might prove costly on a couple of fronts, Gooch promptly switched Foster to the other end. Moxon edged him to second slip 11 overs later and the Yorkshire resistance, if not broken, was certainly buckling. Though not summoned until the 21st over, Childs might therefore have anticipated proving a point to the England selectors.

He sent down 17 overs for 12 runs in his first spell, turned and lifted countless deliveries past flummoxed bats, but earned nothing bar sympathetic applause until he returned to have Sharp taken at short-leg.

Essex had earlier added 43 to their weekend total to gain a lead of 133, Carrick grabbing the two remaining wickets.

Tuesday

Essex's haul of 22 points for beating Yorkshire at Southend yesterday was taken away with interest when, despite the matter being beyond their control, they became the first county to be docked 25 points for producing an unsatisfactory pitch. The loss may be far more serious: the championship leaders are to discuss the future of Southend as a first-class venue and may lose their most lucrative festival week.

More than 20,000 people watched last year's week at Southend and the figure this year looks like being nearly 5,000 more.

Southend Council insist that they prepare the pitches for the festival themselves at Southchurch Park, and Andy Atkinson, the Essex groundsman, is unable to intervene. Unlike the grounds at Ilford and Colchester, Southend is not used for club cricket.

The Southend groundsman, Eric Simpson, with Hampshire until three years ago, dragged nervously on cigarette after cigarette yesterday as a formidable delegation of TCCB pitch experts scrutinised the square.

Within three hours of a nervy Essex triumph, the conclusions of Donald Carr, chairman of the county pitches committee, and Harry Brind, the TCCB pitch consultant, had resulted in the first 25-point penalty for producing a sub-standard wicket. A statement from the TCCB special pitches investigating panel highlighted Essex's impotence. 'The pitch had not been properly prepared and was considered unsuitable for first-class cricket.' it began. 'but there was no suggestion of malpractice on the part of Essex.

Essex cannot be surprised at this sentence, though the feeling persists that, as championship leaders, they constituted a convenient sacrifice to put on the altar of official decisiveness.

Yesterday's decision cut Essex's lead from 52 points to a slightly less formidable 27. Peter Edwards, Essex's secretary-manager said: 'I am extremely disappointed by the decision. I have been in contact with our chairman Doug Insole, who is currently in France, and we expect to release a statement sometime tomorrow.'

Mr Simpson, however, was unwilling to discuss the matter at all.

Wariness about the possible outcome of the inspection doubtless contributed to Essex's struggle towards a target of 107. Indeed, but for another precocious knock from Nasser Hussain, they would have failed to reach the shore.

On the first day Carrick had justified batting first by predicting that the pitch would deteriorate as the match progressed. Hussain's exit to a Sidebottom daisy-cutter bore that out. By then, however, Essex were four short of their ninth championship victory of the summer and Foster duly tonked the next ball over long-on.

Hussain had come in with Essex tottering at six for three, Gooch, playing across the line, Stephenson and Waugh having departed in the opening three overs. Yet while his colleagues fiddled with the erratic bounce, Hussain fairly blazed.

One skied drive might have been reached by a nimbler fielder than Carrick. Sharp was forced to go to hospital after dislocating a finger, his punishment for spilling a tricky running chance at long-leg.

YORKSHIRE

First Innings		Second Innings	
M.D. Moxon, c Foster, b Pringle	27	c Gooch, b Foster	37
A.A. Metcalfe, c Gooch, b Foster	9	c Topley, b Foster	30
†R.J. Blakey, c Foster, b Pringle	12	c Waugh, b Foster	1
D. Byas, c Gooch, b Foster	15	c Hardie, b Pringle	20
P.E. Robinson, c Garnham, b Topley	8	c Garnham, b Topley	47
K. Sharp, b Topley	0	c Hardie, b Childs	16
*P. Carrick, c Hardie, b Topley	0	c Hussain, b Pringle	35
A Sidebottom, c & b Foster	21	c Prichard, b Topley	0
P.W. Jarvis, c Prichard, b Topley	2	c Garnham, b Foster	5
C.S. Pickles, not out	13	not out	27
S.D. Fletcher, c Gooch, b Topley	0	c Prichard, b Pringle	7
Extras (lb 6, nb 2)	8	Extras (b 7, lb 4, nb 3)	14
Total (41.4 overs)	115	Total	239

Fall of wickets: 1–17, 2–49, 3–54, 4–73, 5–74, 6–74, 7–82, 8–86, 9–110.
Bowling: Foster 15–5–30–3; Pringle 13–5–33–2; Topley 13.4–0–46–5.

Fall of wickets: 1–56, 2–62, 3–76, 4–106, 5–146, 6–175, 7–175, 8–182, 9–2!?.
Bowling: Foster 36–10–94–4; Pringle 24.1–5–67–3; Topley 19–7–43–2; Childs 23–13–24–1.

ESSEX

First Innings		Second Innings	
*G.A. Gooch, c Moxon, b Jarvis	11	lbw, b Sidebottom	1
J.P. Stephenson, c Sidebottom, b Carrick	85	c Moxon, b Jarvis	0
P.J. Prichard, lbw, b Jarvis	0	c Blakey, b Sidebottom	13
M.E. Waugh, c Blakey, b Sidebottom	27	b Jarvis	0
N. Hussain, lbw, b Jarvis	21	b Sidebottom	45
B.R. Hardie, b Jarvis	5	b Jarvis	11
†M.A. Garnham, b Jarvis	13	c Pickles, b Sidebottom	0
D.R. Pringle, c Fletcher, b Carrick	37	not out	16
N.A. Foster, c Sidebottom, b Jarvis	0	not out	4
T.D. Topley, not out	25		
J.H. Childs, c Sidebottom, b Carrick	7		
Extras (lb 5, w 1, nb 11)	17	Extras (b 4, lb 9, nb 4)	17
Total (82.4 overs)	248	Total (7 wkts.)	107

Fall of wickets: 1–18, 2–23, 3–120, 4–151, 5–161, 6–163, 7–182, 8–188, 9–228.
Bowling: Jarvis 26–8–76–6; Sidebottom 11–2–40–1; Fletcher 10–0–43–0; Pickles 5–0–22–0; Carrick 30.4–13–62–3.

Fall of wickets: 1–1, 2–1, 3–6, 4–29 5–56, 6–61, 7–103.
Did not bat: T.D. Topley, J.H. Childs.
Bowling: Jarvis 11–0–35–3; Sidebottom 10.2–1–48–4; Fletcher 1–0–8–0; Carrick 1–0–3–0.

Essex (22pts) beat Yorkshire (4) by 3 wkts
Umpires – K.E. Palmer and N.T. Plews

Index